Music on the Move

Music on the Move

DANIELLE FOSLER-LUSSIER

University of Michigan Press
Ann Arbor

Published in the United States of America by the
University of Michigan Press
Manufactured in the United States of America
Printed on acid-free paper
First published June 2020

A CIP catalog record for this book is available from the British Library.

Library of Congress Cataloging-in-Publication Data

Names: Fosler-Lussier, Danielle, 1969– author.
Title: Music on the move / Danielle Fosler-Lussier.
Description: Ann Arbor : University of Michigan Press, 2020. | Includes
    bibliographical references and index. |
Identifiers: LCCN 2020011847 (print) | LCCN 2020011848 (ebook) |
    ISBN 9780472074501 (hardcover) | ISBN 9780472054503 (paperback) |
    ISBN 9780472126781 (ebook) | ISBN 9780472901289 (ebook other)
Subjects: LCSH: Music—Social aspects. | Dissemination of music. | Music and
    globalization.
Classification: LCC ML3916 .F67   2020 (print) | LCC ML3916 (ebook) | DDC
    780.9—dc23
LC record available at https://lccn.loc.gov/2020011847
LC ebook record available at https://lccn.loc.gov/2020011848

Publication of this open monograph was the result of The Ohio State University's
participation in TOME (Toward an Open Monograph Ecosystem), a collaboration of the
Association of American Universities, the Association of Research Libraries, and the Association of University Presses. TOME aims to expand the reach of long-form humanities and
humanistic social science scholarship including digital scholarship. Funding from The Ohio
State University Libraries made it possible to open this publication to the world.

Cover illustration: Map by M. Bourie for Air Afrique. Courtesy of David Rumsey Map
Collection, www.davidrumsey.com.

Contents

Part 3: Mashup

Digital materials related to this title can be found on the Fulcrum platform via the following citable URL: https://doi.org/10.3998/mpub.9853855

Additional materials and teacher resources can be found at musiconthemove.org

Preface

In this book I aim to work out some of the ways in which human connections made through migration and media have shaped music-making. Arjun Appadurai has observed that "any book about globalization is a mild exercise in megalomania," and I am well aware that this project can never be complete.[1] I do not have a "god's-eye view" of the world or its music; I have not even been to all the places discussed in these pages. Yet in an age where the movement of people and music is evident all around us, it seems important to try to think about music in a connected way, tracking not only music that stays in one place but also music that moves.

Although this book undoubtedly reflects my perspective as a college teacher from the United States, I have tried to make the viewpoint inclusive—to frame the discussion so that people who come from many backgrounds will find something here they might relate to. The broad scope of this book means that no topic is treated in full: there is always more to the story than I can tell here.

My training in the United States and Europe concentrated on concert music and, to a lesser extent, jazz. My subsequent growth has been shaped by engagement with many friends and scholars and the music they love and study. This is personal work: I have drawn on the enthusiasm of my colleagues as well as their expertise. The National Endowment for the Humanities Summer Institute on Ethnomusicology and Global Culture, led by Eric Charry, Mark Slobin, Sumarsam, and Su Zheng in June 2011, taught me a great deal and helped me begin to turn my Music on the Move course into this book. When Emily Erken, Alison Furlong, and Austin McCabe Juhnke taught the course, they too made improvements, as did guest lecturers Tracie Parker and Nicholas Poss. The undergraduate students who took the course between 2005 and the present have also assisted in the development of this project—most of all, by bringing me music they cared about and asking me to listen.

I owe a great deal to generous people who have shared their perspectives and corrected many errors along the way. Nathaniel Lew, Marianne Lipson, Joanne Lussier, Benjamin Tausig, and one anonymous reader offered valuable criticism on the whole manuscript. Hyun Kyong (Hannah) Chang, Brigid Cohen, Eric Drott, Luis-Manuel Garcia, Petra Gelbart, K. E. Goldschmitt, Sandra J. Graham, Jeremy Grimshaw, Lynn Hooker, Mark Katz, Ryan Thomas Skinner, Kendra Salois, and Henry Spiller kindly offered their extensive subject matter expertise and vastly improved various sections of the book. To Lynn Hooker I owe particular thanks: without her research and teaching, chapter 2 could not have been written, and her willingness to use this book with her students helped me refine it. Courtney Bryan, Samantha Ege, and Asha Srinivasan were generous in sharing insights, scores, and recordings with me; Soojin Kim allowed me to use a photograph from her research. Louis Epstein's innovative thinking and technical knowledge about digital mapping has shaped this work. Jane Harrison, Dan Jurafsky, Lijuan Qian, Ali Sait Sadıkoğlu, Johanna Sellman, Henry Spiller, and Janet Yu graciously helped with selection, translation, and interpretation of sources. I appreciate Julian Halliday's assistance with the images. And conversations with Gabriel Solis and Olivia Bloechl, who are bringing a global music history into being, helped me adjust my frame of reference.

For partnership in this work I am deeply grateful to Eric Fosler-Lussier, who not only authored the digital maps but also urged me to think about my data in new ways and helped me secure the practical conditions necessary for a phase of intensive writing. His confidence and his sacrifices of time and energy made this book possible. My writing and teaching are further sustained by a network of wonderful colleagues, many more than I can name here. In addition to those listed above, they include Carolyn Abbate, Emily Abrams Ansari, Harmony Bench, Joy Haslam Calico, Maribeth Clark, Daniel Goldmark, Anna Gawboy, David Hedgecoth, Erika Supria Honisch, Lisa Jakelski, Jennifer Johnson, Marian Wilson Kimber, Hannah Kosstrin, Beth Levy, Morgan Liu, Dorothy Noyes, Hye-jung Park, Chris Reynolds, Peter Schmelz, Anne Shreffler, Leslie Sprout, Steve Swayne, Juliet White-Smith, and Reba Wissner.

Funding from the College of Arts and Sciences at Ohio State University helped me acquire the rights to images and audiovisual materials, and a sabbatical in 2017–18 allowed me to finish writing the text. For a subvention that allowed the University of Michigan Press to publish this as an open-access book, I am grateful to the Ohio State University Libraries and the TOME initiative (Toward an Open Access Monograph Ecosystem), a collaboration of the Association of American Universities, the Association of University Presses, and the Association of Research Libraries. A Course Enhancement Grant from the Ohio State University Libraries also supported early development of these materials. Many thanks to Sara Cohen, Susan Cronin, Jon McGlone, Kevin Rennells, Charles Watkinson, and Lanell White for shepherding the book to publication; Joe Abbott for copyediting; and Mary Francis for believing in the possibilities for this book on the Press's digital platform.

Maps

Media Chronology

1877   Edison phonograph invented

1910s   78 rpm records widely available (not the only recording speed)

1925   Electric recording available (via microphones)

1930s   Magnetic tape used by German government for propaganda recordings

1946   Only 0.5 percent of US households have television sets

1947   Magnetic tape available for commercial recordings; can be spliced to edit

1948   33 1/3 rpm long-playing (LP) records available

1949   45 rpm "singles" (1 song on a side) cheaply available

1954   More than 55 percent of US households have television sets

1958   Stereophonic sound, multitrack magnetic tape

1966   Compact cassette tape in wide circulation

1983   Compact discs introduced

1980s   Internet access available to consumers

1998   First music stores appear on the internet

2001   Apple begins selling the iPod. More than 98 percent of US households have color television sets

2002   Streaming begins to become widespread

2006   Apple's iTunes surpasses one billion songs sold

2018   Apple announces it will phase out downloadable music files

Introduction

Most people encounter some kind of music in their daily lives. Some people actively seek out music by making it themselves, attending concerts, purchasing or downloading audio recordings, or using media such as radio or the internet. But music finds even those who don't go looking for it. Music is a persistent backdrop in public places, from the quiet ambient sound in shopping centers to the booming of a loud car radio as it goes by. A friend shares a beloved song; a parent hums a lullaby; a busker plays the saxophone on a street corner. In all these ways, whether requested or not, music is an integral part of our social world.

Take a moment to consider the music you have heard in the past week or so. How much of the music was already familiar, and how much was new to you? How much of the music you heard was chosen by you and how much by other people? When you did choose, what factors helped you decide what to listen to? Each of us will answer these questions differently, and the answers help us sketch our particular social and musical networks. For example, some people find most of their music through direct social contact, like the recommendations of relatives or live performances at religious institutions. Some find their music through the media, at a remove from their personal social contacts; this might happen through television shows or the tips provided by music sellers on the internet: "if you liked this song, try that one." Some might choose a favorite café for its excellent playlist. In any case the music you hear points to a variety of connections in your life, and these connections can support, direct, or even limit your access to musical experiences.

The music you hear may also tell you something about who you are as a person: you may choose particular kinds of music for particular purposes or to make yourself feel a certain way. Some people listen to music because it feels calming, or energizing, or challenging, or fascinating. Workout music differs from the music that accompanies a romantic dinner for two. Many people enjoy musical experiences that help them feel connected to others, like joining a large crowd to sing a traditional song at a college sporting event. Likewise, songs your family has always chosen for weddings or funerals might inspire a feeling of connection with an entire family network and its history.

Some of these effects are internal to one listener, but most of them are also social effects: they take place at least partly in the listener's relationship to social networks. Individuals might prefer music that makes them feel "cultured" or refined, hip or cutting-edge—that is, music that confers social status in some way. Throughout history, groups of people have defined some kinds of music as more important or beneficial than others. For example, European Americans in the United States treated classical music this way in the early 1900s. Collectors, too, take pleasure and pride in having a lot of one kind of music and demonstrating expertise about that music. And some people like to be central players in their musical networks: they like to be the ones to hear a new song first or recommend it to others. In these cases music helps people define their relationships to one another. You can probably name some examples from your own experience.

We might ask, too, about the origins of the music you have heard. To what extent does your music come only from your home country? To what extent is your listening international? Your answers to these questions may depend on your family's history and traditions. If you or your parents are recent immigrants to your country, you might have strong ties to the music from your place of origin and to the communities that support this music. Even families that have been settled in one place for a long time sometimes hold on to special kinds of music from another place, like wedding music or holiday music, that are passed down through generations.

Some people are simply more likely to come across music from far away because of where or how they live. In densely populated places such as Toronto, New York, or Los Angeles, many people cross paths as travelers and immigrants. In places that rarely host foreign visitors, this process happens more slowly. When people move to faraway colleges, undertake church missionary work, or go on vacation, they often encounter music they haven't heard before, and they might bring music with them into their new contexts.

How you get your music might also depend on your access to media. Many people in North America are fans of Japanese animé soundtracks or Jamaican reggae; they may have encountered these cultural forms through travel, but their primary encounter with them more likely comes through radio, television, the internet, or audio or video recordings. Of course, this process is not separate from the process of in-person contact. A friend's recommendation may lead to intense engagement with a particular kind of music through the media, and people who share a passion for a particular music may meet in an online forum, then make contact offline as their common interests grow.

Depending on who you are, some networks that are right in your part of town may be entirely invisible to you. When the Chinese American pop star Wang Leehom (1976–) performed at the Hollywood Bowl in Los Angeles, he filled the venue to capacity with some 17,000 enthusiastic fans. Wang is a major celebrity in East Asia. He has produced 16 albums in Mandarin and Japanese, and he has appeared in several films and dozens of commercials. Yet many white or Hispanic Angelenos have never heard of him, and his concert held no significance for them. The population Wang reached in Los Angeles was primarily a Chinese and Chinese American network, people who live in the United States and follow the East Asian popular music scene.[1] Our networks not only expand our view; they also limit our view according to language or interest so that we fail to cross paths with some people, even our neighbors. What we see through our networks is never all that exists but only a fraction.

Thinking about how music is transmitted within and among communities can help us understand our own places in the musical world and how those places have come to be as they are. Thinking about music this way helps us see that music is not an object: it is an activity, something people do. It exists not only in our imaginations, in performances, and in recordings but also within our social relationships. It runs along the lines of human connection to new places and links people to one another—even when those people are not together in one place.[2] Music can also define our relationships with one another. We are makers, givers, or receivers of music; we assess others based on their favorite music; a fondness for certain music can help us become friends. The transmitters and users of music are all part of this ebb and flow of relationships.

Music in the Global Network

It is a commonplace these days to hear that music, or the music business, is "global." When you think about your own social network, you may notice many threads of connection to music from elsewhere, even though your personal network doesn't literally blanket the globe or connect you directly to every person on Earth. Even the internet, the "World Wide Web," reaches only a little over half of the people in the world.[3] Our media do provide us with a feeling of connectedness—of being able to see everything that's going on or access all the music that has been created. But that feeling is an illusion: some people do not have any access to this form of interconnection, and only a small fraction of the world's music is audible through our network.[4]

Still, this illusion is powerful. Without a doubt we feel as though we are connected. It might fit our intuition better if we think of the "global" not as a blanket covering the world but as a changing network of connecting threads that may extend over distance, with some places and peoples more thickly connected than others. John Tomlinson has called this situation of "complex connectivity" **globalization**. Others have defined globalization as a collection of "flows" of people, goods, and ideas.[5] The anthropologist Anna Tsing has proposed that the idea of the "global" is a way of imagining one's place in the world—a "dream space" that has shaped human ambitions since the mid-1900s. Musicians, environmentalists, human-rights activists, religious groups, marketers, and governments have used this idea to envision controlling the world, making money, or moving societies toward justice and equality.[6]

People have also used the words *global* and *globalization* to describe this sense that music and ideas are moving far and fast. Many commentators say that since the 1980s we have been living in an "age of globalization." Sometimes the use of these terms is an attempt to describe the feeling of living in our times. From the 1960s to the present, air travel has become available to more people, and communications networks are expanding and becoming more comprehensive. Jet-setting business professionals and government officials move among grand international hotels that are nearly the same regardless of location. These developments have led some observers to describe a "time-space compression," in which the ease of travel makes it feel like distances have shrunk. Likewise, advances in communications technology have allowed music, images, and ideas to come at us ever faster, providing more and more information for us to process, which sometimes makes it feel as though we have less time, or the time is too full.[7] If we take the internet as a point of origin for this feeling of time-space compression, we might decide that the era of globalization started in 1989.

The "global" has not always been defined in terms of this feeling, though. Some commentators have emphasized economic globalization, an increased interdependence of financial markets that began in the early 1980s. International corporations, including music and media corporations, operate more and more across borders, hiring workers distant from their headquarters. They even seek to influence the laws of many countries to smooth their path in global operations. Large media companies have pressed governments to increase protections for copyright and intellectual property by enforcing laws against illegal copying of music; this combination of state and corporate power is profitable for the owners of music. Yet economic globalization is not only for the powerful. Disadvantaged low-wage workers migrate to seek better incomes but also send money home and listen to music from home, building economic and social ties between their places of employment and their places of origin.[8]

More recently, scholars have turned to political definitions of globalization. The world is not united by globalization: we have not come together under one world government, nor is there full agreement among nations. But we have developed institutions like the World Bank (established 1944) and the United Nations (1945) that attempt to operate in a truly international way, setting ground rules that apply to all countries. (Of course, the playing field is still not level: many commentators have criticized these institutions for being biased in favor of larger and economically powerful countries.) Furthermore, during the 20th and 21st centuries national governments have vastly extended their reach, establishing permanent military bases, placing information into foreign news media, and using international institutions to govern the behavior of peoples outside their borders. Countries began developing national brands by choosing which music to export as propaganda, and the United Nations initiated programs that protected musical traditions that might otherwise disappear. Those who define globalization politically might mark its beginning during the Second World War.[9]

The word *globalization* as it is used in everyday conversations attempts to capture some or all of these relatively recent trends of interconnectedness. As we have seen, looking at globalization through the different lenses of political, economic, or musical evidence yields different definitions and different historical accounts of what it is, what caused it, and when it started. The term invokes a wide variety of experiences, and it is therefore fuzzy rather than specific. One idea that is common to many theories of globalization is the idea that activity is happening at different scales. Worldwide trends can affect local experiences and habits, and local practices can be absorbed into national, regional, or global action. Music in a neighborhood in the United States may reflect a holiday defined for the whole nation-state—like the fife and drum in an Independence Day parade—or even celebrate a holiday originating on the other side of the globe, like a parade in New York for the Chinese New Year.[10]

Rather than using the terms *global* and *globalization*, I will try to use more specific terms to describe how and why music moves. Still, it is hard to get rid of these words altogether: they are the commonly used shorthand for all this activity and connectedness that feels different from what came before.

In spite of this feeling, music did not start moving around recently. Music has been in motion ever since there were human beings to make musical sounds. **Migration**, or the moving of populations of people from place to place, has been a persistent factor throughout human history, and it has become a pressing concern in our own time. Part 1 of this book describes situations in which music has moved with its makers to new places. When peoples move, they establish new connections as individuals and groups, and these connections have lasting effects on music-making, not only for the migrants but also for those who receive new neighbors. For example, the Romani people, whose ancestors migrated to Europe and the Middle East hundreds of years ago, are not completely integrated; yet their music-making has become a part of European music, and they have changed their playing to adapt to new situations.

Part 2 highlights political, social, and technological changes during the 20th century that brought new possibilities for moving music, including long-playing records, film, television, cassette tape recorders, and digital media. A musical performance is always **mediated** by the various factors that help the music get from its makers to its listeners. Media need not be new or high-tech: a musical instrument is a medium, as is printed music. Sometimes people think of mediation exclusively as a means of **transmission**, bringing music or messages easily from one place to another—and this form of mediation has become important in communication and commerce. But mediation is also built into the very nature of music, for all music requires some kind of making or performance process.

Just as important as the technological development of audio recording was the developing sense of a "smaller world." The United States and the Soviet Union actively solicited political and economic alliances with peoples all over the globe; to support these alliances, the superpowers purposefully increased communication among the peoples of the world. During this period, music was both "pulled" and "pushed" across international borders—in person, on recordings, and by broadcasting.[11] The channels of communication built through these efforts formed a foundation for our time, when music moves quickly across international borders.

When the idea of globalization became popular in the 1990s, people liked to think that in the new era people, money, goods, information, and ideas would zip around in a global network at very high speeds, without obstacles. Nonetheless, as Anna Tsing has pointed out, there is friction in the network: our interconnections across distance are "awkward, unequal, unstable, and creative."[12] Some music moves easily through the network, while other music gets lost in the shuffle. Some routes of travel are encouraged, others discouraged. Some people have access to the network as creators, others as listeners, others not at all.

In part 3, therefore, we look at some of the ways global interconnection supports the flow of music, and we focus on some of the points of friction that impede or direct that flow. We will see that some music-makers have been empowered by access to distant music, using it to craft musical identities for themselves that do not depend on the heritage they received through their families or ethnic groups. We will observe the music industry as it creates and fulfills the musical desires of niche markets, and we will see how constraints built into the global marketplace remain a key factor in the music business. We will also see how migration and mediation work together in the lives of people who have moved: they continue to use both travel and media to maintain contact with faraway homelands.

The conclusion brings together recent assessments of these "flows" and their effects. Some scholars describe the ethical dangers of globalization in more practical terms: loss of local or regional identity, economic exploitation of the poor by the rich, and conflicts over what parts of a musical heritage are worth preserving. Some scholars have mourned the loss of stable identities that results from the movement of people and ideas. These matters remain controversial, partly because different outcomes are observed in different places. The anthropologist Arjun Appadurai (ah-PAH-do-rye) argues that the genie cannot be put back into the bottle; that is, despite these dangers, it may not be possible to go back to a world in which cultures seem distinct from one another. He suggests that the best solution may be to embrace the multiplicity of selves and values that results from globalization.

Tradition, Heritage, and Boundaries

This book makes reference to many groups of people—that is, people who consider themselves to be groups and people who are called a group by others. Boundaries between groups are meaningful to insiders and outsiders alike:

they are an important part of how human beings think about themselves. These boundaries are, in some sense, imaginary: they exist in people's thoughts about themselves in relation to other people. Yet they are also real in that they shape human behavior.[13] Boundaries between groups can be used to create a spirit of solidarity, where each member of a group feels a strong sense of loyalty and belonging. They can also be used to divide people, to promote one group and diminish another.

It is common in conversation and scholarly writing to refer to "a culture," meaning a set of behaviors or beliefs that distinguish one group from another. In the words of Seyla Benhabib: "Whether in politics or in policy, in courts or in the media, one assumes that each human group 'has' some kind of 'culture' and that the boundaries between these groups and the contours of their cultures are specifiable and relatively easy to depict."[14] Once people define and give names to certain groups, they treat those groups and their "culture" as real; naming them seems to nail down those boundaries.[15]

Yet observation of real-world situations reveals that the boundaries between groups are usually movable and often loosely defined. These boundaries are human-made: they are produced through transactions, arguments, and negotiations. In addition to setting political boundaries between nations, people also choose what behaviors they consider "inside the lines" for members of their group and what is clearly outside: what music is good and what is not, who is acceptable to marry and who is not, or which words to choose and which to avoid in particular conversations. According to the music scholar Stephen Blum, "We begin to understand something of what people mean by 'culture' when we hear them arguing about it—comparing one culture with another, or with something they refuse to regard as culture."[16] The philosopher Frantz Fanon argued that separating people into groups may lead us to see the "other" group as a fixed object, incapable of change, with "phrases such as 'I know them,' 'that's the way they are.'"[17]

How we think about groups of people matters. Throughout the 20th century and into the 21st, some countries with multiethnic populations have witnessed vicious acts of **genocide**: attempts to wipe out an entire group, usually identified by ethnicity, race, nationality, religion, or sexual or gender orientation. According to Gregory H. Stanton strong group identity is a necessary precondition of genocide. In the cases Stanton has studied, a large population first defines a minority population by name, drawing a distinction between "us" and "them." The majority then use hate speech against the defined minority, usually claiming that members of the minority group are not really human. Then they organize the power of the state or military to harm the people in the minority group.[18] In recent decades, as majority populations have experienced political and economic uncertainty and migrants have moved to seek refuge from violent conditions, attacks of this kind against minority groups have increased.[19]

Obviously, not every case of dividing people into groups ends in genocide. Yet it is clear that human beings experience groups as a social reality. The perception of groups shapes human behavior, and in some cases the drawing of a boundary between groups can cause harm. In this book we will watch people drawing these lines and using them for purposes of bonding their groups together or excluding people from their groups.

One way that people mediate music is by telling stories about how their music is different from other music—drawing boundaries that define the music.[20] The idea of tradition is one important story people tell to identify a group. **Tradition** is that which is handed down from one person to another. Sometimes people believe that a song has to be very old to be traditional, but that's not necessarily the case. Along with the handing down—the teaching of a song—come the stories about why we sing this song, who the teacher learned it from, and what it has meant in the past. The tradition is not just in the song but also in the story: traditional music "teaches, reinforces, and creates the social values of its producers and consumers."[21] Saying that music is "part of our tradition" usually increases its value, giving it a pedigree that is justified by history and connects today's musician to people in the past.

Another kind of story that delineates who can be part of a group is **heritage**. Heritage is a tradition passed down among a family or kinship group. People often say that heritage means cultivating and preserving musical or other practices as they have existed in the past.[22] It is useful to recognize, though, that the stories we tell today about heritage define the heritage: even though heritage is about the past, people can change ideas about it in the present.[23] Unlike tradition, heritage requires a sense of kinship: it defines the group by pointing to a shared set of historical experiences and, usually, to ethnic or genetic ties. The sense of jazz as a particularly African American heritage, for instance, relies on that sense of kinship.

The act of acknowledging heritage in the present often helps to strengthen belief in those ethnic and genetic ties, using ideas about history to demonstrate the existence of a group. Repatriating Native American artifacts by taking them out of museums and giving them back to the tribes where they originated is an action that is based on the idea of heritage. The individual recipients of the artifacts are not the same individuals they belonged to originally, but both the museums and the recipients perceive that these recipients have a claim on these objects because of their belonging in a particular Native American tribe, ethnically and historically.

Kinship can be a broad concept. A very expansive example of a kinship group is a **nation**, which is imagined as a coherent group occupying a coherent territory. If there is a plausible story that helps people believe they are connected, they can feel that connection, even over great distances. The idea of a nation implies that there is something—a set of customs, a language, a shared musical heritage, a shared history—that unites its members.[24] The idea of a nation can also render invisible the existence of anyone or anything that does not conform to beliefs about what that nation is and who its people are.

We imagine "nations" or "cultures" as unified wholes, yet clearly they are not. Songs sung by the Canadian singer Céline Dion play a vital role in defining stereotypes about love in Ghanaian popular music and literature.[25] Some people in the small Southeast European country of Slovenia enjoy salsa dancing.[26] The generalizations we carry in our heads about what people or nations might be like are **stereotypes**: simplified versions of reality that we use as "good enough" approximations. If we had to actively think about all the detail that we can perceive, all the time, we would go mad: unless we are taken by surprise, our brains make an approximate sketch of the situation and move on. The hazard, of course, is that the approximation may not be accurate enough, creating errors in judgment.[27] As with the example of Wang Leehom in Los Angeles, it is useful to keep in mind the principle that "what you see is not all there is."

Using concepts of culture and nation requires similar caution, for regarding any group's music as a unitary "thing" is apt to lead to inaccurate conclusions. There are aspects of performance style that are unique to each individual player, to each region, and to people who participate in more than one group, more than one tradition. Music changes with every performance, and it changes a lot over time as musicians get new ideas. When music is transmitted from one person to another, it may also gain new meanings just because the new listener interprets it differently.

Some scholars have written about **hybrid** musics—musics that are created by combining two or more different source musics. This term comes from biology: a hybrid is the result of cross-fertilization between two different species of plant or animal. The biological analogy assumes that the source music can be easily divided into separate types that have clear boundaries. Yet musical creativity does not work that way. First of all, the idea of a hybrid assumes that we have precisely distinguished and identified the sources, what they are and to what group they belong. Because musicians freely imitate and adopt music from other musicians as they go along, though, it is impossible to establish an unmixed source for any kind of music. The blending of different musical ideas is not exceptional; it is the norm. In this regard music works like the borrowing of words between languages: it is a process of "constant redefinition and appropriation."[28] Or, in the words of the American composer Lou Harrison, "Don't put down hybrids, because there isn't anything else."[29]

And second, musicians may choose musical styles self-consciously, in part because of the story or group membership that a particular style suggests. A musician may want to present herself as loyal to a particular tradition or as an innovator loosely tied to that tradition. She may want to surprise others by adopting music that is completely different from her heritage or cause a political stir by adopting the music of her enemies. This is not "hybridization" in the manner analogous to biology: the musician's chosen form of expression is purposeful, not an accident of genetics. These choices musicians make can stretch or redraw the boundaries of what we consider a musical style and thereby alter the boundaries of groups of people, as well. For this reason I will avoid the word *hybrid*, describing instead the choices of musicians who mix or blend musics.[30]

Drawing boundaries around musical styles, then, is just as much a contested process as drawing boundaries around groups of people. There are lots of ambiguous cases, and where people choose to draw the boundary reflects evaluative categories like good and bad, ours and not ours. In order to name and talk about music at all, scholars draw borders around types of music, and so do the makers and listeners of music. Yet we need to keep in mind that these borders are human-made and that they are not fixed but negotiable. As we explore how music has moved, we will encounter situations in which a majority adopts the minority's music and situations where the minority adapts to the majority's music, but we will also discover the creation of entirely new types of music for new situations.

PART I

Migration

People have been moving from one place to another for a long time. Evidence from pottery as well as linguistic similarities demonstrates that some four thousand years ago, the seagoing people of the Polynesian islands explored and settled new territories, building a set of trade routes between islands. Likewise, early written histories describe groups of people in motion. Jewish people were forced into exile by famine and persecution. Greek people conquered areas around the Mediterranean Sea and the Black Sea and sent colonies of people to live there, often building walled cities to defend themselves.[1] Although the difficulty of travel in some regions encouraged a settled lifestyle, it is common for populations to **migrate** out of one place to settle in another. Environmental crises, economic ambitions, political conflicts, or the urge to explore have led people to migrate—by choice or by force. In contrast to **immigrants** who migrate into a specific territorial area, we refer to **indigenous** people—descendants of people who originally lived in that specific area or who were living there when colonists arrived. Even though the concept of indigenous people gives us the image of people eternally rooted in one place, it is important to remember that over the course of the long history of humanity, most territories have been used by more than one group.[2]

Music has also always been in motion, for people carry their customs with them when they can. Migrant peoples also come into contact with other groups, whether en route or upon arrival in their new homes. Whether these contacts are friendly or hostile, whether peoples meet on equal terms or not, these encounters often result in an acquaintance with new kinds of music—sometimes also in the borrowing or adopting of that music by the migrants or by the people they meet. On arrival in a new place, migrants have tended to shed customs that are difficult to practice in a new environment. They may change their food ways or stop building instruments for which they no longer have raw materials. They may adapt their musical performance style to fit into a new lifestyle for themselves or to better sell their music to others. In short, migration offers us many opportunities to see peoples coming into musical contact with each other.[3]

Of course, migration has also led people into political conflict. Whereas early in human history transportation was difficult, borders were comparatively easy to cross and frequently in flux. The Roman Empire, for example, had no fixed boundaries: the borders of the empire moved as the emperor and commanders on the ground decided what territory they were willing to defend.[4] In most places the edges of kingdoms or territories were not always marked by physical barriers or policed by guards. By contrast, in our time, crossing borders has become a carefully regulated process—easy for some people, difficult or impossible for others.

This regulation is a result of how human beings have organized themselves. Our globe is carved up into states, which organize people, territories, and governing powers. A **state** organizes a system of laws and boundaries, keeps track of the people living within those boundaries, and defines what rights they are entitled to. States also issue passports, identity papers that mark the citizen as belonging to that state and allow the state to control who enters its territory.[5] Some states, called **nation-states**, are founded on the idea of a **nation**—a coherent group occupying a particular territory, defined by ethnicity, heritage, or some other features held in common.

The citizenship granted by states can mean different things: it might define a legal status, possession of rights and privileges, or economic advantages. It may also offer a collective identity, sentimental attachments, a sense of belonging, or "cultural" ties to the nation-state—that is, shared ways of being that connect a person to the other citizens within that state.[6] For many people there is a strong sense of personal identity associated with the nation-state. If one is French, for example, one might take pride in the habits and practices that come with being French, whether that might be a love of good food and the arts or a 35-hour workweek. This description seamlessly blends elements of the nation (cooking and artistic traditions) with elements of the state (the right to a limited workweek and governmental support for the arts).

Thus, the practical challenges migrants have experienced include not only transportation and finding means to support themselves but also administrative difficulties in gaining and keeping the right to be in a new place (dealing with the state) and the challenge of being perceived as foreign by people who share a strong sense of belonging (dealing with the nation). The presence of minorities within the nation has often been perceived as a threat to national unity. Members of the majority nation have tended to emphasize the difference between migrants and themselves. For example, Muslim immigrants to Europe, many of whom are refugees, face the question of how they might retain some elements of their way of life and yet integrate into European society. In various parts of Europe citizens have expressed fears that Muslim immigrants might refuse to adopt European customs, increase the crime rate, or incite terrorism. Whether they are based on facts or not, these fears encourage citizens to keep migrants out.[7] Migrants can be granted citizenship, partial rights, or no rights at all once they enter a place that is new to them. About 3.7 million people worldwide are "stateless"—they have no citizenship anywhere.[8] Citizenship in a state serves as an important protection: it can also serve as a sharp line of demarcation between those who have rights and those who do not. Saskia Sassen has written that one of the ways we can define citizenship in a given place and time is to notice who is excluded and how the people in power draw the line.[9]

Music does not always acknowledge the administrative borders of nation-states. For example, there are plenty of communities along the US-Mexican border where the arts, information, and money move freely among community members who cross the border regularly.[10] The wishes of individuals and communities about how to live and what to hear often contrast with the way in which a nation-state defines its typical culture.[11] Furthermore, **transnational** forces (that is, forces that act across the borders of nation-states) can render the nation-state less important as they interact with local and regional music-making. In 1999, for instance, responding to the difficulty of breaking into the worldwide market for electronic dance music, the Nortec Collective of Tijuana, Mexico, formulated a new strategy. It began including samples of identifiably Mexican regional musics within its electronic dance tracks—creating a distinctive music with a "local flavor" that was, ironically, easier to market in distant places.[12] Here, a desire to make music available transnationally affected the sound of the music. Thus, we have to be wary of defining music by its place in a national or state system; these are important layers to consider, but there are always broader and narrower fields of view to take into account.

One of the important broader views is that of **colonialism**: the practice of institutional control by one people over another people, their territory, and their resources. From about the year 1500 until the mid-1900s European principalities sent expeditions all over the world, conquering peoples and territories to form **colonies**. The Spanish presence in Latin America; the British presence in the United States, India, Canada, Australia, and Africa; and the US occupation of the Philippine Islands are all examples of colonialism. European powers competed to control trade routes and distant sources of wealth, which included indigenous people as well as material goods such as precious metals and sugar cane.[13] Some colonies were kept merely as points of transit, but in others colonists from the occupying nation settled in the occupied territory for the long term. These colonists faced the usual challenges of migrants but did so from a position of military and political might. They supported themselves and their home nations by taking resources. They imposed new forms of state administration on people who were already there, aligning the operation of the colony with the occupying nation's vision. The colonists established new social hierarchies, defining how they and the colonized people would relate to the occupying nation.

The Spanish occupation of South America and much of North America, for example, established worldwide musical connections. Beginning in 1492, Spanish militias arrived in the Americas, bringing with them African slaves and imposing new ways of life. They destroyed many religious sites belonging to indigenous peoples, replacing them with Catholic churches and missions. The Spanish brought musicians with them and set up church choirs and orchestras to duplicate European musical institutions in the Americas. In Mexico they required Aztec people to attend their churches and sing in the European style. Example 0.1, a piece called *Lamentations of the Prophet Jeremiah*, was written for a choir by Manuel de Sumaya, the chapel master of the Cathedral of Mexico City, in the early 1700s.

Example 0.1. Excerpt from Manuel de Sumaya, "Hieremiae prophetae lamentationes" (Lamentations of the Prophet Jeremiah), performed by Chanticleer. *Mexican Baroque* (Teldec, 1993).
Link: https://doi.org/10.3998/mpub.9853855.cmp.1

Sumaya, a composer of mixed Spanish and indigenous ancestry, mastered the European style: different vocal lines move independently of one another, creating lush harmonies, then come together at the end of each phrase of the text. The words are in Latin, a typical trait of Catholic church music of the time. Outside the church, musicians in New Spain had options: they could make music in the styles Europeans had brought, but they could also create indigenous or African musics, or blend any of these. As travel became easier over the next several centuries, composers and performers trained in the European manner routinely traveled to Europe or the United States, creating international networks that ensured the circulation of music across the Atlantic.[14]

Colonialism has had a dramatic impact on the lives and music-making of both colonized and colonizers, and this impact continues to the present day. Chapter 1 examines the effects of colonialism on music, drawing its key musical examples from Indonesia. We will see that Indonesians who were hired to make music for the Dutch people who ruled their island changed their music-making to suit Dutch tastes. This colonial connection also meant that Indonesian music traveled to Europe and influenced composers there. And even in the present day, traditions invented by visiting Europeans play an important role in attracting new tourists to postcolonial Indonesia.

The other two case studies in part 1 describe experiences of **diaspora**—the spreading out of a population away from its place of origin. In chapter 2 the music of Europe's Roma ("Gypsy") populations in Hungary reveals how the Romani minority have adapted to local performing conditions and made choices that reflect their particular economic circumstances, and how the music of the Roma has become a vital part of European culture. Chapter 3 offers selected examples from the African American tradition. During the three centuries of the slave trade, African communities were disrupted as African people lost the freedom to choose where and how to live. Some historians have traced "survivals": African approaches to music-making that were maintained even after Africans' arrival in the New World. At the same time, African Americans were one of many overlapping populations in North America, and their music both reflected and influenced the music of those other populations. Through these examples we can see that the practice of music changes as musicians meet new audiences and encounter social constraints in new places.

1 Colonialism in Indonesia

Music Moving with an Occupying Force

Music has often circulated along the routes established by trade, warfare, or political alliances, for these activities move individuals and peoples, bringing them into contact with each other. This chapter describes how these relationships have shaped music-making in the tropical Southeast Asian islands we now know as Indonesia. These islands have long been connected to faraway places. In the sixth and seventh centuries CE seafaring traders linked the islands to China, India, the Arabian Peninsula, and East Africa. When the Portuguese explorer Vasco da Gama arrived in the region in 1498, he saw great opportunities for profit in these active commercial networks. The Portuguese inserted themselves into these networks using military force. They terrorized the population of coastal trading towns, built fortified enclaves, and began trading from within those enclaves, using their cannons to protect their transactions and trading partners.

To make this system profitable, King Manuel I stationed administrators, traders, and soldiers in these enclaves to keep them under control. The Portuguese established trading colonies for exchange of goods and reprovisioning ships; plantation colonies, in which they used local or imported labor to gather natural resources for export; and colonial settlements, in which they brought sizable groups of Portuguese people to take territory and forcibly control the population that was already there.[1] As I noted in the introduction, this practice of institutional control by one people over another people, their territory, and their resources is known as **colonialism**.

Some colonies maintained a strict separation between colonizers and colonized, but many produced blended societies that maintained customs from both groups. Often the colonists were men who would marry local women or use them as concubines.[2] Thus, colonialism is one way in which populations from one place end up taking root in another place. Over its long history colonialism has reconfigured the world's peoples and brought musics from afar into contact with one another.

Colonialism is a broad concept about human relationships, encompassing both forcible domination over a group of people and all the social consequences of that domination. Colonial relationships have also determined how the world's peoples have been governed and how they see themselves as part of larger political groupings. The hierarchical combination of a ruling state and its ruled provincial territories is called an **empire**. The hypothetical ideal of a nation-state presumes a homogeneous population who are governed by more or less the same rules (with the notable exceptions of differentiation by gender and social class). By contrast, an empire is a state in which different populations are granted different rights and are subject to different laws.[3] When the Portuguese established colonies, the people they subjugated abroad were treated differently from the people in Portugal. The colonizing forces enslaved the people in the colonies or otherwise put them to use according to profitability and convenience, maintaining control over them through violence.

The Portuguese were not the only Europeans working to establish an empire. The Netherlands, already a banking powerhouse, also sought entry into global trade routes. In 1602 powerful Dutch families formed the private Dutch East India Company, representing stockholders from six cities. The Dutch were at war with Spain and Portugal; this war was fought not only in Europe but also overseas, with the heavily armed Dutch East India and West India Companies standing in for the Dutch Republic in Asia and the Caribbean. The Dutch gained wealth and power by pillaging Portuguese ships and enclaves throughout South and Southeast Asia, coastal Africa, and South America. The Dutch East India Company established profitable trading bases along the coastlines of India, Asia, and southern Africa (fig. 1.1). At the end of the 1600s this private company effectively ruled over 50,000 civilians and 10,000 soldiers.[4]

Conflicts with the British Empire and the difficulty of managing employees at great distances led to the bankruptcy of the Dutch East India Company in 1798. After that, Java, Sumatra, and other territories held by the company became colonies of the Dutch nation-state, the Netherlands. Most of these islands remained under Dutch control (except for brief takeovers by French and British colonial forces) until the Japanese conquered them during World War II. Dutch people lived among the rest of the people on the islands, but they instituted different classes of citizenship, with separate laws applying to

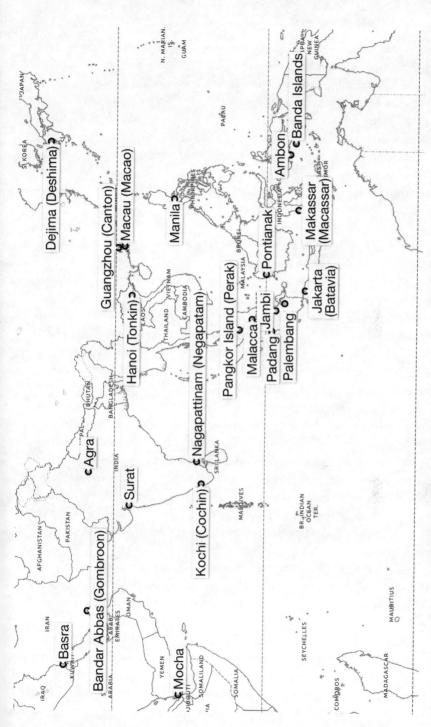

Fig. 1.1. *Music on the Move: Trading Area of the Dutch East India Company. Map by Eric Fosler-Lussier, based on Femme S. Gaastra, The Dutch East India Company: Expansion and Decline* (Leiden: Walburg Pers, 2003), 42. (See https://doi.org/10.3998/mpub.9853855.cmp.2)

groups labeled as European, Indigenous, and Foreign Easterners (covering the large Chinese minority and other non-Indonesian Asian people).[5]

The long-standing European presence in the islands that would become the state of Indonesia has had a formative influence on musical practices both on the islands and in Europe. This chapter describes musical relationships created by colonial relationships, drawing its key musical examples from Indonesia. In these case studies we will see how colonialism made permanent additions to Indonesian musical traditions. Musically, the influence went both ways: colonialism changed European culture, too.

Entertaining the Dutch: *Gamelan* and *Tanjidor*

As colonists who could take what they wanted by force of arms, administrative officials of the Dutch East India Company settled into comfortable lives near their trading base on the island of Java. In the 1700s many moved to the outlying areas of Batavia (now Jakarta) and formed little kingdoms of their own, with "splendid houses and delightful pleasure gardens"—many of them maintained by enslaved people.[6] The colonial officials blended European habits, such as wearing top hats and keeping racehorses, with Javanese habits, such as going barefoot and segregating men from women in public ceremonies. Because most of the administrators' families were Eurasian owing to intermarriage, and their household servants came from the island, the furnishings, food, and music in their homes were often a mixture of traditions.[7]

One such member of this elite social class, Augustijn Michiels, exemplifies the musical mixture as it was practiced at the end of the 1700s. He owned a city estate in Batavia and two properties out in the country, and they were filled with music. According to the historian Jean Taylor:

> Michiels's arrival on one of his estates was like the triumphant progress of royalty, with inhabitants of his lands playing the *gamelan* (an ensemble of Javanese musical instruments) in welcome and all the hamlet heads in procession. Michiels dressed in Indonesian costume and preferred to sit on a mat rather than a chair. His food was Indonesian and his day punctuated with the afternoon siesta. Female slaves waited at table, and his guests were entertained with music from his slave orchestras and by troupes of *ronggeng* (women dancers). At Citrap he also kept *topeng* (masked) dancers in his employ, and his

retainers there numbered 117 house slaves and 48 free servants, in addition to the stable hands and outdoors staff.[8]

This description offers us a glimpse of the hierarchy of power operating in a colonial house, as well as a sense of the intermingling of people and sounds.

One form of music on Michiels's estate was the *gamelan*—a set of percussion instruments, struck with hammers or beaters. A gamelan includes large and small bronze gongs and instruments with metal keys (shaped like the keys of a xylophone) that are struck with a hammer. Depending on the regional tradition, the gamelan may also include singing as well as a variety of non-bronze instruments, including drums, a bowed fiddle, flutes, zithers, and (wooden) xylophones. Although gamelan from Java are the best known in the West, ensembles of gongs and chiming instruments also exist on many of the surrounding islands: only recently did they all come to be called "gamelan." Java's kings employed servants as musicians at their royal courts and kept gamelan in permanent outdoor pavilions. Gamelan music has also been used to accompany ceremonial events in villages, both in religious ceremonies and for festive processionals, such as that of wedding guests.[9] The performance of a gamelan often includes dance or shadow puppetry. The video in example 1.1 gives a sense of what these instruments look and sound like.

> Example 1.1. Excerpt from "Ladrang Slamet" ("Welcoming Music") performed by Studio Karawitan Dahlan Iskan with Siir Natagama Java Orchestra. YouTube. Translation based on Mantle Hood and Hardja Susilo, *Music of the Venerable Dark Cloud* (UCLA Department of Ethnomusicology, 1967), 35.
> Link: https://doi.org/10.3998/mpub.9853855.cmp.4

Gamelan music is organized in layers, which proceed with mathematical precision. The largest hanging gong plays the slowest part, entering to punctuate and define the progress of the music. Smaller gongs, set in cradles, play a melody in the low-pitch range, moving several times as fast as the largest gong. The xylophone-like instruments, which play higher pitches, sound embellishments twice or four times as fast as the middle-register gongs. A piece of gamelan music is organized in repeating cycles: the sounding of the largest gong announces the imminent arrival of the next cycle. The overall effect is one of interlocking strata that create a larger whole, as depicted in figure 1.2.

In example 1.2 you will hear the ensemble playing in **unison** (all together) with an emphatic flourish that gets the piece started. In example 1.3 we hear

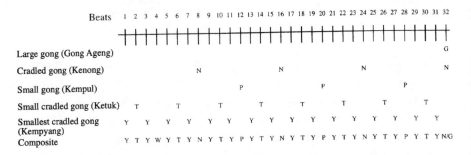

Fig. 1.2. Cyclical pattern in Central Javanese *ladrang* form. Adapted with permission from Henry Spiller.

the layering effect. The music is punctuated at regular intervals by strikes on a large gong, which sounds a little "out of time" (audible in example 1.3 at timepoints 0:03 and 1:01).

> Example 1.2. Distinctive unison passage from "Gending Bonang Babar Layar," recorded at the Istana Mangkunegaran, Surakarta by Robert E. Brown. *Java, Court Gamelan, vol. II* (Nonesuch Explorer Series 79721-2, 2003 [1977]).
> Link: https://doi.org/10.3998/mpub.9853855.cmp.6

> Example 1.3. Layering effect from "Gending Bonang Babar Layar," recorded at the Istana Mangkunegaran, Surakarta by Robert E. Brown. *Java, Court Gamelan, vol. II* (Nonesuch Explorer Series 79721-2, 2003 [1977]).
> Link: https://doi.org/10.3998/mpub. 9853855.cmp.7

The gong marks the last beat of a cycle and announces that a new cycle of music is about to begin. Throughout most of this piece of music, you hear a loud melody that moves very deliberately, at roughly one note every two seconds. You also hear softer notes moving four times as fast as that melody, and some higher, gentle notes move twice again as fast. Your attention probably drifts among these different levels. Javanese musicians would probably say that the real melody emerges from the whole effect, not from any one part.

In contrast, the slave orchestra that played European music on Michiels's estate was a newly created colonial enterprise. Enslaved people in the Dutch colonies were entirely at the mercy of their masters. Most were enslaved for a lifetime, though some female slaves were able to access a measure of freedom by entering Christian marriages with colonists. High-status Europeans required enslaved musicians to play European music on European musical instruments as entertainment during dinners and leisure hours. They also played military music in public parades celebrating the colonial rulers. These small orchestras were highly valued, and slaves who could make music fetched a higher price than those who could not.[10]

The role of these orchestras changed over time. As the power of the Dutch East India Company waned near the end of the 1700s, some Dutch people wanted their blended Eurasian culture to look more like Europe's, so they cultivated European music with renewed intensity.[11] In the 1800s some Javanese held public concert series that included European folk, dance, and military music, as well as symphonies and other works from the European classical tradition. Franki S. Notosudirdjo is an ethnomusicologist who reports that "music was a profession in the colony."[12] A steady stream of imported music arrived from Europe, as well, including music teachers and visiting opera companies.[13]

The enslaved musicians probably participated in both the gamelan and the orchestra. (In 1833, when Michiels died, his family auctioned off 30 enslaved musicians and their instruments.) Notosudirdjo writes that the music the slave orchestras played was European dance music: "the pavane, quadrille, and later on in the 19th century, the waltz, mazurka, polonaise, and pas-de-quatre."[14] Some also played in the style of a military band for parades. These Western musical instruments and styles were part of regular life for European and Eurasian colonists and for Javanese slaves for a few hundred years. They became part of the social norms on the island. The experience of the slave orchestras is believed to be the origin of *tanjidor*, a kind of music that is traditionally made by Javanese people using Western instruments and Western musical forms.[15]

The basis for tanjidor is the European brass band, to which other instruments may be added. The slave orchestras were asked to play European music so that the Dutch colonists could dance. Compare examples 1.4 and 1.5. Example 1.4 is a **waltz**: a European dance popular in the 1800s, famous for its "oom-pah-pah," 1-2-3 rhythm.

Example 1.4. Excerpt from Opening Committee Waltz, Stanford Viennese Ball, 2013. YouTube.
Link: https://doi.org/10.3998/mpub.9853855.cmp.8

Example 1.5 is a sample of tanjidor, entitled "Was Pepeko"—the word *Was* means waltz, and this music retains the "oom-pah-pah" rhythm of its European model.

Example 1.5. "Was Pepeko" (Waltz), performed by Tanji Modern Grup Marga Luyu, directed by Cibong. *Betawi and Sundanese music of the North Coast of Java* (Smithsonian Folkways, 1994 [1990]).
Link: https://doi.org/10.3998/mpub.9853855.cmp.9

In this example you hear a clarinet, trombone, tenor or alto horn, helicon (a type of horn produced in 1800s Europe), snare drum without snares, and bass drum. The ensemble also includes Javanese percussion instruments: you hear gongs and *kecrek* (clashing metal strips mounted on a block and struck with beaters). This kind of music would have played a role as entertainment in a rich colonial house. It is suitable for dancing or just listening.

Although tanjidor originated with slave orchestras, it became a musical tradition in Indonesia, extending after slavery ended in the 1800s. In the early 1900s bands of tanjidor musicians would play for tips at weddings and celebrations of the Chinese and European new years.[16] The tradition was interrupted by both World War II and government policy, but it is still played by Indonesian people in rural areas. Tanjidor ensembles do not play only European music; they also borrow music from the gamelan repertoire, from Chinese music, and from Indonesian popular songs.[17]

Example 1.6 is an example of tanjidor from the north coast of Java. This audio example has some gamelan-like qualities: once it gets going, it includes layered levels of rhythmic patterns that interlock in systematic, hierarchical ways. Typical of tanjidor, it is played on a mix of Western instruments with some Javanese instruments. You hear an oboe-like instrument, a bass drum and snare drum (played without snares, and with hands instead of sticks), a trombone, and some percussion instruments from the gamelan.

Example 1.6. "Gaplek," Tanji Modern Grup Marga Luyu, directed by Cibong. *Betawi and Sundanese music of the North Coast of Java* (Smithsonian Folkways, 1994 [1990]).
Link: https://doi.org/10.3998/mpub.9853855.cmp.10

But apart from the instruments on which this music is played, the music itself sounds nothing like any European model. This is an example of **localization**; that is, a musical practice from elsewhere has been altered to fit local conditions and become part of local traditions.

In the case of tanjidor we see that colonialism had a marked effect on how and for whom music was made. The Dutch used ruthless military force to rule over people on the island of Java. But they also used the force of custom to create and maintain social divisions between ruler and ruled, between Dutch and Javanese.[18] Music played for the rulers' pleasure was one such custom. First under the Javanese kings and then under the Dutch colonial administrators, music was used to delineate a separation between master (who could demand music) and servant (who must play the music the master chooses). Creating and enforcing that separation transformed existing musical practices and introduced new ones. One cannot really say that tanjidor is European music, for it was first made in Indonesia. This musical style has existed there for a long time, but it is not indigenous music. Yet tanjidor is a **traditional** music: Indonesian people hand it down because they value it. This music emerged from contact between peoples and their traditions and from the unequal power relationship built by colonialism.

Java on Display: The Universal Exposition in Paris

The establishment of long-distance connections through colonialism also moved music out of its places of origin. As a result of the colonial relationship between the Dutch and the Javanese, gamelan music from the Indonesian islands became known in Europe. In 1889 the city of Paris hosted a six-month extravaganza called the Universal Exposition. Nation-states and private enterprises sent exhibits of their achievements in arts and letters, as well as examples of their latest technical innovations, which were displayed in a vast Gallery of Machines. The United States was represented by Buffalo Bill's Wild West show, featuring the sharpshooter Annie Oakley; the show dramatized the conflict between white colonists and Native Americans.[19] The Eiffel Tower provided an impressive front door for the Exposition, and live demonstrations of the telephone and the Edison gramophone drew crowds.[20] New train lines were built to carry people swiftly into the city.[21] The Exposition attracted about 30 million visitors over its six-month run.

The Exposition included a large section called the "Colonial Exposition," which included displays of homes from different parts of the world, constructed as living museum dioramas. Within these displays visitors could see hundreds of imported indigenous people who were supposed to represent the daily activities of colonized peoples, including handicrafts and music-making. The organizers of the Exposition treated the people who were on display as specimens, exemplars of their kind, rather than as individual people. A visitor exclaimed, "It was possible to see there twelve types of Africans, besides Javanese, Tonkinese, Chinese, Japanese, and other oriental peoples, living in native houses, wearing native costumes, eating native food, practicing native arts and rites on the Esplanade des Invalides side by side with the latest inventions and with the whole civilized world as spectators."[22] The Javanese village display attracted four to five thousand visitors a day on weekdays and nearly 10,000 on Sundays.[23] Like animals in a zoo, the people on display were given a predetermined diet and were observed closely by anthropologists.

Indeed, the idea of anthropology—studying the customs of a group of people—stemmed from the need to regulate and control colonial populations.[24] Just as the exhibits of modern technology allowed visitors to think of themselves as modern citizens, the exhibits at the Exposition allowed visitors to imagine a whole world, divided into civilized and primitive peoples, with the visitors on the civilized side and the colonized peoples on the primitive side.[25] The souvenir plate in figure 1.3 reveals this division: it depicts the Javanese dancers but also calls their hairstyle "bizarre" and mocks them by comparing them to "primitive firefighters." Visitors to the exhibition did not define "modern" as an absolute quality; rather, they based their judgment of who was modern on comparisons with other peoples, who might be characterized as primitive, indigenous, or folk. Europeans could call themselves modern to draw attention to the difference between themselves and others. At the same time, they did not think of the "modern" as specific to their value system; they believed that it was a universal quality, a norm that everyone around the world should aspire to.[26]

Whereas European music was presented in scheduled concerts in concert halls during the Exposition, music from Europe's colonies was offered within the diorama displays at the Colonial Exposition. These performances were framed as a way of bringing the experience of the world directly to Paris: if Europeans did not want the inconvenience of traveling, they could see the genuine inhabitants and customs of other lands at the Exposition. The press framed these exhibit-performances as an educational event, but their primary attraction lay in the vivid experience that stimulated Europeans' imaginations with thoughts about faraway places.[27]

It appears that viewers and listeners at the Javanese pavilion heard some Sundanese (from west Java) and some Javanese music. But they did not receive explanations about what they were seeing and hearing in these performances. Indeed, it is likely that they could not hear everything: the exhibits were not fully separate, so the sounds from different exhibits and the crowds blended together. It may have been hard for witnesses to even identify what they heard

Fig. 1.3. Detail from a souvenir plate from the Universal Exposition depicting the Javanese dancers. The plate reads: "Javanese. The Javanese dancers have bizarre hairstyles with helmets, which caused Lili to say when she saw them: 'Oh! Papa, look, primitive firefighters.'" Collection Radauer, www.humanzoos.net. Used by permission.

as music, let alone listen to it with full attention. Nonetheless, many visitors were captivated by the musical performances: by hearing what they perceived to be primitive music, they could better understand themselves as "modern" people.

French people had already been exposed to ideas about Asian music, but those ideas had been presented to them through their own music. In the late 19th century French composers of **concert (or "classical") music** were interested in faraway places; they wrote operas and songs about those places. But most French citizens would not have had the chance to travel abroad, nor would they have heard Asian music as it was performed by Asian people. The Dutch had sent a gamelan to Paris as a present several years before, but no one knew how to play it, so it remained a museum piece. The Exposition was thus a rare opportunity to witness this music in person.[28]

The musicologist Sindhumathi Revuluri has described how some French listeners tried to write down the sounds of the gamelan for later study or performance. They found the rhythms difficult to capture, both because they were novel and because they fit so poorly into European understandings of music.[29] One scholar, Julien Tiersot, met privately with the Javanese musicians to have them play the music again more slowly, so he could hear it better. He wrote down excerpts in the European system of symbols used for classical music (music **notation**), along with a great deal of verbal description of the performances. Of course, the European system for capturing music on paper could not capture many elements of the gamelan performance. These instruments were not tuned to the notes of a Western musical scale, so presenting them in Western notation was inaccurate. Louis Bénédictus went still further, altering the Javanese music to fit French concepts. In a publication entitled "Bizarre Musics at the Exposition" he remade the gamelan music into pieces that could be played on the piano.[30] These pieces reduced the complexity of the gamelan to what could be played by one person and eliminated the special resonant sound of the metallic gamelan instruments. Bénédictus also changed the melodies so that they would reflect a French idea of tunefulness. Yet, as Revuluri has pointed out, they are not typical French piano pieces of their time. Bénédictus's versions did capture some of the rhythmic density, percussive textures, and sudden shifts in timing that seemed special about the gamelan.[31]

The Exposition reflected an attitude typical of its time: a fascination with the "other" people of the East. Fascination with the unfamiliar is known as **exoticism**: this fascination is fueled by the knowledge that the observer has more power than the observed "other." The particular kind of exoticism that focuses on an imaginary East is called **orientalism**.[32] Some French listeners were charmed and enraptured by the gamelan music in this way. One eyewitness, Émile Monod, wrote that "like the crystalline sounds of faraway bells, the plaintive peace of this languid tonality seems to express vague pains and cradles us deliciously."[33] He found the gamelan charming precisely because it was different, and he used orientalist stereotypes of the unknown East ("languid," "vague") as well as sensuous language ("pains," "cradles us") to express that attraction.

Some people heard the gamelan as evidence that people in the colonies were indeed primitive, as compared to the modern people of Europe. Monod reported: "The Javanese gamelan, the Arabian oboes, the Annamite [Vietnamese] violins, etc. are of great interest from the point of view of the history of music; the interest is less from the point of view of production for these instruments have not changed for centuries. Conversely, European music has progressed constantly."[34] The French musician Claude Debussy (1862–1918) admired the gamelan for the new and complex sounds it offered. Reversing

Monod's claim, Debussy wrote that "if we listen without European prejudice to the charm of their percussion we must confess that our percussion is like primitive noises at a country fair."[35] Where the critic was eager to use the music as an occasion to point out the superiority of the French, Debussy rejoiced in new sounds from afar. Both the disdain and the fascination are elements of orientalism.

What Debussy loved about this music was not necessarily the same thing individual Javanese might have loved about it; he was interested in new musical ideas from the Western perspective, and the Javanese system offered a way of making music outside of the Western tradition of harmony. Oddly, gamelan music also appealed to Debussy's French national pride. This was not because the Javanese had anything to do with the French. Rather, because so much of traditional classical music was German in origin and was dominated by German composers and techniques, some French musicians of Debussy's generation were looking for nontraditional, non-Germanic ways of organizing their music. As far as Debussy was concerned, music that presented a new alternative was welcome.

During and after the Universal Exposition, the arts became a means to express an awareness of colonized peoples and the social inequality of colonial relationships.[36] Debussy experimented with using the sounds of Javanese gamelan in his own compositions. Listen again to some of example 1.3, recalling its different layers of rhythmic activity, some moving slowly, some moving twice or four times as fast. Then compare example 1.3 to example 1.7. Example 1.7 is a piano piece called "Pagodas," completed in 1903. The texture of this piano music at timepoint 0:52 closely imitates that of Javanese gamelan music, with different, pulsating layers of activity.[37] By the end of the piece (timepoint 4:34) Debussy has introduced a very fast layer of ornaments above the slower activity.

Example 1.7. Claude Debussy, "Pagodas," performed by Sally Pinkas, Dartmouth College, 2014. Used by permission.
Link: https://doi.org/10.3998/mpub.9853855.cmp.12

Debussy imitated the gamelan in other ways, too. Sometimes the performers of a gamelan play in unison to create a dramatic effect. You can hear an example of this effect in example 1.2 at timepoint 0:13. Debussy used this effect in "Pagodas" (example 1.7) at timepoint 2:23, among other places. Especially at the climax of Debussy's piece (starting timepoint 4:02), low notes on the piano imitate the strokes of the largest gong.

As Revuluri explained, Debussy's imitation was far from exact: it is like a reminiscence of what he heard at the Exposition, translated into a French musical style and transposed to a Western musical instrument. A gamelan and a piano are tuned differently. Debussy often uses groups of six rather than four fast notes, creating an imprecise wash of sound. Most important, his piece is not organized in cycles. Instead, it follows a classic European form: it begins by introducing musical ideas, moves away from them in the middle, then returns to those ideas at the end. Nevertheless, the overall effect is an unmistakable imitation of the gamelan sound.

Ultimately, Debussy became dissatisfied with the fashion of borrowing ideas from afar. He wrote that Western versions of folk music "seemed sadly constricted: the additions of all those weighty counterpoints had divorced the folk tunes from their rural origins."[38] Here Debussy fell back on a particular idea of indigenous authenticity—the belief that the music had been played in a certain way since the dawn of time and should not be altered.[39] Of course, no music is eternally the same. In this particular case individual Javanese composers had been adding to the gamelan tradition, creating individualized and identifiable works with titles, for at least a hundred years. The music scholar Richard Mueller has connected Debussy's statement to the composer's frustration in revising his Fantasy for Piano and Orchestra. Debussy found that despite his efforts, he could not reconcile the subtly changing texture of gamelan music with European music in a way that satisfied him.[40]

Debussy's desire to leave the Javanese music untouched, in its supposedly natural state, was a romantic idea. This kind of thinking is like that of the anthropologists who treated the Javanese on exhibit as if they were specimens from another time, not another place. Thinking about groups of people as distinct unto themselves and totally separate in a way that nothing can overcome is characteristic of colonialism, which maintains rigid social divisions between groups to preserve a power structure. At the same time, though, Debussy felt an urge to experiment with these sounds himself, to make something new out of them, in part precisely because of the feeling of utter difference, utter novelty. Debussy was motivated by attraction to the music but also by the exoticism (and the racism that often comes with the exoticism) that was characteristic of his time. Debussy was not the only one who felt this fascination. Some European musicians even traveled to Java to hear gamelan music.[41]

What are we to make of Debussy's appropriation of the sound of gamelan music? It is not exactly theft, for the gamelan musicians lost neither the ability to play their music nor income as a result of Debussy's composing "Pagodas."

From a musician's perspective, the reuse is also not that unusual: musicians have a tendency to remember and imitate sounds they like, playing with them and incorporating them into their own music. Still, borrowing across colonial lines with an attitude of exoticism seems troubling, as it delineates a difference of power, with a wealthier and more powerful European person drawing on music made by less powerful people of color.

The literary scholar Homi Bhabha, who has spent his career studying the phenomenon of colonialism, calls situations like this **colonial mimicry**. According to Bhabha the colonizer makes an imitation of the Other that reforms it but keeps it recognizable, creating "*a difference that is almost the same, but not quite.*"[42] In this context appropriating the music of a people can be a way to show power over them. But to create an imitation, the colonizer must engage with the colonized people, studying their ways, and this engagement threatens the wholeness of the colonizer's culture by introducing foreign elements into it.[43] Colonial mimicry creates new, blended artifacts and practices and shows how, once an empire is established, colonizers and colonized peoples are locked together in an uncomfortable but unavoidable relationship.

Indeed, even after Debussy stopped imitating gamelan music, some of its effects lingered in his music. Debussy had used six notes in the place of four to represent the quickest rhythmic level of the gamelan sound. He found that he liked that effect. He used it again in other pieces of music, and it was eventually absorbed into the French style of Debussy's time. As Revuluri has explained, this effect, which began as an imitation of a French idea of Asian music, was no longer audibly Asian.[44] Yet there it remained, a trace of the colonial relationship that was dramatized for Europeans at the Exposition.

Music and the Tourist Trade: Balinese *Kecak*

Another effect of colonialism is that it changes the marketplace for music in the colonized location, bringing in audiences from afar who make demands on performers. Even after colonies become independent (decolonization), tourism along trade routes established by colonists has delivered visitors; as audiences they, too, affect the musical scene. An excellent example of these effects is a practice called **kecak** (ke-chock), cultivated by amateur and professional musicians in Bali, a small Indonesian island east of Java. Kecak is a form of dance and drama accompanied by a special kind of vocal chanting on the syllable *-cak* (chock), performed by a male chorus.

At the time when kecak originated, this kind of chanting was performed in two different situations: a traditional sacred trance chant called *sanghyang dedari*, which was not performed as a drama, and a secular (nonreligious) form that is highly theatrical. In the sanghyang dedari ritual the "cak" chanting is used to accompany the dancers who enter an altered mental state; there is also a female chorus. In secular kecak the chanting of the male chorus is a form of entertainment that adds excitement to a drama (the female chorus is omitted). Balinese performers view these as separate kinds of performance: one is a religious rite, whereas the other is an artistic spectacle performed for tourists. According to I Wayan Dibia, a practitioner of kecak, both the sacred and secular versions are still performed, though the secular one is now much better known.[45]

In the secular form of kecak, heard in example 1.8, the male chorus, dressed in checkered sarongs over short trousers, sits on the ground in concentric circles. The chorus, which is responsible for the "cak" chant, takes on various roles to support the drama: sometimes they portray a monkey army or an ogre, at other times the wind or a garden. Sometimes the chorus sings in unison; at other times the chorus uses short syllables in interlocking rhythms that create a sound of busy complexity.

Example 1.8. Choral presentation of "cak" syllables. Excerpt from a kecak performance in Uluwatu, Bali. YouTube. Good faith effort has been made to contact the videographer.
Link: https://doi.org/10.3998/mpub.9853855.cmp.13

I Wayan Dibia has described the chant as a "voice orchestra," presenting through vocal means the melodic phrases and rhythmic patterns that reflect those of the traditional Balinese orchestra (gamelan). Figure 1.4 shows one possible rhythmic pattern for the chanting. Performing ensembles can choose from among several different rhythmic patterns of this interlocking kind.[46]

A chorus leader chooses the tempo for the performance and cues the chanters to perform loudly or softly. A beat keeper imitates gong sounds with his voice, sometimes joined by members of the chorus. A narrator tells the story. Occasionally, we also hear solo singers, and sometimes the whole chorus sings a melody together. In kecak solo dancers perform intricate gestures that distantly recall the formal dance traditions of Balinese royal courts. Meanwhile, the gestures of the chanting chorus are informal: they sit cross-legged, stand, wave their arms, or bow in a praying gesture as the story requires.[47]

In a later excerpt from the same kecak performance (example 1.9) we meet

beats	1	2	3	4	5	6	7	8
group A		x			x			x
group B	x			x		x		
group C	x				x		x	

Fig. 1.4. Diagram of interlocking syllables in kecak. The numbers across the top mark successive points in time. Separate groups within the chorus say "cak" at different time-points to create an interlocking pattern. This pattern was taught to me by Jeremy Grimshaw in 2011.

Sita, the wife of Rama, who is the noble incarnation of the god Vishnu. Sita has been abducted. Near the start of the excerpt Trijata enters: she is the niece of the evil demon king Rahwana, but she has become Sita's friend during her captivity. Sita and Trijata dance in an elegant and courtly manner, which befits their elevated social status. This scene includes a mournful song about Sita's fate as a prisoner; sometimes we also hear narration through the spoken word. You can see the solo singer sitting among the chorus members, facing the camera. The chant is a nearly constant presence, sometimes loud and sometimes soft.

Example 1.9. Sita in captivity; entrance of Trijata. Excerpt from a kecak performance in Uluwatu, Bali. Good faith effort has been made to contact the videographer. Link: https://doi.org/10.3998/mpub.9853855.cmp.15

Partway through the performance, the warrior monkey Hanuman enters: he has been sent by Rama to contact Sita. At first she rejects him, but when he shows her Rama's ring, she knows why he has been sent. In return she gives him a flower to take back to Rama.[48] Especially noticeable in example 1.10 is the interaction between the performers and the tourists who have come to view the kecak performance. Although Sita and Trijata do not acknowledge the tourists, Hanuman makes a great stir by engaging the tourists, sitting with them, posing for pictures, and even checking tourists' hair for bugs, as a monkey might. The tourists respond with typical tourist behavior, laughing and chatting. One even steps out into the performance space to take a photo of Hanuman with evident delight.

Example 1.10. Hanuman interacts with the audience. Excerpt from a kecak performance in Uluwatu, Bali. Good faith effort has been made to contact the videographer. Link: https://doi.org/10.3998/mpub.9853855.cmp.16

The secular form of kecak has its origin in the 1930s. The German musician and artist Walter Spies, who had lived in Bali since 1927, was visiting a Balinese historic site. Spies was serving as the choreographer for a film entitled *The Island of Demons*, and he wanted a dramatic musical performance that would be exciting for the film. Spies suggested that the kecak sacred chant be combined with a dramatic performance of scenes from the Ramayana epic, an ancient Hindu poem, and he worked with the Balinese dancer I Wayan Limbak to realize his vision.[49] According to Limbak, who played a role in Spies's film, "The final form of the kecak was the result of a collaboration between Spies and village elders, with Spies determining the theme of the dance and its timing."[50] The film contained an exorcism scene, which represented the sacred sanghyang dedari ritual in abbreviated form, without the trance element. This was the first time the ritual was presented in a non-religious context, though in recent years musicians have permitted tourist access to the sacred form.[51] Although Spies seems to have played a significant role in the founding of this performing tradition, he insisted that the secular kecak was a Balinese creation.[52]

Indeed, Balinese people made this kind of performance into a tradition of their own. The Ramayana epic was already a thousand-year tradition in Bali, familiar to performers and audiences on an island where Hindus form the majority of the population.[53] The importance of this Hindu drama had been reinforced by the Dutch administration, which promoted Hinduism in the 1920s as a way to contain Islam in the Indonesian islands.[54] The musician I Gusti Lanang Oka and the businessman I Nengah Mudarya brought Spies and Limbak's version of kecak to the village of Bona, refined its formal structure, and established "The Abduction of Sita" as a favorite scene.

Kecak also benefited from the Dutch policy of "Balinization"—that is, preservation of Bali in what the Dutch thought of as a pristine state. The Dutch colonized Bali much later than Java; beginning in the 1840s and continuing until 1908, they conducted military campaigns against the Balinese kingdoms that resulted in the violent deaths of many Balinese. That the European press covered this violence embarrassed the Dutch, who wanted to be regarded as benevolent colonizers. To repair their reputation, in the 1920s the Dutch forbade modernization in Bali and encouraged the restoration of the arts as they had been practiced in the destroyed kingdoms. This effort produced a self-consciousness among Balinese people about their own artistic life and how they wanted it to be understood by others. Outsiders typically viewed Bali's arts and rituals as untouched by the West, but in fact these traditions had been revived and altered under Dutch influence.[55] Spies's activities were part of a growing tourist industry that supported and encouraged these revived rituals.

In the 1930s Bali was promoted to tourists as "the last paradise": artists in the village of Bona continued performing kecak to entertain tourists arriving on Dutch steamships. Yet there is no record of Balinese people attending these performances, which appear to have been made exclusively for tourists. After the 1960s, kecak troupes were established all over Bali, especially in the south. The movement of large numbers of tourists supported the development of this long-standing institution of Balinese music. Today there are about 20 troupes that regularly perform kecak.[56]

Kecak is community-based music: people from a particular village work together to sustain a schedule of regular paid performances. Rather than using the income for personal needs, most of the money goes to community goals such as securing a water supply or restoring a temple. To fulfill this function, kecak is still performed for tourists. The people who organize kecak performances are in close contact with hotels, restaurants, and tourist agencies. Some troupes have permanent contracts with hotels.[57]

Over its 90-year history kecak has been subject to larger political and economic forces. During the Second World War Japan occupied most of the islands in the region, and many residents of the islands suffered war crimes. After declaring independence in 1945, Indonesians experienced years of violence and political instability as nationalists in favor of independence clashed with those who remained loyal to the Dutch. Under the "Old Order" Sukarno regime (1945–67) conflicts between Muslims and other religious groups overlapped with conflicts between communism and capitalism and between democracy and authoritarianism. From 1965 to 1967 the Indonesian Army and its vigilantes, supported by the US government, killed between a half million and one million people, many of them ethnic Chinese or actual and alleged members of the Communist Party. Under these conditions tourism declined sharply. Furthermore, Balinese nationalists hated the idea of foreign entities using their island as a museum, so they dismantled the Balinese tourism industry.[58] Under the authoritarian but stable Suharto regime (the "New Order," 1967–98), though, tourism was actively encouraged again, in part because Indonesia needed the income. In 1969 a new international airport opened at Denpasar, making Indonesia easier to reach.[59]

With this new wave of tourism came increased attention to the possibilities for revitalizing and promoting many kinds of Indonesian music, including kecak. Most notable is the effort to standardize kecak performance.[60] In early kecak, performances presented fragments of the Ramayana epic; they did not attempt to tell the story in full, and even major characters could be omitted. They could also perform stories from other sources. Since the 1970s, though, kecak includes only certain standardized scenes from the Ramayana, and the selected story is presented in a more complete form. In kecak of the 1930s the chorus wore everyday clothes. Their costume has become more uniform over the years, with checkered sarong and red sash, as well as white dots on temples and forehead. Differences among kecak performances have become less a question of a director's artistic vision and more a question of whether well-trained soloists are available for key roles.[61]

Today, that process of standardization persists. If one troupe makes an innovation, it spreads quickly and becomes standard. Indeed, this standardization is enforced by the marketplace. The ethnomusicologist Kendra Stepputat has pointed out that most tourists arrive at kecak performances on the recommendation of other travelers, guides, printed guidebooks, or hotel employees. Kecak troupes pay guides and tourist agencies to bring people to their performances, and they rely on these channels of communication. The tourism industry has real power over the content of kecak: tourist agencies or guides can and do refuse to send tourists to performances that do not adapt.

Of course, foreign tourists typically have no idea of these market pressures. They know that kecak is unique to Bali and that it is a "must-see" cultural attraction. Under the influence of their tour guides tourists overwhelmingly experience kecak as "authentic," meaning that they perceive it as part of the long-standing heritage of people on the island, a tradition practiced by the entire population, handed down from generation to generation from time immemorial. There is no way for them to see that kecak is produced for their benefit and has always been made for tourists, not for Balinese people.[62] In the case of kecak the invented tradition elicits from outsiders that feeling of experiencing authenticity.

This situation is not as unusual as it might seem. Eric Hobsbawm has pointed out that many traditions are "invented": that is, they are constructed for the needs of the present, but they are made to seem valid by the use of symbols, rituals, and ideas from the past. The **invented tradition** is in large part a matter of representation. Appropriating older symbols helps to create the sense that the new practice is "authentic" or legitimate; it can help people feel part of a group; and it can help convince people of a new idea by couching it in familiar, traditional terms. According to Hobsbawm, traditions are invented more frequently in times of rapid change, and they frequently remind individuals of their citizenship, providing "flags, images, ceremonies, and music" that help them feel part of a nation.[63]

It is often not obvious that a tradition has been "invented." In the case of kecak the invented tradition is designed to seem ancient. It tells a story known to be more than a thousand years old, and the style of presentation retains the resonance of ritual even though its religious elements have been removed. The solo dancers' costumes look as though they belong to a courtly culture from another time. Even in the 1930s, the staging cultivated a sense of mystery. A visitor named Bruce Lockhart recorded in his diary that to enter the perfor-mance, one had to descend into a dark temple courtyard, lit only by torches. A Balinese performer gave Lockhart the impression that every male from the neighboring village was part of the presentation and that this performance was a regular social ritual in the villages.[64] That the chorus wears relatively little clothing and chants rapidly on a single syllable conforms very well to visitors' own stereotypes of indigenous peoples. Barbara Kirshenblatt-Gimblett, an expert on the presentation and performance of heritage, proposes that this kind of performance is a form of virtual reality: it lets tourists see what they want to see by creating it for them.[65]

All of these strategies have worked for the marketing of kecak. According to Stepputat a narrator on the National Geographic Channel described kecak in these terms in 1996: "On the island of Bali, man becomes the animal of its origins—this is the famous monkey dance called the kecak. Over a hundred men portray an army of chattering apes from the Hindu epic poem Ramayana. There is no orchestra, only the primeval sounds of the chorus."[66] This percep-tion of the kecak and the people who perform it as "primitive" forms a rela-tionship between the tourist and the performer, between the Balinese and the visitor. Appealing as it is, kecak allows visitors to understand themselves as "modern" people in contrast to the presentation they see—even though the performers are their contemporaries. (This situation might remind us of the Universal Exposition of the 1880s.) Playing to other people's insulting stereo-types is a tactic known as **strategic essentialism**: this tactic has allowed Bali-nese communities to access tourist dollars for their own purposes. As tourism constitutes some 30 percent of the Balinese economy, the cultivation of these stereotypes has proven to be a resource for postcolonial Indonesians.

Of course, kecak *is* a traditional music: it is taught by one performer to another, enabling group cohesion and earning money for community proj-ects. Saying that kecak is an invented tradition does not make it less valid or meaningful than any other tradition. Rather, it is a way to point to the purposefulness by which kecak has been created and sustained. A tradition need not stretch back to the dawn of time to be real, and sometimes people craft their traditions to seem older than they are. Kecak would not fulfill its social purpose if tourists did not believe it was an old tradition. Giving that ancient impression is itself part of the tradition, as true of kecak in the 1930s as it is today.

Kecak serves as a reminder that what we can know from watching a performance is only part of what is really going on. Historians of the arts read many kinds of contextual clues: letters and photographs, interviews with musicians and bystanders, and observations about social relationships and the flow of money. No matter where a person stands in the scene—as a bystander, as a tourist, as someone who talks to the performers, as a viewer of YouTube—she or he will have access to only a partial perspective. What looks like an ancient practice to the outsider may merely be staged for the outsider's benefit.

This question of perspective is especially important for understanding the legacy of colonialism. Early in the 20th century, more than 500 million people lived under colonial rule. Over the course of the 1900s, many of these colonies declared independence and became sovereign nations, a process known as **decolonization**. But long-established colonial relationships could not be erased overnight. Our present-day world bears the scars of these relationships.

Indonesian Music in the World

Given that the Indonesian islands have been so intimately connected with other places for so long, it is not surprising that some of their music has become important abroad. The ethnomusicologist Maria Mendonça has identified active gamelan groups in many places. We might expect to find these groups in the Netherlands, given the former colonial relationship, and in Singapore, Taiwan, and Japan, given trade routes. But gamelan ensembles also exist in the United States, Great Britain, the Czech Republic, Poland, Australia, and New Zealand. Mendonça explains that most of these groups have flourished not because of Indonesians migrating to these places but because people with no heritage ties to Indonesia experience an affinity for this music.[67] Gamelan has been **deterritorialized**—unlinked from the place where it originated.

Since Debussy's encounter with gamelan in Paris, gamelan has become not just a one-time encounter with an exotic curiosity but also a part of educational and musical institutions. In England and Wales gamelan was included in the National School Curriculum for Music. Educators have been attracted to the sense of working together that is required to play interlocking parts. One teacher noted that gamelan is a lesson in civics: "you have to be responsible to everyone else in the group, no matter which part you play."[68] On the most practical level, a gamelan can be large enough to accommodate a whole class of schoolchildren, and the level of difficulty of different parts varies, so different musical abilities can be accommodated within the group. Because few Indonesian people live in Britain, gamelan seems egalitarian: it does not belong to some members of the group more than others. For some of the same reasons gamelan has become a beloved institution at many North American colleges and universities.[69]

Why has gamelan become a worldwide phenomenon, while other kinds of Indonesian music have not? This situation is a good example of Anna Tsing's idea of "friction": some kinds of music move easily and gain a foothold in new places, and others do not.[70] In the case of gamelan the musical values of European and Euro-American listeners have garnered this music institutional support. Gamelan has been treated as a "classical" (or court) music by scholars; indeed, it has been researched since the 1920s, sometimes with the financial support of the Dutch government. As a court music with a long history, gamelan could be taken seriously in the West as a tradition analogous to European classical music. After Old Order Indonesia successfully exhibited gamelan at the 1964 World's Fair in New York, the Indonesian government sold 10 sets of gamelan instruments to colleges and universities in the United States. Though the sale was inspired by a need for hard currency, this gesture also supported the propagation of gamelan in academic institutions outside Indonesia.[71]

According to Sumarsam, a Javanese American ethnomusicologist, "the colonial legacy has brought about a complex society in which individuals' and institutions' viewpoints cannot be sorted in terms of a simple inside-outside dichotomy."[72] The various efforts that colonial and postcolonial governments made to establish, reestablish, or publicize musical traditions gave gamelan support within Indonesia but also made gamelan seem to outsiders like a tradition of central importance. The outsiders' positive view then encouraged Indonesians to maintain that tradition. For instance, echoing the Exposition of 1889, the New Order regime continued to support gamelan as an emblem of Indonesia, sending Javanese and Balinese gamelan and dance to represent Indonesia at the 1970 World Exposition in Osaka.[73] This action aimed to satisfy world opinion with a music that had proven recognition and appeal, as cultivated during the colonial period. In contrast, contemporary Indonesian popular music—much more popular than gamelan with listeners in today's Indonesia—has struggled since the 1970s under changing regulations about what kinds of music and dance could be broadcast over government-controlled radio and television. As Indonesian government officials believed this less dignified music was unfit to represent Indonesia, it found little support for international visibility.[74]

In the widespread adoption of gamelan the institutional legacy of colonialism is still present. East Asian, European, and North American institutions have demonstrated a preference for a "classical" or courtly music over a popular one, for an established tradition over newer ones, and for music that seems like ritual over transparently commercial music. These preferences accord with the priorities imposed by Europeans and carried on by the postcolonial governments of Indonesia. Musicians' choices to innovate or to preserve tradition and listeners' choices about which music to prefer reflect contemporary circumstances, but they are rooted in many layers of practices and values from the past. These layers include what the music means and has meant to generations of people of many ethnicities, as well as the ways in which colonizers and colonized people have interacted to shape and reshape the tradition over time.[75]

The situation of gamelan in today's world reveals that colonial relationships do not end when the colony becomes independent. The administration of any colony alters social and political norms, moving people around geographically and creating unequal power relations among them. After a colony breaks off the political relationship with a colonizer, the social and economic relationships created by colonialism often remain active. Even as they change, these relationships provide a network of connecting threads, shaping the pathways along which music moves.

2 The Romani Diaspora in Europe

Mutual Influences

A **diaspora** is a whole population or ethnic group that moves out of one place of origin, usually scattering to different places. (The word *diaspora* comes from the word *spore*—seeds in the wind, a "scattering" of people.) The term is often applied to Roma, Jews, and Africans who have been displaced from their original homelands for a variety of reasons. Most diasporas are involuntary or semivoluntary, not a happily chosen option. The movement of people and their practices and habits from one place to another has sparked musical interchange as populations come into contact. Taking the Roma as a case study, this chapter explores how the scattering of people affects music-making. We will see that even in diaspora, people can create and maintain meaningful connections that span distances and cross national borders.

Who Are the Roma?

The Roma are a diasporic people, a minority group of Indian descent. Scholars believe there are about 15 million Roma in Europe, several million in the Middle East, and about one million in North America, although the population figures are uncertain. There are many different language and cultural groups of Romani people. The term *Roma* comes from the Romani language and means "people." In recent years some European Roma have rejected the disparaging name *Gypsies* (derived from *Egyptian*, with negative connotations of being "gypped" or cheated) and adopted the term *Roma* as a way of talking about their diaspora as a whole. Joining their common political interests has enabled a more unified effort to obtain legal protections that are routinely denied them in their various countries of residence. Not all groups welcome this collective identity, though: the Sinti, who are scattered throughout central and western

Europe, prefer to use their own **ethnonym** (ethnic group name). Nonetheless, for the sake of convenience, I will adopt the widely recognized term *Roma* to refer to the diasporic population in general. An adjective form, useful too as a name for the language, is *Romani*—as in "the Romani people."

As people of North Indian origin, ancestors of Roma migrated to other parts of Asia, where some of their descendants remain, as well as to Europe. Continuing persecution and the search for employment introduced nomadic customs for some groups of Roma, although the overwhelming majority have been settled for decades or centuries. How the Roma diaspora began is unclear. Some histories suggest that thousands of Indian musicians were deported from India into the Sassanid Empire (now Iraq, Iran, Afghanistan, and Azerbaijan) to provide entertainment. Other accounts suggest that Arabic invasions of India caused waves of outward migration. It appears that over generations the Roma gradually made their way through the Byzantine Empire, moving farther into the Balkans, Greece, and the Slavic regions.[1]

During the 1400s and early 1500s small groups of Roma migrated to many parts of Europe, as far away as Spain and Scandinavia (fig. 2.1). They found creative ways to keep themselves safe as newcomers: acting the role of Christian penitents or pilgrims or using (often forged) letters from nobles or the pope stating that they should be allowed to travel. People in Europe wanted the Roma to provide skilled service as musicians, herbalists and healers, fortune-tellers, horse-traders, metalworkers, and manufacturers of weapons. But when the Roma entered these trades, they offended the local artisans, who lost business to them. Most Europeans viewed the Roma as criminals and intruders or believed them untrustworthy because they were far from their place of origin and had dark skin. Sometimes they were accused of witchcraft and punished without a trial or even hunted and murdered.[2] In eastern Europe some rulers valued the services of the Roma and allowed them to remain. Often they were paid in food rather than money, which increased their dependence on the goodwill of the rulers. In Wallachia and Moldavia, then part of the Ottoman Empire, the lords enslaved almost all of the Roma, keeping them as skilled laborers.[3]

Because Romani customs seemed strange, European governments enforced assimilation; that is, they wanted Roma to act more like the people around them. Beginning in the 1640s, the king of Spain attempted to force Romani people to adopt Spanish customs. In the Habsburg Empire Empress Maria Theresa encouraged assimilation by requiring the Roma to settle and pay taxes from the 1740s onward. She tried to dilute their racial identity by letting them

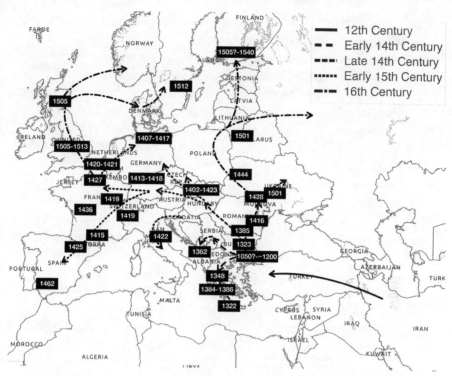

Fig. 2.1. *Music on the Move:* Migration of Romani people into Europe. Map by Eric Fosler-Lussier, based on Lev Tcherenkov and Stéphane Laederich, *The Rroma*, vol. 1 (Basel, CH: Schwabe, 2004), 83. (See https://doi.org/10.3998/mpub.9853855.cmp.18)

marry only non-Roma, and she prohibited them from setting themselves apart by their clothing, their language, or their professions. Aside from encouraging the diasporic Roma to stay put, these measures failed. Most Roma did not entirely give up their own traditions, even if they adopted local habits when required to do so. Most continued to use the Romani language alongside whatever local languages they needed, such as German, Slovak, Spanish, Hungarian, Bulgarian, or French. Integration has had marked effects—the Romani language includes many borrowed words from local languages—but efforts to extinguish Romani traditions and ethnic traits were largely unsuccessful.[4]

Persecution has followed the Roma throughout their history, even to the present day. Almost two-thirds of the Roma in Nazi-occupied Europe were killed in the Holocaust; the Roma received no postwar reparations from the German government, and the killing of Romani people was not fully acknowledged until the late 1970s.[5] Policies that took Romani children away from their families to encourage assimilation persisted in Switzerland until the 1970s and were prominent in the communist East Bloc countries. Romani who have endured forced sterilization, police brutality, and routine denial of access to education have sought redress in the European Court of Human Rights.[6] Although Romani people have lived in Europe for centuries, they have not always been offered a sense of belonging.

Even so, the Roma have played a significant and distinctive role in European musical culture. Because many Romani people were musicians and entertainers by profession, they interacted a great deal with the other populations of every region they visited, and many of them became adept at performing musical styles of those regions. Playing whatever style of music people would pay to hear is a form of social and economic **assimilation**—changing their behavior to fit the expectations of the dominant group—that has been useful for diasporic Romani people in many parts of Europe.

The majority cultures around them have shaped how the Roma minority make their music, but their music has also had a noticeable impact on the people around them. Not only have the Roma taken on the musical styles of regions where they live and work; they have also helped to define what those regional styles are. What is known worldwide as Hungarian music is hard to separate from the Romani style of playing. Flamenco, one of the most recognizable musical styles of Spain, was developed by the Calé, or Spanish Roma. Sinti jazz (also called Manouche jazz) is a distinctive style of music that originated in Paris. The interplay of the Roma and Sinti with the peoples around them makes a useful case study, helping us to see the ways in which diasporic people adapt to new places and shape musical life in those places.

Hungarian "Gypsy" (Romani) Music: Integration and Tradition

The music of Hungarian Roma provides an excellent example of the strategies by which diasporic people fit socially and culturally into the societies in which they live. Because they have adapted over time to a variety of social circumstances, different groups of Roma have developed different musical practices. The two largest groups of Hungarian Roma are the Romungro and the Vlach Roma. The Romungro are Hungarian Roma who have historically been integrated into Hungarian society, most of them urban. Most of them speak more Hungarian than Romani; many of them have lost their Romani language skills altogether. Documents from the 1700s tell of "Gypsy music" ensembles who were hired to provide party music and dance music at the courts of princes and dukes. This evidence demonstrates that Romungro musicians were integrated into the fabric of life for ethnic Hungarians, even though they participated as a separate social class, as hired help at parties. Today they continue to be employed as professional musicians but also work in a variety of other jobs. They still experience discrimination in education, although the number who have access to universities is growing.[7]

Romungro Music

The popular music that Romungro (integrated, Hungarian-speaking) musicians play for Hungarian listeners has long been known simply as "Gypsy music"—even though it has also been strongly associated with Hungarian identity. In the words of the musicologist David Schneider, "'Gypsy music' refers to the popular music often performed in cafés or restaurants in regions historically belonging to Hungary by professional musicians who are frequently ethnic Romanies."[8] For a long time people made no distinction between the "Hungarian" style of music and the "Gypsy" style: Hungarians thought of the music Romungro people played as Hungarians' own (after all, it was made for them), and Western Europeans thought the Hungarian and the Gypsy style were one and the same because both Hungarians and Roma seemed foreign to them.[9]

Very often a single piece of Romungro music includes a slow section ("music for listening") followed by a fast section ("music for dancing"). This slow-fast sequence is a holdover from a popular Hungarian dance style of the late 1700s. In addition, Romungro musicians often played Hungarian tunes; and they adopted the violin and the clarinet, two Western European instruments, as the most prominent lead instruments in their bands. In short, the music known as "Gypsy music" has long blended ethnic Hungarian elements with a style of performance particular to Romungro musicians.[10] This style is not intrinsically ethnic—it can also be adopted by non-Romungro musicians— but it has been associated with Roma because so many Roma people in Hungary made a living as professional musicians, playing this music.

The video clip in example 2.1 shows musicians performing "Gypsy music" in a restaurant in Budapest. There is a clear social separation between the entertainers and the restaurant patrons; however, the Romungro do share the space of the restaurant with its Hungarian patrons, and the patrons evidently enjoy the music. The music at the beginning is an example of the slow (listening) style. The music sounds very romantic: the violinist plays fast notes "around" the main notes of the melody as ornaments and often hesitates and holds out notes to prolong the listener's suspense. You see and hear a lead violin (playing the melody); a *cimbalom*, a hammer dulcimer that can play either melody or background chords; and some backup stringed instruments, the bass and second violin, which typically fill in harmony along with the cimbalom, or play "oom-pah" off-beats in fast music. Sometimes a band like this also includes a clarinet as a second lead instrument.

Example 2.1. Lajos Sárkozi, Jr., and his ensemble playing at the Százéves restaurant, Budapest. Video by Willem Gulcher, used by permission. Good faith effort has been made to contact the performers.
Link: https://doi.org/10.3998/mpub.9853855.cmp.19

Listen to example 2.1, and notice the changes in tempo (speed). The lead violinist, Lajos Sárközi Jr. (LYE-osh SHAR-keh-zee), dictates the pace of the music, and as in the previous example, there are pauses, hesitations, and very fast passages with lots of notes. In the slow section that opens the clip, the group lingers on each harmony while the violinist provides the ornamented, dramatic melody. The changes in tempo and some of the ornamental flourishes are **improvised**: Sárközi decides on these in the moment. At timepoint 1:49 he leads the group to move slightly faster, and the progression of time becomes a little more regular. In this section, even though the tempo is still slow, we start to hear a steady "oom-pah" pulse in the background some of the time. At timepoint 3:44, the violinist pauses, then begins a section in the fast style ("music for dancing"). The violinist introduces a new tune that sounds more like "fiddling," with a steadier stream of notes, and the chord changes become more frequent. The musicians play at a quick and comparatively steady tempo, accompanied by "oom-pah" patterns in the bass and second violin. Even at this fast tempo, the lead violinist takes some liberties, arriving at the main beat a little before or a little behind everyone else and leading the whole group to speed up toward the end. This purposeful imprecision adds to the feeling of spontaneity in the performance, keeping the listener in moment-to-moment suspense about what is coming next.

The **virtuosity** of the lead violinist and the cimbalom player is an important part of the performance. Virtuosity means technically difficult playing (such as playing two notes at once or a series of extremely fast notes): the person who plays this way is called a virtuoso. To play this music well requires that the performers be as dramatic and showy as possible. Sárközi comes from a Romani family with a long musical tradition: his father is also a well-known performer. The younger Sárközi (1991–) developed his virtuosity at Hungary's premier school of music, the Liszt Academy of Music in Budapest. The "Gypsy" style is not his only occupation: he is also an expert performer of jazz, including but not limited to the Manouche jazz tradition developed in France.

Minority and Nationhood

The integration of Romani people into European societies as professional musicians has presented both opportunities and challenges. Like other Romani people in Hungary, Romungro musicians face discrimination in housing, education, and other social services. Still, their ability to entertain Hungarian listeners has provided them an income and a distinctive social role. As the musicologist Lynn Hooker has shown, this "integrated but not equal" status has shaped how people understand their music.

Perhaps because Romani performers are so often thought of in racist terms, the question of who should take the credit for "Gypsy music" has been raised throughout the music's history. In 1854 a Hungarian scholar warned that "trusting the preservation and distribution" of the national music "only to Gypsies" could lead to a serious misunderstanding: "it must not be a matter of surprise if foreign musicians begin to doubt the true Hungarian character of the national music customarily performed by our Gypsies, and if they regard this as being Indian Gypsy music rather than Hungarian music."[11] Some Hungarians wanted the credit for Romani musicians' innovative playing to be given to Hungary rather than to the Roma themselves.

This sentiment was in accord with the Hungarian **nationalism** of the time. Nationalism can encompass not only an investment in the nation's political success but also promotion of its artistic achievements. It is important to remember that nationalism is based on a belief in shared genealogy, history, or ethnicity; in a nation that saw itself as ethnically Hungarian, Roma were outsiders, no matter how long they had been there. From the Hungarian ethnic nationalist point of view, the musical basis of Hungarian "Gypsy music" was entirely Hungarian, including musical features that had been present in Hungarian folk songs for centuries. The Roma were merely hired performers who had adapted to the Hungarian style: they filled a social need, since gentlemen might compose a song but would certainly never perform one in public for money. Given the low social status of Romani people, many Hungarian critics have been unwilling to see them as creative partners in forming the national style of Hungary.

In the early 20th century, ethnomusicologists confronted this question. They acknowledged that Hungarian "Gypsy music" was Romani in origin, but they claimed that it was no good: it was merely popular music that had been corrupted to appeal to the masses. They blamed the Roma for demeaning the national style, and they went looking for "pure" musical performances among ethnically Hungarian peasants in rural areas.[12] This idea of "purity" was both an unattainable ideal and a racist one. It is unusual for a given ethnic group or a given music to maintain firm, clear boundaries over centuries. In particular, Eastern Europe's history is full of migrations that encouraged the mixing of peoples and musics. This quest for a purely "Hungarian" tradition can be understood as a product of the pressures of the time, as well as ethnic bias: many peoples during this period claimed their national traditions as a point of pride, and Eastern European nations wanted to establish their own identities more firmly. Still, the desire either to strip the credit for "Gypsy music" from the Roma or to vilify the music altogether is striking, given the ongoing popularity of this music in Hungarian public life. This controversy demonstrates that even when the majority culture has adopted the musical contributions of a diasporic minority, that adoption has not always been wholehearted.

In contrast, Franz Liszt (1811–86; pronounced "List"), a 19th-century musician of Hungarian descent, thought that the uniqueness of Hungarian music was primarily attributable to the Roma. Liszt insisted that Romani performers should receive credit for their musical creations; of course, Hungarian music critics were outraged.[13] People in Western Europe were reasonably willing to accept Liszt's story because the Hungarians, being of a different language group, already seemed peculiar. Furthermore, Western Europeans were susceptible to **orientalism**: they enjoyed reading about "oriental secrets" and hearing vivid, exciting performances. Whether these performances were defined as Hungarian or Gypsy was not very important to them; indeed, they did not recognize the difference between the two. Ironically, the way people in Western Europe thought about Hungarians was similar to the way Hungarians thought about the Roma. Believing that some people are exotic "others" can make their music seem more attractive, even as it also creates a disparity of opportunities between the two groups.

Vlach Roma Music

The second most populous subgroup of Romani people in Hungary are known as Vlach Roma (sometimes spelled Vlax; the final sound is a "kh" at the back of the throat). The Vlach Roma are descendants of the Roma who were enslaved in Wallachia and Moldavia. Those who moved into Hungary after their emancipation in the 1850s lived in rural areas, were not well integrated into Hungarian language and culture, and tended to preserve the Romani language. They maintained their own musical styles, distinct from the styles of the urban Romungro.[14] Traditionally, Vlach Roma were not professional musicians but artisans: for generations many were metalworkers or wood-carvers. As the rural Vlach musical tradition developed, these Roma typically made music among themselves, for their own use. Whereas the Romungro adopted some Western European instruments (like the violin) for their music-making, the music of the Hungarian Vlach Roma places far more emphasis on the human voice.[15]

Like Romungro music, the traditional music of Vlach Roma people can be either slow or fast. Songs in the slow style are typically laments: they express longing, sadness, or frustration. Example 2.2 is a lament called "Grief, Grief." This song is not accompanied by instruments, and it is comparatively simple. The melody generally moves from higher notes to lower notes, like a sigh, and it has a mournful tone. The tempo is variable, and the singer uses both the timing of his phrases and the quality of his voice to express sorrow. You can also hear that the music-making is interactive, with audience comments inserted into the singer's pauses. These are the lyrics to "Grief, Grief":

Grief, grief,
If I could catch you,
I would bind you into my apron,
I would push you into the [river] Danube.

Into the Danube, into the [river] Tisza,
'cause I'm alone;
I have neither father nor mother;
I will die.

Oh, how God has damned me,
And there's nothing I can do,

I have to suffer,
Mother, I must die!

This whore has killed me,
Let misery eat her!
She's eaten my head,
Let poverty destroy her!

I don't sleep for nights on end,
I just keep thinking;
I always think about
What I could do?

I grew up in poverty,
Motherless and fatherless,
And I grew up
Among the many good boys.

My young life, mother,
I live in sorrow,
But I have to know
That I grew up as an orphan.[16]

Vlach Roma songs in the slow style often refer to being orphaned or discon-nected from family. Among Romani people, separation from one's family is one of the worst tragedies imaginable—and a common one throughout their history of persecution.

Example 2.2. Mihály Várady, "Grief, Grief," *Gypsy Folk Songs from Hungary* (Hungaroton 18028-29, 1989 [1976]). Courtesy of Naxos USA.
Link: https://doi.org/10.3998/mpub.9853855.cmp.20

In contrast, the Hungarian Vlach Roma fast song style often emphasizes happier themes. This is music for dancing, usually performed at parties with friends and extended family. This kind of song is produced in a distinctive way: people use their mouths to imitate the sounds of the string bass and other instruments to maintain a steady rhythm. (The closest analogy in Western tradition is beatboxing. The technical term for this strategy is **oral bassing**.)

Vlach Roma dance music can be accompanied with hand-clapping, spoons, or other rhythm sounds. If another instrument is available, it may be used, but the foundation of this music is the singing and the rhythm created by the oral bassing.

Listen now to Mihály Kolompar's "You Are Not That Sort of Girl" (example 2.3), which illustrates the Vlach Roma fast song style. This song is sung by just one singer. It is a lighthearted, flirtatious song, in which the singer playfully denounces a girl who might not return his affections. The singer alternates lyrics in Hungarian and Romani with oral bassing. He conveys the tune not only with singing but also with **vocables** (syllables that do not carry linguistic meaning) and trumpet-like buzzing with his lips:

> You aren't that pretty, only your eyes are pretty.
> Because of your curly black hair, soon I'll die.
> This gypsy girl didn't give me any grub.
> I asked her for it, but she didn't give it to me; she gave me brandy.[17]

Example 2.3. Mihály Kolompar, "You are not that sort of girl." *Music on the Gypsy Route* vol. 2 (Frémaux and Associés, 2004). Used by permission.
Link: https://doi.org/10.3998/mpub.9853855.cmp.21

Example 2.4 is one more Vlach Roma fast song, called "Who Has Been There." This example shows how two singers can perform this style of dance music. A woman's voice introduces the oral bassing; then she sings the main tune, with words in Hungarian and Romani, while a man joins in with oral bassing as accompaniment. Other people join in as the song continues. This kind of singing might be heard at a festive family party, with different people taking over the music-making so that everyone has a turn to dance.[18]

Example 2.4. "Who has Been There," song attributed to "the daughter of Limchi, in Végegyháza, the Buje." *Gypsy Folk Songs from Hungary* (Hungaroton 18028-29, 1989 [1976]). Courtesy of Naxos USA.
Link: https://doi.org/10.3998/mpub.9853855.cmp.22

This historical distinction between integrated and nonintegrated populations has broken down in recent years. From the early 1970s onward, a revival of folk music and dance in Hungary encouraged the exploration of many kinds of traditional music. Through formal classes or informal folk-dance evenings, amateur and professional folk dance enthusiasts brought rural music and musicians into urban environments.[19] The 1980s saw a boom in **world beat** (also called **world music**): the mass-marketing of recordings of many different ethnic groups and traditions.[20] These trends have brought Vlach Roma music greater visibility and brought Vlach Roma people opportunities and connections. The Vlach Roma performing group Kalyi Jag has capitalized on the appeal and novelty of this music. Their recordings, like the song "The Night Girls" (example 2.5), have made this music accessible internationally. So have the "Gypsy punk" musicians in the New York band Gogol Bordello.

Example 2.5. Excerpt from Kalyi Jag, "La Ratjake Cheya" (The Night Girls). *The Gypsy Road: A Musical Migration from India to Spain* (Alula Records, 1999). YouTube. Link: https://doi.org/10.3998/mpub.9853855.cmp.23

The Hungarian Vlach Roma are only one among many Romani groups. Despite the linguistic connections that tie them together, different groups have distinctive musical styles and practices. For instance, compare the Greek music in example 2.6 with the Romungro and Vlach Roma examples.

Example 2.6. Panajótis Lókos, Jórgos Pátzis, and Jórgos Jorgíou, "Khoròs Gáïda" (Bagpipe dance), recorded in 1977. *Gipsy Music from Macedonia* (Topic Records TSCD914, 1996). Link: https://doi.org/10.3998/mpub.9853855.cmp.24

The lead instrument in example 2.6 is a zurna, a reed instrument like an oboe. This music bears no resemblance to the Romani music typically performed in Hungary. Because the Roma are a diasporic population, scattered like seeds throughout many places, they have adapted their musical practices to suit their situations.

To sum up our story so far, there are important differences between the musics of different diasporic Romani groups. As we saw in the contrast between the Romungro people (Roma who have historically been integrated into Hungarian-speaking society) and the Vlach Roma (who have historically lived and made music apart from ethnic Hungarians), whether a particular group is economically, socially, and artistically integrated into the surrounding community affects the development of their tradition over time. Integration of a minority population with the majority may or may not mean altering aspects of one's own language, music, or customs in exchange for better opportunities.

"Gypsiness" in European Classical Music

Romani music (particularly the Romungro style) was consciously incorporated into the **concert music** (*or* **"classical"**) tradition of Central and Western Europe. People referred to the classical adoption of the Romungro style as the "Hungarian style"—believing that Romungro and Hungarian music were the same thing. This appropriation was part of a widespread preoccupation with foreign "others." Until the late 1600s the Turkish (Ottoman) Empire reigned in Southeastern Europe, including most of Hungary, extending to the outskirts of Vienna. It's not surprising that the Austrians and Germans were preoccupied with Turkish and other "Eastern" peoples during this time: this preoccupation inspired a fad of caricatured imitations of Eastern music in Western music. The point was not to portray other people's music accurately but to present a kind of "foreignness" in music. "Gypsy music" (the Romungro style) became one of the styles available to composers of classical music in Western Europe.[21] When discussing the stereotyped version of the people or the music, I will use the term *Gypsy*, even though it has pejorative connotations: this is a way to distinguish the stereotype from the lives and performances of Romani people.

European musicians typically did not imitate the Romungro style directly, but they used enough of its key features that the result was recognizable as "Gypsy." These borrowings usually included the presence of an individual instrument or voice (often violin or clarinet) played with heightened drama or expression, rhythmic flexibility (with a tendency to speed up or slow down dramatically), and a high degree of virtuosity. We hear these elements in example 2.7, the second movement of Joseph Haydn's String Quartet op. 54, no. 2.

Example 2.7. Joseph Haydn, String Quartet, op. 54 no. 2, second movement, performed by the Dudok Quartet. YouTube. Used by permission. Link: https://doi.org/10.3998/mpub.9853855.cmp.25

(In the European classical tradition a "movement" is a self-contained section within a multisection piece of music.) Haydn did not call this work "Gypsy," but many others have recognized Romungro features in it. A string quartet usually includes one slow movement, and it was a challenge for the composer to maintain the listener's interest at a sedate pace. In this movement Haydn solved the problem by allowing the violin to play a highly ornamented melody that moves at a variable tempo, in the manner of the Romungro slow style.

In comparison to a Romani performance there is less room for improvisation in Haydn's quartet: the piece is written down in music notation, and changes in the melody's speed are specified precisely in the violin part. The violin's runs of quick notes are still slower than what a Romani musician would play, but within the context of what is typical for the classical string quartet, the overall impression is still one of unusual freedom and flexibility.[22] In addition, Haydn chose an ordinary minor scale (a common Western scale pattern) rather than the altered notes characteristic of Romungro performance. This music is a distant echo of Romani performance, not an attempt to faithfully recreate it. This strategy was used occasionally by later composers, too: Johannes Brahms's Clarinet Quintet (1891) includes a slow movement that follows Haydn's model (example 2.8).

Example 2.8. Excerpt from Johannes Brahms, Clarinet Quintet, second movement, performed by Quatuor Modigliani with Sabine Meyer. YouTube. Link: https://doi.org/10.3998/mpub.9853855.cmp.26

Composers of Haydn's time (1732–1809) frequently borrowed ideas from dance music or popular tunes. Romungro bands were gaining fame by playing in Hungarian courts during Haydn's career, so he likely came into direct contact with their music.[23] For Haydn the Romungro style was just one of many useful musical "topics" to draw on and did not likely reflect a particular point of view regarding the Roma people.[24]

During the 1800s, though, the stereotyped idea of the "Gypsy" began to permeate popular culture. Gypsy characters were featured in opera and operetta (such as the famous *Carmen*), and imitations of the Gypsy style of instrumental music flourished.[25] The idea of the Gypsy had symbolic value for literate Europeans who lived in and around courts and cities. They were increasingly aware that their lives were constrained by rigid customs. Many of them imagined the Roma as freer than they were: unconstrained by European rules of decorum and able to wander at will. (In this kind of thinking, "wandering" is a stereotype: many Roma were settled, but other Europeans continued to imagine them as nomadic.) Franz Liszt published a long book called *The Gypsy in Music*, in which he praised the Roma for having a connection to nature that urban Europeans lacked: "The pleasures invented by man can never prove other than sickly and insipid to the man accustomed to drink from the cup which Nature offers him, intending him to enjoy every drink and to relish every drop. Of what value are town-baubles to the man who enjoys braving the winter, and feeling the fire of his cheeks resisting its cold breath—who prefers being alone and unsheltered from its biting rod?"[26] Liszt noticed that Romani people were frequently poorly housed and clothed, but he insisted that these conditions merely reflected their brave refusal of European norms. To him the Roma seemed strangely separate from "civilized" society, wild and ungovernable. Their music, likewise, seemed to come from their fiery, independent souls: "The masters of Bohemian art, eminently inspired, will not submit to any laws of reflection or restraint. . . . They give free course to every caprice and turn of fancy."[27] The Roma thus offered not only an attractive musical style but also a way for Europeans to imagine what it would be like to live a freer, more "natural" life—without the inconveniences of actually doing so.

These beliefs about the Roma exemplify **exoticism**. Composers have frequently chosen to use musical ideas that convey the idea of distant places, precisely because "away" may seem more exciting than "home."[28] Yet the Roma were not geographically distant from Europeans: this kind of exoticism differentiated people by skin color, clothing, music, social class, and behavior, not by distance. Perhaps because these "others" were close to home, most Europeans perceived them not as distant curiosities but as dangerous. Exoticism is a kind of imaginary thinking that crosses social boundaries: typical cases involve people with higher social status fantasizing about those whom they perceive to be their inferiors. When Romani music was incorporated into classical music, it became a way of making European classical music more exciting, with a definite flavor of having crossed a boundary to experience something dangerous.

Franz Liszt offers a particularly interesting case of blending Romani music and European classical music. Liszt was born in Western Hungary, but he learned to speak Hungarian only as an adult; most of his writings were produced in French. Still, he had intense feelings of national pride in Hungary. Liszt especially valued the virtuosity of Hungarian Romani music: although his book included a great deal of racial stereotyping, it also conveyed deep admiration for the thrilling virtuosic performances Romani musicians offered. Liszt himself was a virtuoso on the piano as well as a composer. Both in his concerts and in his compositions he tried to capture the excitement and passion of Romungro performances.

Some of Liszt's most famous piano works are his "Hungarian Rhapsodies," which directly imitate Romungro music. By calling these works **rhapsodies**, Liszt indicated that they were not piano pieces of any ordinary kind but impassioned, poetic musical outbursts. His Hungarian Rhapsody no. 2 (example 2.9) includes both slow and fast sections, closely modeled on Romungro practice.

Example 2.9. Franz Liszt, Hungarian Rhapsody no. 2, performed by György Cziffra. *The Masters Collection: György Cziffra* (Hungaroton HCD32814-16, 2019). Courtesy of Naxos USA.
Link: https://doi.org/10.3998/mpub.9853855.cmp.27

In the slow section a simple melody has been decorated with ornamental flourishes and dramatic changes in tempo. The beat is stretched and compressed in the Romungro tradition, with pauses and rushing ahead for dramatic effects.

Later in the piece, we hear an amazing imitation of the sound of the cimbalom, the hammer dulcimer commonly used by Romungro ensembles. Although this music is played on the piano, a standard Western instrument, this passage sounds like the cimbalom player's hammers quickly hitting the strings. We also hear a shift from slow, dramatic music to fast, hurried music (example 2.9, timepoint 6:00 to 7:32). Now that you are familiar with its "Gypsy" features, listen to the entire Hungarian Rhapsody no. 2. At the end of the rhapsody it sometimes sounds as if it might veer out of control as it accelerates to an exciting close.

Liszt's adoption of Romungro performance is substantially different from Haydn's. Whereas Haydn echoed just one element, the melodic freedom of Romungro performance, Liszt aimed to capture the specific instrumental sounds of a Romungro band, as well as the rousing spirit of its performance. Although Liszt wrote about Romungro people as an exotic race, he also esteemed them enough to pay close attention to their playing and even imitated them as precisely as possible in his own compositions and performances. Liszt's exoticism includes not only racist denigration but also affectionate admiration: a complicated blend of ideas that may be uncomfortable for us to recognize. Exoticism typically relies on this mixture of attraction and repulsion, fascination and loathing. It allows audiences to imagine contact with someone they believe is utterly different from them while also containing that contact within the frame of a performance that the audience can feel comfortable about. Liszt's music carries with it some of the excitement and some of the distinctive features of Romani performance. It also stirs the audience's imagination about the stereotyped "Gypsies," activating whatever prior knowledge or prejudices they carry with them. Those ideas are not separate from the music: they are part of what makes the performance fascinating.[29] Furthermore, these ideas are still present today. Romani musicians use this fascination to attract listeners by playing Liszt's rhapsodies in concerts and restaurants, and commentaries on Romani music often refer to the same exoticizing stereotypes that were common among Liszt and his contemporaries.[30]

There is no doubt that Liszt received great professional benefit from his use of Romungro music. He was esteemed as a concert performer and cheered by audiences all over Europe. Liszt's virtuosity was legendary: figure 2.2 is a caricature of him at the piano that shows him as having eight arms, the only way anyone could conceive of his playing music so complicated and fast. This virtuosity was not only an effect of the Romungro style, for he was a stunning pianist who played many kinds of music. But Romungro music provided a vehicle for showcasing his virtuosity that became a distinctive brand for him. (The giant sword in the caricature marks him as "Hungarian," as it was a gift to him from the Hungarian city of Pest; but the cartoonist was also making fun of Liszt's and Hungary's pompous nationalism.)[31] In addition, the Romungro style was a novelty: it allowed Liszt to bring new and exciting elements to his concerts, building a distinctive reputation. Liszt's Hungarian branding was good for business: the Rhapsodies drew people to his live performances; then he published them as printed sheet music in several different versions. Because he was an international performer with access to the music publishing market, Liszt stood to benefit financially from the Romungro style in a way that Romani musicians could not.

Indeed, the "Hungarian style" (that is, the domesticated European version of the Romungro style) flourished in European music. Johannes Brahms (1833–97) published four books of "Hungarian Dances" that sold very well. Most of them are based on borrowed tunes. The Hungarian Dances were piano pieces composed for four hands—two players sitting at one piano, playing together—a highly sociable form of music-making. In example 2.10 you can see the two players' enjoyment as they work together to coordinate the dramatic changes of tempo.

Example 2.10. Excerpt from Johannes Brahms, Hungarian Dance no. 5, performed by the Passepartout Piano Duo. YouTube.
Link: https://doi.org/10.3998/mpub.9853855.cmp.29

Fig. 2.2. "Liszt-Fantaisie." Anonymous caricature of Franz Liszt, *La vie Parisienne*, 3 April 1886. The original caption reads: "Liszt and his saber: He has renounced it today, after recognizing that he would do more damage with just the piano and his two hands. A strange specimen of the octopus species. Eight hands at four octaves each, thirty-two octaves!!!" Reprinted in Richard Leppert, "The Musician of the Imagination," in *The Musician as Entrepreneur, 1700–1914: Managers, Charlatans, and Idealists*, ed. William Weber (Bloomington: Indiana University Press, 2004), 42.

This music is significantly easier to perform than Liszt's virtuosic Hungarian Rhapsodies: Brahms's pieces could be played by dedicated amateurs who had pianos in their homes. Yet they still featured the hallmarks of the "Gypsy" style: fast-moving melodies, minor keys, variable tempos, and "oom-pah" accompaniments. A passage of high fast notes near the end of example 2.10 might recall either fiddling or the sound of the cimbalom but not with the exactness of Liszt's rendition.

It is noteworthy that composers of European classical music did not borrow all the elements of Romungro music. Some features, like fluctuations in tempo and the presence of a leading voice or instrument, were easy to accommodate. But some features of Romani music were subdued or absent in European classical composers' imitations. The bright or piercing tone quality is usually markedly reduced. The non-Western scale or melody patterns used by Romani musicians were usually "regularized" into a form of the minor mode. Perhaps most important, where Romani music includes a significant amount of improvisation, classical music was a written tradition: although there is always room for interpretation, the notes and instructions for performing them are usually present on the printed page. So even though Haydn's or Brahms's "Gypsy" style emulates a sense of free-spiritedness, the features that make the performance seem improvised are all specified in advance.

This choice to **appropriate** (or take) certain musical features was probably based on what features the European classical composers found appealing, dramatic, or interesting and what features could easily be accommodated by performers on standard Western instruments. As it was used in European classical music, "Gypsy music" appropriates some features of Romungro music, but not all, and integrates them into a preexisting type of music, Western classical music.

This appropriation was designed to please Europeans who had the means to purchase printed music. Brahms's Hungarian Dances provided a way for people who had pianos in their homes to enjoy the "Gypsy" style. Even people who would never encounter a Romani person became familiar with the style. At the same time, this feeling of familiarity could be deceiving: knowing these pieces was vastly different from knowing or understanding Romani people and different even from hearing them perform in person. Although the music might provide some knowledge of Romani music, we might say that such knowledge has been **mediated** multiple times. It has passed from Romani performance, through the European classical composer's selective listening, the composition of a new version for different instruments, that version's publication in sheet music, to its interpretation by other musicians. Much like a whispered game of "telephone," the content and meaning has changed in the process. People at the end of the chain may understand something very different from what was expressed at the beginning.

The gap between the Romani experience and the mediated version of that experience has sometimes caused grief. Many Europeans have maintained an affection for the popular cultural manifestations of "Gypsiness" yet have expressed a revulsion for real, living Romani people.[32] Though Roma have lived in Hungary for hundreds of years, society grants them much less "belonging" than it allows to ethnic Hungarians and only under certain conditions. Yet there is also a strange intimacy in the way that Romani music has been absorbed into the musics of Europe's ethnic majorities. Romani musicians created some of Europe's most distinctive national styles, and the ongoing confusion between what is "Hungarian" and what is "Gypsy" (or what is "Spanish" and what is "Gypsy") testifies to the connections between the ethnic majority and minority populations.

One cannot say that the diasporic Romani and the majority populations among whom they live are entirely separate; neither are they fully integrated. Rather, they remain in tension with each other but tightly bound together. Like the people in Europe's faraway colonies, the existence of Romani people allowed Europeans to define and imagine themselves as white, modern, and civilized: selves were defined against the perception of "others." Defining some people as outsiders, however, only increased their importance in the European imagination. As Stuart Hall has said, the outsider is "absolutely destined to return . . . to trouble the dreams of those who are comfortable inside."[33] In Europe's persistent preoccupation with Romani people we can see how thoroughgoing this impact has been. Complex relationships of this kind are typical of situations involving diaspora.

Eurovision 2017 and Romani Representation

The preoccupation with Romani music remains evident in our time. In May of 2017 the Romani Hungarian singer Joci Pápai (YO-tsee PAP-ah-ee) created great excitement among Roma and other ethnic minorities when he reached the finals of the Eurovision song contest.[34] This international contest, held every year, allows each European nation (and sometimes other nations) to submit one **pop song**. The songs are all performed live on television and via webcast. Eurovision estimates its audience at upward of 180 million people, reaching approximately 36 percent of the viewing public in its service area.[35] After semifinals and finals the contest's winner is chosen by a combination of online and phone voting from the public and juries located in the participating countries. Over the years the Eurovision contest has been a highly visible event where nations represent themselves: through a selected song each nation effectively chooses how others will see and hear it. On one hand, the need to represent the nation to others often results in the use of stereotypes of that nation; on the other hand, some artists use their performances to critique those stereotypes. A few even make direct political statements, which violates the contest rules. The contest is a useful way to see how stereotypes are evolving as peoples present themselves through the media.[36]

Joci Pápai (1981–) is not the first Romani person to advance in the Eurovision song contest. Esma Redžepova (with Vlatko Lozanoski) represented Macedonia in 2013; Sofi Marinova represented Bulgaria in 2012; the group Gipsy.cz represented the Czech Republic in 2009; and Marija Serifović won the contest as Serbia's representative in 2007. Yet this participation has been rare. Though the contest's organizers have mandated inclusion of minorities in the national competitions, over the past few decades Romani performers have experienced discrimination in the national contests in Bulgaria, the Czech Republic, Hungary, Turkey, and Serbia. These performers faced a significant backlash in the press: many people argued against allowing Roma to represent their European nations.[37] Because of this history, media coverage in 2017 repeatedly emphasized Pápai's ethnic identity as Romani. This fact was mentioned in every article about him. Writers implicitly framed his presence as a triumph over adversity, though the nature of that adversity went unmentioned.

Indeed, it is remarkable that Pápai was selected as Hungary's representative. In today's Hungary the police and other state officials routinely persecute Roma. It is not unusual for state authorities to openly state racist stereotypes as reasons for continuing school segregation and employment discrimination. In 2014, for example, a Hungarian judge characterized the Roma as "a group of people who stand apart from the traditional values of majority society, and whose lifestyle is characterized by the avoidance of work and the disrespect of private property and the norms of living together."[38] Nonetheless, negative public feeling about Roma was evidently not uniform enough or strong enough to keep Pápai from winning. As the victor in the Hungarian national contest, he was chosen through a combination of public voting and a jury of popular Hungarian musicians: the final vote was the public's.[39] But, as the ethnomusicologist Carol Silverman has pointed out, music has long been one of the acceptable professions for Romani people in Eastern Europe. In this context, where "Roma are powerless politically and powerful musically," it may have been easy enough for Hungarians to accept Pápai's performance.[40] As we will see, it is also possible that his conscientious presentation of Hungarian identity overcame objections to his ethnicity.

The 2017 Eurovision Song Contest took place in Kiev, Ukraine, with the widely advertised theme, "Celebrate Diversity."[41] The international public relations director for the event, Viktoriia Sydorenko, explained: "It's all about Europe: each country is so different, but at the same time comes together by sharing common values. This diversity of cultures makes us stronger as we complete each other."[42] Ironically, in preparation for the arrival of thousands of visitors to the contest, the Kiev City Council burned several Romani neighborhoods that were visible near highways and railways, permanently forcing about 350 people from their homes and rendering them destitute. Volodymyr Netrebenko, who backed the effort, explained: "We, as the titular nation, should do everything in our power to create a safe environment for all citizens in the territory of Ukraine"—thus relying on the stereotype that Roma are dangerous criminals and firmly excluding them from the category of citizens.[43] The city council glossed over this persecution using xenophobic stereotypes; they called it an effort to "Clean the city" or "Protect your house, neighborhood, your city, your land."[44] The city of Kiev thus ensured that visitors would not see Roma people—except for Pápai—while in Kiev to enjoy the contest.[45] An activist, Sergey Movchan, has accused Ukraine of using the Eurovision Song Contest to set up a false face—claiming to "celebrate diversity" when in fact the government has suppressed many aspects of diversity.[46]

For the contest Pápai wrote his own song, entitled "Origo" (origin). His performance, seen in example 2.11, begins with singing in Hungarian that alludes to the four-line pattern of an "old-style" Hungarian folk song, a celebrated part of Hungarian ethnic national heritage.

Example 2.11. Joci Pápai, "Origo," Eurovision Song Contest 2017. YouTube.
Courtesy of Eurovision.
Link: https://doi.org/10.3998/mpub.9853855.cmp.30

This choice is significant because many Hungarians have hypothesized that this style of song existed in Hungary before the influence of Roma: it is the music they imagine as "purely" Hungarian.[47] Yet in the song's words Pápai makes reference to the stereotype of Roma as travelers: "I was born to be a wanderer." From the first 30 seconds of the song a Hungarian audience receives mixed signals of both Hungarian and Romani identities. The audience outside Hungary would be unlikely to recognize any allusion to folk song; to them, the words about being a wanderer (stereotypical Rom) probably seemed the more potent message.

After two verses (timepoint :26), Pápai uses the same plaintive tone for the song's chorus. According to Pápai, "the chorus is Romani but it doesn't actually have a specific meaning. The Jálomá part. It is just a way gypsies use their voice in music all the time."[48] Though vocables are associated with fast music for dancing among the Vlach Roma, here Pápai uses them in a slower pop song to make the song sound more "Romani." The tune is not Romani, however; it is shaped much like the melody of the Hungarian verse. During the chorus a dancer becomes visible. The dancer's bare midriff and her swaying hips are reminiscent of the "belly dance" style associated with Turkish and Balkan Roma. Her costume includes a wide skirt, with which she makes sweeping movements: these movements are common in stage portrayals of "Gypsies," as are her "hand flower" gestures. By drawing on several well-known ways of presenting the Roma from different places, the dancer presents a Romani folksiness in a general way that many Europeans would recognize.[49]

Next (timepoint :45), the energy of the song increases with the introduction of a dance beat. A violin also enters, an evident reference to the Romungro tradition; at the same time, Pápai also uses a water can as a percussion instrument, a common practice among groups that popularized the Vlach Roma tradition among the general public. The violin is more restrained than one would expect from a virtuoso. It is repetitive, as one expects in a popular song, but it does include ornaments that hint at the style of playing one might hear in a Hungarian restaurant. Over the dance beat we hear a repetition of the verse, the chorus, and the violin interlude, which now includes a very brief couples' dance for Pápai and the dancer: reminiscent of the Hungarian national dance called *csárdás*, this is another element that looks "traditional" or "folk-like."

Then Pápai begins to rap (timepoint 1:52). It is a distinctive sound, as Hungarian is a percussive language with long and short syllables. With the change to rap the tone of Pápai's delivery shifts from plaintive to angry. Here Pápai's first-person lyrics use a rhetorical strategy from the American and worldwide tradition of **rap music**, outlining his own biography as a struggle and demanding recognition. Pápai's music is his God-given "weapon," he argues, a power that expresses grief but also inspires fear and respect in others: "you hear my melody and you already know my name." At the end of the rap, at the words "tears of thousands are streaming down my guitar," the dancer drops to the floor, looking distressed; Pápai cradles her face, lifting her up and appearing to comfort her, and she returns to her dancing. Although this is probably the most political moment in the song, its meaning is conveyed obliquely: nowhere are Roma referred to in the lyrics, and nowhere does Pápai articulate the specific grievances that elicited the "tears of thousands."

"Origo" offers the listener a remarkable blend of traits. In three minutes it manages to convey a strong sense of Hungarian tradition to Hungarians, while also signaling a transnational Romani identity and membership in the international pop music industry to a broad swath of international listeners. Reviews of Pápai's performance called attention to its "Gypsy" elements: this part of the blend was meant to be legible internationally, and it was.[50] Yet the song does not represent a particular strand of Romani tradition; rather, it mixes Romani elements from many places to make a more generic, more "universal" Romani identity.

Although Pápai's performance may have raised the visibility of Romani people, it did not inform audiences about their continuing struggle for equal rights. With its conspicuously blended styles, Pápai's performance can be understood as a purposeful "Celebrate Diversity" event. After selecting a Romani man to represent Hungary, Hungarians and the Eurovision Song Contest can claim to be inclusive and multicultural, even as the persecution of Roma continues all around them. The musical visibility of Roma is promising, but it may not deliver a meaningful change in circumstances.

The media studies scholar Anikó Imre has described musicians like Pápai as being "suspended between the global media and the nation state."[51] To gain access to an international platform, Romani musicians have had to conform to particular expectations. Imre describes how state officials and music industry executives have "hand-picked" exemplary performers to elevate to fame but also required that these performers distance themselves from their Romani traditions in favor of a broader kind of appeal. Sometimes this has meant singing in Hungarian instead of Romani, singing patriotic songs about the Hungarian nation-state, or playing demeaning roles.[52] The performers may be well paid, and they may also gain entry to the international market, for their music has become an identifiable commodity on the world stage. Some, like Pápai, have succeeded in combating certain stereotypes (dirtiness, criminality) but not others (wandering, exoticism).[53] The romantic stereotypes are also a valuable selling point: popularizing "Gypsy music" has meant capitalizing on those stereotypes, which only reinforces their power.

The same musical and personal flexibility that has long been a survival strategy for the Romani diaspora is again in evidence here: to make their way, Roma have adapted, performing the roles asked of them by different patrons. Those patrons now include the Eurovision Song Contest, the nation-state of Hungary, patriotic or nationalist Hungarians, and online buyers of "world beat."

It has been difficult for the Roma to break out of their limited roles as outsiders. They are spread among many lands, some have no language in common, and the laws and policies of the different nation-states where they reside vary widely. Nonetheless, using the human rights frameworks of the European Union and the United Nations, during the past 60 years Roma have organized an international movement to advocate for themselves.[54] This movement has meant a change in how some Roma see themselves. Instead of identifying only with people in their own local groups, they are seeking the connections among different groups of Roma throughout the diaspora—beginning to think of themselves as a nation without a state, even a "virtual nation."[55] Along these lines Pápai's decision to reference a variety of Romani musical and dance elements may be based in political as well as ethnic solidarity. This larger group identity is more visible to outsiders and therefore more effective in advocacy.

The international Roma movement has attracted funding from international nongovernmental organizations (NGOs). Within and alongside that effort some Romani musicians have found ways to use their distinctive appeal to address social problems.[56] The Athe Sam (We are here!) festival, held annually in Budapest between 2007 and 2011 and sporadically since, blends music, theater, film, and visual arts with panel discussions and educational events about Roma history, culture, and politics. The festival includes both Romani and non-Romani performers, and it has been marketed to tourists as well as locals. This, too, is an effort at visibility: gaining the understanding and trust of neighbors far and near might encourage those neighbors to support the movement for Romani civil rights. By using the arts to bring people into a more direct conversation about citizenship and rights, these musicians are moving out of the entertainer's role and into the role of advocates. As of this writing, the progress of this agenda remains uncertain: because government officials often regard Romani voices as politically oppositional, these forms of public expression remain tentative and subject to censorship. Yet some continue these efforts, hopeful that they can shape a dialogue about what it means to be Roma in diaspora within a multicultural Europe.[57]

3 The African Diaspora in the United States

Appropriation and Assimilation

The music of the United States is the product of peoples in motion. From the beginning the colonies that would become the United States consisted of over-lapping immigrant groups who moved into territories inhabited by Native American peoples. The earliest large groups of white colonists arrived from England, Scotland, and the Netherlands in 1607. African people arrived in North America more or less continuously between 1619 and the 1850s as a result of the slave trade, the largest forced migration in world history (fig. 3.1). Depending on their origins, resources, and the freedoms granted or denied them by law and custom, these groups lived under vastly unequal conditions. The forced labor of enslaved Africans became a mainstay of the economy in the colonies, and the social relations created by slavery shaped every aspect of US society, including music-making.[1] The music African Americans created in the United States has played an extraordinary role in the musical life of the Americas and the world.

The practice of slavery in the colonies that would become the United States began as indentured servitude but evolved into a hereditary, permanent caste. Early in the 1600s, servitude was based not on skin color but on religion: people who had not been Christian before coming to America were judged to be slaves. Nonetheless, the practice of slavery hardened into a system based on **race**—the assignment of social distinction based on color or other elements of physical appearance, in this case white citizens' unshakable conviction that brown-skinned people were inferior—and enforced by law. The concept of race has no basis in human biology, but as an imagined fact that has affected how people interact with one another, it has shaped ideas about music and the conditions in which music is performed.[2]

The history of African American music is difficult to reconstruct; almost none of this music was written down until the 1800s, so scholars have relied

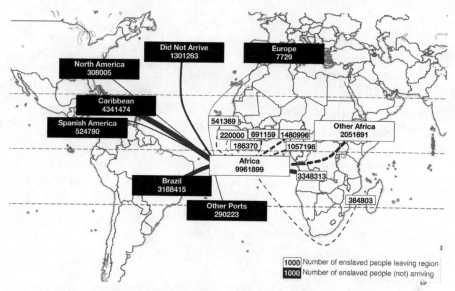

Fig. 3.1. *Music on the Move:* Trans-Atlantic Slave Trade Voyages. Map by Eric Fosler-Lussier. This map depicts the transportation of enslaved people from Africa as listed in *The Trans-Atlantic Slave Trade Database* in the decades between 1580 and 1860, grouped by regions where they arrived. White boxes and dashed lines indicate departures; black boxes and solid lines indicate arrivals. Voyages for which the major place of sale could not be imputed were removed from this visualization: the number of enslaved people who did not arrive at their destination (many died, but some possibly escaped) is represented by the difference in the number of persons leaving Africa and those arriving at destination ports. The excellent database at slavevoyages.org describes the research behind this map and more detailed visualizations. (See https://doi.org/10.3998/mpub.9853855.cmp.31)

on eyewitness accounts, most of them by white observers. Nonetheless, the mixture of diasporas has made the United States what it is, so scholars have tried to learn all they can about how these musics came together. This chapter describes two musical products of African diaspora in the United States—the blues and spirituals—with an eye toward the ways in which the social circumstances shaped the development of African American traditions.

The Blues: Made in America

Scholars generally acknowledge that enslaved Africans brought their musical traditions to the United States. Historical records mention that some slave traders required Africans to bring their musical instruments with them. On slave ships traders used whips to force captives to sing and dance—a form of shipboard exercise that entertained the traders and "aired" the captives to prevent disease.[3] Once in the United States, enslaved Africans continued to make music on African and European musical instruments. Many firsthand accounts from colonial America describe group dancing and singing on Sundays, as well as songs to accompany manual labor.[4]

After the Louisiana Purchase, in 1803, some slaveholders moved west and south, taking enslaved people with them to cotton plantations in Arkansas, Mississippi, Tennessee, Louisiana, and eventually Texas. Some of the musical instruments we associate with those parts of the rural southern United States closely resemble African traditional instruments. The banjo appears to be a version of the long-necked lutes played by itinerant minstrels in the West Sudanic Belt, the transitional savannah area between the Sahara Desert and Equatorial Africa that runs from Senegal and The Gambia through Mali, northern Ghana, Burkina Faso, and northern Nigeria. By contrast, one-stringed instruments, played with a slider against the string, are traditional in the music of central Africa: they are an antecedent of the slide guitar tradition in the southern United States. Another kind of one-stringed instrument is the "mouth bow," which is plucked or strummed while held against the mouth. This instrument, played in the Appalachian and Ozark regions of the United States, is part of the musical traditions of Angola, Namibia, and southern East Africa.[5] The presence of these instruments offers tangible evidence that Africans brought their own ways of music-making to the Americas.

Because slave owners bought and transported slaves at will, though, Africans typically could not stay together in family and community groups that maintained these traditions. The extent to which African ethnic groups were able to maintain contact among themselves in the Americas is debated by historians: there is some evidence that ethnic clusters persisted in some places, but most scholars describe the African experience in the Americas as one of profound dislocation for families and communities.[6] Considering this disruption, some scholars have wondered about the possibility of **survivals** or **retentions** from African music—that is, whether some traits persisted from the traditional musics that Africans brought with them.[7] In contrast, the music scholar Kofi Agawu argues that these terms imply too much passivity; rather, Africans and people of African descent actively guarded and preserved their musical heritage.[8]

What is certain is that Africans continued to develop and adapt their traditions in the Americas; they also initiated new musical traditions. The blues are an exemplary case. The **blues** are a tradition of solo singing, developed by African Americans in the United States in the mid- to late 1800s, that gives the effect of highly personal expression. Early blues often described hard work and sorrow, but they also treated broken relationships, money problems, and other topics—sometimes seriously and sometimes with a wry sense of humor. The lyrics are cast in the first person: "I'm leaving this morning with my clothes in my hand . . ."; "I didn't think my baby would treat me this way. . . ." The first-person lyric does not mean the blues are autobiographical; rather, the singer creates a speaking persona and a vivid situation with which the listener can identify.[9] Most melodic phrases start at a relatively high pitch and descend. In addition, the singer might use wavy or inexact intonation, producing an expressive and highly variable sound that may resemble a complaint, a wail, even a provocation. In early blues there might be just one accompanying instrument, often played by the singer: guitar, banjo, fiddle, mandolin, harmonica, or piano. As blues gained in popularity and record companies began issuing recordings, that simple accompaniment was often replaced with a small band.

The poetic form of the blues is a three-line verse: the first two lines have the same words, and then the third line is a conclusion with new words:

Lord, I'm a hard workin' woman, and I work hard all the time
Lord, I'm a hard workin' woman, and I work hard all the time
But it seem like my baby, Lord, he is dissatisfied.[10]

This verse form maps onto a musical structure, the "12-bar blues": each line consists of four bars (units), each of which comprises four beats (time-units felt as pulses). This form can be repeated, bent, broken, or ignored as the musician wishes. The tempo is slow, and the rhythm has a characteristic "swing," giving the listener the sense that there is an underlying pattern of long and short notes on each beat. The overall texture is not complicated. Often the instrument drops out, or simply keeps the beat while the singer sings one phrase, and then comes in with more interesting material after that phrase. This kind of musical back-and-forth is known as a pattern of **call and response**.[11] Mississippi Matilda Powell's "Hard Workin' Woman" (example 3.1) is a blues composition that exemplifies all these features.

Example 3.1. Mississippi Matilda Powell with guitarists Sonny Boy Nelson and Willie Harris, Jr., "Hard Working Woman," recorded 1936 in New Orleans. *Mississippi Blues Volume 3, 1939–1940* (Document Records DOCD-5671, 2002). Used by permission. Link: https://doi.org/10.3998/mpub.9853855.cmp.33

Gerhard Kubik is an ethnographer—that is, he seeks to record and analyze the practices of particular groups of people. For many years he has tried to understand the connection between African music and the African American blues tradition in the southern United States. Kubik traveled through Africa and made numerous field recordings; he then compared specific elements of those field recordings to the earliest existing recordings of the blues. Kubik was careful to note that there are limitations in this method: by comparing recordings made decades apart and continents away, one cannot determine a "family tree" for the blues. Music was not routinely recorded until the 20th century, so there is no way for us to hear precisely how the blues tradition developed during its early years. And certainly the recordings Kubik made in the 1960s cannot be "ancestors" of blues recordings from the 1920s! Rather, Kubik tried to identify characteristic elements of musical traditions—traits that might be preserved over time—that would suggest a kinship between those traditions. Like a family resemblance to a distant cousin, these traits hint at a relationship; but as we will see, there is also much in the blues that reflects their distinctly American origins.

Kubik's research suggests that musical traits from two different parts of Africa contributed to the blues. One is an ancient lamenting song style from West Africa that was associated with work rhythms, which Kubik calls the "ancient Nigritic" style. These songs would be accompanied by the repetitive motions and sounds of manual labor, like the sound of the stones used for grinding grain. Kubik recorded example 3.2, sung by a person he identified only as "a Tikar woman," in 1964 in central Cameroon.

Example 3.2. Grinding song attributed to "a young Tikar woman," recorded by Gerhard Kubik in central Cameroon, 1964. *Africa and the Blues* (Neatwork AB-101, 2001). Used by permission.
Link: https://doi.org/10.3998/mpub.9853855.cmp.34

The grinding tool that accompanies the song produces a "swinging" rhythm. The singer's melody begins high and descends with each phrase, and the phrases are of roughly equal length. The words of this song, like those of typical early blues, are a lament and a work song: "If you don't work you cannot eat. I am crying about my fate and my life."[12] Kubik identifies these features as survivals within the blues style. He compares the example from the Tikar woman in Cameroon with the blues singing of Mississippi Matilda Powell (example 3.1). Powell's thin, breathy vocal quality also resembles that of the Tikar woman.

The other style Kubik identifies as a possible cousin of the blues is an Arabic-Islamic song style that developed among the people of the West Sudanic Belt, particularly the Hausa people of Nigeria and Niger. Unlike the ancient Nigritic style, the Arabic-Islamic song style was urban and cosmopolitan: it flourished around major cities and courts. This kind of music was made by a single person, accompanying himself on an instrument. As the singer was an entertainer who would move from place to place, this tradition consisted of solo songs that were not connected to community music-making. An example offered by Kubik is the song "Gogé," performed by Adamou Meigogué Garoua, recorded in northern Cameroon in 1964 (example 3.3).

Example 3.3. Solo song by Adamou Meigogue Garoua, accompanied by bowed lute, recorded by Gerhard Kubik in northern Cameroon, 1964. *Africa and the Blues* (Neatwork AB-101, 2001). Used by permission.
Link: https://doi.org/10.3998/mpub.9853855.cmp.35

The distinctively raspy vocal style of this example sounds vehement and sometimes exclamatory, the words declaimed theatrically. Most of the phrases descend in pitch, and the singer's voice often slides between pitches or moves quickly among ornamental notes. The combination of voice with instrument is also distinctive: during the sung phrase the fiddle is silent, but between phrases the fiddle comments with melodies of its own in a call-and-response pattern. We also hear in this song the characteristic **"blue" notes** (bent or pitch-altered notes) associated with blues.

Kubik compares Garoua's song with a blues by Big Joe Williams, "Stack O'Dollars" (example 3.4), recorded in 1935 in Chicago.

Example 3.4. Excerpt from Big Joe Williams, "Stack O'Dollars," played on a guitar, a one-string fiddle, and a washboard. Recorded in Chicago, 1935 (Document Records BDCD-6003, 1991). YouTube.
Link: https://doi.org/10.3998/mpub.9853855.cmp.36

As in the Garoua example, Williams uses his voice to make many different qualities of sound. Sometimes he speaks in a raspy voice; sometimes his melody reaches up to become a wail. Throughout, he bends notes, glides between notes, and adds ornaments. The call and response between the singer and instruments is present here, too. For these reasons Kubik identifies a link between these elements of the Arabic-Islamic song style and the African American blues.

In short, Kubik finds it likely that musical traits from different groups of people, and different parts of Africa, contributed to the blues tradition in the United States. But the Arabic-Islamic and ancient Nigritic song styles were not like stable "ingredients" that simply mixed together to form the blues, nor were they handed down only among people who belonged to the ethnic groups from which these styles came. That is, blues were not a "heritage" music in this genealogical sense. During the slave trade, family and ethnic groups suffered disruption and dislocation. The migration of slave owners and the sale of enslaved people to distant regions meant that members of different African ethnic groups were mixed together and dispersed widely among European American communities. The blues were not cultivated only among West Sudanic or West African ethnic groups in the United States. So how did these elements of song traditions take root, or become **localized**, in their new environment?

In Kubik's view the prominence of certain traits in blues is not explained by who brought these traits to the United States (heritage). Rather, these traits became widespread because they were useful and attractive to black people in the particular environment of the South in the 1800s; that is, this music spread as a tradition, passed from person to person.[13] Musicians can learn both songs and techniques fairly quickly: when they hear something they like, they may imitate it and adopt it as their own. Kubik thinks there was a kind of selection process; for example, musical traditions involving drums were frequently suppressed by slave owners, so traditions without drums flourished. That blues could be performed by one person with any instrument that came to hand made it an inexpensive and mobile musical form that was hard to take away. Unlike louder forms of group singing and dancing, the blues were less likely to attract unwanted attention in an oppressive and controlled environment. Blues singers could use the themes of suffering, overwork, and loneliness derived from the ancient Nigritic style to describe their experiences and to speak for their communities. Furthermore, the 1890s saw the rise of Jim Crow laws, which limited economic and social opportunities for African Americans; but because slaveholders had exploited black people for entertainment as well as work, white Americans remained willing to accept African Americans as entertainers.[14] In all these ways the blues had expressive and practical advantages.

Appropriation, Authenticity, and the Blues

The blues are much more than the sum of these African traits. Many aspects of the American context, including various audiences and commercial markets for the blues, were vital in shaping the history and content of this music. When black blues musicians traveled to perform in tent shows and vaudeville theaters (1890s–1920s), they found an audience of mixed ethnicities with an appetite for popular song. Soon white singers picked up this style of singing and the three-line form of the blues song. Composers of popular songs, many of them Jewish American, wrote blues and published them as sheet music (1910s). Many of these popular songs—some labeled as "blues," some just incorporating aspects of the blues—were issued on commercial recordings (1920s).

In the 1930s and 1940s, folklorists—some sponsored by the US government—went looking for southern folklore and "rediscovered" the rural blues, which by then seemed utterly different from the widely known commercial forms of blues. Elvis Presley (1950s) and the popular singers of the British Invasion (1960s) not only took African American blues singers as their models but also recorded their songs, often without attributing them to the original songwriters.[15] By the late 1960s the blues were recognized around the world as distinctively belonging to the United States. They were used in US public relations abroad and widely imitated.[16] We have already seen in chapter 2 an instance in which the musical practice of a minority group becomes a symbol and a point of pride for the nation at large. (Recall that the "Hungarian" music for which Hungary is most famous is Romani music.) To extend Kubik's line of thinking: the blues spread among people of many ethnicities because the style and themes of this music appealed to many musicians and audiences.

Yet, in the face of persistent social and economic inequality, one might wonder whether this kind of appropriation can happen on fair terms. **Appropriation** means taking something as one's own. Musical "taking" is, of course, a special case: if someone adopts a musical style or idea, the person from whom it was adopted can still play the music that has been taken. For this reason musical appropriation is sometimes called **borrowing**, which has a less negative connotation. A more neutral-sounding term for the spreading of music is **diffusion**—an intermingling of substances resulting from the random motion and circulation of molecules, as in chemistry. As the metaphor of diffusion involves no human actors at all, just the movement of music from one group to another, this idea seems to attribute the movement of music to a natural process—like talking about globalization as a "flow" without saying who caused that flow. But appropriation is a purposeful choice, and a personal one: as we saw in the case of Liszt (chapter 2), the act of taking music as one's own reflects the taker's values and biases.

If we want to think about it in neutrally descriptive terms, we might say that the circulation of ideas is merely what has happened, and still happens, in the ebb and flow of music-making. Musicians have long taken sounds and ideas from others, repurposing or altering music to suit their own purposes. But appropriation can also mean theft. **Cultural appropriation** occurs when a member of a group that holds power takes intellectual property, artifacts, knowledge, or forms of expression from a group of people who have less power.[17] Most definitions of cultural appropriation assume that "cultural" groups and their musical practices have clear and firm boundaries. They do not: music may be made differently even by members of the same group, and group allegiances are often hard to define. But people use the idea of cultural appropriation to address a real problem: if the powerful take music from the less powerful, what are the consequences? To put it bluntly: is this appropriation more like a complimentary form of imitation or more like a colonial extraction of resources?

One form of harm that can come about through cultural appropriation is that powerful people profit more from the music than do the less powerful people who made the music first. In the early days of the blues African American performers did earn money through in-person performance and recordings. Still, their earnings were modest. Recording and publishing companies often cheated musicians who lacked access to expert advice about contract and copyright law. Many media outlets preferred to play recordings by white musicians, further limiting black musicians' opportunities to profit.[18] During and after the 1960s, rock bands such as the Rolling Stones, Cream, and the Allman Brothers certainly reaped far greater monetary rewards from the blues than did the African American blues musicians whose songs they played. At the same time, the blues revival that spread the blues among Americans of other ethnicities increased professional opportunities for African Americans. Some musicians of this generation, such as B. B. King and Buddy Guy, attained considerable wealth and prestige, as well as a place in the spotlight. As the black blues musician Muddy Waters reportedly said of the Rolling Stones, "They stole my music but they gave me my name."[19]

Cultural appropriation can also make practitioners of the appropriated music feel that they have been misrepresented. The revivalists' attraction to the blues was based in part on insulting exoticist stereotypes about African Americans and their lives.[20] In a 1998 history Leon Litwack wrote that "the men and women who played and sang the blues were mostly poor, propertyless, disreputable itinerants, many of them illiterate, many of them loners, many of them living on the edge."[21] This account describes African Americans as hapless, mysterious, and utterly different from other Americans who might encounter their music. These stereotypes emerge from long-standing categories of racist thinking that have been difficult to unseat. Historically, the advocates of segregation had justified their position by claiming that African Americans were weak, dependent, and incapable of progress, effectively relegating them to the enforced boundaries that slavery had created. These habits of thought persisted even as many white Americans embraced the blues, and they remain a key part of the image of the blues.

Instead of seeing the blues as an art form requiring expertise, some observers have viewed the blues as the natural product of African Americans' mysterious lifestyle. Eric Clapton, the lead guitarist of Cream, noted that it had taken him "a great deal of studying and discipline" to learn the blues, whereas "for a black guy from Mississippi, it seems to be what they do when they open their mouth—without even thinking."[22] The stereotype operating here makes a hard distinction between folkloric music (handed down by tradition, eternally the same) and commercial music (sold in a marketplace, constantly changing). As we saw in chapter 1, the idea of the "modern" had been used to draw distinctions between non-Europeans and Europeans, and between the savage and the civilized.[23] Clapton's statement set his own creativity apart from that of African Americans, failing to acknowledge the individual creative effort of black blues artists.

Some people have argued that cultural appropriation is harmful because they want to preserve the authentic musical practice—for instance, recovering the blues as they were long ago rather than allowing for changes in the tradition. **Authenticity** is perceived closeness to an original source; judgments of authenticity are made with the aim of recovering that real or imaginary original. People who seek authentic blues take pleasure in a folk experience they have imagined for themselves as rural, untouched by commerce, and laden with suffering: they hope to find a true point of origin where the music first sprang into existence. Yet this argument is based less on historical facts than on present-day values, which emphasize distinctions between folk and commercial music and between origins and current uses. Authenticity is not a property of the blues; rather, it is a story that people tell about the music and its makers, a story that emphasizes heritage and the difference between "them" and "us."[24]

In seeking authenticity, people often treat "cultures" as clearly delimited from each other, and they look for a source that is identifiably from only one group, not mixed or "hybrid." The problem with this kind of thinking is that reality is more complicated. As best we can know it from the limited documentation that survives, the history of the blues does not support a clear distinction between folk and commercial music. Far from untouched by commerce, African American artists took advantage of opportunities to make money through music. Oral histories of the rural blues suggest that some blues musicians traveled from place to place to earn a living as entertainers, acquiring new material and making innovations in their performances along the way.[25] The blues became known to the wider public in the 1900s and 1910s, as African American musicians performed the blues and other music professionally in theaters and circus sideshows. Blues musicians heard, and sometimes imitated, the vaudeville performances.[26] When the blues were "discovered" by record companies—and of course one can hardly call it a discovery, as the music was already flourishing—African American performers willingly recorded their music for commercial markets.[27] These recordings, in turn, fostered a new generation of blues musicians in the South, who learned to play from the recordings instead of from local musicians.[28] In one way or another most musicians tailor their music to the demands of audiences, and African American musicians are no exception.[29] Here we see a limitation of Kubik's theory or of any theory that tries to define a thing by going back to its origins. Some elements of African music came together in the blues, but the context of traveling shows and commercialism in the United States was also an essential factor in the music's development.

The mistaken focus on authenticity at the expense of other musical values **reifies** music—that is, makes it into an object rather than an activity. When blues became not just a manner of performance, but also a folk artifact to be recorded for posterity or a musical form to be copied, it became more like an object to its borrowers, losing the flexibility of live performance and changeable tradition.[30] Once that happens, there is a risk that all performances will be measured against that "original" version. Holding the original as the highest standard disincentivizes creative development of the tradition.

Focusing on authenticity can also assign to music-makers a rigid set of group characteristics that differentiate them from other groups. The belief that all members of a certain group have particular inherent attributes is called

essentialism: it is a way of making stereotypes seem truthful by saying they are a permanent part of the people they represent. The blues were especially attractive to white musicians in the 1960s who wanted to seem oppositional to the social status quo. But by emphasizing the authenticity of the tradition, they relegated African Americans to being part of history rather than part of the present day, as Clapton did. They essentialized African Americans as the unchanging folk source of the music and named themselves as the innovators.

Claims about authenticity are not only produced by white people who want to reify the blues. They have also been used by people who want to protect African American ownership of the blues tradition. This line of thinking has sometimes been called **strategic essentialism:** a disempowered people's temporary use of stereotypes about themselves to promote their own interests—in this case, to guard a valued heritage against a specific act of appropriation.[31] In the early 1960s, a volatile period in the civil rights movement, the critic Amiri Baraka wrote a searing critique titled "The Great Music Robbery" in which he addressed white appropriations of African American music. He objected because white musicians were earning so much profit and praise for playing black music but also because the blues represented specific African American experiences. Baraka went so far as to call the idea of a white blues singer a "violent contradiction of terms": not because the blues were a genetic inheritance of black people but because the common experience of discrimination, reflected in the blues, bound black people together as a group.[32] The absorption of black music into American music, explained Baraka, changed the meaning of black music and even felt like erasure of black people and their experiences. "There can be no inclusion as 'Americans' without full equality, and no legitimate disappearance of black music into the covering sobriquet 'American,' without consistent recognition of the history, tradition, and current needs of the black majority, its culture, and its creations."[33]

At the same time, though, saying that black people are fundamentally different from other Americans reinforces that social separateness and the stereotypes that support it. The music scholar Ronald Radano has argued that Baraka's criticism essentializes African Americans by assuming they all share similar origins and experiences. Telling the story of black music as if it were entirely separate from white music not only misrepresents history but also reinforces a false belief in fundamental racial differences—and this belief can then be used to justify continuing discrimination.[34] Baraka did recognize the danger of essentialism: in a different essay he emphasized that committed musicians of any color could learn the "attitudes that produced the music as a profound expression of human feelings."[35] This statement means that African American music is an open tradition in which people of various ethnic origins might learn to participate, if they are willing to try to understand black musicians' perspectives and experiences.

Thus, the objections to cultural appropriation boil down to economic exploitation and disrespectful representation.[36] One could try to respond by discouraging appropriation. Yet people who use the charge of cultural appropriation as an effort to prevent traditions from mixing can also cause harm, perpetuating essentialist stereotypes. Thinking of the blues as an unchanging essence encourages white audiences to ignore African Americans' further development of that tradition—or of other traditions. Worse, thinking of African Americans as people who only produce blues or spirituals unjustly limits their artistic freedom. In the words of the philosopher Kwame Anthony Appiah, "talk of authenticity now just amounts to telling other people what they ought to value in their own traditions."[37] Musical appropriation across lines of social power seems generally to have this ambivalent quality: it can cause real harm to real people, yet trying to prevent appropriation can also cause trouble by encouraging inflexible and stereotypical thinking about groups and differences. This dilemma is built into life in the United States because of the violent and unequal circumstances by which the nation developed. The particulars of any musical borrowing among peoples in the United States may reinforce that violence, or work against it, or try to find a way past it; but it is always there to be grappled with.[38]

The Spiritual: Mutual Influence and Assimilation

Both European Americans and African Americans have nurtured traditions of religious singing, or "spiritual song." Whereas some of the African American music used for entertainment developed separately from European American traditions, religion offered a point of contact between black people and white. During the 1600s and 1700s some groups made efforts to convert enslaved people to Christianity. In the North enslaved people were often considered part of the household, and they were encouraged to sing psalms and hymns as part of prayer services. Missionaries visiting the South pressed for conversion, but slaveholders decided whether and what to teach the enslaved people under their control. Generally, African Americans in the South received less religious instruction than their northern counterparts, in part because of a fear that literacy would empower them. The 1700s saw the rise of African American churches in both South and North. In the North these churches grew and developed their own collections of hymns, but southern whites feared that black churches were aiding in the organization of slave rebellion, so they disbanded them.[39] Some scholars have speculated that pervasive segregation by race in the southern United States helped to preserve African American musical practices.

From the 1720s through the 1800s people in the United States participated in several waves of religious fervor, commonly known as the Great Awakening. During the Second Great Awakening (1800–1840s) itinerant evangelical preachers defied conservative Protestant slaveholders by hosting camp meetings, lively outdoor worship experiences that might last a week, attended by thousands of people. These evangelical meetings encouraged excited and emotional expressions of faith instead of rehearsing old-fashioned, carefully written sermons; this value harmonized with already existing African American musical practices. Camp meetings were interracial events, typically attended by black and white alike, even by enslaved people, and they were sometimes led by African American preachers. The degree of social mixing across racial lines would vary from place to place, and sometimes African Americans had to stand or sit separately from white participants. Nonetheless, the religious practice of the camp meeting offered an opportunity for European Americans and African Americans to find common ground in the language and practice of Christianity and taught some European Americans to regard African Americans as real people with souls and spiritual lives.[40]

Singing of religious songs played a prominent role in these Christian camp meetings. Observers recorded that African American attendees contributed "boisterous" singing at the meetings and often stayed up all night singing hymns after other attendees had gone to bed.[41] A Methodist preacher, John F. Watson, was concerned because the style of this worship differed substantially from white Protestants' musical renditions and did not meet their standards of respectfulness: "In the *blacks*' quarter, the coloured people get together, and sing for hours together, short scraps of disjointed affirmations, pledges, or prayers, lengthened out with long repetition *choruses*. These are all sung in the merry chorus-manner of the southern harvest field, or husking-frolic method, of the slave blacks. . . . With every word so sung, they have a sinking of one or other leg of the body alternately; producing an audible sound of the feet at every step. . . . What in the name of religion, can countenance or tolerate such gross perversions of true religion!"[42] Watson complained that African Americans were using words and music that were not officially sanctioned by any religious denomination. Another frequent complaint was that African Americans performed worship music with energetic dancing. African Americans differentiated the kind of body movement they would perform at a "shout" (worship) from the kind of movement they would consider dancing, but to white outsiders their bodily engagement in worship seemed disrespectful. Even as white listeners marveled at a kind of singing that was strange to their ears, coming together to sing helped African Americans identify themselves as a community, both within and out of earshot of European Americans.

Watson's description of "short scraps" helps us understand how African Americans' Christian camp meeting music worked. Though many had become familiar with the words and music of European American Christian hymnbooks, this music was used from memory and only in part. The worship leader would often sing a line, either from a hymn or improvised on the spot, and have the congregation repeat it, alternating the call of the leader with the response of the congregation. A similar practice, called **lining-out**, had been used in the British Isles before it was exported to the colonies. At the same time, this practice of alternating lines was also consistent with the call-and-response form that African Americans used in work songs. In the British practice lining-out tended to stick closely to the words in a hymnbook: it was a way of teaching illiterate congregants biblical stories by rote. In contrast, African Americans freely combined lines of Christian hymns with improvised words of praise. The leader could move from one idea to another, and the congregation would follow.[43] An observer in the 1880s wrote: "When the minister gave out his own version of the Psalm, the choir commenced singing so rapidly that the original tune absolutely ceased to exist—in fact, the fine old psalm tune became thoroughly transformed into a kind of negro melody; and so sudden was the transformation, by accelerating the time, for a moment, I fancied that not only the choir but the little congregation intended to get up a dance as part of the service."[44] Frequently, African Americans added memorized choruses from other hymns that were well known among the congregation as the spirit moved the leader, even if this resulted in mixing of the original hymn texts or entirely new statements of faith.

Scholars typically refer to this genre of African American singing as the **folk spiritual**. The audio recordings we have of folk spirituals were made long after the 19th-century camp meetings. Researchers have read eyewitness accounts, listened to the later recordings, and made their best guesses about how African American spirituals might have sounded in that time. The written historical sources can be compared to living people's knowledge of the spiritual. As the singer and scholar Bernice Johnson Reagon has said of her childhood during and after the Second World War, "As I grew up in a rural African American community in Southwest Georgia, the songs were everywhere."[45]

African American folk spirituals were sung in groups, generally with no instrumental accompaniment. The words of these songs focus on themes from the Bible, with particular attention to stories of liberation. These included Daniel's deliverance from the lion's den; the journey of the Hebrew people from their captivity in Egypt to freedom; and the figure of Jesus as a liberator from sin. Frequent allusions to being a people chosen by God assert a sense of self-worth and confidence in a better future.[46] Though the spirituals have sometimes been called "sorrow songs," they express a variety of emotions, from longing to rejoicing.

In example 3.5 the Blue Spring Missionary Baptist Association of southwest Georgia blends improvised preaching and improvised singing.[47]

Example 3.5. Deacon Richard Diggs and the Blue Spring Missionary Baptist Association Delegation, "Traditional Prayer with Moans," recorded at the Smithsonian Institution National Museum of American History, 1989. Bernice Johnson Reagon, compiler, *Wade in the Water, vol. 2: African American Congregational Singing: Nineteenth-Century Roots* (Smithsonian Folkways with National Public Radio, CD SF 40073, 1994).
Link: https://doi.org/10.3998/mpub.9853855.cmp.37

The congregation in this recording sings ecstatically in answer to the preacher's message. The leader speaks or sings a phrase, and the congregation speaks or sings in return. Not all of the singers in this congregation are "in sync." Some start just a little before others as they decide in the moment what to sing together by listening carefully to each other. The ethnomusicologist Charles Keil has argued that this slightly "out of time" feeling gives this music its dynamic and engaging qualities.[48] Each singer has a great deal of freedom to sing the music in her or his own way: some offer embellishments around the main pitch or create harmonies.

The United Southern Prayer Band of Baltimore's rendition of "Give Me Jesus" (example 3.6) is congregational spiritual singing in the African American tradition. Like the preceding example, this music was recorded in the

1980s, but it includes many of the features scholars believe were part of the tradition from long ago.

> Example 3.6. United Southern Prayer Band of Baltimore, "Give Me Jesus," recorded at the Smithsonian Institution National Museum of American History, 1989. Bernice Johnson Reagon, compiler, *Wade in the Water, vol. 2: African American Congregational Singing: Nineteenth-Century Roots* (Smithsonian Folkways with National Public Radio, CD SF 40073, 1994).
> Link: https://doi.org/10.3998/mpub.9853855.cmp.38

It is a joyful and participatory style of singing. One has the sense that the congregation is spontaneously moved to involvement by lifting their voices, stomping their feet, and clapping their hands. That the song is repetitive means that everyone can participate, whether or not they knew the song beforehand; this kind of repetition was characteristic of camp-meeting songs.[49]

We might compare this rendition of "Give Me Jesus" to a recording of a white congregation in Kentucky singing the hymn "Guide Me O Thou Great Jehovah" (example 3.7). This recording illustrates the practice of lining out a hymn: the leader sings each line of the hymn, and the congregation answers in a call-and-response pattern. In this and other ways this singing is very like the above examples from African American congregations.

> Example 3.7. "Guide Me O Thou Great Jehovah," Ike Caudill leading the Indian Bottom Old Regular Baptist Association congregation, Letcher County, Kentucky. From the Alan Lomax Collection at the American Folklife Center, Library of Congress. Courtesy of the Association for Cultural Equity.
> Link: https://doi.org/10.3998/mpub.9853855.cmp.39

We hear a deep engagement in worship and repetition that allows for broad participation, as well as a heterophonic singing style in which participants are free to add ornaments or harmonize. Note, though, that we hear no foot-stomping or hand-clapping; this performance is more restrained physically.

Scholars have historically had difficulty sorting out how the mutual resemblance between white and black spiritual song styles developed. Beginning in the 1930s, some suggested that African Americans took British American tunes for lining-out and "Africanized" them—much in the same way that Romungro musicians took Hungarian folk melodies and approached them in their own special style.[50] This theory pained African Americans: in Reagon's words, "Leading scholars claiming an objective, scientific method of research and analysis studied our work and ways of living and declared us incapable of original creativity."[51] But there is growing agreement among scholars today that most of the tunes did not come from British traditions: African Americans used ideas from Christianity but made their own songs about those ideas and performed them in their own ways.

It is reasonable to believe that the spiritual is a truly American creation and that contact between black Americans and white Americans shaped the music of both populations.[52] The melodies and the freely improvised and recombined words we hear in this kind of spiritual singing are consistent with what we know about older African American practices. African Americans incorporated Christian religious ideas and found lining-out compatible with their own call-and-response singing. As testified to by Watson's complaints, this practice seems to have had a meaningful influence on white singing, especially in the southern United States, through camp meetings.

The Spiritual and Assimilation

The folk spiritual is still a living tradition. Yet, like most living traditions, it has engendered offshoots and been borrowed and transformed in a variety of ways: these transformations are also part of the continuing story of how music moves. In the Civil War era spirituals were used by abolitionists as propaganda for their cause: these songs showcased the suffering of African Americans under slavery. On one hand, musically minded white listeners could find common ground with black singers in appreciation of the spiritual. On the other hand, the danger of essentialism arises here again: images of suffering African Americans were sometimes used to affirm white superiority and racism.[53] This misperception was also a highly conspicuous element of the popular entertainment called minstrelsy. Featuring skits and musical numbers, minstrel shows depicted black people as comical, pathetic, the butt of every joke. African American intellectuals objected to this kind of portrayal and looked for ways to counteract it. They aimed to present African Americans in a manner that would gain respect among European Americans, especially among the educated Protestants of the North who might be sympathetic to the cause of free African Americans.

As the ethnomusicologist Sandra Graham has described it in her book, *Spirituals and the Birth of a Black Entertainment Industry*, the African American colleges founded after the Civil War (now usually known as "historically black colleges and universities," or HBCUs) worked hard to change public perceptions of black people. Music was one tool for change. H. H. Wright, dean of the Fisk Freed Colored School (now Fisk University) in Nashville, Tennessee, recalled that "there was a strong sentiment among the colored people to get as far away as possible from all those customs which reminded them of slavery." Wright reported that the students "would sing only 'white' songs."[54] Ella Sheppard (1851–1914), assistant director and founding member of the choir at Fisk, explained that "the slave songs were never used by us then in public. They were associated with slavery and the dark past, and represented the things to be forgotten. Then, too, they were sacred to our parents, who used them in their religious worship."[55] But with the encouragement of their music teacher, the white missionary George White, the Fisk choir began to sing a few spirituals on campus alongside their repertoire of hymns, popular parlor songs such as "Home Sweet Home," and a few selections of European classical music.

That the Fisk choir sang primarily "white songs" is an example of **assimilation**: people within a minority or less powerful group changing their behavior to be more like a dominant group. We might think of assimilation as a companion concept to appropriation: it emerges from contact between groups who have unequal authority. By singing music associated with white people, the Fisk students sought to distance themselves from perceptions about black people as slaves. Many white people associated cultivated choral music with social privilege and respect: the Fisk students surely hoped that this kind of singing would mark them as educated people who belonged in polite society.

The Fisk Jubilee Singers made their first concert tour under the direction of George White in 1871 to raise funds for a building project at Fisk. They sang in churches and theaters alike, and their program consisted of the "white songs" they had customarily performed. In 1872 they added a few spirituals to their repertoire, and these quickly became so popular that they came to dominate the Jubilee Singers' concert programs. Yet the spirituals were not sung as they had been in worship. The melodies were made regular in a way that conformed to the musical tastes of middle- and upper-class white people. Some songs were sung as solos or in unison, but some were set in four-part harmony, a technique borrowed from European music. In this style individual singers had fewer opportunities to improvise: one description of the Jubilee Singers praised their "precise unison." Yet they did preserve some of the rhythmic features of the spiritual, such as accented notes placed off the beat, that white listeners found surprising.[56] These assimilated versions of folk spirituals are called **concert spirituals**.

The Fisk Jubilee Singers were recorded early in the twentieth century; they probably sounded different then than in the 1870s, but this recording of "Deep River" still offers us some insight (example 3.8).

Example 3.8. Fisk Jubilee Singers, "Deep River." *Fisk University Jubilee Singers, in chronological order*, vol. 3, 1924–1940 (Document Records DOCD-5535, 1997). Used by permission.
Link: https://doi.org/10.3998/mpub.9853855.cmp.40

In this example we hear four-part harmony and a very smooth style of vocal delivery. There is no spontaneity or call and response in this music, as one might hear in the folk spiritual. Instead, "Deep River" is presented in a choral style that reflects the European ideals of precision and harmony.

Over the course of six and a half years the Jubilee Singers raised $150,000 for Fisk, a staggering sum. (The map in fig. 3.2 shows many of their tour stops.) On the heels of this success the Hampton Agricultural and Industrial School (now Hampton University) and the Tuskegee Normal School for Colored Teachers (now Tuskegee University) soon founded their own groups of Jubilee Singers, aided by published sheet music of the Fisk group's songs. The printed versions further altered the songs: they were written down according to norms of Western classical **notation**, in major and minor keys, even though in performance these melodies did not entirely conform to those keys.[57]

Graham has called the concert spiritual an act of "translation": an intentional transformation that made the spiritual understandable and valuable to white audiences.[58] White audiences could imagine that they were hearing the reality of the plantation, and the spirituals excited a sense of exoticism. One observer cited the choir's "wild, delicious" sound; another delighted in the "strange and weird" music that recalled the harsh conditions under which African Americans survived.[59] At the same time, the sound and the social aspiration of the concert spiritual were shaped by the institutions of higher education that sponsored them. The idea that African Americans needed to accommodate themselves to white norms in order to win respect reflected a sad reality of the day; this, more than anything else, shaped the sound of the concert spiritual. These performances succeeded in winning a great deal of praise and money from white listeners, though this affirmation was accompanied by a sense of exotic difference.[60]

In the early 1900s the spiritual became an increasingly popular source for

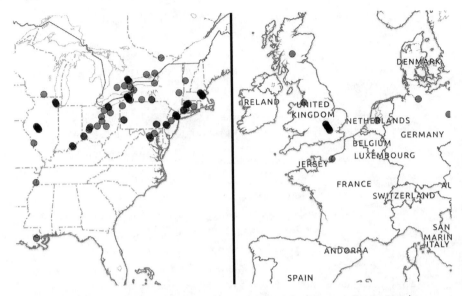

Fig. 3.2. *Music on the Move:* Concert Tours of the Fisk Jubilee Singers, 1871–80. Map by Eric Fosler-Lussier based on an original map and research by Elizabeth Lacy and Louis Epstein. Darker or overlapping dots indicate multiple performances. (See https://doi. org/10.3998/mpub.9853855.cmp.42)

choral pieces and songs to be presented in the format associated with a classical music concert. Harry T. Burleigh was part of the generation of African Americans born after Emancipation. A composer and singer, he studied at the National Conservatory of Music in New York. He composed many of his own songs in the art music tradition, but his arrangements of spirituals circulated more widely, and he was a key figure in developing interest in the concert spiritual among classically trained musicians. During the Harlem Renaissance (ca. 1917–35) artists such as Langston Hughes, Jessie Fauset, Duke Ellington, Roland Hayes, Paul Robeson, William Grant Still, Augusta Savage, and Hall Johnson focused on the creation of a positive African American identity through the arts.[61] Part of their purpose was to find a less folksy, more modern expression of identity that they hoped would engender respect for black people among their white peers. Literacy had long been withheld from black people, so they wrote. Acknowledgment of their music as art had been withheld, so they composed.[62]

The Harlem Renaissance brought the concert spiritual, sometimes also called the "neospiritual," into the spotlight again. Musicians began performing concert spirituals as solo songs with piano accompaniment. The tradition of performing spirituals in this way comes from the classical music genre of the **art song**—a formal and prestigious kind of classical performance. Songs of this type were popular in the United States in the 1800s because they could easily be performed in middle-class homes.

A strong proponent of the concert spiritual was Paul Robeson. He performed spirituals in concert alongside other music representing the peoples of the world, with the purpose of claiming equal respect for all. The arrangement of "Sometimes I Feel like a Motherless Child" for voice and piano we hear in example 3.9 was made by Lawrence Brown. Brown regularized the melody into orderly phrases with an unobtrusive accompaniment of simple chords. Robeson adopted some elements of dialect—singing, for example, "chile" for "child"—which was a characteristic marker of the concert spiritual at this time. Still, he projected his voice in the manner expected in classical music performance. This kind of performance contradicted the ideas about African Americans that were expressed in minstrel shows: the concert spiritual presented African American music as equal to, and similar to, European classical music.

Example 3.9. Paul Robeson with Lawrence Brown, "Sometimes I Feel Like a Motherless Child," *Songs of Free Men* (Columbia/Odyssey 1942, reissued on Sony Classical, 1997).
Link: https://doi.org/10.3998/mpub.9853855.cmp.43

The concert spiritual was controversial, even among African Americans who were committed to improving their social status through the arts. Zora Neale Hurston (1891–1960), an anthropologist, folklorist, and writer who took part in the Harlem Renaissance, believed that only the spontaneous folk spirituals were authentic. She saw the concert spiritual as artificial, restrictive, and not really African American any more: "These neo-spirituals are the outgrowth of glee clubs. Fisk University boasts perhaps the oldest and certainly the most famous of these. They have spread their interpretation over America and Europe. . . . There has not been one genuine spiritual presented. To begin with, Negro spirituals are not solo or quartette material. The jagged harmony is what makes it, and it ceases to be what it was when this is absent. Neither can any group be trained to reproduce it. Its truth dies under training like flowers under hot water."[63] Intellectuals like Hurston questioned the practice of assimilation. They valued new economic and educational opportunities, but they were also looking for the best ways to preserve their traditions. Hurston felt strongly that the concert spiritual was a kind of domestication, making the spiritual easier for white people to understand while removing some of its essential features. This kind of adaptation changes the appropriated music into something new; and if the original music is beloved, this transformation can cause distress for those who love it. The problem of authenticity arises here again: some African Americans wondered if keeping a strict separation from European traditions was the best way to keep valued parts of their tradition alive.

The concert spiritual has crossed racial and national lines. Today, many church, community, and college choirs of varying ethnicities sing concert spirituals all over the world. Sometimes they imitate African American vernacular English, but often the language has been transformed into a more standard version of American English. Most characteristic of today's concert spiritual, regardless of the racial identity of the singers, is a crisp precision of delivery.[64] In this recording of "Wade in the Water," sung by the Howard University Choir (example 3.10), you hear a meticulous choral sound: as in European classical choral music, a conductor coordinates the performance.

Example 3.10. Harry Burleigh, arranger, "Wade in the Water," performed by the Howard University Chamber Choir, 1993. Bernice Johnson Reagon, compiler, *Wade in the Water*, vol. 1: *African American Spirituals: The Concert Tradition* (Smithsonian Folkways with National Public Radio, CD SF 40072, 1994). Link: https://doi.org/10.3998/mpub.9853855.cmp.44

This music also lacks the spontaneity of the folk spiritual tradition. Any bodily motion (swaying, clapping) is either organized (everyone doing it together) or suppressed altogether. In these ways the concert spiritual has been distanced from African American folk approaches to performance. Even so, this concert spiritual retains from the African American tradition imagery of enslavement, escape through the water, and difficult journeying.

As a living musical tradition the spiritual has proved to be a music of extraordinary versatility, inspiring musicians of many traditions. It has also continued to be a valuable tool for those who choose to assimilate. The first female African American composer to win recognition in the classical music world, Florence Price (1887–1953), was conservatory-trained and framed her work within the Euro-American concert music ("classical") tradition. She composed symphonies and other works for large ensemble, some piano music, and many songs. Her *Black Fantasy* (Fantasie nègre, example 3.11), composed for solo piano in 1929, is an arrangement of the spiritual "Sinner, Please Don't Let This Harvest Pass."

Example 3.11. Florence Price, "Fantasie nègre" (Black fantasy), performed by Samatha Ege. Used by permission.
Link: https://doi.org/10.3998/mpub.9853855.cmp.45

But at first it is not recognizable as such. We hear a stormy and passionate introduction that uses techniques borrowed from the European classical composers Frédéric Chopin and Franz Liszt. (Recalling that Liszt appropriated others' music, we might notice that all music is subject to reuse and further appropriation.) Only after that introduction is the spiritual melody heard (timepoint 0:58), but it is still decorated by the techniques Chopin used to ornament a songlike melody. This music is difficult to play: it reflects the virtuosic tradition of 19th-century piano music.

Through *Black Fantasy* and other works, Price sought to bridge the gap between African American traditions and the European American classical tradition. The difficulty of the work and its resemblance to classical piano works made a bid for respect and inclusion in that tradition, even as the spiritual melody offered content new to that tradition. In Price's day most white Americans still had not thought of African American music as an art form but only as a kind of folk practice that did not require training, effort, or creativity. Price's music demolishes that distinction, bringing ideas from African American music into the classical music tradition and insisting that this, too, is art.[65]

Troubled Water (1967), a piano piece composed by Margaret Bonds (1913–1972), continued the tradition of using spirituals to bridge traditions. Bonds's music blurs the lines among different genres of music more completely, accompanying the spiritual melody with elements from classical music and jazz. *Troubled Water* (example 3.12) is a concert piece for piano, based on the spiritual "Wade in the Water."

Example 3.12. Margaret Bonds, "Troubled Water," performed by Samantha Ege. *Four Women: Music for Piano by Price, Kaprálová, Bilsland, and Bonds* (Wave Theory Records, 2018). Used by permission.
Link: https://doi.org/10.3998/mpub.9853855.cmp.46

The piece has three main sections and a coda (a brief ending section). It begins with an ostinato (a repeated pattern) in the bass, a feature that frequently appeared in jazz piano performances of that era. The ostinato continues throughout the first and third sections of the piece, underneath a statement of the "Wade in the Water" melody that is harmonized in jazz style. When we hear the melody again in the contrasting middle section of the piece (from timepoint 1:37 to 2:49), the accompaniment makes reference to classical piano works that represent water through rippling cascades of notes—especially Claude Debussy's "Reflections in the Water" from *Images*. The third section of Bonds's piece returns to the ostinato, and it is like the first section, though it also reintroduces some of the rippling water ideas near the end of the section. *Troubled Water* closes with a forceful statement of the spiritual melody.

In our day the blending of traditions is commonplace and usually intentional: the composer makes choices about how to express herself not only on the basis of tradition (what has been handed down to her by teachers or kin) but also by how she wants to be perceived and what she wants to represent. As Margaret Bonds and Florence Price sought entry into the classical music world, they could have chosen to assimilate completely, abandoning the musical markers associated with African American music. Instead, African American music became a resource for them and a point of pride that distinguished their music from others'. This piano music reflects the paradoxical views of the Harlem Renaissance: though black artists might choose to assimilate to improve their standing in a white-dominated country, they also continued to respect and cultivate the traditions associated with black Americans.

The relationships created by the scattering of people through diaspora are multifaceted and durable, involving many kinds of interaction and mutual influence. As individual American musicians make their particular musical choices, they act within or against racial identities defined by America's colonial and diasporic history. Although the concept of race has no basis in science, race has often been treated as a social fact that defines or limits artistic heritage and community membership. Nevertheless, it is easy to see that in the United States musical traditions have become intertwined, with borrowings in many directions. In the experiences of the African American and Romani diasporas we can see many instances of the troubled and violent relations between diasporic minorities and their majority neighbors. At the same time, we can recognize the musical relationships created by diaspora as complex and significant forces that have shaped the development of music in countless ways. Once we have observed how these relationships work, we might use words like *heritage* and *tradition* with caution, for music is not only "handed down" within a family or other group, but also "handed around" through appropriation, assimilation, and other borrowing practices. These practices are not an exception: they are a typical part of how music moves.

PART 2

Mediation

Part 2 of this book focuses on developments in recorded and broadcast media that have helped people move music. It also examines how media strategies and international politics encouraged nation-states to move, support, or suppress music. Chapter 4 illuminates the introduction of recording technology, the development of the international record trade, and some of the effects recording has had on the movement of music. Folk song collectors traveled far and near, moving music from rural areas to cities and creating archives of valued sounds; these archives would change how people thought about their musical heritage. The development of a large consumer market for recordings has encouraged the creation of improbable combinations of sound—from artificially edited representations of nature to the mixing of traditions in "world music." At the same time, recorded music has also become part of live performances, thanks to the artful combination of recordings in turntabling and electronic dance music. Because these performances can themselves be recorded or re-recorded, our environment includes a vast variety of mixed musics.

Technologies of recording and broadcasting have served the interests of people who want to move music for particular purposes. Chapter 5 reveals the role of nation-states in moving music across international borders, a process that encompasses the movement of people, as well as the strategic use of media. Both Japan and Turkey made sweeping musical reforms when their governments imported music as a means of modernization. During the Cold War, nation-states used musical style to distinguish themselves from one another and to shore up international alliances. The United States, China, and the Soviet Union also regulated the content of musical performances, attempting to limit the expression of social dissent, yet the circulation of audio recordings and the availability of broadcasts made music much harder to control. In this period people began thinking of the world as a system in which each state offered its particular, characteristic music: though each country presented its own version of heritage, the form and character of these performances became somewhat standardized as these versions toured from country to country. Both modernization efforts and Cold War competition increased the number and variety of musical connections among people in different places.

4 Sound Recording and the Mediation of Music

For listeners, the introduction of sound recording brought with it the means to hear voices or music with no performer present. A live performance offers a special feeling of immediacy; being present in the same space as a performer, or performing oneself, is a vibrant form of human awareness. Listening to music from a recording is a different experience, though it may be no less vivid. A performance is **mediated** if there is somebody or something between the maker and the listener: any kind of musical recording (like an mp3 file or a long-playing record), a broadcasting organization (like YouTube or a television station), a recommendation service (like Pandora), or a subscription service (like Apple Music). Each of these things that might come between performer and listener is a medium, and in the plural we call them media. We can also say that a recording mediates the musical experience.

When the performer and the listener are in the same place, within earshot, that performance might feel "immediate" (not mediated). Yet all art is mediated. When performer and listener are in the same place, the medium for transmitting musical ideas might be a musical instrument or the human voice. Often multiple media operate at the same time: in a song that has words, the voice is a medium that conveys the words; and the words are a medium that conveys thoughts. Between the composer and the performer there may be (for example) printed sheet music, correspondence instructing the performer how to play, or demonstration recordings, or all of these. Human beings often take no notice of all the levels of mediation at work in their environment: they skillfully negotiate paths through a network of meaningful activity.[1] This awareness gap creates a paradox: even though music is a highly mediated activity, the feeling of immediacy has often been important to how people have perceived music.

Even the written word can mediate music. Some pieces of music, called program music, are meant to be accompanied by poems or titles that spur the listener to imagine the meaning of the music more concretely. Other kinds of verbal information, too, can mediate our listening. A newspaper review of a live concert might change the listener's opinion of what she heard. If the listener thinks Itzhak Perlman is a superb violinist, and then the next morning reads that Perlman is playing poorly these days, this news may retrospectively color the listener's memory of the performance. This, too, is a kind of mediation: it comes between the listener and the performer, changing the listener's perspective, even if it happens after the fact. Sometimes people think of mediation exclusively as a means of **transmission**, bringing music or messages from one place to another. But mediation is also built into the nature of music, for all music requires some kind of making or performance process.

Nonetheless, the ability to reproduce music by technological means has invited some people to think in new ways about mediation: in the recording era music's mediated nature has become more noticeable. Even in the early days of recording, the ability to send recorded audio to distant places built global commercial connections and helped individuals living far from their places of origin feel a connection with those places. Recording has changed how communities imagine their past as well as their present: preserving musical performances allows a sense of connection through historical time. Recording technology has also enabled new creative activities. Most popular music today is made directly in the recording studio, as it is being prepared for distribution, so creating art and distributing it are no longer separate processes. Whether it is evident as transmission or as creation, then, mediation is a key component of our artistic lives.

Moving Music: A Global Industry

Commercial recordings and the machines that could play them became available in the United States in the 1890s as cylinders, then around 1910 in the form of discs, with a playing time of about three minutes per side.[2] Immediately, many recording companies began competing to supply consumers with playback machines and recorded music. From the beginning these companies were globally connected. In a quest for new content and new markets, US and European record companies searched the world to collect music for reproduction on records. In the first decade of the century, the Victor Talking Machine Company sent representatives to Japan, the Philippines, Korea, and China.[3] Its competitor, the London-based Gramophone Company, developed large markets in Egypt and China. Gramophone also set up factories for pressing records in India, Russia, Spain, Austria, France, and Germany.[4] Odeon Records, based in Berlin, Germany, established itself worldwide before World War I, opening a record-pressing plant in Buenos Aires, Argentina; and the French company Pathé Frères developed business connections throughout Asia, North Africa, and the United States.[5]

By the 1930s, people had access to recorded music in many places—in homes, in public venues, or broadcast over developing radio networks.[6] The existence of these recordings created star performers all over the world. Musicians could now gain popularity not only in the places where they performed in person but also more broadly within their language groups and regions. For some performers, star status changed their lives: in India and China the music of socially stigmatized female performers, such as courtesans and prostitutes, sold well and even became acceptable for listening in homes.[7] Genres of music that featured brief selections and a sound that was easy to record, like solo song, became more famous. Genres that could not easily be performed in front of the recording horn, like choral music, were recorded less frequently.[8]

Many of these recordings were intended for sale in or near the places where they were recorded: Malayan music to Malayans, and so forth. (Often this meant recording in Malaya, sending the recording to be manufactured in Calcutta, then sending the copies back to Malaya for sale.) As a result of colonial occupation and long-standing trade routes, however, multiethnic settlements existed all over the world. Colonists who lived far from their countries of origin and diasporic people eagerly purchased records from "home."[9] In **cosmopolitan** (internationally connected) cities listeners demanded recorded music in a variety of languages and styles, and international corporations transported records to meet that demand.[10]

For example, the Lebanese company Baida Records sold its recordings not only in the Middle East and North Africa but also in the United States to Arab American immigrants.[11] Example 4.1, "Raqs Fahala," is a Baida recording of Arab music, probably made before 1911.[12]

Example 4.1. Mahmoud Al-Rashidi, "Raqs Fahala," recording of Arab music, probably made before 1911 (Baida Records 272A). YouTube.
Link: https://doi.org/10.3998/mpub.9853855.cmp.47

This music is a *raqs*—that is, a piece of dance music—attributed to Mahmoud al-Rashidi. You will hear an introduction played in **unison** (all instruments playing the tune together). This unison section comes back several times throughout the piece. In alternation with the unison section we hear a soloist playing the *oud*, a lute-like instrument. Every time the oud plays, its music is new and possibly **improvised** (made up or altered in the moment of performance, not beforehand). These solo sections are accompanied by an **ostinato** (repeating pattern) played by percussion instruments, and the whole ensemble plays short interjections between the oud's phrases. In the second half of this short piece a solo violin takes the place of the oud. This is a simple musical form that alternates between a repeated refrain and new material. As early records could include only a few minutes of music per side, this simplicity suited the medium.

This and many other examples demonstrate that the new availability of audio recordings succeeded in moving music among diasporic populations. By the beginning of the 1900s, immigrants from many parts of the world had arrived in the United States. In the first decade of the century US record companies initiated targeted marketing campaigns in many languages to encourage immigrants to purchase records of music from their homelands.[13] It was often cheaper and more convenient for record companies to make these "ethnic records" in the United States, so the companies also recorded musicians from a variety of immigrant groups.[14] Example 4.2 is a **polka**, an example of Polish ethnic dance music, recorded in 1927 in Chicago.

Example 4.2. Excerpt from "Polka Wiewórka" (Squirrel Polka), with Stanisław Kosiba, clarinet (Victor 80475, 1927). YouTube.
Link: https://doi.org/10.3998/mpub.9853855.cmp.48

This music features a clarinet playing a jaunty and repetitive tune over a steady "oom-pah, oom-pah" accompaniment played by stringed instruments. This music's phrases are of regular length, and there are pauses at regular intervals: these features make the music suitable for social dancing.

Because of their broad appeal as entertainment music, these recordings could be sold to immigrants in the United States, in the immigrants' countries of origin, and in other places that shared a language or musical preferences with them. Thus, the advent of recording enabled a variety of international activities that gave many peoples access to each other's music. Diasporic populations felt closer to home as the record industry's activity strengthened musical connections between homelands and their diasporas. Colonizing nation-states also built radio broadcasting systems for their colonies: this investment of state money encouraged the making and sharing of records to be played on the air.[15] People gained new access to music that may have been unfamiliar before; for example, the French musician Darius Milhaud noted in 1930 that recordings from Tunisia, Argentina, and Greece had become available in France.[16] The circulation of recordings also built new connections between urban and rural people. Rural music could now be heard in cities and, to a lesser extent, vice versa.

The ability to amplify and record sound, and to manipulate recorded sound for new effects, has shaped what music can be made and how music can move. In the remainder of this chapter we will consider some of the ways in which people have used sound recording to connect listeners across distance and time, even inspiring imaginative connections that had not existed before.

Archiving Sound

Before they had access to the phonograph, ethnographers who studied folk music tried to write down the music using music notation as they listened. This procedure was cumbersome and inaccurate. Sometimes the ethnographers even stopped the musicians in the middle of a performance so they could scribble down what they heard. In contrast, the phonograph allowed the ethnographer to record a complete performance all at once and then listen again and write down the music later.

This method was sometimes still awkward. Percy Grainger (1882–1961), an Australian-born musician who collected folk songs in Great Britain, reported a performer's complaint that singing into the recording horn was like "singin' with a muzzle on." Since high notes would sound distorted if they were sung close to the horn, Grainger moved the singers' bodies around as they were singing (fig. 4.1). In his view, "having their heads guided nearer to, or further from, the recording trumpet" was still less disruptive than stopping the performance to write.[17] Grainger hoped that, eventually, recording would replace the need to write down the songs at all, for the written version could never capture all the nuances of the performance.[18]

Figure 4.2 shows Grainger's written version of a song he collected, sung by Joseph Taylor (b. 1832, death date unknown). We see in this image that Grainger tried hard to capture some of Taylor's special vocal effects. Grainger noted the singer's "slide" between notes, and he placed accent marks (>) over notes that received extra stress. He pointed out variations in loudness even within a single note: these are marked with the symbols < for growing louder, > for growing softer, as over the words *try* and

Fig. 4.1. Postcard photograph of Percy Grainger and Evald Tang Kristensen recording Danish folk singer Jens Christian Jensen, 1922. Photographer unknown. Grainger Museum Collection, University of Melbourne, 2017/41-1/34. Reproduced by kind permission of the Estate of George Percy Grainger.

round. The written version also served the scholarly purpose of comparison: Grainger put asterisks (*) over notes that were sung differently on different recordings, or he wrote the alternative versions underneath. Yet listening closely to the recording Grainger made, a listener may notice other effects he could not capture in writing. Whereas the written version provides a way to compare performances in detail and could even be used as instructions on how to perform the song, the recording captures the performance in a way that preserves the distinctive sound of the singer's voice. Audio example 4.3 is an excerpt of the song Grainger collected, which was sung by Joseph Taylor.

> Example 4.3. Excerpt from "The White Hare," sung by Joseph Taylor. Recorded by Grainger on July 9, 1908. *Voice of the People, vol. 18* (Topic Records, 1998). Link: https://doi.org/10.3998/mpub.9853855.cmp.51

By archiving audio, people understood tradition and heritage in a new way. Recording allowed collectors to imagine that they could gather up all the musical traditions of the world and preserve them. (One British collector audaciously declared in the 1930s that he and his colleagues had recorded every British folk song; he thought all that remained to be done was to study small variations in performance.)[19] The social conditions of the time encouraged this interest. At the beginning of the 20th century many people were thinking

8.—THE WHITE HARE.

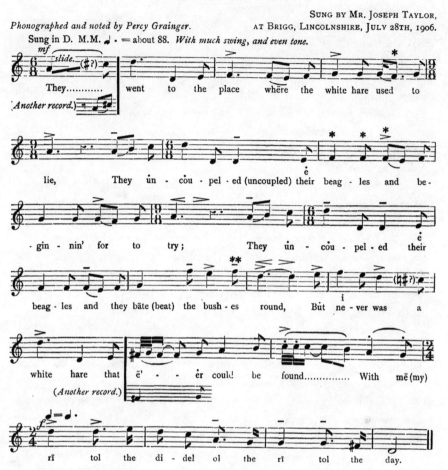

Phonographed and noted by Percy Grainger.

SUNG BY MR. JOSEPH TAYLOR,
AT BRIGG, LINCOLNSHIRE, JULY 28TH, 1906.

Sung in D. M.M. ♩. = about 88. *With much swing, and even tone.*

Fig. 4.2. Grainger's detailed transcription of "The White Hare," sung by Joseph Taylor. From "Songs Collected by Percy Grainger," *Journal of the Folk-Song Society* 3, no. 12 (May 1908): 189–90.

about what it meant to be modern. Over the past few generations ways of life in urban areas had changed quickly as a result of the Industrial Revolution. Once recordings became a prominent medium for listening, some observers imagined that different groups of people would make more and more similar music over time, losing the special traits that made them distinct from one another.[20] Collectors such as Grainger and Béla Bartók began collecting rural music in order to document it before it died out amid the pressures of modern life. They worried that rural people, exposed to popular music, would give up their old ways of making music. Once these recordings were made, scholars and artists often used them to discuss or define a heritage as a fixed and stable thing (**reifying** it).

The desire to create and maintain a definable heritage had some strange effects. Some collectors interfered with the traditions they studied: they urged the people they recorded to sing "the old way" and instructed them not to change their music. Some even altered the songs they collected to "restore" them to hypothetical original versions, erasing the individual variations in hopes of finding the authentic "original."[21] Here we might recall the idea of authenticity as a perception of closeness to an original source: the relationship of these collectors to folk song is like that of some fans to the blues. The collectors' idea of the music was rooted in their own values. When they examined the music, they were hoping to find a particular history, and they were even willing to change the music they found in the present to make it fit their idea of what their past should be like.

For some collectors the archival collection became more important than the live performing tradition: whereas the live performance was ephemeral and changed every time, the archive seemed authoritative and unchanging. Having a tangible collection of recordings allowed people to experience heritage as a fixed entity, provable and permanent. Many collectors were inspired by nationalist feelings: they were interested in distinguishing their national musics from others' and in developing hierarchies of value to demonstrate their music's excellence. The British Folk Song Society, of which Grainger was a part, used folk songs to define and mediate a particular idea of British music. The society's work inspired an outpouring of distinctly British concert music compositions based on those songs.[22]

Yet composers and nation-states also used audio archives to purposefully change or invent traditions. Amid a large-scale modernization effort in the 1920s and 1930s the Turkish government instituted a program of folk-song collection with the goal of making music more compatible with European traditions. (Turkey's admiration for Europe and disdain for "the East" during this period has sometimes been called **occidentalism**, as a mirror image of Western Europe's orientalism.)[23] As the Turkish poet and activist Ziya Gökalp explained, "Our folk music has given us many melodies. If we collect these and harmonize them in the Western manner, we shall have both a national and a European music."[24] Thousands of songs were recorded by phonograph, then written down in European-style notation and classified into categories.

Turkish radio personnel then selected particular songs that fit into their new vision of modern music—and altered those songs as they thought necessary. They "corrected" features they believed reflected the individual styles of folk singers rather than a group identity. They arranged the songs so that they could be performed by a chorus, which would not have happened in the countryside.[25] Example 4.4 is a song belonging to this new genre, known as **Turkish Folk Music**. This kind of song was recorded and broadcast on the radio as a demonstration of both heritage and modernization.

Example 4.4. "Genç Osman" ("Young Osman"), performed by the Ankara Radio Folk Music Group. *Folk and Traditional Music of Turkey* (Folkways FE 4404, 1953). Link: https://doi.org/10.3998/mpub.9853855.cmp.52

State and radio officials asserted that the new music was truly Turkish because it was based on their archived recordings, but of course the state was not obligated to reproduce the music exactly as it had been archived.

The Turkish and British reworkings of folk-song practices are **invented traditions**: the collectors designed their collecting and publication activities for the needs of their present day, but they used music that seemed old to make their activities seem valid and authoritative.[26] In other words, they were making heritage: building a virtual version of the past. Although these activities depended on a belief that the sound recording was a faithful or "authentic" representation of the music "as it really was," when the makers and users of recordings moved music from rural to urban settings, they added new meanings and enabled new uses of these musical sounds.

Taking and Giving Back Sounds

In many cases the archiving of folkloric sound on recordings has promoted cultural appropriation. (Indeed, the Turkish example discussed above is an example of a nation-state's appropriation of folk music.) Countries that have

sponsored song-collection projects have tended to be those that have colonized other peoples—typically wealthy countries with strong institutional
support for the arts—or those seeking to become more powerful. By contrast,
peoples whose songs are collected tend to be those that were colonized.[27] In
their eagerness to learn about music from other places, collectors have sometimes taken music of less powerful people in ways that do harm to those people.[28] Often the collector earned royalties by publishing the recordings or by
publishing observations about the music-makers, while the music-makers
themselves earned nothing. Sometimes the musicians who were recorded were
compelled to sing under embarrassing or humiliating conditions, or the
recording was made without the performer's consent.[29]

Scholars and archivists have long considered how to make this situation
more fair. One option is to **repatriate** recordings—that is, return them to the
peoples or places of origin. Like cultural appropriation itself, repatriation
raises sticky questions. If the original performer is deceased, to whom should
the music be repatriated? To the direct descendants of the performer or to
members of their ethnic group? Since people move, this choice might mean
sending the recording to a place where the music was never heard at the time
of its recording. Or should the recording be repatriated to people now living
in the place where the music was made? They might have no connection to
that music. If a recording was made without permission or under coercive
circumstances, should it be heard today at all?[30]

The problem of ownership further complicates these questions. Under US
law, only writing or music set down in a "fixed form" is entitled to **copyright**
protection. Songs passed down from person to person, but not recorded, have
not been regarded as "authored" works but rather as a product of community
life. (The legal tradition of copyright, which originated in Great Britain, certainly favors European means of conveying artistic traditions. It will be discussed further in chapter 7.) This practice entitles the folk-song collector who
writes down the music and publishes it to payment for that publication and
any recordings of the written song. Meanwhile, the person who originally sang
the song likely receives nothing. Furthermore, if the recording is published far
away from its point of origin, the original performer and community might
not even have access to the recorded version of their own music.

In the case of a unique art object or other artifact, the decision to return
the object to its original owners or their descendants would mean that the
archives or museum cannot keep it. Because recorded music can be duplicated
as many times as necessary, this constraint might not apply. Still, most libraries

and archives have strict policies against duplicating recorded material.[31] When a collector deposits material in an archive, the archive and the collector typically agree to a binding set of conditions for the use of that material. It is difficult for the library to do anything other than what was specified at that time. Native American peoples whose folklore was recorded have sometimes asked not only for a copy of their music but also for all copies (including the master), because ethnographers made recordings of rituals that are considered private or suitable for hearing by only one gender.[32] Many archives have resisted such claims, as they mean the loss of access to that material. Yet, increasingly, repatriation projects are taking these concerns into account and entering negotiations with the peoples whose music was recorded.

The relationship between the recorder and the musician is not always combative, however. The anthropologist Aaron Fox has described a meaningful and revealing case of repatriation.[33] In 1946 a music collector, Laura Boulton (1899–1980), visited the town of Barrow, in northern Alaska, to collect Iñupiat (Eskimo) music. Boulton made recordings of dance songs and children's music, and she wrote down her interpretations of this music, despite her lack of knowledge of Iñupiat language or musical practices. Joseph Sikvayugak (1898–1979), a community leader, sang on most of the recordings (fig. 4.3). He assisted Boulton throughout her time in Barrow, though she gave him little credit in her subsequent writings. Boulton earned a considerable amount of money from royalties from her recordings, which were deposited at Columbia University in New York, inaccessible to the Iñupiat. Ten years after Boulton's visit, Sikvayugak purchased a reel-to-reel tape recorder and continued to make documentary recordings of his community's music.

A researcher, Chie Sakakibara, traveled to Barrow in 2004, carrying copies of Boulton's recordings and a letter from Fox, the director of the archives at Columbia University, expressing willingness to share the recordings. Over a few years Iñupiat communities, which share close kinship ties, spread the word and requested further copies of the recordings. As a result of hearing these recordings, Sikvayugak's grandchildren, the brothers Riley and Vernon Sikvayugak and Vernon's spouse, Isabell, formed a group to begin performing these songs again.

Present-day Iñupiat people see that their heritage and traditions have been disrupted; indeed, this disruption was already apparent during Boulton's visit. In 1946 the US government was building a naval research laboratory in Barrow, changing the character of the community and its means of livelihood. Iñupiat people faced pressure to assimilate. Missionaries discouraged their rit-

Fig. 4.3. The Sikvayugak brothers perform as Laura Boulton makes a recording. Courtesy of the Archives of Traditional Music at Indiana University.

ual music; and as there were no local schooling options, young people were sent to boarding school, where they were separated from the traditions of their community. At these schools teachers shamed Native American students who spoke their native languages or sang the songs they had learned at home. According to Fox, Joseph Sikvayugak believed, as Laura Boulton did, that recording could capture and preserve a tradition at a time of great cultural change. His grandchildren, hearing his recorded voice, are reviving that tradition because it is meaningful to them.[34] This recreation is not identical to the original, nor is it meant to be: it is a collaborative process to make something valuable in and for the present day.[35]

Authenticity and the Hyperreal

When audio recording was first invented, its primary use was to capture sound as evidence of what had really happened. For example, recording two people making a verbal agreement allowed later listeners to verify the sound of the individuals' voices. The feeling of authenticity that people attached to folk-song recordings reflected that belief: if it was recorded, it must really have happened in precisely that way.

Early versions of the recording equipment allowed the user to record or play back sound from a disc or cylinder but offered no way to modify the recording. Technologies for modifying sound after it was recorded came considerably later. One of the first ways to manipulate the sounds on a recording was **overdubbing**. Musicians would make a recording, then replay that recording and play their instruments along with it at the same time to create a composite recording, then replay that composite and play instruments along with it again, until they had all the parts they wanted. When musicians began overdubbing in the 1940s, the process was extremely cumbersome. The tracks the musicians recorded first would come out sounding weaker and less distinct when they were recorded from playback over and over.[36]

Not only was this kind of technical manipulation difficult, but many people also criticized it as inferior because of the persistent ideal of authenticity. When the jazz clarinetist and saxophonist Sidney Bechet (1897–1959) used overdubbing to play all the parts on a recording of "The Sheik of Araby" by himself in 1941, the record was denounced by other jazz musicians as a kind of parlor trick. In example 4.5 you hear Bechet playing soprano and tenor saxophones, clarinet, piano, bass, and drums. This recording was marketed as a novelty record, "Sidney Bechet's One-Man Band."

Example 4.5. Excerpt from "The Sheik of Araby," performed by Sidney Bechet's One Man Band (Victor 27485-A, 1941). YouTube.
Link: https://doi.org/10.3998/mpub.9853855.cmp.54

A fellow jazz musician, Mezz Mezzrow, complained that the recording was "neurotic and bestial," with no community spirit.[37] Mezzrow could not trust a recording that represented a fictional performance that never really happened: it seemed profoundly strange and inauthentic.

Recording on magnetic media, in which people captured sounds on long pieces of wire or metal-coated tape, became more widely available in the mid-1940s. These technologies afforded composers further possibilities to create sounds that corresponded to no real-world performance. In 1944 an Egyptian composer, Halim El-Dabh (1921–2017), recorded a women's healing ceremony outside Cairo on a wire recorder; he then manipulated the sound using the resources of a local radio station. In an overdubbing process like Sidney Bechet's, El-Dabh played the recording in an echo chamber, then re-recorded the resulting sound several times. He also edited out the consonants that defined the women's sung words and the initial attacks of drum sounds but kept the resonant quality of voices and the decaying drum sound.[38] The resulting music, audible in example 4.6, is strange and ghostly: it sounds recognizably human but distant and disembodied. Like Bechet, El-Dabh made recordings that did not just preserve "real-world" events: they used recorded media for artistic as well as practical purposes.

Example 4.6. Halim El-Dabh, "Ta'bir al-Zar" ("The Expression of Zar"). Excerpt under the title "Wire Recorder Piece" on *Crossing into the Electric Magnetic* (Halim El-Dabh Records, LLC, 2001). Reproduced by kind permission of Deborah El-Dabh. Link: https://doi.org/10.3998/mpub.9853855.cmp.55

A few years later, the French radio technician Pierre Schaeffer (1910–95) made "noise music" by painstakingly editing together miscellaneous sounds from the environment that had been recorded on discs: trains, singing, coughing, a harmonica performance, pots and pans, and so forth. By carving a groove into the disc that formed a closed circle instead of a spiral, Schaeffer could make sounds repeat (or "loop") as the disc spun around and around in the same groove, then record that repetitive loop on a second phonograph. In one of Schaeffer's "noise studies," called "Étude pathétique" (Study in pathos; example 4.7), we first hear pot lids and plates being dropped and spun on a kitchen floor; then, without warning or pause, we hear a train passing close by. Not only does this music refuse to reflect a single musical performance; it also purposefully violates any kind of logical listening. Schaeffer disorients listeners by allowing them to imagine the sounds being made in a certain place and then making those listeners rethink what they have heard by changing the imagined setting or the action unpredictably.

Example 4.7. Excerpt from Pierre Schaeffer, "Étude pathétique" (Study in pathos) from *Études de bruit* (Noise Studies). *Panorama of Musique Concrète (1948–55)* (London: Ducretet-Thomson Records, 1955). YouTube. Link: https://doi.org/10.3998/mpub.9853855.cmp.56

Schaeffer used recording as a way to divorce music from real-life experience: what we hear in these works cannot be mapped onto a clear mental image of human or mechanical activity.[39] The idea of recording music had become detached from the idea of recording reality or performance as it really happened: the audio recording itself became a way of making music. It is not that the artifice of recording became invisible; rather, musicians embraced the artifice as one of the valid tools for making music.[40]

Over time, methods for editing recorded sound have become more and more sophisticated. Magnetic tape could be cut apart and spliced together or run backward, but digital sound files can be manipulated or combined in many more ways, and individual sounds can now be altered or created digitally. As the archive of recorded sound has grown over the past 140 years, more and more music from the past has become available for reuse by museums, nation-states, and individuals. The person making a recording today can access a dazzling array of raw material: enormous amounts of recorded music from past and present, recordings of ambient sound, and newly created sounds. In effect, the sound editor has a "god's-eye view" of the sonic landscape. These technologies allow the creation of virtual worlds—immersive experiences that may seem "more real than the real"—sometimes called **hyperreal**.[41]

The ethnomusicologist Steven Feld, who spent years doing research in Papua New Guinea, made a recording that exemplifies the hyperreal. From the 1970s to the 1990s Feld spent time with the Kaluli people, learned about their lives, and recorded their music. Feld deplored corporate oil exploration, logging in the rainforests, and the arrival of evangelical missionaries, for he believed these changes placed the Kaluli under the domination of outsiders who controlled travel, education, and jobs.[42] To draw attention to the situation and raise funds for rainforest preservation, Feld made a recording that documented Kaluli life—not as it was when he was there but as he imagined it might have been at some time in the past, before the encroachment of technological modernity. This recording was marketed as "endangered music" in the 1990s, at the height of consumer interest in "world music."

Feld spent a lot of time recording the ambient sounds of the rainforest—birds, insects, and water noises—and carefully edited out the sounds of helicopters, airplanes, and the bells of the missionaries' churches. In the editing process, he layered the natural sounds with recordings of Kaluli musical performances to place the listener inside the recreated rainforest scene, hearing ambient sounds and human music together. The resulting recording, released in 1991, mimics the progress of a 24-hour day, with the insects and frogs of night giving way in the daytime to human work, play, and ceremonial activities—all accompanied by natural background sounds—and then nightfall.[43]

Example 4.8 is called "Making Sago." We hear a group of women singing and talking as they complete the morning chore of beating and scraping sago, the starchy core of a palm tree, a common food in the Pacific Islands. The sounds of their work are audible, as are the bird and insect sounds of the surrounding rainforest. Human whistling that imitates birdsong is a remarkable characteristic of Kaluli music.

Example 4.8. Ulahi, "Making Sago," recorded by Steven Feld. *Voices of the Rainforest* (Rykodisc RCD 10173, 1991; Smithsonian Folkways HRT15009, 2011). Link: https://doi.org/10.3998/mpub.9853855.cmp.57

Feld's recording is a carefully developed fictional world: a created soundscape that places the listener in the pristine rainforest as it no longer exists in Papua New Guinea.

Feld recognized the irony. He, a scholar committed to truthful representation, had produced a fictional soundscape. Most listeners who encounter "Voices of the Rainforest" cannot tell by listening how much of it is true-to-life or what has been edited out. Indeed, this recording only succeeds if it feels real to the listener. Even if the listener has read Feld's notes and knows how this soundscape was constructed, the recording encourages the suspension of disbelief, for the voices and sounds of the rainforest are close by, right in our ears.[44] The power to create such a vivid illusion relies on the feeling of authenticity that was present in early uses of sound recording: the evidence of our senses can make the experience feel real even if the ascertainable facts tell us it is not.

Feld framed his intervention as an effort to make known the beauty of Kaluli customs and of the rainforest—erasing intrusive sounds to remind listeners of the possibility of living and making music together with nature rather than against it.[45] Yet Feld's advocacy does not represent the viewpoints of Kaluli people. He acknowledged that many on the island would not care about this reconstruction of their "lost world" because their economic interests are now tied to logging and oil. Feld's representation of the Kaluli sound-world does not address the Kaluli at all: it was an attempt to attract North American listeners' attention and cultivate an emotional attachment in hopes of stimulating action to preserve the rainforest. Moving these sounds was an intervention, meant to alter the beliefs and emotions of people at a distance.

Mixes and Mashups

The examples discussed above show that new music can be made partly or entirely out of other recorded music. Another influential example is **turntablism**, a technique that black, Caribbean American, and Latinx hip-hop musicians developed in 1970s New York City. From the 1970s to the present day, turntablism has traditionally relied on old technology—the turntables used to spin recorded discs for playback—as well as a mixing board and a large personal collection of vinyl long-playing records (LPs). The turntable artist creates a new live performance by playing selections from LPs on two turntables, using the mixing board to play the sound from one turntable or the other, or even both at once.[46] Once a practice local to New York, turntablism is now practiced in many places—yet another example of widespread appropriation of an appealing technique.

This form of creative expression can create new sounds—like, for instance, the distinctive scratch heard when the disc jockey (DJ) pulls the record backward to replay the same bit of music again. The expert turntablist moves quickly, creating entrancing rhythms and blends of sounds by combining and repeating many sounds from multiple records. This video of the Japanese turntablist DJ Kentaro (example 4.9) demonstrates his technical and artistic virtuosity. Kentaro has marked the discs so that he can access precisely the excerpts he wants and spin them from the desired spot each time. He has also altered the discs by adding tape and letting the stylus drag on the label of a disc to create a rhythmic hissing sound. His choice of source LPs places his performance in the African American tradition: this performance makes reference to the African American tradition of rap (spoken-word music), including the classic Run-DMC song "You Be Illin'," as well as the dance beats of 1970s funk.

Example 4.9. DJ Kentaro, performance recorded at the DMC World DJ Final, 2001. Published on YouTube by DMC World Championships, 2012. Link: https://doi.org/10.3998/mpub.9853855.cmp.58

Turntablism is only one of many kinds of music that use other recorded music as a source. The disco, funk, and R&B that turntablists often borrow can also be sampled digitally. **Digital sampling** is a logical outgrowth of turntablism: instead of playing excerpts from vinyl LPs, brief selections of music are digitally copied from recordings of music or other sound and placed into new musical contexts through editing. While turntabling is a live, in-person performance, digital sampling happens in the recording studio.[47] Sometimes the sample functions as a recognizable quotation from another piece of music. Part of the appeal of music that is based on sampling is the pleasure of recognizing those quotations. At other times the quoted material is so transformed that it is hardly recognizable. It might be a hidden part of the musical texture or go by in an instant as a sound effect.

Rhythmic repetition has been fundamental to much of the dance music that has developed since the 1970s, and technologies of recorded sound have enabled musicians to make musical forms based on mechanical repetition. Looping, or repeating a short excerpt of music again and again to form a continuous pattern, is a very basic kind of sound editing. **Electronic dance music** relies on the manipulation of prerecorded music through looping and turntablism. In live performance the DJ makes a loop repeat, as a foundation for a longer passage of music, while also adding other layers of musical elements that change over time. These elements may come from vinyl records, but they are more typically digital samples from an enormous variety of recordings. The excerpts vary widely in style, but they are selected so that they can conform to the dance beat the DJ has chosen.

The virtuosity of the DJ, like that of the hip-hop turntablist, consists in selecting these changing elements, sequencing them, and making artful transitions from one to the next. The transitions from one passage of music to the next can be smooth and gradual or surprising, even witty. Listeners judge a DJ by the musical taste of her or his selections—they value musical samples that are unknown or rare—and by the DJ's technical prowess of combining them in the moment while keeping the dance beat going.[48] Marea Stamper (1977–), who works under the name "the Black Madonna," is a Chicago-based DJ whose music embodies these kinds of virtuosity. Her May 2017 set at the Lente Festival in the Netherlands lasted almost two hours and included music from many sources, including funk, disco, pop, rock-jazz fusion, Latin music, and the work of other DJs.[49]

More than an hour into this set, we hear a synthesizer play a "ramping up" gesture, and we hear women's voices chiming in repeatedly on the syllable "oh" (this excerpt is example 4.10). Here Stamper reuses a mix from a group called Metro Area.[50] Soon we start to hear flourishes of stringed instruments that sound like the background interjections of a disco recording. The disco elements become more audible, and then the disco song emerges with its vocal part intact. This is a 1981 song called "I Hear Music in the Street," by a now-forgotten band called Unlimited Touch; Black Madonna speeds up the song to match the beat of the preceding music.

Example 4.10. Excerpt from The Black Madonna's set at Lente Kabinet Festival, 2017. Soundcloud.
Link: https://doi.org/10.3998/mpub.9853855.cmp.59

Two minutes later, yet another song fades in. Throughout her performances Black Madonna raises and lowers the amount of bass to control the energy in the room.

According to the ethnomusicologist Luis-Manuel Garcia, some of the pleasure of electronic dance music comes from this process of transformation over time. As they dance, people experience both the consistency of the persistent beat and the transitions and transformations of the other musical elements. Long stretches of music create an immersive and absorbing experience. Like Feld's "Voices of the Rainforest," the Black Madonna's creations build a sonic world that feels like a distinct reality. Garcia found that participants in dance parties in Chicago, Paris, and Berlin tend to regard these parties as an entirely separate space from the rest of their lives, a "temporary dismantling of the everyday."[51] Participants aim to conceal their social class and some other markers of identity in order to lose themselves in the dance party.[52] The Black Madonna reports that "I am at my most in-tune—my best self—when the music lifts the whole room together, and all the separations between us dissolve for a little while."[53]

Electronic dance music travels. Not only do these remixes circulate on recordings and across the internet, but the musicians and the dancers also circulate from place to place. At any given event the crowd may consist of locals, immigrants, and tourists, and some tourists may have flown in specifically for this event. From one cosmopolitan city to the next the parties are not identical, but they can share similar musical practices and social expectations. This network is not evenly "global," but it does create loose ties among partygoers within and sometimes even between world regions.[54] Thus, the DJ and producer Fernanda Arrau, based in Santiago, Chile, plays at clubs and festivals throughout Latin America and internationally.[55] The Afghan producer Shuja Rabbani, based in Dubai, is seeking to make this kind of music more widely known throughout the Middle East, particularly in places where it has been denounced or suppressed by Islamist authorities.[56] This global appeal is not surprising. Because electronic dance music is based on the reuse of previously recorded music, its content is flexible: one can represent one's own heritage, someone else's, a "neutral" electronic sound, or any blend of elements. These musical compilations then recirculate as recordings that can be sampled again, yielding a vast wash of music-about-music.

In the 1980s, alongside the development of turntablism and the mixing and remixing of dance music, yet another kind of mixing became popular. Music from different parts of the world became a fad in the international music industry, supported by consumer enthusiasm for diversity and by large record companies with a wide reach. Some recordings marketed under the category **world music** (or **world beat**) came from a single tradition that seemed novel to listeners in North America and Europe. Others were made by Western recording artists who mimicked music from afar. Still others were international collaborations that blended traditions. As Western popular music styles came to be practiced in many places, there was more common ground for such collaborations, like the one between popular musician and promoter Peter Gabriel and the Senegalese pop star Youssou N'Dour.[57] These world beat projects were not the earliest recordings to involve blending of this sort, but they were notable for their number and especially for the peculiarity of the blends. (Although this kind of music is most commonly called world music, I will refer to the genre as world beat, because the phrase "world music" inappropriately appears to represent the whole world of music.)[58]

There are several words for blends of this sort. The creator of a **mashup** edits recordings together to make a purposeful combination of musics that are perceived to be very different in origin or style. That perception of difference is important because it gives the mashup a feeling of whimsical improbability. A more general category that includes mashups is a **mix**—music that is created by combining two or more different source musics. (In a mix the musics need not be extremely or comically different.) Sometimes people use the biological term *hybrid* for this process. The idea of a "hybrid" implies that the source music can easily be divided into separate species that have clear boundaries.

As we saw in the case of electronic dance music, not all mixes maintain the illusion of clearly separate sources. The world beat mixes of the 1980s, in contrast, used source music that had already been marketed to consumers as distinct species, carefully labeled with backstories that located the music in specific times and places of origin. One such species was the women's choir called Mystère des Voix Bulgares (Mystery of the Bulgarian Voices), which sold many records in the 1980s. Journalists discussed the singers using the language of exoticism: one critic referred to their "hypnotizingly foreign beauty." But their publicity materials also gave lavish descriptions of their authenticity. To North American audiences, the recording seemed to present a genuine East European folk music that had been hidden from the West but was now being revealed. Example 4.11 presents Mystery of the Bulgarian Voices singing a song called "Guro Is Looking for a Bride."

Example 4.11. Excerpt from Krassimir Kyurktchijski, "Guro is Looking for a Bride," performed by Mystère des Voix Bulgares/Angelite. *A Cathedral Concert* (Verve World 314 510 794-4, 1988). YouTube.
Link: https://doi.org/10.3998/mpub.9853855.cmp.60

This music is notable especially for its **dissonance** (the clashing of one note against another). This is a difficult effect to achieve in choral singing, and it is very different from the choral singing styles that had been familiar to Western listeners.

The Mystery choir's artistic impression relied on cultivating the belief that they were folk musicians from the countryside. The women wore folk costumes, spoke no English on camera, and demonstrated a carefully cultivated modesty of appearance and demeanor. Despite the impression given to the media, however, this music only loosely reflected Bulgarian folk practice. For comparison listen to example 4.12, a recording of folk singing from Bulgaria.

Example 4.12. "Gel Yano," performed by the Bistritsa Grannies and their Grand-Daughters, Bistritsa, Bulgaria.
Link: https://doi.org/10.3998/mpub.9853855.cmp.61

Compared to the Mystery choir's polished choral performance, this singing excerpt has a rougher edge. The excerpt begins with vigorous whoops, and the singing women repeatedly maximize the clash between notes by modifying the pitch of the note up and down repeatedly.

The Mystery choir's imitation of this style standardized the pitch and removed those in-the-moment pitch modifications so that each performance is the same, and they used this kind of harmony with tuneful dance songs that could seem catchy to Western ears. Most record-buyers did not know that the Mystery choir's highly polished "folk style" was made by professional musicians. In Eastern Europe and in communist parts of Asia from the 1950s to the 1980s, many nation-states founded national folk ensembles that modified traditional folk practices into stage performances, especially useful for export. This music was meant to give the impression of being folk music, without

Fig. 4.4. Album cover of *From Bulgaria with Love*, by Mystère des Voix Bulgares. The folk costumes are a ubiquitous part of the choir's presentation; the gun indicates their origin in a Communist country, which would have been regarded as unsafe and unfree by Western European and US audiences.

calling attention to its nature as an invented tradition. The women of the Mystery choir appeared in folk costume on their album covers; the presence of a gun pointed at the women on the cover of their album "From Bulgaria with Love" (1992) underscored that they had come from Cold War Eastern Europe, which was perceived in the West as mysterious and dangerous (fig. 4.4). Consumers in the West did not seem to care that this music was professionally arranged; it was easy to avoid thinking about this factor, as the marketing emphasized authenticity. That feeling of authenticity greatly enhanced consumers' appreciation for the music.[59]

The Mystery choir's dissonant choral sound was novel for a while, but American and European record-buyers did not demonstrate a deep interest in the details of Bulgarian choral singing. Once the Bulgarian women had completely saturated the limited market for their records, they began to collaborate with other groups to provide more novelty. One noteworthy collaboration is the pairing of the Bulgarian women (singing under the updated name "Angelite" [an-ge-LEE-tay]) and the Central Asian "throat-singers" of Tuva.

Tuva is a remote province on the Siberian/Mongolian border where the primary historical livelihood is sheepherding. Throat-singing is a technique that excites more resonant frequencies than do usual uses of the voice. This technique produces rich low notes and flute-like overtones high above. In keeping with the traditional outdoor occupations of Tuvan people, the overtones can be made to imitate natural phenomena, such as the singing of birds.[60] Example 4.13 is Anatoly Kulaar, singing "Borbangnadyr with Stream Water." First we hear the sound of a stream; then Kulaar's voice comes in, vibrating to imitate the rushing of the stream. Audible at timepoint 0:47 and again at 1:24 are the whistle-like overtones, which are produced by the voice itself (not a whistle).

Example 4.13. Anatoly Kulaar, "Borbangnadyr with Stream Water." *Tuva, Among the Spirits* (Smithsonian Folkways SFW CD 40452, 1999).
Link: https://doi.org/10.3998/mpub.9853855.cmp.63

Recordings of Tuvan throat-singing became popular as a novelty among world beat listeners in the early 1990s. Like the Bulgarians, some throat-singers embarked on worldwide tours and made television appearances. They encountered the same problem as did the Bulgarians: once a Western listener has heard some throat-singing, the novelty fades. To keep people buying new recordings, the Tuvans and the Bulgarians discovered that mixes could renew the novelty of their singing. They also toured together.

Example 4.14 comes from a track called "Legend" that the Bulgarians and Tuvans recorded together. As collaborations go, the match between the Tuvans and the Bulgarian women's choir is inventive: both groups feature unusual vocal styles. Although Tuvan throat-singers do not traditionally sing in groups, they do sing together on concert tours in the West, as they do here. This piece of music begins with the Tuvan singers. At timepoint 1:17 the Bulgarian choir enters with a chant-like melody, which sounds like a separate layer of music. The two groups stay quite distinct from each other in this recording; they sing in different registers (low and high), and each retains its own characteristic style of singing.

> Example 4.14. Excerpt from Angelite with Huun Huur Tu and the Moscow Art Trio, "Legend." *Fly, Fly, My Sadness* (Jaro Records, 1997). YouTube.
> Link: https://doi.org/10.3998/mpub.9853855.cmp.64

Though in "Legend" the constituent musics in the mix are not fully integrated, another song, "Lonely Bird," integrates them much more closely. "Lonely Bird," excerpted in example 4.15, includes less of the signature sound of either group.

> Example 4.15. Excerpt from Angelite with Huun Huur Tu and the Moscow Art Trio, "Lonely Bird." *Fly, Fly, My Sadness* (Jaro Records, 1997). YouTube.
> Link: https://doi.org/10.3998/mpub.9853855.cmp.65

Rather, the two choirs sing together as background for a soloist, using syllables like *ah* and *doo* rather than words from either of their languages. Some of the promotional material for this CD suggests a secret, ancient connection between the Bulgarian and Tuvan peoples, as if they are long-lost cousins who are now coming together to make music. No historical evidence supports this improbability. Rather, the suggestion is just intended to cultivate the listener's belief that the music is authentic.

This phase of the marketing of world beat coincided with the 1980s and 1990s, when many people expressed optimism about globalization. During this period, mixes of distant, completely unrelated music became commonplace. The world beat fad made a great deal of music from around the world commercially accessible, yet almost all of this music had a short shelf life, just like other kinds of popular music. The public that purchased this genre of commercial music demanded musical novelty that reflected exotic difference but also suggested global connectedness. Once the consumer was familiar with isolated examples of music from many ethnicities, marketers sought to hold their attention through improbable combinations of styles and sounds. The more improbable the combination, the more consumers marveled.

This business of mixing musics—making music about music—is curious. This kind of music-making transparently relies on editing technology to create mixes of sound that never existed as live performance. The pleasure of the blended music, however, rests on our beliefs about authenticity and hybridity: we are pleased when we recognize the original "ingredients," but the artfulness of combining these ingredients often takes center stage. The existence of mixed musics has not eclipsed the old-fashioned experience of authenticity. Rather, it playfully engages that experience, letting us experience both difference and assimilation at the same time. As listeners, we do not have trouble accepting these musics-about-music as real: they are just part of our mix.

5 Music and Media in the Service of the State

Earlier chapters of this book demonstrated that politics on a vast, even worldwide scale—sometimes called **geopolitics**—can cause people and music to move to new places through migration or technological mediation. This chapter examines situations in which other kinds of geopolitical relationships caused music to move across international borders in the service of **states**.

When we think of a globe with the countries outlined on it, the boundaries represent states. A state is an administrative unit that claims territorial boundaries, enumerates its **citizens**—the persons who are affiliated with the state—and grants rights to those citizens. (The state can also withhold rights.)[1] Historians sometimes describe states as if they were human actors; that is, they might say that "Colombia appealed to the International Court of Justice." Though the people doing the appealing are individuals, they are acting on behalf of the entire administrative apparatus—with its power and authority behind them—and on behalf of all the governed people. People have given states the right to use certain kinds of violence to keep order within their boundaries or to defend their boundaries.

Some of the countries on today's globe are governed as **nation-states**, which organize territory and people according to overlapping considerations of state and nation (the human sense of belonging to a coherent group in a particular territory). According to the political scientist Benedict Anderson, a **nation** is an "imagined community." That is, people who do not know each other personally can perceive a sense of solidarity and commitment to each other and recognize each other as fellow citizens. The sense of a nation's coherence may be based on ethnicity, heritage, or other factors held in common. The link between the people exists in their perceptions—hence "imagined," in Anderson's terminology—but they act on nationality as a real fact about themselves and others. Words or actions that are based on that sense of solidarity and advocate for the empowerment of the nation are called **nationalism**.[2]

The identification of nation and state as a single entity does not describe real life in most places, because mixed or overlapping populations are a norm. In some states citizenship is defined at least in part by a person's genealogy. Other states, though, encompass multiple distinct groups who think of themselves as nations, and some states give rights to citizens irrespective of national belonging. Under colonialism European states managed faraway territories, and they defined different rights for different groups of citizens. Since colonial administrators often drew state boundaries that did not correspond to national groups, some of these newer nation-states have been troubled by intergroup conflicts.[3] India, for example, is a state containing many nations, and the borders of many African states are drawn in ways that divide rather than unite people who share a language. For diasporic peoples, or for colonized peoples whose borders were drawn by others, questions about who counts as a full citizen of the state have remained important. Citizenship in a state does not offer perfect protection: states have often done violence to their own citizens, as well as to those people perceived as not belonging.

Anderson believed that media helped create nations: once a group of people shared printed books and newspapers, they could all relate to the same information and thereby relate to each other. Sharing media reinforces and helps to standardize a common language and common expectations.[4] At the same time, this unity is almost always incomplete or temporary: different citizens or groups argue about how their nation should be defined, and that definition changes over time. Music can be an important part of how people make themselves feel like a national group or even how they define their nation.[5]

Individuals make musical choices, but states can also use music to advance the interests of their power or their people, both within and outside their borders. Spreading information, music, or ideas that promote a particular agenda is called **propaganda**—for it propagates ideas. Propaganda need not always be negative. States use propaganda to achieve a wide variety of outcomes, and a state can direct propaganda to people within or outside its borders. The case studies described in this chapter demonstrate that states have pushed music into places outside their borders and pulled music in from outside. The music that moved has sometimes served as propaganda, conveying ideas that support a particular point of view. Often, this point of view has had to do with defining a nation or a state or establishing a relationship among groups of people. The examples in this chapter also demonstrate that propaganda is not only a function of the printed or electronic news media. As we will see, states have used live performance, as well as music transmitted by other means, to create relationships.

"Pulling" European Classical Music into Japan and Turkey

The decision to pull music from elsewhere into a state has often been motivated by political concerns. For centuries European empires held a great deal of economic and military power and reigned over large territories, putting pressure on other states to "keep up" for fear of losing their independence. Some states sought to ally with or even emulate Europeans. Alliances could take the form of trade or diplomatic relations. States could also affirm a relationship by instituting musical or literary connections.[6]

In the late 1800s and early 1900s Japan and Turkey undertook large-scale projects of adopting European practices. The process of rapidly changing administration, education, and citizen behavior to emulate Europeans was known as **modernization**. The equation of "European" with "modern" is noteworthy. The American sociologist Edward Shils observed in the 1950s that for peoples outside Europe and the United States, *modern* means "the model of the West detached in some way from its geographical origins."[7] Thinkers in many parts of the world had come to believe European missionaries' accounts of European superiority, and some even referred to their own civilizations as "backward" or "sick."[8] In the Japanese and Turkish cases the adoption of European music was not a forced result of colonialism: the decision to import ideas was made by the importers based on their own assessments of where power lay in the world. Furthermore, there was no one standard for modernization: individuals, nations, and states developed their own definitions of what it meant to be modern, and these ideas changed over time.[9]

From 1633 until 1853 the military government of Japan maintained a policy of isolation from other peoples. This policy did not entirely eliminate knowledge of music from outside the country, but it did minimize foreign influence.[10] In 1868 Emperor Meiji took power and initiated radical changes in policy, lifting the ban on Christianity and encouraging rapid modernization through adoption of Western practices. Observing developments elsewhere in the world, the emperor had concluded that as a matter of security Japan should emulate Europe's technological and military developments.

European church music arrived with missionaries, and military band music came to Japan as part of a broader adoption of military culture.[11] Soon thereafter, the government of Japan decided to implement Dutch and French methods of education. As the music critic Kōichi Nomura described it, "Music and singing were included in the school curricula of advanced foreign countries"—and adopting European methods was taken as a sign of progressive thought.[12]

In 1879 a music educator, Shūji Izawa, presented a plan to the minister of education. Izawa said he did not know of any cases where foreign music was successfully imported and that it would be impossible to entirely replace Japanese traditional music with Western music. "By blending Eastern and Western music," he wrote, Japan could "establish a kind of music which is suitable for the Japan of today"—that is, modern Japan.[13] At great expense the Japanese government created a second music education system to teach European music, running in parallel with already existing Japanese music institutions and practices. The Yamaha corporation, today the world's largest maker of musical instruments, began manufacturing keyboard instruments in Japan in 1887. The Japanese state sponsored composers of European-style music, some of whom studied in Europe or the United States.

The *Inno Meiji* Symphony (1921), written by Japanese composer Kōsaku Yamada (1886–1965), is a **symphonic poem**: a piece of music for European-style orchestra that conveys a story or idea. In this music Yamada presented the story of Japan's modernization under Emperor Meiji. In example 5.1, an excerpt from the beginning of the piece, the music is slow and ethereal, as if referring to a timeless past. We hear brief interjections of jingling rattles and a hollow-sounding woodblock.

Example 5.1. Excerpt near the beginning of Kōsaku Yamada, "Inno Meiji" Symphony. Tokyo Metropolitan Symphony Orchestra, conducted by Takuo Yuasa (Naxos 8.557971, 2007). YouTube.
Link: https://doi.org/10.3998/mpub.9853855.cmp.66

Europeans typically used these sounds as stereotypes that represented "the East" (i.e., orientalism). As Yamada was European- and US-trained, it is not surprising that he borrowed this strategy of representation.[14]

About five minutes into Yamada's *Inno Meiji* (example 5.2) we hear a march, trumpets blazing and drums pounding: this music conveys the image of military power.

Example 5.2. Excerpt near the middle of Kōsaku Yamada, "Inno Meiji" Symphony. Tokyo Metropolitan Symphony Orchestra, conducted by Takuo Yuasa (Naxos 8.557971, 2007). YouTube.
Link: https://doi.org/10.3998/mpub.9853855.cmp.67

After some turbulence, including a direct conflict between the military sounds and the woodblock (perhaps between the West and Japan), the music slows. In the European tradition, the oboe and flute heard at this point traditionally represent the countryside ("pastoral" music). The strings follow with a peaceful tune. A few minutes later the military instruments come into conflict with a gong—another stereotypical orientalist sound—which interrupts as if someone had raised an objection.

The middle of the piece evokes a sense of uncertainty: the vague trilling strings and wandering harmony sound like "waiting" music that lacks direction. Emerging from this uncertainty, we hear the wail of a *hichiriki* (hee-chee-ree-kee), a reed instrument from the Japanese classical tradition of *gagaku* that imitates the sound of a mournful human voice. The hichiriki is accompanied by plodding low strings and drums, creating an effect recalling funeral marches from the European orchestral tradition (example 5.3).

Example 5.3. Excerpt near the end of Kōsaku Yamada, "Inno Meiji" Symphony. Tokyo Metropolitan Symphony Orchestra, conducted by Takuo Yuasa (Naxos 8.557971, 2007). YouTube.
Link: https://doi.org/10.3998/mpub.9853855.cmp.68

Yet at the end of the piece the strings swell energetically and return to a light-hearted tone, mixing the pastoral and military elements we heard before and ending cheerfully.

The particular mix of celebratory and mournful elements in this music suggests a possible interpretation: leaving Japanese traditions behind was difficult, but the nation would overcome this difficulty. That Yamada told the story using a European orchestra, with a Japanese instrument prominent only in the funeral march portion of the piece, reinforces this perspective. Composed in 1921, this music looked back on the struggles of the 1880s from a time in which modernization had already been accomplished. Fittingly, the piece uses the tools its author defined as modern to convey its story about modernization.

Turkey underwent a similar process of modernization in the aftermath of World War I. The Republic of Turkey was established as a nation-state in 1923, following the breakup of the Ottoman Empire and a subsequent revolution against Western occupation. The new republic's first president, Mustafa Kemal, was called Atatürk—"father of the Turks." As Turkey had lost the portion of its territory that lay in Europe, Atatürk decided to assert Turkey's continuing European identity by remaking the nation-state on European principles.[15] Atatürk minimized the role of Islam in government, gave women significant legal rights, and ordered the nation-state's historians to emphasize the shared roots of Islam and Christianity. By Atatürk's command the Turkish language would now be spelled with Latin letters; time would be measured by the Gregorian calendar, dating from the birth of Jesus; and Turkish personal names would correspond to the European form (a given name and a family name). Turkish people would dress like Europeans, giving up the traditional fez. Countless new books urged Turkish people to be more like Europeans in their day-to-day lives. These efforts did not convince Europe to embrace Turkey, but they did alter Turkish intellectual life, convincing educated Turkish people of their joint heritage with the West.[16] For Atatürk, being modern was the same as being European, and he could force people to modernize.

With these reforms came dramatic alterations in music education. European concert music had already been available in Turkey for more than a hundred years, existing alongside Arabic-Persian **monophonic** music—that is, music consisting of a single melodic line.[17] Melodies in the Turkish art music tradition were complex and highly ornamented, built on musical scales (called *makam*) that were incompatible with European scales. Atatürk called Turkish monophonic music "primitive" compared to European harmony, and he named European music as the "universal" to which Turkey should aspire. Atatürk prohibited radio performances of Turkish art music and closed the schools that taught it, and he institutionalized European music across the Turkish educational system.[18] In contrast, peasant (folk) music became a populist symbol of the Turkish nation: the government encouraged its performance and sponsored folk-song collecting trips.[19]

Ahmed Adnan Saygun was one of the first generation of Turkish composers to receive this Westernized education. He also studied at the Paris Conservatory and spent parts of his career as a folk-song collector. Saygun's *Yunus Emre*, completed in 1943, is an example of **oratorio**—a European genre of music that blended religious content with the storytelling and singing style of opera.[20] (Handel's *Messiah* is a well-known example.) Yunus Emre was a Turkish Sufi mystic whose poems conveyed messages of divine love and the transitoriness of life. Emre's verses were well known in Turkey, acceptable to Islamic clerics and secularists alike. People sang them in Islamic religious practice as hymns (called *ilahi*) but also taught them to children as nursery rhymes.[21] Saygun ordered the chosen poems so that the trajectory of the whole oratorio moves from pessimism to optimism.

The Turkish government demanded that music should be both Turkish and European at the same time. Saygun walked this tightrope in a variety of ways. Sometimes he borrowed or modified recognizable Turkish melodies that other people had associated with Emre's verses, but he did so in an altered form. Sometimes he wrote new music that imitated the characteristics of Turkish folk songs. Sometimes he composed music with no relation to Turkish materials at all.[22]

As the musicologist Emre Aracı has pointed out, at the end of the first section of *Yunus Emre* we hear the words and melody of a well-known ilahi tune, which would have been recognizable to Turkish listeners. Example 5.4 is one version of this tune, called "I am the lamenting waterwheel."

Example 5.4. Excerpt from Burhan Çaçan, "Dertli Dolap—İlahi." *Ilahiler—Kasideler* (Bayar Müzik, 1998). YouTube.
Link: https://doi.org/10.3998/mpub.9853855.cmp.69

The basic melody is simple, moving by steps up and down a scale. It includes expressive turns that would fall "between the notes" of a European scale. All voices sing the melody in unison; a stringed instrument plays along with them, and a drummer keeps time.

Saygun's version (example 5.5) slows the ilahi tune down, keeping much of its basic contour but altering its tuning so that it fits into a European scale.

Example 5.5. Excerpt from Adnan Saygun, "Dertli Dolap," no. 5 chorale from *Yunus Emre*. Orchestra of the Ankara State Opera and Ballet and Ankara State Opera Chorus, conducted by Hikmet Şimşek (Ankara State Opera A-91.0001, 1991). Translation adapted from Abdur Rahman, https://thecorner.wordpress.com/2018/12/28/dertli-dolap-reflections-on-endless-trouble-is-my-name/, with help from Ali Sait Sadıkoğlu. YouTube.
Link: https://doi.org/10.3998/mpub.9853855.cmp.70

The tune is first presented by a chorus singing in two parts, in harmony, but the parts are so close together that they approximate the expressive turns of the ilahi version. In the second phrase the voices get further apart and more distinct. In subsequent phrases the harmony becomes richer, with more separate voice parts. The ilahi melody remains audible, but the harmony parts move more and more independently so that the different voice parts change notes at different times.

It is particularly noteworthy that Saygun chose a musical form (oratorio) associated with Christianity. Even more striking is that in several sections of *Yunus Emre* he imitated the style of the German composer Johann Sebastian Bach, who wrote music for Christian churches. Bach composed many **chorales**, pieces that took Christian hymn melodies and added harmony to them so they could be sung by a choir or congregation in church. Example 5.6 is a Bach chorale, "Who Has Struck You Thus?" In this example, and in chorales generally, the different voice parts sometimes move from syllable to syllable in sync but sometimes move independently of one another; they come together and pause at the end of each phrase. The tune moves mostly in steps up and down the scale: it is audible in the highest voice part. The voices in Saygun's chorale move in a similar way, evoking the music of Bach.

Example 5.6. Johann Sebastian Bach, chorale "Wer hat dich so geschlagen" ("Who has struck you thus") from the St. John Passion. WDR Radio Orchestra and Chorus (Westdeutsche Rundfunk, 2018). YouTube.
Link: https://doi.org/10.3998/mpub.9853855.cmp.71

Saygun's setting of the ilahi tune took advantage of the fact that a simple hymn melody could be harmonized regardless of its source: a skilled composer could as easily write harmony for an Islamic tune as a Christian one. The particular harmonies Saygun chose were not like Bach's; he tried to retain some of the sound of makam, not recreating the Turkish scale faithfully but rendering some of what he called its "color."[23] In blending Islamic and Christian religious elements, using European music that was acknowledged as "universal" along with known Turkish music, Saygun managed to create a work that met the government's criteria for Turkishness and Europeanness.

On the scale of geopolitics Japanese and Turkish efforts toward modernization are excellent examples of pulling music: these states chose to import music that fulfilled their purposes. In both cases European colonialism inspired the pulling. As rulers envisioned themselves making closer connections to the centers of power, they imagined that importing music could strengthen international relationships. Turkish leaders, for example, hoped that adopting European music would help Europeans see Turkey in a better light. The imported music could also change how states related to their own citizens, for Western music was part of a comprehensive propaganda effort to persuade citizens to make the effort of modernization. If citizens refused to conform, states compelled them to change by controlling the availability and content of their education. Certainly, not all citizens in Japan and Turkey embraced the sudden imposition of unfamiliar musics. In both states later generations would moderate their admiration for Europe and further develop their own criteria for what counted as "modern."

Music in the Cold War: Polarization and Integration

The movement of music through propaganda intensified during the Second World War and the Cold War. In the 1930s, concerned that German propaganda might win Latin Americans to the Nazi cause, the US government sent ballet companies and other artists on tour throughout the region.[24] In wartime, governments on all sides made radio broadcasts and short films, sending out information or misinformation that served their interests and adding music to make the broadcasts more attractive. The experience of worldwide warfare inspired individuals and governments to think about faraway people and imagine how order could be reestablished.[25]

With the founding of the United Nations (UN) in 1945, nation-states became increasingly important in people's thinking about both geopolitics and personal belonging. Under the nation-state model individuals and regional groups in many places saw themselves as citizens belonging to nation-states, and they empowered nation-states to act on their behalf to maintain order within their borders and defend their borders against outsiders. In turn they conceived "the new world order"—one order, not many—as a system of nation-states.[26]

Within this system conflicts between "superpower" states played an outsized role. After the end of the Second World War the formerly allied Soviet Union (Union of Soviet Socialist Republics, or USSR) and United States held irreconcilably conflicting goals. The USSR was an empire ruling over many nations across Eurasia. Its leaders believed they had a historic mission to establish communism as an economic and political system in as many world societies as possible. Seeking to modernize, in the 1920s and 1930s the USSR had built a state-controlled economy to transform an agrarian empire into an industrialized one. The Soviets proposed to export this vision of what it meant to be modern to developing and decolonizing nations.[27]

The United States was also an empire: at the end of the war it occupied

Japan, southern Korea, and part of Germany, as well as islands in the Caribbean and the Pacific. US leaders aimed to maintain and expand the large network of allies cultivated during the war, with the purpose of discouraging communism and encouraging economic development based on capitalism. The United States offered the rest of the world its own means of being modern: "democratic and equalitarian, scientific, economically advanced and sovereign," with a high standard of living and an emphasis on personal and corporate freedoms.[28] The conflict between the US and the Soviet Union was not only political and military but also **ideological**—based on systems of thought and values.

This conflict was called a "cold" war because the United States and the Soviet Union did not engage in direct military conflict, though they maintained hostility toward each other and built vast stores of armaments. The US-China relationship was similar. Yet the Cold War did include many armed conflicts, uprisings, and protests—most notably in Korea and Vietnam but also in Soviet-occupied Eastern Europe, Latin America, Africa, and the Middle East. Although these conflicts, shown in figure 5.1, appeared to be local matters, the opposing sides in each conflict were supported by the United States or its European allies on one side, the Soviet Union or China on the other. Through proxies the superpowers fought each other for dominance all over the world. If any one country tipped toward communism, the United States would fear it was losing its power, and if any one country tipped toward capitalism, the Soviet Union would feel threatened. Many states, including Yugoslavia, Indonesia, Egypt, and India, declared themselves "nonaligned": the superpowers were trying to win them over, but they had not chosen one side or the other.

During this era individuals began to imagine their nation-states differently: they started to see their own nations in relation to this global system of world alliances and conflicts. The desire to cultivate alliances meant communicating more, and rapid developments in technology supported this aim. The use of communications media did not replace travel; on the contrary, nation-states used all the means at their disposal to push their political and musical ideas into distant places or to pull in politically or musically desirable ideas from afar.

The technologies of recording and broadcasting contributed to this pushing and pulling of music. The German and US governments had refined audio recording using magnetic tape during World War II, and long-playing (LP) records were first introduced in 1948. These allowed more than three minutes

Fig. 5.1. *Music on the Move*: Superpower interventions during the Cold War. This map represents military interventions instigated or supported by superpowers during the Cold War. Map by Eric Fosler-Lussier after Mike Sewell, *The Cold War* (Cambridge: Cambridge University Press, 2002), 116–17. Further data from J. Patrice McSherry, "Tracking the Origins of a State Terror Network: Operation Condor," *Latin American Perspectives* 29, no. 1 (1 Jan. 2002): 38–60; and Gregg A. Brazinsky, *Winning the Third World: Sino-American Rivalry during the Cold War* (Chapel Hill: University of North Carolina Press, 2017), 231–69. See also Mary Dudziak, *War-Time: An Idea, Its History, Its Consequences* (New York: Oxford University Press, 2012), 137–56. (See https://doi.org/10.3998/mpub.9853855.cmp.73)

per side, so a much wider range of music could be recorded than ever before. The US government shipped LPs of American music (classical, jazz, folk, and popular) to US libraries in other countries for use in live public programs and radio shows. By 1968, consumers could buy magnetic cassette tapes and portable tape recorders: these tools allowed music to circulate unofficially in the Soviet Union and China, among other places. Some of the Cold War musical interactions discussed in this chapter would have happened without recording media, but some of them depended on the availability of those media.

Just as world politics became polarized during the early Cold War, so did the politics of musical style. In 1948 the Central Committee of the Soviet Communist Party sharply criticized several famous Soviet composers, saying that they had "lost contact with the people" and done "immeasurable harm to the development of Soviet music."[29] This was not the first Soviet censure of musicians, but its threatening tone drew international attention. In the party's view music should be understandable by everyone, praise the nation, support the Communist Party, and represent the aspirations and character of the working class.[30] Taken as a whole, these loose criteria were known as **socialist realism**. They applied to all the arts in the Soviet Union and in the Soviet-occupied states in Eastern Europe. Given that the Soviet state had exiled, imprisoned, or killed dissident writers in the 1930s, composers took these admonitions seriously.[31]

Shortly after this criticism, in 1949, the Soviet musician Dmitri Shostakovich (1906–75) composed a work for chorus and orchestra called "Song of the Forests." The words convey approval of the government's postwar reforestation program and optimism about the future of the Soviet Union. At the beginning of example 5.7, which comes from the fourth movement, we hear a children's chorus.

Example 5.7. Excerpt from Dmitri Shostakovich, "Song of the Forests," end of movement 4 and beginning of movement 5, performed by Yuri Temirkanov, the St. Petersburg Philharmonic Orchestra, the St. Petersburg Chorus, and the Boys' Choir of Glinka College. From *On Guard for Peace: Music of the Totalitarian Regime* (BMG, 1998). YouTube.
Link: https://doi.org/10.3998/mpub.9853855.cmp.74

The style of this music is sweet and cheerful, with an atmosphere of happy participation. A few minutes later, a full chorus of adult voices comes in, and the orchestra plays a buoyant march. The trumpets and drums add a militaristic sound, projecting the nation's strength. In every way this music overtly praised the state and its actions: it is propaganda aimed at Soviet citizens.

Shostakovich's colleague Galina Ustvolskaya (1919–2006) completed the first movement of her Piano Sonata no. 2 in 1949, after the Soviet censure of musicians, but this piece does not reflect the Soviet criteria for public music. Ustvolskaya knew when she composed this music that she could not publish it: it was composed "for the drawer"—that is, for her private purposes. The first movement of this two-movement piano work (example 5.8) is introspective and dissonant.

Example 5.8. Excerpt from Galina Ustvolskaya, Piano Sonata no. 2, first movement, performed by Marianne Schroeder (HAT HUT records, 2017 [2010]). YouTube. Link: https://doi.org/10.3998/mpub.9853855.cmp.75

At the start of the movement we hear a gentle, dissonant chiming. But soon this gentleness gives way to an intense, clangorous marking of time, like the tolling of a large bell. This music bears no resemblance to the optimistic political music demanded by the government. The Soviet government's restrictions did not stop the composition of the sonata, but they did keep it from being heard in public spaces until 1967. The sonata was first published in 1989.[32] Meanwhile, Ustvolskaya continued to teach at the Leningrad Conservatory and maintained a public persona that conformed to the state's wishes, writing film music and brief, cheerful pieces.

In the classical music world of postwar Western Europe, the Soviet censure of composers was greeted with alarm, partly because it diminished the expressive freedom of artists and partly because the overtly propagandistic musical style seemed repellent. In some regards the musical and the political judgments seemed to be two sides of the same coin. The National Socialist state had used music as propaganda to build pride in German heritage. Coming just after World War II, the Soviet regulation of artists' output seemed to resemble the Nazi use of art as propaganda.

Some Western thinkers and some composers of concert music responded by seeking to make music that could not be used as propaganda. Perhaps the most extreme example is *Structures Ia*, composed in 1952 by the French musician Pierre Boulez (boo-LEZ, 1925–2016). Boulez said he wanted to remove "absolutely every trace of heritage"—that is, any conventional elements that would convey meaning, ideas, or expression.[33] Using a process of composing called **serialism**, Boulez used preplanned sequences (series) of notes, durations, accents, and loudness to keep himself from creating music that relied on conventional techniques. Serialism had existed before the war, but the postwar revival of interest in this technique can be taken as a direct response to the Soviet insistence that music have political purpose.[34] This piece of music (example 5.9) deliberately does not convey any kind of political or social agenda.

Example 5.9. Excerpt from Pierre Boulez, *Structures Ia* (1952), third movement, performed by Alfons and Aloys Kontarsky (Wergo WER 6011-2, reissued 1992). YouTube. Link: https://doi.org/10.3998/mpub.9853855.cmp.76

If Soviet or Nazi propaganda promised listeners a sense of moral superiority or political engagement, *Structures Ia* resisted making such promises.

Certainly, music composed by serial methods was not the only kind of music being produced in Western Europe during this time. In fact, because of its elite nature, it had only a small following. Even among his peers, Boulez was in the minority: quite a few other European composers of his generation were attracted both to socialism and to socialist realist musical principles.[35] But for a while this music gained a disproportional amount of institutional power in Europe and the United States. University music departments hired composers who used serial methods; the composers won Pulitzer Prizes and Guggenheim Fellowships; and some critics and musicians claimed that this music demonstrated the superior technology and logic of "the West" (Western Europe and the United States).[36]

Thus, as the political division between the Soviet Union and the West intensified around 1950, some people on each side worked hard to define their side as the polar opposite of the other. The more the Soviet Union urged its composers to produce understandable, melodious music, the more some composers in the West produced difficult, unmelodious music. The more the Soviets required that composers produce music that served political purposes, the more composers in the West wanted to make nonpolitical music. In turn, the Soviets routinely denounced the "New Music" of Western Europe as inhuman, distorted, and unacceptable.

The divide between Eastern and Western Europe, and more broadly between the US-influenced and the Soviet-influenced world, was often called the Iron Curtain, implying that no connection or transit was possible between the two sides. Yet this mirror-image activity, doing the opposite of what the enemy does, built a kind of connection. Both parties looked closely at what the other was doing and responded directly to it by doing the opposite or by criticizing it in print and broadcast media. Musical or political dissenters on each side felt the attraction of the other side's music and used it as a model for their own music-making. Even though many people thought about the Cold War conflict as division, the constant critique of musical values created a kind of global integration: a sharing of musical ideas at a distance.[37]

"Pushing" Music to Represent the Nation-State

Another kind of global integration came from states' use of musical performance in propaganda. US officials noticed a sudden expansion of Soviet-sponsored music programs throughout Latin America, the Middle East, and East Asia in the early 1950s. Concerned that the Soviets had gained an advantage, the United States began sponsoring foreign tours, aiming to outshine Soviet and Chinese musicians. The US musicians were supposed to perform well, build warm personal connections with citizens of other lands, and create a positive impression of the United States. Thus, throughout the early Cold War years the superpowers and many other nation-states pursued their propaganda aims by sending musicians to perform all over the world—an action known as **musical diplomacy**.

Soviet musical exports focused on virtuoso concert soloists such as David Oistrakh and Sviatoslav Richter, the distinguished tradition of Russian ballet, and choral and dance performances with a folk flavor reflecting socialist realist values.[38] Each national group within the empire was supposed to contribute a distinctive and carefully curated artistic style, with the Soviet socialist realist style serving as an overarching concept for them all. Example 5.10 is an example of that folk-flavored style.

> Example 5.10. Excerpt from Igor Moiseyev State Academic Dance Ensemble, "Kalmyk Dance." YouTube.
> Link: https://doi.org/10.3998/mpub.9853855.cmp.77

It is a carefully choreographed professional performance that imitates some aspects of folk dance practiced by a tiny minority group in the Caucasus, the Kalmyk people. The state-sponsored group performing in this example, the Igor Moiseyev Ensemble, toured extensively abroad to represent the Soviet Union. They developed a generic socialist realist "folk ballet" style, to which they added some gestures characteristic of the different national groups they claimed to represent.[39]

Though the Moiseyev ensemble's performances were unfailingly upbeat, the performance concealed the tragic situation of the Kalmyk people. The Soviet government had deported this entire ethnic group to Siberia in 1943, where officials separated them and suppressed the use of the Kalmyk language. They were allowed to return in 1956, after which their dance could join the national repertoire—even as their language fell into disuse. Persuasive onstage, the Soviet portrayal of many nations within one peaceful empire rang hollow.

Recognizing musical diversity as its biggest asset, the United States sent many kinds of music abroad: symphony orchestras and soloists for concert music, jazz, folk music of Native American and Appalachian peoples, blues, religious choral music, gospel, and rock 'n' roll. Famous soloists and even large orchestras went on tour; these spectacular performances highlighted both the quality of music-making in the United States and the wealth of a country that could ship so many people and instruments. Professional and collegiate jazz bands demonstrated that the United States recognized the importance of African American music. US officials sent serial or avant-garde music to people who might be impressed by it; they also sent popular music where they thought it would make the best connection with the public.[40]

These musical presentations not only disseminated music to new places; they also created meaningful personal contacts across vast distances. People living far from urban centers were often surprised and grateful that the superpowers sent them musical performers. This flattery reinforced an emotional connection among citizens of different countries. In their ambassadorial role performers frequently met with other musicians in the countries they visited, sharing tips or equipment (such as new reeds for saxophones, a rare commodity in some parts of the world). American choirs sang in East Asian Protestant churches and met university students there. Sometimes US jazz musicians were greeted by expert fans who had already learned about their music from radio broadcasts or records: the musicians remembered these conversations warmly.

After the United States and the Soviet Union signed an exchange treaty in 1958, they also exchanged musicians with each other. These visits offered one of few ways in which US and Soviet citizens could talk to the "enemy."[41] The use of music in diplomacy encouraged both the musicians and their audiences to regard themselves as an active part of Cold War cultural competition and cooperation. Even citizens who watched the tours from home felt pride in their music's success abroad and enjoyed seeing themselves and their countries in a positive light.

Pushing and Pulling Culture: Paul Robeson

The life of Paul Robeson (1898–1976), an American singer and public intellectual, demonstrates the power of geopolitics in moving music through travel and media during the Cold War. A member of the Harlem Renaissance generation, Robeson began his career onstage and in film, with major roles in *Porgy and Bess*, *Show Boat*, and *Othello*. From 1922 on, he also performed concert spirituals with the pianist Lawrence Brown (example 3.9). His rich baritone voice won praise from the press and appealed to interracial audiences.

Like many Americans of his era, Robeson supported international socialism following the Soviet model. He believed that socialism was a way of allying the US struggle for African American civil rights with struggles against racism and colonialism all over the world (fig. 5.2). To express these sympathies, Robeson began to include in his concert programs labor songs—songs with working-class and socialist content. For example, Robeson's album *Songs of Free Men* (recorded 1940–44) includes a performance of "Joe Hill," a song about a Swedish American labor activist who was executed for a murder he likely did not commit. The song, a dreamed conversation with Hill, concludes that Hill's work to organize workers would live on in others' efforts to secure workers' rights.

Although Robeson's voice had a trained sound, he did not cultivate an operatic vocal style but often chose a simple, even folksy tone. In 1934 he traveled to the Soviet Union, where he observed "a complete absence of racial prejudice," and he sent his son to high school there.[42] In the 1940s he protested against anti-Semitism and racial segregation; he also kept Soviet songs on his programs.[43]

Once the Cold War started, though, the American public and the US government feared socialists. During the "Red Scare," support for free speech deteriorated, and people believed to be communists were watched closely by government agents or fired from their jobs. Despite these threats and several attempts on his life, Robeson would not be intimidated. After 1947 he made more political speeches, and police patrolled his concerts. In 1949 an Associated Press reporter misrepresented the text of one of Robeson's European speeches. In the ensuing media frenzy the US public turned against him, and the matter was taken up by the House Un-American Activities Committee (HUAC).[44] Veterans' groups and politically conservative organizations held protests against him, and music critics and audiences shunned his performances.

Fig. 5.2. Paul Robeson leads shipyard workers in singing "The Star-Spangled Banner." National Archives of the United States, via Wikimedia Commons.

Robeson's August 1949 concert in Peekskill, New York, drew thousands of protesters. White supremacists burned a cross and hanged an effigy of Robeson, threatening to murder him. The demonstrators blocked the road and instigated fistfights and beatings, but the police refused to respond to the violence. A week later, 25,000 listeners and some 3,500 protesters attended the rescheduled concert; after the performance the protesters injured concertgoers by throwing rocks at their cars.[45] The threat of violence only further discouraged audiences from attending Robeson's concerts. Yet Robeson remained openly critical of US policy, often using words that echoed Soviet policy statements. For example, he attacked American military interventions in Asia as a form of colonialism, saying that US troops should fight the Ku Klux Klan instead of North Koreans.

Throughout this period Robeson lived under constant FBI surveillance. Stores refused to sell his recordings. Concert promoters declined to book dates for him. His name was removed from *American Sports Annual*, where his status as an All-American football player was recorded.[46] Even African American leaders turned against Robeson because he was "adding the burden of being red to that of being black"; that is, his actions made black people seem like communists, further discrediting them in the eyes of whites and making it harder for them to advance the cause of civil rights.

In 1950, citing a "state of emergency" due to international tension with the Soviet Union, the US Department of State revoked Robeson's passport. The inability to perform abroad reduced Robeson to penury. In 1947 he was earning $100,000 a year, but by 1952 he was making only $6,000 a year. Yet the effort to contain Robeson backfired. He was already well known abroad, but his de facto imprisonment in the United States drew further publicity to his cause. One State Department official called Robeson "one of the most dangerous men in the world" in 1955. The state could not control Robeson's influence.[47]

The US government's attempt to control Robeson's movements was thwarted by mediation. Although he could not travel abroad, he spoke and gave concerts by telephone to large audiences in England, Germany, and Wales. A recording of Robeson's singing was played to symbolize his presence at a peace conference in Warsaw, Poland. Robeson sent recorded greetings to groups of people all over the world; one of them was for the Bandung Conference of nonaligned states, where Asian and African leaders convened to strategize against colonialism. He gave a symbolic concert at the border of Canada, his singing amplified through loudspeakers so that his voice could be heard by 40,000 people outside the United States.[48]

As one Soviet commentator explained, "you can arrest the singer but you cannot arrest his song."[49] Recorded media and technologies of transmitting sound bridged the gap between Robeson and the people he wanted to reach. During this period Robeson became one of the most famous individuals in the world. In particular, people who wanted to end the practice of colonialism in Africa and South Asia found his message attractive and continued to popularize his ideas in the press. They also advocated for the return of Robeson's passport.[50]

As part of its Cold War strategy, the Soviet government publicized Robeson's situation, using it to demonstrate the unfairness of the United States government and its oppression of both communists and African Americans. Soviet officials sought direct contact with Robeson and promoted his music through frequent radio broadcasts.[51] In 1952 they awarded him a state honor, the International Stalin Prize for Strengthening Peace Among Peoples. In January of 1957 the Soviet newspaper *Pravda* printed a message of greeting ostensibly from Robeson to Soviet citizens, which emphasized that he would like to visit them but couldn't because of the US government. Robeson was both "pushed" and "pulled." He initially sought out the connection with the Soviet

Union in the 1930s, but in the 1950s the Soviet Union also chose to import his music for political reasons.

In June of 1958 the US Supreme Court ruled that the State Department had no right to deny Robeson's passport because of his "beliefs and associations." Robeson was welcomed as a hero in the Soviet Union. When he arrived, the public already knew him as a friend. The documentary film *Speak of Me as I Am* offers evidence that the Soviet use of Robeson's music was highly effective. In the film a Russian interviewee reported, "At school we discussed his concerts. It was unusual—we'd never heard foreign singers on the radio before." A pair of Russian factory workers described Robeson warmly: "He was like us. He came from a working-class family. We understood each other. He stood for peace."[52] Thus, it seems likely that the Soviet media campaigns to promote Robeson within the USSR helped make him a star outside his home country. This warm relationship ended abruptly in 1961, however, when Robeson angered Soviet officials by challenging their prejudice against Jewish people.[53] He gave further performances internationally, but his health was declining, and he would never regain the public acclaim he had once enjoyed. He died a recluse in 1976.

Robeson's case illustrates an important aspect of Cold War psychology. The travel restrictions imposed by Iron Curtain countries, the United States, and others made people much more curious about what they were missing. This curiosity created markets for music from distant places and encouraged individuals and states to "pull" music into their own environments. The political criticism of musical performances only fueled the curiosity and thereby the movement of music.

Pulling Music: Rock in the Cold War

Politically cultivated curiosity had an important effect on the spread of other kinds of music from the West into the Soviet Union, Eastern Europe, and China. The extent of censorship waxed and waned over the years, but starting in the late 1940s, a good deal of American music became inaccessible in communist countries. Some citizens living under repressive governments imported rock and popular music from the United States because this music carried connotations of political freedom and personal liberation. (The US government had carefully nurtured these connotations through radio propaganda, and it also facilitated the transportation of musical recordings.)[54]

China offers a compelling case of "pulling" music across borders on political grounds. The People's Republic of China was established as a communist state in 1949 under Mao Zedong (Mao Tse-tung). After disastrous economic and social reforms, the Communist Party launched the Cultural Revolution. Ostensibly a campaign for "stamping out old ideas" to transform the arts and education, the Cultural Revolution became a reign of terror. The state and angry mobs executed hundreds of thousands of people and persecuted millions, seizing property, forcing people from their homes, and destroying libraries and religious sites.[55] Between 1966 and 1976 the government enforced artistic norms along the lines of Soviet socialist realism. As in the Soviet Union, officials promoted some kinds of music and forbade others, controlling public spaces, media, and imports of recorded music.[56]

The state's chosen music therefore dominated public life. During the Cultural Revolution the Chinese state encouraged the composition of popular songs and operas on communist themes and imported the ebullient choral music style of socialist realism from the Soviet Union. Example 5.11, "No Communist Party, No New China," is typical of this style of choral music. Large, well-disciplined choirs, all singing the state's message together, served as a metaphor for the united support of communism.

Example 5.11. Excerpt from "No Party, No New China." From "The Little Red Record," performed by the Chinese Red Army Choir (FGL Productions, 2002). YouTube. Link: https://doi.org/10.3998/mpub.9853855.cmp.79

The music is a march with triumphant trumpets and drums, suggesting military strength. The voices sing a tune based on a pentatonic (five-note) scale, signaling the particularly Chinese character of this strength. The words reinforce popular belief in the power of the state and the party.

The Cultural Revolution created massive social unrest. Members of the communist youth movement (the Red Guards) were rewarded for reporting disloyalty. These accusations tore apart communities and families. Schools and universities were closed, creating an ill-educated "lost generation" of people who were used to settling problems by violence or bribery.[57] After 1976, under Deng Xiaoping, the government still controlled public spaces and the media, but Chinese citizens had a little more exposure to Western popular music through the presence of foreign-exchange students, the illegal import and circulation of copied cassette tapes, and concerts in bars of foreign-owned hotels in major cities.[58]

In the early 1980s state officials continued to promote *tong-su* songs, gentle popular songs with words supporting the government.[59] The Chinese state had also begun to allow the import of Cantopop (short for Cantonese pop) love songs, most of which came from Hong Kong. Faye Wong's "Love without Regrets" (example 5.12, from 1993) is a good example of Cantopop. The lyrics contain no political content, seeming to comment only on an interpersonal relationship:

I'll face the future with my own blind obsession
Can't you feel that I have to respect myself?
How can people go on so long and still not understand?
Even if I must leave you, I refuse to regret.[60]

The music of "Love without Regrets" is equally inoffensive: Wong sings a predictable melody with a light, sweet vocal tone. Despite its geographical proximity to China, Hong Kong was at that time still a British colony, with separate political and economic systems. Many mainland Chinese regarded Hong Kong's Cantopop as modern, in part because of its association with Western pop music, and they found its nonpolitical qualities safe and appealing.[61]

Example 5.12. Excerpt from Yuan Wei-Ren and Faye Wong, "Love Without Regrets," from *Love Without Regrets* (Hong Kong: Cinepoly CP-5-0091, 1993). Translation from Cantonese by Dan Jurafsky. YouTube.
Link: https://doi.org/10.3998/mpub.9853855.cmp.80

At the same time, though, some Chinese musicians embraced rock music—not one of the state's chosen styles. The song "Nothing to My Name" (1985), written and performed by Cui Jian (tsway jon, 1961–) is a famous example. In live performance the song begins with a slow introduction, played on a Chinese bamboo flute (*dizi*) accompanied by chimes and cymbals. When the heavily amplified voice comes in, accompanied by electric guitar, the contrast is palpable (example 5.13).

Example 5.13. Excerpt from Cui Jian, "Nothing to my name," live performance at Stanford University, 2008. YouTube.
Link: https://doi.org/10.3998/mpub.9853855.cmp.81

In this music, as in Yamada's *Inno Meiji* Symphony decades before, particular sounds bring to mind their imagined places of origin. The audible contrast between the dizi flute and electric guitar establishes that the premise of the song involves a contrast or combination of Chinese and Western ways of thinking. Cui Jian purposefully uses a rough style of singing, which differs markedly from tong-su songs and Cantopop.

The words of "Nothing to My Name" do not make an explicit political point. Rather, they allude to escape and suggest a conversation with a reluctant partner ("When will you come with me?" and "I want to make you free"). These ambiguous words about longing and conflicting feelings could refer to a personal relationship or to a political circumstance:

How long have I been asking you,
When will you come with me?
But you always laugh at me,
For I have nothing to my name.
I want to give you my hope.
I want to help make you free.
But you always laugh at me,
For I have nothing to my name.
Oh, oh . . . when will you come with me?[62]

Despite the song's indirectness, listeners have most often interpreted it in political terms. The lyrics of this and other rock songs of the time point to disillusionment and a desire for better alternatives.

Until the 1980s most rock music in communist countries was either **underground** (played in private without the government's knowledge) or **unofficial** (the government knew but wouldn't or couldn't stop it). Not everyone who made unofficial music was a political dissenter: but it is difficult to completely separate the attractions of the music from its association with the West.[63] During the early 1980s rock music in China circulated on cassette tapes; it could also be played in small private clubs, supported by foreigners.[64] Police knew about these clubs and quietly monitored their activities; for this reason we might call Chinese rock an unofficial music during this period.

In 1989 activists—many of them students—occupied Beijing's Tiananmen Square for seven weeks, demonstrating against China's corruption and economic stagnation. During the students' protest in Beijing, they sang Cui Jian's "Nothing to My Name" as an anthem that reflected their desire for something new. The Chinese Army put down the rebellion in Beijing, forcing soldiers to kill several thousand of their fellow citizens. In another city, Chengdu, police beat hundreds of protesters to death. Some reports suggest that the state executed hundreds of dissenters and imprisoned tens of thousands. Even today, Chinese people cannot discuss the events of 1989 openly for fear of imprisonment. People who are too young to remember may not know of the uprising at all, as the state maintains tight control over education and public speech.[65]

Because of the brutal suppression of the students, after Tiananmen Square many Chinese stayed away from songs with implicit political messages. Even so, after 1989 rock music continued to appeal to some students. They connected it to nonconformist attitudes and behavior, including long hair for men, blue jeans, and critical opinions of the government. That the student protesters in Tiananmen Square had sung Cui Jian's music endowed rock with political meaning. As a result the Chinese government could no longer ignore rock music.

The government quickly neutralized the dissenting power of rock. The state started allowing rock music concerts—not all the time and not everywhere, but the standards were loosened. By permitting rock music, officials took away some of its power as an unofficial or countercultural phenomenon. The government blunted Cui Jian's revolutionary reputation by allowing him access to media and inviting him to official state events. In July of 2005 Cui Jian appeared at the "Great Concert on the 60th Anniversary of the Victory of World Anti-fascist War," a state-sponsored event, in Beijing. With the government's stamp of approval it was harder for Cui Jian to come across as rebellious. At the same time, government control of the media meant that censors could limit his airtime, making him seem less important to audiences. Because the state exerts so much control over citizen behavior, state policy directs what can and cannot be heard.

This strategy successfully limited the political effectiveness of rock as protest music. With the economic reforms of the 1990s and 2000s Chinese musicians have found economic opportunity, so they are less likely to rebel. The majority of Chinese popular musicians know it is in their financial interests to maintain cordial relations with government officials. In 2000, for instance, a band manager called Cui Jian "an irresponsible shouter," implying that musicians can get further by not engaging in protest.[66] Mainland Chinese broadcasters still avoid rock music, and it has only a small public presence, even though illegally imported compact discs continue to supply listeners with rock from abroad.[67]

The diasporic Chinese who watched the events of Tiananmen Square on television, and those who were exiled as a result of the protests, value the political symbolism of Chinese rock music. When Cui Jian performed on college campuses in California—a US state that includes a large population of Chinese and Chinese American people—"Nothing to My Name" evoked an overwhelming response. At Stanford University (example 5.13) audiences cheered when they recognized the flute introduction of "Nothing to My Name" and sang along with every word. Rock had been "pulled" into China to express rebellious feelings, but then diasporic Chinese people "pulled" Chinese rock music into their own environments as they participated from afar in China's evolving political situation.

A World Showcase

Since the founding of the United Nations in 1945, nation-states and individual citizens have pushed and pulled music across international borders—often for purposes of political expression. Soon after the United States and the Soviet Union began routinely sending their musicians abroad, other states began similar programs. Given that many kinds of music existed within the borders of any one country, representing one's nation to others meant making choices about what music was most "representative"—or simply "best." Government officials made these judgments, sometimes according to their own preferences and sometimes under pressure from a ruling majority who wished the nation-state to be perceived in a certain way.[68] Whether the performances were live or mediated, the presentation of music abroad was an opportunity for the nation to produce an image of itself as part of the world.

Thus, the formal act of representing one's country abroad through music served as a state propaganda strategy. But during the Cold War a wide variety of people, including musicians and publics all over the world, embraced the idea that music stands in for the nation-state.[69] These performances were not just representations of nationhood; they helped citizens and others imagine the nation as a real, coherent entity.[70] By defining what the state is, these performances also give that definition power in people's lives and open that definition up to arguments from those who do not think it fits.[71]

The idea that nations should contribute to a world showcase of "cultures" reflects the kind of thinking that led to the founding of the United Nations at the end of the Second World War. At that time not all peoples—not even the majority of peoples—lived in nation-states. Nonetheless, the UN model was based on the idea of a democratic community of states—"the world order"—and that idea became a norm for thinking about how countries could live together peaceably.[72] As decolonization accelerated in the 1950s and 1960s, each of the newly decolonized nations sought to define an identity for itself that could be understood by other people in the world. By having a defined "culture," each nation-state could support its claim that it was real, unique, and worthy of statehood.[73] The idea of a UN-style showcase of "cultures" presents an orderly picture of the world, in which each group of people is known and valued. As we saw in the case of the Kalmyk people, the showcase may also disguise the world's more complicated, heterogeneous, and conflicted realities.

By the 1960s, many nations had established state-sponsored music or dance ensembles along these lines. The Ballet Folklórico de México, a troupe developed by Amalia Hernández in 1952, became an official state dance company in 1959. (Since 1964 it has operated as a private nonprofit with extensive corporate support.) The dancers frequently convey widely recognizable stereotypes—mariachi music, swirling red skirts, and the "Mexican hat dance" with sombreros (example 5.14).

Example 5.14. Excerpt from Ballet Folklórico de México de Amalia Hernández, "Jalisco." YouTube.
Link: https://doi.org/10.3998/mpub.9853855.cmp.82

By placing the dancers into symmetrical geometric formations on the stage, the choreography borrows not only from regional dances of Mexico but also from European classical ballet.

In a nod to Mexico's populations who identify as indigenous or *mestizo* (mixed), the ensemble also makes a point of presenting dances that represent indigenous American life before contact with the Spanish. In the absence of reliable historical information, these dances draw musical and gestural inspiration from European portrayals of "primitive" peoples through modern dance, like Igor Stravinsky's *Rite of Spring*, which was first performed in France in 1913. To demonstrate the idea of "primitive" people, the choreography of *The Rite of Spring* was purposefully heavy, including stomping of feet and repetitive motion in lines or circles (example 5.15).

Example 5.15. Excerpt from Igor Stravinsky, *The Rite of Spring*, performed by the Joffrey Ballet, 1987. YouTube.
Link: https://doi.org/10.3998/mpub.9853855.cmp.83

The harshness of the music was supposed to seem modern, but the gestures evoked prehistoric times. The Ballet Folklórico de México's piece called *Azteca* (example 5.16) draws on similar ideas and gestures about ancient rituals. It, too, fuses ancient and modern ideas. *Azteca* calls on viewers to embrace indigenous heritage as part of Mexico's identity, while also framing Mexico as part of the international showcase of nations. Although Mexico's population includes people of African descent, they are not represented in the troupe's offerings.[74]

Example 5.16. Excerpt from Ballet Folklórico de México de Amalia Hernández, "Azteca." YouTube.
Link: https://doi.org/10.3998/mpub.9853855.cmp.84

These various representations of Mexican heritage mean different things to different people. The choreographer Anthony Shay has witnessed the patriotic and enthusiastic responses of Mexican audiences. For people of Mexican descent living outside Mexico, especially in the southwestern United States, Ballet Folklórico performances cultivated pride in Mexican heritage. In response, several University of California campuses and the Los Angeles County School District formed similar dance companies. Shay notes that these ensembles did not want to replicate folk dances exactly as they may have been performed in Mexican villages. Rather, participating in these dances created a mediated experience of heritage and ethnicity that they valued. People not of Mexican origin, in the United States and elsewhere, may experience Ballet Folklórico performances as imagined tourism: warm and festive, the dances present both novelties and ideas that are familiar from media portrayals of Mexico.

Strangely, the construction of a "United Nations" model of musical performance transformed each nation-state's chosen musical practices and made the differences among them less apparent. Many of these "national" touring ensembles performed in similar ways.[75] They typically emphasize folk cultures that seem old or indigenous but present them formally on a stage, as in a European concert hall. The dances are carefully choreographed by a professional in such a way that they can easily be televised. Vivid costumes and stereotyped gestures convey the distinctive national qualities of the performance— even if these differ markedly from how contemporary people in that nation might dress or dance. All of these traits work to establish a national "brand" that represents the nation-state to its own people and to the world—but in a form that seems familiar and comparable to other such performances. The philosopher Kwame Anthony Appiah has described this increasingly standardized system as "a collection of closed boxes."[76] Shows of this kind continue to the present day. Through them the nation-state can push particular ideas both to its own citizens and to faraway others.

Thus, pushing and pulling music helped nation-states establish themselves as "modern," define their values as distinct from the values of others, and project those values outward to the world. Performances of this sort embody a kind of connectedness: in deciding what musical offerings to present on the world stage, state officials took the opinions of other states and peoples into account. Likewise, individuals who participated in the pushing and pulling worked to build symbolic and practical connections that felt meaningful to them. Across the 1900s these self-conscious efforts created a world where choosing music might mean taking a political position, forging an alliance, or granting a sense of belonging. More and more, people were making these choices within a worldwide system of musical representation.

PART 3

Mashup

The third and final part of this book explores how migration and mediation have worked together to shape musical practices of the recent past. In chapter 6 we see that the ease of transmitting music through recording and travel has left a mark on individuals' thinking about their own music-making. The American composers Lou Harrison, Terry Riley, and Olly Wilson worked in the Euro-American concert tradition but also brought in music of other traditions. The American popular songwriter Paul Simon chose to draw on the music of the South African singing group Ladysmith Black Mambazo. The ability to join a tradition of one's choosing (rather than inheriting one from forebears) derives from the sense—new during this era—that all traditions are accessible through recorded media and are available for appropriation. Strategies for borrowing have changed over time. Though this first generation of composers highlighted their borrowings in conspicuous ways to demonstrate political and social affiliations, US composers of a later generation—Barbara Benary, Asha Srinivasan, and Courtney Bryan—take a subtler approach, melding their borrowed music into more seamless wholes. Nonetheless, their borrowings remain meaningful to them and to their audiences.

Chapter 7 focuses on the ways in which the recording industry has clashed with music-makers and listeners, both in the US and abroad, and on the ways in which conflicts about ownership and piracy shape the production and reception of music. Copyright is protected asymmetrically in ways that advantage Europe and the United States. Copyright enforcement efforts have led to violent interventions in the Global South, and music creators in Latin America, South Asia, and Africa have had difficulty using copyright to protect their work from being exploited internationally. Brazilian efforts of this kind, led by former minister of culture and singer/songwriter Gilberto Gil, offer an opportunity to think about alternative models of ownership.

Building on the insights from earlier chapters, chapter 8 uses the theory of Nestór García Canclini to discuss artists' strategic selection of musical styles in a globally networked world. The chapter begins with a consideration of the musical connections forged by the Korean diaspora in the United States. Korean American musicians are using old and new strategies of mediation to create and maintain personal and commercial links with Korea. We then turn to several examples of hip-hop made outside the United States. Musicians who appropriate rap may not all have the opportunity to travel widely, but they can access music from abroad via media. The artists discussed here—Yugen Blakrok, Soultana, and Mayam Mahmoud—draw on African American musical styles, blending that music with their own customs and beliefs to create music that reflects their own points of view.

My conclusion brings together Arjun Appadurai's and Nestór García Canclini's ideas about cultural violence with Philip Rieff's ideas about the role of value judgment in maintaining cultural order. Rieff highlighted what he saw as an ethical danger of postmodern diversity: how are we to make decisions if we lose the ability to judge certain texts or certain selves as "better" or "worse" than others? Canclini describes the ethical dangers of globalization in more practical terms: loss of local or regional identity, economic exploitation of the poor by the rich, and conflicts over what aspects of heritage should be preserved. Yet Appadurai argues that the genie cannot be put back into the bottle: despite these dangers, it may not be possible to go back to a world in which cultures seem distinct from one another and some superior to others. He suggests that the best solution may be to embrace the multiplicity of selves and values.

6 Composing the Mediated Self

The Canadian communications scholar Marshall McLuhan wrote in 1964 that because of media, "the globe is no more than a village." He believed that the media were creating a worldwide sense of involvement in others' lives, even over vast distances. Where people formerly might have associated only with people from their immediate communities, television brought into homes the images and voices of unfamiliar people, as well as their music and art. McLuhan called the media "extensions of man," as if they wired our nervous systems to a network, making our eyes and ears reach further than they ever could before. Having to pay attention to all that input could overwhelm people, but it could also make them feel a new "interdependence with the rest of human society." These extensions created an uncanny intimacy, even with faraway people: "Everybody in the world has to live in the utmost proximity created by our electric involvement in one another's lives." The "global village" is now a cliché, but McLuhan was one of the first to describe how communications media might be changing human social life.[1]

Would that process of becoming connected "make of the entire globe, and of the human family, a single consciousness?" McLuhan expected that peoples would become more similar as a result of this connectedness and especially that the less powerful would feel pressure to conform. Part of his concern was that the media was already an industry: having rented out our nerve endings to corporations, we are now subject to the input those corporations choose.[2] Even as McLuhan thought about profound changes in African and Asian lives, he also believed that global connectedness was "de-Westernizing" people in Europe and North America.

This intuition corresponds to some of what we already know about how music moves. As we saw in chapter 4, the nature of sound recording and the distribution of those recordings changed a great deal during the 20th century. The Cold War years saw the development of new kinds of media, and individuals and nation-states created new reasons to move music across borders, both personal and political. If we take McLuhan's ideas seriously, we must consider the possibility that this transformation also made a change in people themselves: in how they think and behave and in their preferences and opinions.

Writing in the 2000s, the anthropologist Thomas de Zengotita tested McLuhan's theories by observing present-day behavior. De Zengotita's theory of mediation suggests that people who live in a "mediated" way are indeed different from their "less mediated" forebears.[3] Of course, experiences have been mediated by newspapers and books since the invention of printing with movable type (in China around the year 1040; in Europe in the 1420s). The history of mediation goes back much further if we count the circulation of ideas in oral or handwritten forms. Still, de Zengotita and McLuhan argue that with television and other 20th- and 21st-century mass media, we encounter a more complete transformation of what it means to be a person. Here are some of de Zengotita's key ideas about how mediation affects our experiences.

Being the recipient of media changes people by sheer flattery. You are constantly addressed, your attention requested, your tastes complimented. Information you want is brought directly to you, hundreds or thousands of times a day, by advertising and other media. All this information seems to be addressed to you, personally. De Zengotita calls the result of this kind of mediation the **flattered self**. He claims that the flattered self has a kind of **god's-eye view**—everything that person might wish is all available, all the time.[4] When a person goes looking for some music (say, the examples of Chinese rock music discussed in this book) and for some reason cannot find that music quickly on the internet, it is easy to become annoyed and feel personally thwarted. We have developed expectations that we will be able to get whatever we're looking for, with only modest effort. That effect is the god's-eye view. Of course, not everything is equally accessible—it is the **appearance and expectation of total accessibility** that defines the worldview of the mediated person.

This appearance of accessibility is grounded in real experiences. We saw in chapter 4 that audio recordings helped make music more accessible: with the introduction of long-playing records in 1948 that trend continued to accelerate. Moreover, in the 1960s air travel became affordable for the first time. It became possible for ordinary people to go somewhere very far away just because it seemed interesting. This kind of travel differs radically from permanent, one-time migrations, in which people frequently have no choice about where to go or whom to interact with. Rather, with all this choice some individuals began to experience culture as a kind of buffet: a musician could sample the music of the world through recordings and travel, borrowing at will.

Another part of being a flattered self is **thinking that one's own opinion should be heard by the world**. This effect manifests itself in social media, where people broadcast their opinions and activities publicly, and on television shows in which many people, no matter how badly they sing, have a chance to be heard and judged by millions of listeners. The people who feel directly spoken to by media, and those who always feel free to offer their opinions or judgments in return, are flattered selves. As we will see, many musicians of the generation that came of age between the 1940s and the 1960s believed they had something urgent to communicate through their music: they aimed not merely to entertain or engage their listeners but also to use music as a particular kind of expression that was both personal and political.[5]

According to de Zengotita, the fact that music or food can represent social class or ethnic origin is not unusual. The era of mediation brought a heightened awareness of that representation and frequent opportunities to represent themselves to the world in self-conscious and carefully chosen ways. **Heritage**, all that is passed down within a family or ethnic group through the generations, still plays a significant role for most people. But the mediated person need not continue in the musical tradition she has inherited. With the increased accessibility of music through a variety of media, and the dazzling array of options for representing oneself, the flattered self makes choices about how she wishes to make music and how she wants to be perceived.

In the discussion of African American traditions (chapter 3) we saw that some thinkers used the idea of **authenticity** to emphasize and reify heritage, drawing distinctions between groups of people. This concept of authenticity derived from the purposeful social distinction that separated "folk" from "modern" peoples and presumed a stable connection among people, their habits, and a particular place ("These are real Swedish meatballs"; "This is a genuine Appalachian folk song"). In the case of the African American concert spirituals in the Harlem Renaissance, intellectuals argued about whether concert spirituals were "authentic"—that is, whether a musical practice that showed signs of assimilation truly represented African American heritage or a watered-down, false version of that heritage. Once we are aware of choices and of mediation, the idea of authenticity may lose some of its force. Today, some people would take the perspective that both kinds of performance are valid options—that individuals may choose how to represent themselves through music. This is a highly mediated way of looking at the world. Others might defend the "realness" of boundaries and insist that we can tell true from false, authentic from inauthentic. I will return to these perspectives in my conclusion.[6]

The identification of styles, habits, or artifacts with a particular ethnic origin, social class, or political issue continues to operate very strongly for mediated people, in that people who feel invested in a certain ethnic group or political issue choose certain styles of music that they think represent them and their cause. But again, this is a *choice* of representation. The link between the music and other aspects of social identity is not automatic or given at birth, nor does it appear to be limited by geography, nationality, or similar factors. Each mediated individual gets to choose for themselves out of a whole world of available possibilities. Choices about how to present oneself have existed for a very long time, but the vast array of choices and the sense that one is continuously broadcasting those choices seem characteristic of our historical moment.

De Zengotita points out that deciding whether mediation is good or bad is extremely difficult, because the exact same forces contribute to both the good and the bad aspects. The same global, multinational record companies that enable greater access to diverse cultures may also be accused of causing market pressures that crush the initiatives of small record labels in low-income countries. The borrowing of music may create a meaningful positive relationship, or feel like theft, or both at the same time.[7]

De Zengotita is well aware of the fundamental inequity in the world situation that allows some of us to be flattered, mediated selves, while some of us have little or no access to such options and choices. In his terms you have to live in the "real" world all the time if you have no access to the options and choices presented by the "mediated" world. Some people do not have financial resources that enable choice. Some people live under political or military duress and are forced to do things a certain way. Some people are just not tied into the global economy through media, and they might not have access to options. Because the rest of the situation of mediation is ethically murky—it is often hard to decide what is better or worse—the inequity of access seems to be the main aspect of mediation that can be criticized in ethical terms.[8]

The examples considered in this chapter connect de Zengotita's and McLuhan's theories of mediation with the politics of musical style established during the Cold War. The political pressures that people experienced during that period and the new availability of music through various media combined to shape musicians' choices. Through recordings and travel US musicians working in the 1960s and thereafter had access to a wide variety of music (providing them with a god's-eye view of world music). They could choose among a vast array of musical styles, and appropriate one or several of those styles. Crucially, they based their choices on social, political, and ethical considerations—some to assert a sense of connection, some to highlight their personal criticism of the world around them. In all these ways these musicians seem to be the first generation of music-makers to carry the new "mediated" attitude that de Zengotita describes. We will also encounter some US musicians—most of them younger—who, in their own ways, absorbed and extended the lessons of the "mediated generation."[9]

Paul Simon: Musical Appropriation and the Mediated Self

First, we should establish how the mediated self thinks about and appropriates music. The making of Paul Simon's album *Graceland* offers useful insight. Simon (1941–) made the album with extensive cooperation from the South African musical group Ladysmith Black Mambazo, whom he first heard on a cassette tape around 1984. It was inconvenient that the musicians were South African: the United Nations (UN) had placed that country under international sanctions because of the South African government's segregation of people by racial categories (apartheid), its massacres of black Africans and other people of color, and its arbitrary detentions of protesters.[10]

The United States abstained from the UN's resolution until 1986, so, as a US citizen, Simon could legally travel to South Africa.[11] At the same time, many other countries had suspended musicians' travel to South Africa. Simon went, but his breaking of the UN boycott drew heated criticism. In response to these accusations Simon said that he was supporting black South Africans, paying them triple what they would receive in the United States, and giving them an international outlet and visibility. The UN Anti-Apartheid Committee looked into the case and decided that Simon did not violate the spirit of the boycott since he had not supported the South African government in any direct way.

Simon had a point. Because *Graceland* was such a huge hit, it transformed the careers of the African musicians involved. The South African group Ladysmith Black Mambazo had been recording since the 1960s and had been on the radio in Africa. After they recorded with Simon, they became international celebrities. The group's bass player, Bakithi Kumalo (1956–), defended Simon's relationship with the African musicians:

Bakithi has little patience with critics who brand Simon a cultural plunderer or musical imperialist. "Well, I've been asked this question many times, even by my own people. To be honest, I don't see anything wrong." He says thoughtfully, "I tell people, 'Listen, this is my life. I'm a musician. Whoever calls me and says, hey, let's play South African music'—why not? Because that pays my bills, you know, that takes care of me! . . . I don't see any problem with Paul learning and getting involved with South African music. If he didn't do it, I don't think anybody else would!"[12]

Even many years later, everyone involved with the recording remains sensitive about the ethical issues that the project raised.

Simon was also an attentive listener. The ethnomusicologist Louise Meintjes has pointed out that *Graceland* skillfully includes characteristic elements of South African music. The distinctive sound of **mbube**, choral singing that juxtaposes a chorus of low voices against a high lead singer, is evident throughout much of the album. Example 6.1, "Wimoweh," sung by Solomon Linda's Original Evening Birds in 1939, exemplifies the characteristic texture of mbube.

Example 6.1. Excerpt from Solomon Linda and the Original Evening Birds, "Mbube," (Singer Bantu Records, G.E. 829, 1939). YouTube.
Link: https://doi.org/10.3998/mpub.9853855.cmp.85

Simon's song "Homeless," in example 6.2, offers a similar sound: low voices singing in harmony and a high voice soaring above.

Example 6.2. Excerpt from Paul Simon with Joseph Shabalala and Ladysmith Black Mambazo, "Homeless." *Graceland* (Warner Brothers 9 25447-2, 1986).
Link: https://doi.org/10.3998/mpub.9853855.cmp.86

Simon's album also draws on the South African genre of **mbaqanga**, or township jive. (The *q* in *mbaqanga* is pronounced as a tongue-click.) According to Meintjes this music recalls mbaqanga both in the choice of instruments—especially the electric bass—and the way the instruments engage in interplay with the voices.[13] The song "Akabongi" (example 6.3), sung by the Soul Brothers in 1983, illustrates some key features of mbaqanga.

Example 6.3. Excerpt from Soul Brothers (David Masondo, Moses Ngwenya, and Zenzele "Zakes" Mchunu) performing the song "Akabongi." *Isicelo* (originally Munjale Records MUNG 4000, 1983; re-release on Soul Brothers Records CDSBL 1001, 2005). YouTube.
https://doi.org/10.3998/mpub.9853855.cmp.87

The solo guitar is prominent at the beginning of the song, with a playful little "warming up" tune. Once the drums come in and the groove starts, we hear the bass guitar as a driving force. Voices singing in harmony alternate with a small group of backup instruments. Simon's song "Diamonds on the Soles of Her Shoes" features similar strategies. Although the song begins with a slow introduction in the style of mbube, about a minute into the song (at the start of example 6.4) we hear a brief guitar solo, much like the one that started the Soul Brothers' song.

Example 6.4. Excerpt from Paul Simon with Joseph Shabalala and Ladysmith Black Mambazo, "Diamonds on the Soles of her Shoes," *Graceland* (Warner Brothers 9 25447-2, 1986).
Link: https://doi.org/10.3998/mpub.9853855.cmp.88

Almost immediately the groove starts, with a prominent part for the bass guitar. Unlike the Soul Brothers, Simon sings the verses alone, but like them, he includes interludes by a small group of backup instruments (example 6.5). Later in the song, we hear a chorus, singing in harmony on the syllables "ta na na na" in a way that recalls mbaqanga.

Example 6.5. Second excerpt from Paul Simon with Joseph Shabalala and Ladysmith Black Mambazo, "Diamonds on the Soles of her Shoes," *Graceland* (Warner Brothers 9 25447-2, 1986).
Link: https://doi.org/10.3998/mpub.9853855.cmp.89

Simon has emphasized in liner notes and interviews that the musicians worked collaboratively to create *Graceland*. Still, a video about the making of the album includes a revealing moment. Seated at the mixing board, Simon shows how he created a demo recording of the song "Homeless," overdubbing his own voice several times to create the harmony he had in mind for the chorus of the song. "It's all me," he says (fig. 6.1).[14] The video goes on to describe how Simon and Ladysmith Black Mambazo changed the harmony together, but the concept of the song was evidently Simon's.

At another moment in the video Simon demonstrates how the characteristic sound of the album was created through mixing, blending his own ideas with the sounds composed by the South African musicians. Discussing the song "Boy in the Bubble," Simon explains that, to his ears, the drum at the start of the song sounds "so African." But he then demonstrates at the mixing board how he altered the soundscape to conform to his own idea of what "Africa" sounds like. He recorded the characteristic sounds of the accordion

Fig. 6.1. Paul Simon at
the mixing board. Still
from *Classic Albums:
Paul Simon Graceland*
(DVD, Eagle Rock Enter-
tainment/Isis Produc-
tions, 1997).

and the prominent bass guitar line but added synthesizer, bells, more drums, and multiple tracks of his own voice in the background. Again, it's "all him."[15]

At the mixing board we could say that Simon is a flattered self with a god's-eye view of all the available sounds. He can make each one louder or softer; he gets to choose the final mix. He occupies a highly empowered position. That power comes both from the technology—he is the one who has access to the mixing board—and from his position in the web of social relationships. He pays the other musicians, so he gains the right to manipulate their sounds as "raw material" and make choices about the final product.

Does this borrowing differ from Liszt's adoption of the Romungro style (chapter 2)? In that case Liszt tried to adopt or imitate the essential features of Romani music in order to make his own music seem livelier and full of passion. He found their lifestyle and their music exotic (charming because unfamiliar). So far, the cases seem similar: Simon, too, was charmed by the sound of South African music, which was novel to him, and he wanted to incorporate that sound into his own music. Yet Simon's technology of imitation is quite different. He has a mixing board: he can take ownership of other peoples' sounds and blend them with his own. In some ways the resulting imitation is seamless: it is difficult to tell whose ideas are whose.

The ethnomusicologist Veit Erlmann has complained about this aspect of Simon's music. He called the "seamless" quality an offensive form of **cultural appropriation**. In Erlmann's view Simon created an inauthentic facsimile of African music, as if Simon had a hand puppet of Ladysmith Black Mambazo and was telling it what to say and how to be "African." Erlmann saw this project as selfish: Simon was the center of his own universe, and he took for his own purposes everything that could be foreign, absorbing it all into his own music. In other words Erlmann saw Simon's flattered self as a serious problem: Simon was so invested in his god's-eye view that he failed to understand the other musicians' perspectives.[16]

But the musicians involved in making *Graceland* have stated in no uncertain terms that they were delighted to work with Simon, that they found the process worthwhile, and that they appreciated the musical and economic opportunities the collaboration brought them. Though Louise Meintjes rightly pointed out that the songwriting contributions of South African musicians are credited inconsistently and sometimes downplayed on the album, guitarist Ray Phiri insisted that "there was no abuse."[17] The positive and negative elements of this collaboration are difficult to untangle.

The question of borrowing between the United States and other countries calls to mind all the questions of inequality raised in studies of colonialism and globalization. Economic barriers make it difficult for even well-intentioned individuals to meet on equal terms. McLuhan wrote that the existence of any kind of frontier between unequal societies stimulates frantic activity on the part of the "less developed" side, creating in them the desire to catch up or modernize.[18] Yet as we saw in chapter 5, during the Cold War the need for alliances also prompted frantic activity on the part of superpower nation-states as they attempted to win over nonaligned peoples throughout the world. Simon's interest in traveling to collaborate with South African musicians echoes this push to make connections; it also reflects the interest of Ladysmith Black Mambazo in "catching up" by gaining access to international audiences. Economic and political boundaries generate excitement in part because the stimulus for connection creates multifaceted meanings on all sides.

The Paul Simon case shows that mediation not only connects people but also reinforces the noticeable inequality between those who can mediate their experiences at the mixing board and those whose music is appropriated as raw material. We might recall here the discussion of cultural appropriation in chapter 3, which highlighted unequal credit and earnings. Simon's music and the concerns that come with it are characteristic of the 1980s, when **world beat** (sometimes called **world music**) became a category for record sales. The *Graceland* album's great success was not an isolated incident: the phenomenon of Western musicians promoting or appropriating music from elsewhere was common (as we saw in chapter 4).[19]

This question of creative control shapes how we interpret what is going on.

McLuhan saw the mediated self from the receiving end: the mediated person is part of the "masses" who effectively rent out their nerves and senses to the media industry but may not make their own art. For people who have access to and control over the distribution technology, though, the mediation process looks vastly different. Think again about Paul Simon at the mixing board: recording technology makes us aware of other people's music (in his case South African music) in a way that may encompass ownership (of a recording), desire to participate (through travel), collaborative interaction (making a recording together), and creative control (at the mixing board). All these activities offer plenty of space for musical inventiveness. That empowered sense of creativity is characteristic of the mediated self.

A Mediated Generation: Representing Oneself through Chosen Styles

Many members of the generation that came of age in the 1950s and 1960s believed that the Euro-American (or "Western") tradition of **concert music**— often called "classical" music—was too rigid: they chose to blend a variety of ideas and sounds from outside that tradition into their music. The music of Terry Riley (1935–) offers another case of purposeful borrowing; unlike Simon's, Riley's borrowing involves an imitation of style rather than a direct incorporation of sounds. Riley is from California, a virtuoso pianist and composer. In his youth he was influenced by serial music (like Pierre Boulez's *Structures Ia*, discussed in chapter 5), but he then turned away from that technique. Far from wanting to separate his music from the conventional meanings of daily life, Riley wanted to transform life through music. He has referred to his own music as "psychedelic cosmic opera," an "expansive experience."[20]

From 1970 on, Riley immersed himself in the study of North Indian (Hindustani) classical music.[21] Music from this tradition typically unfolds as a long, gradual process, starting at a low pitch and moving slowly, then increasing in intensity and speed and encompassing higher pitches in the musical scale. This process may last several hours: the listener's satisfaction comes from paying attention to the music's revelations over time.

North Indian music typically includes a drone: a note that is held steady over a relatively long time. In example 6.6 we hear a drone starting at the very beginning of the track.

Example 6.6. Shahnai ensemble of Hira Lal, "Raga Mishra Kafi." *North India: rudra veena, vichitra veena, sarod, shahnai.* Anthology of Traditional Music, UNESCO collection (Auvidis, 1989 [1974]). Used by permission of Smithsonian Folkways Recordings.
Link: https://doi.org/10.3998/mpub.9853855.cmp.91

Playing above that drone, we hear instruments called *shahnai* (a double-reed instrument, like an oboe). These instruments are frequently played in pairs: the melodies of the two intertwine with or echo each other more and more as the piece goes on. Soon a pair of drums, called *tabla,* joins in, increasing the energy and giving the music a more steady rhythmic pulse. If you listen for a while, you will notice the melody getting more expansive and the energy and complexity of the music increasing over time.

In 1976 Riley composed a piece that imitates this kind of music, entitled "Across the Lake of the Ancient World." A drone is present in some parts of this piece (we hear the opening in example 6.7) but not as consistently as it would be in North Indian music; sometimes it goes away for a while, then returns.

Example 6.7. Excerpt from Terry Riley, "Across the Lake of the Ancient World." *Shri Camel* (CBS Records, 1988 [1980]). YouTube.
Link: https://doi.org/10.3998/mpub.9853855.cmp.92

Instead of using reed instruments (the shahnai), Riley chose a Yamaha electric organ, which has a similar reedy tone. But Riley's most essential borrowing for this piece is the Hindustani practice of increasing complexity and rhythmic interest as the music goes on through time. Riley crafted a gradual introduction of material that offers a satisfying sense of expansion. As "Across the Lake of the Ancient World" goes along, the music becomes more rhythmically active, and the melodic lines become more intertwined with one another, much like the trajectory of Riley's Hindustani models. Example 6.8 includes a short selection from the middle of the piece, a pause, and then a selection closer to the end.

Example 6.8. Second excerpt from Terry Riley, "Across the Lake of the Ancient World," *Shri Camel* (CBS Records, 1988 [1980]). YouTube.
Link: https://doi.org/10.3998/mpub.9853855.cmp.93

As would be true in the Indian tradition, this music has improvisatory elements: the listener has a sense that every performance is unique, not repeatable.[22]

Riley, who was not born into the North Indian musical tradition, chose this musical practice specifically as an alternative to the Euro-American classical tradition. His attraction to Hindustani music was founded in part on ideas about how society should be different: when he rejected the serialism of the 1950s, Riley sought an alternative to Western music that would provide a sense of countercultural mysticism. The musical process that gradually unfolds engages the listener in a process of transformation—even an expansion of consciousness—that seemed utterly different from what Western concert music could offer. Riley's choice represented a commitment to transformative listening of this kind. To Riley, and to his listeners, this choice also made a statement: non-Western ways of being might affect us in ways that our own Western practices and values cannot. Riley did not assimilate into Hindustani ways of life; rather, his musical borrowing exemplifies admiration for Hindustani music, as well as a desire to replicate its effects, both musically and spiritually.

Like Riley, Lou Harrison (1917–2003) sought alternatives to his Western training. Harrison studied composition with Henry Cowell, who was important both for his radical socialist politics and his interest in all kinds of music. Harrison lived in San Francisco, California, for much of his life. There, on the Pacific Rim, Asian influences were much more prevalent than elsewhere in the United States. San Francisco has a large Chinese community, and Harrison encouraged his students to hear Chinese opera there. Along with Cowell, Harrison was a very early advocate of pacifism and multiculturalism (even in the 1930s, before multiculturalism had been named). Harrison spent time in Japan, Korea, and Taiwan in the early 1960s; he also studied with Indonesian musicians in the 1970s and visited Indonesia in the 1980s.[23] These were not fleeting interests but long-standing and serious ones. With his partner, William Colvig, Harrison constructed two sets of gamelan instruments, now located at San José State University and Mills College.

Harrison idealized what he called "Pacifica" (Asian/Californian culture) as opposed to "Atlantica" (East Coast/European culture). He persistently referred to Europe as "Northwest Asia," trying to marginalize Europe's importance in favor of other places. Harrison consciously intended to disrupt or overturn the established hierarchy that gave special status to European music: he wanted to create a level playing field where all music could be equally valued and used by whoever wanted to use it.[24] Harrison presented a musical model of Pacifica by adopting many features of Asian music in his own compositions. Even before his first trip to Asia, he began borrowing ideas from Asian music, adding the pentatonic (five-note) musical scale and bell-like sounds to his compositions.

Spending several months in Korea and 20 days in Taiwan, he learned to play several instruments: the Korean *p'iri* and the Chinese *guan* (both wind instruments with a reedy sound) and the Chinese *sheng* (mouth organ), *zheng* (a stringed instrument, like a lute), and *dizi* (flute).[25]

Among his many musical influences Harrison deliberately included Chinese traditional music. In the Cold War United States this was a pointed political gesture. With communist China considered a major threat to American security and proxy wars with the Chinese taking place in Korea and Vietnam, to claim Chinese culture as a peaceful alternative to US-style politics was profoundly countercultural. Harrison's composition *Pacifika Rondo* (1963) made such a claim: this multimovement piece protested against American military action and the atom bomb, imitating musical styles from all around the Pacific basin as a sign of solidarity with Asian peoples. Harrison used the serial technique and an imitation of a military band to represent the harshness of the US nuclear attack on Hiroshima, Japan. With musical styles standing in for peoples and their actions, this choice seemed like a claim of allegiance to Asian values and a condemnation of Western values.[26]

In Harrison's "Music for Violin and Various Instruments" (composed in 1967, revised in 1969) he combined the Western violin with an ensemble of instruments from other parts of the world: a reed organ (based on the Chinese sheng), percussion, psaltery (a harp-like instrument based on the Chinese zheng), and four *mbiras* (thumb pianos), an instrument developed by the Shona people of Zimbabwe. Rather than just borrowing the instruments, Harrison often built his own copies of them. Remaking the instruments allowed Harrison to tune them according to his personal musical preferences; the retuning also allowed instruments from a variety of origins to sound good together.

In the third movement of "Music for Violin and Various Instruments" (example 6.9) we hear the mbiras (thumb pianos) prominently. The first mbira player plays many of the same notes as the violin, while also tapping on the instrument with his fingers and stomping on the floor: these techniques make the piece sound a little less like concert music and more like folk music. The tune is vaguely Asian in style; it uses a pentatonic scale, which has often been used in Western music to mark "Asian-ness."[27] The entire movement consists of variations on a short phrase. In some variations arching extensions of the phrase grow more intricate and ornamental; in others lively syncopation is added, making the music more dance-like. The movement has a clear overall structure that includes repeated sections; this is a feature retained from Western classical music.

Example 6.9. Lou Harrison, "Music for Violin and Various Instruments," movement 3. Performed by Lou Harrison, Richard Dee, William Bouton, and William Colvig. Reissued on *The Music of Lou Harrison* (CRI American Masters CD 613, 1991). Link: https://doi.org/10.3998/mpub.9853855.cmp.94

Harrison's blending of elements makes this music a representative of no one tradition: it is an effort to combine beautiful sounds from different traditions, making what Harrison called "planetary music."[28]

Harrison has been criticized for borrowing only the distinctive sounds from non-Western musics: he typically did not borrow overall organizational plans. Even the sounds were altered in the process of borrowing, as Harrison rebuilt the instruments. Harrison did not seek to transform his listeners' consciousness by asking them to hear music in unaccustomed ways, as Riley did. Rather, Harrison organized sounds within the musical structures typical of Western art music and within the social structure of the Western concert setting.[29] Much like Claude Debussy, Harrison expected his listeners to rejoice in the new sounds and in the sense of affiliation with foreign peoples those sounds brought with them. By borrowing sounds, Harrison was not trying to recreate other kinds of music faithfully; indeed, his music includes elements that would not otherwise have been heard side by side. Yet the way he used these sounds from afar purposefully evokes a sense of "foreignness," reminding the listener that other worlds and ways of being are possible.

We might think of Harrison's strategy as trying to use positive elements of exoticism without the negative ones. The historian Christina Klein has described Americans' fascination with Asia in the 1950s and 1960s. US involvement in Asia during World War II, the Korean War, and the Vietnam War ensured that the idea of Asia was ever-present for Americans, not only in the news but also in popular culture. Musicals such as *The King and I* and *South Pacific* presented stereotypical clashes of Asian and Western characters who seemed irredeemably different from one another.[30] But Americans who wanted to criticize US military actions in Asia found in Asian music an appealing resource for expressing solidarity with Asian people. By adopting elements of Asian musics as their own, Riley and Harrison made personal statements reflecting this political commitment.

In the music of Olly Wilson (1937–2018) we can hear a complex working-out of self-definition with respect to multiple musical traditions. Wilson, a scholar and a composer, held a PhD in music composition. He spent a year in West Africa in the early 1970s, and he wrote articles analyzing similarities between the music of West Africa and that of African Americans. As an African American who belonged to the generation after the Harlem Renaissance, Wilson chose to connect to the African American tradition and to consider what about his American life has any connection with Africa. Like many members of his generation Wilson was particularly inspired by **pan-Africanism**—the idea that Africans and members of the African diaspora share a common heritage.

In 1976 Wilson composed a piece called *Sometimes* for a singer and tape: the tape contains electronic noises and voices. This piece is based on the **concert spiritual** "Sometimes I Feel like a Motherless Child," which we heard in example 3.9. In *Sometimes* Wilson manipulates the spiritual in various ways. Sometimes we hear fragments of its tune, sometimes entire recognizable phrases; these phrases are sung by the vocalist or appear on the tape as echoes. Meanwhile, the inclusion of noises and distorted sounds on the tape creates a neutral, severe landscape, much like the strange sounds heard in old science fiction movies (example 6.10, timepoint 1:40–3:24).

Example 6.10. Olly Wilson, "Sometimes," performed by William Brown. *Other Voices* (CRI SD 370, 1977), re-released on *Videmus* (New World Records 80423-2, 1992). Link: https://doi.org/10.3998/mpub.9853855.cmp.95

In some parts of *Sometimes* (like example 6.10 at timepoint 5:10–6:55) the music sounds like multiple voices speaking or singing at once, which is analogous to the traditional congregational singing of spirituals. The voices on the tape, however, also sound ghostly, distant and disembodied, and the singer's part disintegrates into howls and other nonverbal sounds. The words "I feel like a motherless child" are reflected in the anguished distortions of the singing voice and the sense that the voice is alone in a hostile environment. By referring to the spiritual and being performed in this particular way, *Sometimes* calls forth the traumatic history of African Americans in the United States.

In another passage (example 6.10, timepoint 11:20–12:58) the word *mother* is broken up into syllables and played with, more for the sound and rhythm of the syllables than for their meaning. This musical strategy resembles the jazz tradition of "scat," where the singer plays with sound and meaning. But, again, it is also a way to make the spiritual a less coherent song, for at this point the spiritual has been torn to shreds.

Wilson was educated in the serial tradition and in what is broadly called **New Music**—the extension of the Euro-American "classical" tradition into experimental or tradition-breaking practices. (Boulez's music, discussed in chapter 5, belongs to this genre.) While some practitioners of New Music attempted to deny "meaning" in music, preferring to think of music as abstract sound, Wilson deliberately used the academic language of electronic music to create meaning: "I attempted to recreate within my own musical language not only the profound expression of human hopelessness and desolation that characterizes the traditional spiritual, but also simultaneously on another level, a reaction to that desolation that transcends hopelessness."[31]

There is an interesting irony about Wilson's choice of musical styles. Wilson was trained in the modern postwar musical style represented by tape manipulation—it was *his tradition* by virtue of his education—yet he also recognized that style as potentially alienating to listeners. So he juxtaposed that style against the voice that sings the spiritual—which was *also his tradition*, by heritage and by choice—and makes the spiritual sound like the only human voice within an alien landscape. In thinking about his place between the two traditions, Wilson often quoted the African American sociologist W. E. B. DuBois: "One ever feels his two-ness,—an American, a Negro; two souls, two thoughts, two unreconciled strivings; two warring ideals in one dark body, whose dogged strength alone keeps it from being torn asunder."[32] Although Wilson acknowledged the descriptive value of DuBois's idea of doubleness, he also said that musical practices constantly adapt or blend to accommodate new situations: "As an individual living at the end of the twentieth century, I have inherited a rich legacy of musical practices from throughout the world, and I have reveled in all of it."[33]

Even though *Sometimes* is concert music in the Euro-American tradition, it also draws on aspects of African and African American music that Wilson defined in his research. Apart from making direct reference to the spiritual, it also embodies what Wilson called a **heterogeneous sound ideal**; that is, it includes many dissimilar textures, voice qualities, and layers of sound. Wilson identified this heterogeneity as a key feature of African diasporic musics.[34] Whereas this sound ideal is most characteristically heard in the nonblending sounds of Duke Ellington's jazz orchestra or the varying vocal tones of a blues singer, the use of voice and electronic sounds is an extreme version of the same principle. Setting many different sound qualities into contrast with each other helps bring out the human drama of the spiritual in a new way. The combination of styles Wilson uses is profoundly personal, reflecting his own array of social and musical commitments.

In sum, the first-generation mediated musicians discussed thus far—

Simon, Riley, Harrison, and Wilson—exemplify de Zengotita's vision of what it means to live in a mediated age. It is easy to see that they worked from a god's-eye view: they took advantage of their access to an enormous variety of music not only through historical and present-day sound recordings but also through travel. They could reach outside the limits of their education or upbringing to ally themselves with many kinds of music. As Harrison put it, "I always used just what I wanted when I wanted it or needed it."[35]

Second, these musicians made self-conscious musical choices based on political values or social affiliations. By choosing a tradition to use, they also adopted at least some of that tradition's connotations and used those connotations as a form of branding. Wilson made a personal statement from an African American perspective that also used the resources of concert music. Harrison and Riley were trying to introduce Eastern practices as an alternative to Euro-American culture. Riley also wanted to encourage alternative listening practices. Trained to extend the classical music tradition, they tried to modify the system of musical values they had inherited by adding new sounds from other traditions. The sense of difference that they hoped to create depended on the music's political and social connotations, as well as on the novelty of the sounds themselves.

Third, these first-generation musicians believed that their musical choices made meaningful public statements. We see them as individuals communicating with the world or commenting on it; they had a sense that their own opinions were important and worth conveying to the world. They were willing to bend or break the conventions and boundaries of their inherited musical traditions to serve their individual tastes and convey their political messages. This sense of self-importance seems to parallel what de Zengotita calls the flattered self, the self of the mediated era that always wants to tell the world what it thinks.

Introducing elements from outside the concert music tradition allowed these composers to present novelties to their audiences. For those who were associated with New Music, novelty was essential; for Simon, too, it served as a selling point. Nonetheless, as much as these composers were motivated by an element of self-interest—taking whatever one wants—they also pushed North American listeners to broaden their definition of "respectable" music. Music's meaning reflects social **conventions**: that is, a community's shared expectations of what constitutes good music. By identifying themselves with musics of Asians, Africans, and African Americans, Riley, Harrison, Wilson, and Simon asked listeners who were used to Euro-

American concert music to take these musics seriously—presenting them not as lesser "others" to Western concert music but as peer musics worthy of interest.[36] This worldview resembled the United Nations' vision of a community of nations in dialogue with one another—except that the UN's vision did not include the mixing of the traditions.

Amid the larger dramas of the Cold War and the civil rights movement, these composers' musical statements also seemed political. By rejecting or modifying elements of their training in elite forms of Western music, they declined an alliance with the United States as a superpower, allying themselves instead with peoples who were marginalized, some of whom called themselves nonaligned or even enemies of the United States. Musical borrowing and mixing sometimes served as a way for musicians to define a sense of individuality and commitment in relation to a social context where musical style was already political. Given the available definitions of what a musician should be and do, these musicians rejected those definitions and created new ones that fit the stories they wanted to tell about themselves and their world. This, too, is a mediated selfhood—not necessarily a bad one. Being able to define oneself musically offered musicians meaningful opportunities for social and political participation.[37]

Next-Generation Mediated Selves: Benary, Srinivasan, Bryan

Musicians who came along after Riley, Harrison, and Wilson have mixed musics more and more flexibly, often blurring the boundaries so much that the listener can no longer distinguish what has been blended with what. Barbara Benary (1946–2019), a generation younger than Harrison, developed a particular fascination for the **gamelan**. A composer, performer, and ethnomusicologist, she studied gamelan as a college student; she then spent time studying violin in Madras, India. On her return to New York she played the violin with the Philip Glass Ensemble, which was experimenting with music based on repetition. As a young professor at Rutgers University she taught traditional gamelan performance to her students; at the same time, she was a member of the experimental music scene in New York, playing with a group called "New Music New York."

Benary also founded a gamelan in New York, called Gamelan Son of Lion. (The name Benary means "Son of Lion" in Hebrew, so the gamelan was marked as her own; indeed, she built and tuned it herself, with Harrison's work as inspiration.) She left Rutgers in 1980 and moved to New York, composing and working with the gamelan full time. In her compositions Benary aimed for a loose mingling of musics in which neither is required to accommodate the other or, in Benary's own words, "a marriage in which neither partner is asked to convert."[38]

Gamelan Son of Lion does not perform traditional gamelan repertory from Indonesia; rather, the ensemble has served as a workshop for performances of newly composed music. Whereas in Harrison's music it seems critical that the listener recognize the "foreign" sources, in much of Benary's music the Asian origin of the instruments seems almost incidental. This approach was controversial within Benary's circle of musician friends: some disapproved of using the traditional instruments of the gamelan "as a set of sound producing objects" without pointing to the Indonesian tradition.[39]

A piece called *Braid*, which Benary composed in the 1970s, is organized around the repetition of a fixed series of notes that covers all the available notes in the gamelan's scale (called *pelog*). In that regard the concept is like that of the serial music of the 1950s, mentioned in chapter 5.[40] Benary designed the series like this: from the starting point go three notes up the scale, then one note lower; following this cycle, the player ends up back at the starting point (fig. 6.2). Players move through the piece by repeating the first two notes of the pattern over and over, then (whenever they like) dropping the first note and repeating the second and third notes over and over, and so on. The three parts are offset from each other in time, so they sound "interlocking"—but the organization of the piece has otherwise nothing to do with the organization of gamelan music. As we hear in example 6.11, the overall effect is repetitious but luminous, as the chiming sound of the instruments is attractive and resonant.

Example 6.11. Barbara Benary, "Braid," performed by Gamelan Son of Lion. *The Complete Gamelan in the New World* (Folkways FTS 31312, 1982 [1979]). Used by permission of Smithsonian Folkways Recordings. YouTube. Link: https://doi.org/10.3998/mpub.9853855.cmp.97

Braid rewards attentive listening: as we get used to the repetition of pitches, the introduction of each unfamiliar note offers a small but refreshing change. Like Riley's, this music is based on incremental, gradual changes, which are intended to draw the listener into a state of contemplative attention—a strategy sometimes called **minimalism**.

This appropriation of gamelan music conveys a different sentiment than

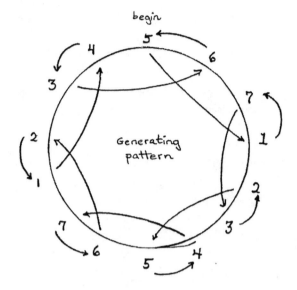

Fig. 6.2. Barbara Benary, *Braid*, generating pattern. *Gamelan Works*, vol. 1, *The Braid Pieces* ([New York]: Gamelan Son of Lion, 1993), 2. The numbers refer to the degrees (step numbers) of the seven-note scale.

did Riley's or Harrison's adoptions of Asian music. Riley and Harrison wanted their listeners to recognize the source of their borrowings: in order for the political meanings they associated with their music to be effective, the listener had to at least get as far as the generalization "that sounds Asian." In contrast, unless the listener happens to be familiar with the Indonesian tuning of the scale or the chiming sound of the gamelan, Benary's music makes no reference to any specific place or people.

Rather, *Braid* more closely resembles other minimalist pieces that were based on "found sounds," snippets of spoken-word audio that would be looped into repetitive blurs.[41] The composer Steve Reich's 1966 tape piece *Come Out* exemplifies this technique. In it the voice of Daniel Hamm, a black man arrested for a murder he did not commit, describes the bruises he sustained when he was beaten during his arrest. His words are grim: he says he had to "open the bruise up and let some of the bruise blood come out to show them" that he was really injured. Yet Reich (1936–) treats the words as musical sound rather than as a meaningful statement. The words "come out to show them" repeat until they lose their verbal sense; then the tape loop is played against itself but offset in time (example 6.12). Later, Reich manipulates the loop further, creating peculiar blurring effects.

Example 6.12. Excerpt from Steve Reich, "Come Out," *Reich Remixed*
(Nonesuch PRCD 8762P, 1999 [1967]). YouTube.
Link: https://doi.org/10.3998/mpub.9853855.cmp.98

In these pieces both Benary and Reich acted as mediated selves: what they took as "found sound" was someone else's art or someone else's voice. Indeed, the voice (or in Benary's case the instrumental sound quality) retains some of its recognizable qualities even as it has been metamorphosed. As the music theorist Sumanth Gopinath has pointed out, Reich's use of Hamm's recognizably black voice points to many possible meanings: the struggle for civil rights, the violence done to persons (as violence is done to the voice on the tape), and the imprisonment of African Americans.[42] Although the vestiges of Indonesian music that remain in Benary's *Braid*—the sound quality of the gamelan and the tuning—point to a vague "elsewhere," the piece itself seems quite abstract.

Like Riley's, Benary's demand that the listener pay close attention to small changes points to a way of life that contrasted with US life in the 1960s (or today). Most of the composers who made minimalist music had some attachment to music from other parts of the world. At the same time, Benary's use of gamelan seems to bear much less predetermined meaning than do Harrison's, Riley's, or Reich's borrowings: there are fewer cues that point the listener to interpret the music in a particular way. Although the listener who has prior knowledge of gamelan may associate Benary's *Braid* with Indonesian music, those without such knowledge seem more likely to accept the piece as "found sounds."

The composer Asha Srinivasan (1980–) also works with blended traditions in a New Music context. Srinivasan comes from a family of musicians and immigrated to the United States from India as a child. In her childhood Srinivasan learned about Carnatic (South Indian) musical traditions, but her interests drew her to the Western music available through US public schools. Through undergraduate and graduate study in the United States, she has acquired expertise in a variety of Western musics, including composition for electronic instruments. As an adult she has chosen to explore Indian music again by studying it on her own. In a video posted online, she refers to herself and her music as "hybrid": she freely blends elements of various traditions together.[43]

Srinivasan's *Janani* exemplifies that mixture. The 2009 version of *Janani*, which means life-giver or mother, is composed for a piano and four saxophones. In Carnatic music a *raga* (or mode) consists of a particular collection of musical notes, associated with certain characteristic ornaments and bent notes, that provides a basis for improvisation. Srinivasan explains that the piece makes use of two ragas: one that shares her mother's name, Lalitha (example 6.13), and another that is her mother's favorite, Ahiri (example 6.14).

> Example 6.13. Raga Lalitha, audio examples at the website Raga Surabhi.
> Link: https://doi.org/10.3998/mpub.9853855.cmp.99

> Example 6.14. Raga Ahiri, audio examples at the website Raga Surabhi.
> Link: https://doi.org/10.3998/mpub.9853855.cmp.100

When *Janani* begins, we hear a drone played on the piano, but the sound is not made by pressing the keys: the player reaches inside the piano to pluck the strings repeatedly, occasionally sweeping a fingernail across them to create a dense resonance (example 6.15). The sound quality of the plucked piano strings resembles that of a *tambura*, an instrument that exists in Carnatic and Hindustani traditions, whose strings sound a drone (example 6.16).

> Example 6.15. Asha Srinivasan, *Janani*, saxophone version, performed by Michael Mizrahi, piano; and Sara Kind, Jesse Dochnahl, Will Obst, and Sumner Truax, saxophones. Recording provided courtesy of the composer.
> Link: https://doi.org/10.3998/mpub.9853855.cmp.101

> Example 6.16. Excerpt from B. Balasubrahmanian, "Tambura (N. Indian)," Wesleyan University Virtual Instrument Museum. YouTube.
> Link: https://doi.org/10.3998/mpub.9853855.cmp.102

The saxophones enter with a narrow range of notes near the drone note, then gradually expand, presenting more and more of the raga at a flexible, unhurried pace. This strategy is very like the introduction to a performance of Carnatic music. Beginning at timepoint 2:35 in *Janani* (example 6.15), the pace becomes steady: the introduction of a regular pulse corresponds to the next phase one would expect if this were an Indian piece. The music builds to a point of maximum intensity, only to pause suddenly at 4:30. The rest of the piece moves at a brisk pace while exploring the Ahiri raga. From 4:52 most of the ensemble keeps the rhythm while the soprano sax wails above them: a similar texture is heard in both North and South Indian music, usually as a reed instrument accompanied by drumming.[44] Although the overall progression of a slow and free section, followed by the introduction of a steady pulse and the gradual intensification of energy, resembles Carnatic music, the time-scale of the piece does not: at about seven minutes, *Janani* proceeds much more concisely through the sequence.

Even as it relies on Indian models for its form and choice of notes, this music also resonates with both jazz and New Music. The choice of instrumental sounds plays a key role here. The technique of plucking and sweeping the piano's strings, which in *Janani* sounds like a tambura, originated with Henry Cowell, who composed experimental piano pieces in the 1920s (example 6.17).

Example 6.17. Henry Cowell, "The Banshee," Sonya Kumiko Lee (piano), film by Johnny Kwon. Used by permission.
Link: https://doi.org/10.3998/mpub.9853855.cmp.103

The choice of saxophones for this piece is compelling, too. Depending on what previous experience the listener brings, this sound can mean different things. For a listener familiar with South Indian music, the sound of the saxophone resembles that of the *nagaswaram*—a larger version of the shahnai we heard earlier in this chapter. Music for this instrument is often lively and loud, and two or more can be played together, as in example 6.18.

Example 6.18. Excerpt from "Nagaswaram or Nadaswaram," Nagaswaram performance at Thirugukkungudi in Tamil Nadu. Performers not named. Good faith effort has been made to contact the videographer.
YouTube, video posted by indiavideo.org
Link: https://doi.org/10.3998/mpub.9853855.cmp.104

For listeners who are unfamiliar with the Indian referent, the high wailing of the saxophone and the many expressively bent notes in *Janani* may recall how saxophones have been used in **jazz**. For example, Johnny Hodges's solo "I Got It Bad," recorded with Duke Ellington and his orchestra in 1958 (example 6.19), makes full use of the instrument's expressive qualities, with a great deal of glissando (sliding between notes).

Example 6.19. Excerpt from Duke Ellington and Johnny Hodges, "I Got it Bad," 1958 videorecording. Duke Ellington Live in '58 (DVD, Reelin' in the Years Productions, 2007). YouTube.
Link: https://doi.org/10.3998/mpub.9853855.cmp.105

Srinivasan has notated the glissando effect in the performers' instructions for *Janani*, and she instructs the player to emphasize them, making them "long and deliberate."

Another characteristic effect is the way the saxophone section of a big band often plays together with precision. We hear such an effect in example 6.20, "Three and One" performed by the Thad Jones and Mel Lewis Orchestra. The players play as one, in close harmony: even the fast notes and bent notes stay in sync with each other.

> Example 6.20. Excerpt from Thad Jones and Mel Lewis Orchestra, "Three and One," featuring Jerome Richardson, Jerry Dodgion, Joe Henderson, Eddie Daniels, Pepper Adams, saxophones, as performed on "Battle of the Bands." YouTube. Link: https://doi.org/10.3998/mpub.9853855.cmp.106

This "tight" style of playing remained an important element in virtuosic jazz as well as in New Music. In the late 1960s and 1970s the saxophonist Anthony Braxton began performing what he called "creative music," which appealed to people from concert music and jazz circles who were looking for edgy modern music. That sense of being up-to-date and novel was a key element of New Music just as it was for avant-garde jazz musicians: Braxton worked between these musical communities, connecting them. Braxton's style featured a great deal of fast unison playing—for instance, in his *Composition 40M* (example 6.21).[45]

> Example 6.21. Excerpt from Anthony Braxton Quartet, "Composition 40M," performed by Anthony Braxton, Kenny Wheeler, Dave Holland, and Barry Altschul. Montreux Jazz Festival, 1975. YouTube, video posted by crownpropeller. Link: https://doi.org/10.3998/mpub.9853855.cmp.107

The tight precision we hear among the lower saxophone parts in *Janani* at timepoint 6:07 resembles this virtuosic manner of performance and connects *Janani* to the traditions of New Music as well as jazz.

A fan of Euro-American concert music might bring still other reference points to their hearing of *Janani*. At timepoint 2:35, the moment at which the pace becomes quicker and the beat more regular, the lowest-pitched saxophone sets up a busy pattern. Starting at timepoint 2:51, the higher-pitched saxophones play a new melody high above. This moment feels like a new beginning—it might remind a concert music fan of Darius Milhaud's *Creation of the World*, a European ballet from the 1920s that begins with a prominent saxophone solo over repetitive patterns (example 6.22).

Example 6.22. Excerpt from Darius Milhaud, "Creation of the World," performed by Kaleidoscope Chamber Orchestra. Used by permission. YouTube.
Link: https://doi.org/10.3998/mpub.9853855.cmp.108

Srinivasan may not have intended all these resonances between *Janani* and other musics: different listeners will bring different kinds of knowledge to the piece and make different associations. One of the things that makes Srinivasan's music remarkable is its place at the nexus of many kinds of music. Listeners may enjoy the music whether they hear any, all, or none of these resonances, for *Janani* is exciting to listen to, with pacing that draws the listener in and an energetic conclusion. In a note accompanying the piece on her website, Srinivasan identifies the ragas and their connection with her mother but does not emphasize all the ways in which *Janani* draws on Indian music.[46] Unlike Riley or Harrison, Srinivasan does not require her listener to consider the particular sources or referents of her music, nor does she rely on a particular interpretation of what "India" might mean. Rather, her music stands open for listeners to make meaning of it themselves.

Courtney Bryan is a composer and pianist whose expertise includes concert music and jazz. Bryan composed *Yet Unheard*, with words by Sharan Strange, for a memorial concert. Its first performance took place in 2016, on the first anniversary of the black activist Sandra Bland's death in police custody in July of 2015. Unlike Olly Wilson's *Sometimes*, in which New Music and African American traditions contrast with each other, Bryan's piece absorbs a variety of elements into a more seamless personal style.

Yet Unheard (example 6.23) begins with tones that are dissonant (sounding harsh together) and slide downward (timepoint 0:27).

Example 6.23. Courtney Bryan and Sharan Strange, "Yet Unheard," performed by Helga Davis with the La Jolla Symphony and Chorus conducted by Steven Schick, 2018. Video courtesy of UCSD-TV.
Link: https://doi.org/10.3998/mpub.9853855.cmp.109

This kind of sound has traditionally been used by concert music composers to signal lament. As more instruments enter, they play in imitation: groups play similar parts but begin at different times so that they overlap (from timepoint 0:52). When the harp and flute come in (timepoint 1:19), they play melodies that wind around on an upward path. Bryan's overlapping patterns of sliding string sounds recall a piece of European **New Music** from the 1960s, Krzysztof Penderecki's *Threnody for the Victims of Hiroshima*—another work laden with grief and horror (example 6.24, especially the passage after timepoint 2:27).

Example 6.24. Krzysztof Penderecki, "Threnody for the Victims of Hiroshima" performed by the Finnish National Radio Orchestra conducted by Krzysztof Urbánski. Link: https://doi.org/10.3998/mpub.9853855.cmp.110 (listen at timepoint 1:47 to 3:32)

At the same time, Bryan's use of imitation and dissonance brings to mind the very beginning of Johann Sebastian Bach's St. Matthew Passion, an **oratorio** that dramatizes the story of the death of Jesus as told in the Gospel of Matthew. Bach's melodies, too, share the winding quality of Bryan's harp and flute lines: they turn back on themselves, as if they are knotted up (the Bach is example 6.25). In both cases the introduction acts as a framing device, setting the stage for the particulars of the drama.

Example 6.25. Excerpt from Johann Sebastian Bach, instrumental introduction and chorus "Come, ye daughters" from St. Matthew Passion, performed by the Munich Bach Choir and Orchestra, directed by Karl Richter. YouTube. Link: https://doi.org/10.3998/mpub.9853855.cmp.111

The words of *Yet Unheard* also allude to Bach's Passion. Bryan's chorus begins with "Mother, call out to your daughter" (example 6.23, timepoint 1:40) much as Bach's chorus starts with "Come, daughters, help me lament" (example 6.25, timepoint 2:02). In both pieces the chorus acts as narrator and commentator, and solo voices act as particular characters (fig. 6.3). The stories of Bach's and Bryan's oratorios resonate but differ in important ways. Bryan's music, like Bach's, portrays the death of an innocent. Bach's oratorio ends with a choral lament after the crucifixion of Jesus: the Christian Passion story ends in darkness, before the Easter resurrection. But in the introduction to *Yet Unheard* the chorus urges us to "push back hatred's stone" and hear Bland's voice—a reference to the Easter narrative, when Jesus's friends push back the stone and find he is no longer in the tomb. Like Jesus, Bland spent "three days in a cell": this comparison offers a possibility of resurrection through memory that is not possible in actuality. Through this mixture of imagery Bland seems to be at once dead and resurrected—simultaneously mourned and present in spirit.

Indeed, we hear her presence. At timepoint 2:53 of *Yet Unheard* (example 6.23) a solo singer enters, singing words written from the perspective of Bland herself, recalling the day she died. In Bach's oratorio Jesus, the central character, hardly speaks at all, but the words presented from Bland's perspective take a central place in Bryan's narrative. The soloist's voice edges painfully upward,

Fig. 6.3. Singers in a performance of the chamber version of Courtney Bryan's *Yet Unheard*, Ojai Music Festival, 2017. *Pictured from left:* Joelle Lamarre, Gwendolyn Brown, Helga Davis, Julian Terrell Otis, and Davóne Tines. YouTube: www.youtube.com/watch?v=XiklJQEC5kl

accompanied by mysterious flute trills that yield to a military-sounding trumpet when she asks: "And my power, robust, unbidden, was it too much on display? Did that drive his anger to kill me that day?" The frequent presence of the jangling, metallic triangle contributes to a sense of emergency in this music.

Immediately thereafter, on the words "Didn't he kill me that day," the singer adds one phrase that sounds like it is built on a **blues scale**; it descends into the lowest notes she can produce (timepoint 4:36). Hints of blues appear again at "Tried to kill my dignity too" (timepoint 5:52) and in the choir's response on the words "black people" (timepoint 7:02). These references are fleeting, and they quickly surrender to the overall tense sound of the work. Perhaps the suppression of the blues references reflects the choir's message at that point: "We've forgotten how to imagine black life. . . . Our imagination has only allowed for us to understand black people as a dying people." Only at the end of the piece (after timepoint 14:06) do we hear a last bit of blues when the singer, as Bland, wails above the choir and orchestra, "Won't you sing my name," an outpouring that descends along a blues scale as it disappears again into the abyss of the singer's lowest tones.

The music Bryan has created in *Yet Unheard* draws on multiple sources—oratorio, New Music, blues—to achieve its effects. Yet the experience of the music does not suggest quotation or mashup but an unrelenting outpouring of grief. That is not to say that there is no trace of Bryan's African American heritage here; indeed, the work as a whole is framed as an outcry specifically from the African American community, echoing the hashtag #sayhername that Black Lives Matter activists used to protest police brutality. As a 21st-century composer, Bryan chooses various musical styles for her compositions; she is free to move among the traditions as she wishes and to integrate them as she pleases.

The "first-generation" mediated composers described in this chapter appropriated music for various reasons: one reason was to signal a political allegiance. In the music of the three "next-generation" composers discussed here—Benary, Srinivasan, and Bryan—the overt signaling of difference has become more subtle. These composers still choose musical styles based on what each style means to them and what it can convey to listeners. But they draw less attention to the markers that proclaim appropriation—allowing different musics to meld together into something new. The emphasis here seems to be on a smoother integration of different materials, creating something that may not immediately reveal itself as "mixed." Bryan aptly characterizes herself as a "composer and pianist beyond category."[47] No preexisting genre label is sufficient to describe her creative contributions.

Globalized Generations

As we saw in the early chapters of this book, musical borrowing, assimilation, or appropriation across lines of power have had stakes both political and personal. In cases where the socially empowered borrow music from the less powerful, appropriation has often felt like disrespect or theft. Those effects persist in the mediated era, yet the wholesale appropriation of styles has also become commonplace and a matter of individual choice. As a large and growing archive of recorded music is available for reuse, and travel and circulation of media have made it possible to know more kinds of music, composers have begun to treat it all as available for their use. Sometimes an element of exoticism plays a role in the selection of music to borrow, but often, as we have seen, the purposeful choice of a style has also served as a form of personal expression, a means of representing oneself and one's allegiances in a particular way.

In chapter 8 we will return to the idea of appropriation for the purpose of making blended music. The Argentinian anthropologist Néstor García Canclini describes appropriation of this kind as a creative act of the individual, and he asks us to examine closely the strategic nature of appropriation. What is the borrower trying to accomplish through musical appropriation? Is the composer gaining entry to places or ideas that would otherwise be forbidden? Is the composer developing a personal identity that is meaningful and distinct from peers' identities? Does the appropriation make this composer seem more modern or more traditional?

We know that musicians habitually pick up new and fascinating sounds, possess them, and sometimes weave them into their own music-making. For the first mediated generation described in this chapter, borrowing was often a refashioning of identity: rejecting some part of their prior education, composers appropriated music to flag their opinions and affiliations clearly. The next-generation composers discussed above proceeded in various ways. In the tradition of New Music, Benary's appropriation was absorbed into an abstract musical process, losing its Indonesian associations. Srinivasan and Bryan, like Wilson before them, participate in more than one "home" tradition. Unlike Benary, Bryan and Srinivasan do not conceal their source music, but they do minimize the contrast between traditions, creating a thorough blend. As composers who move between New Music and other traditions, they might use this blending as a means for moving back and forth—or for resolutely standing in the doorway, giving up neither identity in favor of the other.

7 Copyright, Surveillance, and the Ownership of Music

Before the existence of sound recording, people could own printed sheet music for their use in reproducing music, or they could know and play music from memory, but they could not own the sounds themselves. With the advent of recorded media, sounds could be captured on wax cylinders, disc-shaped gramophone records, magnetic tape or wire, small cassettes for personal use, or compact discs. All of these are physical, tangible media that a person can own. Playing recordings at home became a realistic option for many people. Owning sounds was an exciting activity in its own right: many enthusiasts amassed large collections of recordings.[1] The owners of recordings could also move them from place to place, sell them, or give them away.

Physical recording media (compact discs, DVDs, cassettes, and other formats) are still very important in the worldwide circulation of music, encompassing about half of all music sales in the world.[2] To a great extent this is a matter of availability. As of 2018, only about 55 percent of the people in the world had internet access (fig. 7.1). Broadband or high-speed internet (which is most useful for moving music) is even more limited. Cell phones can also move digital music from place to place. As of late 2017, about 66 percent of individuals in the world had cell phones.[3] As we will see, however, physical media continue to play a role in moving music because their use cannot as easily be observed from afar.

With the capacity for making recordings widely available came opportunities to make money selling the recordings. Yet music remains an unusual kind of commodity for buying and selling because it is essentially intangible. What does it mean to own music, then? Karl Marx, who described the capitalist system in the 1860s, identified two kinds of value. An object can have **use value**: things satisfy human needs, so people use them. Every commodity has use value; this kind of value resides in the difference of this particular com-

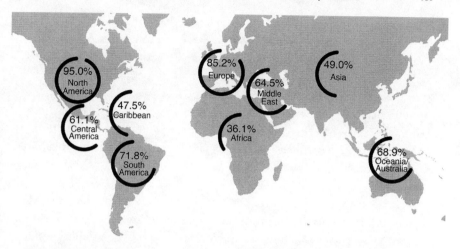

Fig. 7.1. *Music on the Move:* Internet Usage Rates by Region, 2018. Map by Eric Fosler-Lussier. This map shows the percentage of people in each region estimated to have internet access (broadband, mobile, or dial-up) in June of 2018. Data from www.internetworldstats.com. (See https://doi.org/10.3998/mpub.9853855.cmp.113)

modity from other commodities. For example, I think my favorite song is different from all others; and my car keys open only my particular car.

The second kind of value is **exchange value**: things that are useful can be exchanged for other things. Exchange value makes different objects comparable to each other. For example, a hammer might cost me $9.99, and a music download might cost me $9.99. Their functions are different, but their exchange value is equivalent. Only when items change hands by being bought, sold, or traded do they acquire "value" in this sense.[4]

In their ordinary lives many people tend to think about music primarily in terms of its use value. When a parent sings a lullaby, both parent and child might enjoy the song, but no payment changes hands. In today's world people often assign music exchange value in addition to its use value. Concerts demand high ticket prices, and music can be recorded onto an object or encoded as a digital file that is bought and sold like anything else. To the music industry, music is a commodity that can be sold for profit.

Sometimes these two views of music come into direct conflict.[5] Adrian Strain, the global communications director of the International Federation of the Phonographic Industry (IFPI), explained in 2014 that the music industry's principal aim is to assign exchange value to music and make it available for purchase. That is, the companies want to **monetize** musical experience: turn it into money. Strain said, "We are a *portfolio industry* that is monetising all the different ways consumers access music. From CDs to downloads. Subscription to ad-supported services. From music video to performance rights."[6] In Strain's world monetizing musical experiences is good because it enriches record companies. Many in the industry would also argue that this process also supports musical creativity because it funds the purchase of more music from musicians. Nevertheless, the premise that music should be monetized is not universally accepted. As we will see, music circulates in the marketplace differently in different parts of the world, depending on the social norms that define music's value.

Despite the intangibility of music, part of the process of making recordings looks like manufacturing in any industry. Record companies like Sony or Warner Music pay to record music in recording studios and to duplicate and package physical copies of the recordings in factories. They also generate and sell digital audio files, collections of encoded ones and zeroes that can be decoded into musical experiences. Ownership of the manufacturing resources—Marx would call them the "means of production"—is tangible, physically real. More important, though, record companies also own the intangible legal right to reproduce, publish, sell, or distribute the content of the recording. This right, which is protected by law in many parts of the world, is called **copyright**. (Music that has been written down is also covered by copyright, which adds another layer of ownership and complexity. This chapter will deal primarily with recordings.)

To obtain the copyright, the record company buys the labor of the musician, who assigns the copyright to the company so that the company will promote and distribute the music. The company also takes most or all of the profit. The musician may receive royalty payments for each sale, but this usually happens only after many units are sold (e.g., more than 100,000 copies) and intermediaries such as streaming services are paid. The companies justify this practice on the grounds that they have to recoup their costs for finding musicians and making, duplicating, and publicizing the recordings.[7] The most valuable part of what the record companies own is not the technology they use to reproduce the music but the legal right to reproduce that particular music. Companies sometimes refer to this ownership as **intellectual property**—an intangible, yet valuable, owned resource.

This system of ownership, developed in the early 1900s, earned record companies excellent profits. It is no surprise, then, that the advent of the internet, file sharing, and downloading worried the managers of these companies.

Everyone who has access to a microphone and a laptop or smartphone can make recordings, and it is easy to copy a digital file. Unauthorized copies of recordings threaten the companies' interests by violating their copyright, jeopardizing the investments the record companies have made in acquiring the rights to these songs. One trade group representing the music industry claims that as a result of online file sharing, sales of recorded music on compact discs fell 23 percent between 2000 and 2005.[8]

Illegal copying of recordings is not a new problem. After the Phillips corporation introduced compact cassette tapes to the consumer market in 1963, individual users could easily record music from the radio, from other recordings, or from live performances. They immediately began to make creative use of this technology—not only copying music they wanted but also making **mixtapes** on which they creatively chose a sequence of music to record. In the 1980s, record companies advertised the slogan "home taping is killing music" in hopes of persuading people to honor their copyright, and they labeled those who make illegal copies "pirates."[9] The sharing of digitally encoded music files on compact discs, portable hard drives, or the internet has only increased the ease of copying and the quality of the copies. **Piracy** rings around the world either distribute music for free over the internet or make illegal CDs to sell. The recording industry spends an enormous amount of money and effort trying to prevent these activities.

Because there are so few barriers to copying and distributing recordings, protecting the ownership of recorded sounds is the paramount problem in the music industry today. The rest of this chapter deals with the ownership and distribution of music, with particular attention to how copyright enforcement affects the movement of music on a worldwide scale. As individuals, record companies, and governments fight over ownership rights, a great deal of money is at stake. Also on the line is individuals' artistic freedom to mix and remix music, as well as the rights of people who own copies of audio recordings to use those recordings as they please.

What Does It Mean to Own Copyright?

Copyright law is intended to promote the creation and public availability of useful works and incentivize creativity by ensuring that artists get paid. In the United States, copyright law protects original works in a fixed form, including literary works, musical works and their lyrics, dramatic works, choreography, pictorial works or sculpture, motion pictures, audio recordings, and architecture. No registration is required: once a work is in a "fixed form," it is protected by copyright for a period of 75 to 120 years after the death of the author, depending on when and where it was made and the nature of the material.[10] (Once the copyright period has expired, the work is in the **public domain**, available for use by anyone.) For music, a "fixed form" may mean either an original work that has been written down or an analog or digital recording.

As we saw in chapter 4, the reliance on fixed forms sets certain kinds of music apart from others. When US copyright law began covering music in 1831, legislators considered only sheet music in European-style music notation, which captures melody and rhythm in a fixed (written) form. In 1897 copyright expanded to cover public performances of printed music.[11] As folklorists began collecting and writing down music, and as sound recording of folk singing became available, these practices broadened the scope of music captured in fixed form. Yet, more often than not, the copyright has been held by the person who made and published the recording, not by the person who created the song. As the poet and folk singer Aunt Molly Jackson put it, "Since I left my home in Kentucky in 1931, I have had my songs that I composed translated in 5 different languages and records made out of my songs but I have never received one cent from anyone."[12] Copyright law does not protect all creators equally. Furthermore, the securing of copyright on a song known to many people may inhibit further development of that song, as artists have to pay licensing fees to the copyright holder to reuse or remake it.[13]

Once a work is copyrighted, US law restricts duplication of it, except in certain circumstances. Someone who wants to make a copy can claim **fair use** based on four factors: the purpose and character of the use, the nature of the copyrighted work, the portion of the work used relative to the whole, and the effect of the use on the market for the copied work. If a use is educational, takes only a small part of a work, and does not encourage people to use the copy in place of the original, a claim of fair use might be legitimate. Copying a whole poem or track of music to distribute widely or resell, however, would not be deemed acceptable.[14] The courts have established certain uses as fair: making one copy of a recording to a computer and one to another device for portability, making a "backup copy" for personal archiving, and making a noncommercial copy for a friend, as on a mixtape.[15] Apart from fair use, US law specifies some other legitimate uses of copyrighted work, most of them pertaining to educational settings or transformative artistic use such as parody.

Legal protection for sound recordings is extremely complex: the law has changed to keep up with current customs and technologies. When and where a recording was made has determined what its users can do with it; in 2018 the US Congress enacted legislation to attempt to regularize enforcement.[16] As of 1976, copyright holders had the right to control the copying, distribution, and public display of the protected work and the making of derivative works based on it. Except in the case of freely available, noninteractive network broadcasts (such as over-the-air radio), they could demand a licensing fee in exchange for any of these activities. Similar protection for digital streaming was added in 1995.[17] Copyright is enforced by action of the copyright holder; that is, the holder has to find out someone has violated her or his copyright and sue them. Protecting a copyright involves significant resources of time and money. As the large record companies have the most at stake, they actively defend their copyrights through lawsuits and other means both in the US and internationally.

The Cat-and-Mouse Game of Copyright Enforcement

Copyright ownership of recorded music is concentrated among the "big three" international corporations. The largest, US-based Warner Music Group, controlled about 25 percent of the market as of September 2018. Universal Music Group, an American company owned by the French media conglomerate Vivendi, controlled about 24 percent. Sony Music Entertainment, a Japanese company with studios in the United States, controlled about 22 percent. Each of these groups issues music recordings under a variety of **record labels** (or brands).[18] Independent labels unaffiliated with these companies control the other 29 percent of the market.[19] Of course, there are also privately made recordings that are not sold on any official label, and a great deal of content is distributed on social media such as YouTube. This independent fraction of the musical economy is hard to document. Taken together, the revenue from the sale of recorded music amounted to $15.7 billion in 2016, according to record industry figures.[20]

Since the 1950s, the US recording industry has been represented by the Recording Industry Association of America (RIAA), a trade group that tracks the sales figures for the industry. The RIAA spends between three and seven million dollars per year lobbying the US government to enact tighter copyright controls and enforcement.[21] The international organization affiliated with the RIAA is the IFPI, which is based in London but has regional offices worldwide. Like the RIAA, the IFPI tracks sales and advocates for copyright enforcement but on an international scale.

The large media companies, RIAA, and IFPI routinely claim that illegal downloading and copying hurts their legal and economic interests, yet this claim has not yet been proven. For years the RIAA and IFPI have emphasized the "value gap"—the difference between what companies actually earn by selling music and what they imagine they could be earning if all illegal copying came to an end. Of course, because the industry does not have direct knowledge of user activities that are outside its control, the "value gap" estimate is based on guesswork. The trade organizations guard their sales figures closely, so no one else can confirm the truth of their data. The argument about lost revenue has surfaced every time consumers gain the ability to copy music on their own equipment in a new way. In response media companies have attempted to litigate remedies based on their estimates of harm (including, for instance, proposing a royalty tax on blank tapes, assuming they will be used for copying).[22]

To combat illegal duplication of copyrighted music, the large media companies began creating **digital rights management** (DRM) systems that use technical means to prevent copying. The most notorious of these cases unfolded in the mid-2000s. Sony had released more than five million audio CDs with a DRM package that could damage computers. When a user put the CD into a computer drive, a license agreement appeared that asked the users to give up many of their rights, including the right to make digital copies, the right to leave the country with the audio files, and the right to sue for damages if the software caused harm. Even if the user clicked "I do not accept" after seeing the agreement, Sony's CD still installed hidden software onto the computer. Sony's software made the user's system vulnerable to virus attacks. Worse, it included spyware that informed Sony about the user's listening habits, and if the user tried to remove the software, it could permanently damage the CD drive of the computer. Users sued Sony, and Sony paid to settle the court case in January of 2006. Sony's system was only one of a hodgepodge of strategies tried during this decade, including the use of digital "watermarks" that would permanently label files and the manufacture of devices that would not permit the copying of watermarked files.[23]

These DRM systems had several serious drawbacks. First, they did not deter the major piracy operations but only discouraged casual, small-scale copying by less determined people. Second, these systems actually took away rights from the user by preventing instances of legal copying. A 1998 US law known as the Digital Millennium Copyright Act made it illegal under most circumstances to break into or reverse-engineer any DRM or "technical protection" systems.[24] For example, if a teacher wanted to copy an excerpt for educational use, that would be fair use, which is legal, but DRM prevented the copying, and it was illegal for the teacher to circumvent the DRM.[25] In effect, the major record companies arrogated to themselves rights that belonged to users. (The US Copyright Office has since acknowledged this kind of problem and tried to outline some exceptions.)[26] Third, some kinds of DRM, including Sony's, have operated like spyware, reporting on the user's computer activity without the user's consent. Record companies considered secrecy necessary, because if users could see how DRM worked, they could more easily defeat it. Yet the idea that corporations would gather information about users in their private homes disturbed many users.

After several lawsuits DRM technologies fell out of favor, but the attempt to regulate user behavior only became more urgent as peer-to-peer file sharing over the internet grew. In 1999 the US-based file-sharing website Napster began enabling the easy peer-to-peer sharing of music files; it was soon joined by Kazaa (Dutch, later based in Vanuatu), Grokster (Nevis, West Indies), Pirate Bay (Sweden), and others. The RIAA and its international affiliates pursued legal action against these entities. These lawsuits proceeded slowly, in part because of the complexity of international agreements about trade and telecommunications. Efforts to suppress file sharing failed: new sharing sites sprang up as others were shut down.

The RIAA next tried to attack copying by finding and punishing the users of pirated files. By hiring online investigators to trace individuals' internet protocol (IP) addresses, the RIAA identified college students who used university networks to download or share music. Between 2003 and 2008 the RIAA pursued legal action against about 35,000 individuals.[27] The RIAA also threatened to sue universities that refused to identify students by their IP addresses. In 2007, for example, Ohio State University turned over the names of more than a dozen students to the RIAA; most of these students settled the lawsuits out of court, paying several thousand dollars each.[28] This strategy frightened some students into buying music legally, but it did not come close to eliminating file sharing.

By 2008 the RIAA had found a new strategy: demanding that internet service providers (ISPs) monitor individuals' usage and cut off those who appeared to be sharing files illegally.[29] Like the strategy taken with the universities, this action relied on the ISPs' ability to survey the traffic of files over the internet and identify particular users. The chair of the RIAA, Mitch Bainwol, believed that if users knew they were being watched, piracy would decline: "Part of the issue with infringement is for people to be aware that their actions are not anonymous."[30] When the Grokster file-sharing service was taken down as a result of a lawsuit, a notice appeared on its website stating that the specific IP address of the user's computer had been logged, with the words: "Don't think you can't get caught. You are not anonymous."[31]

As of this writing, the major music corporations have begun to discourage the use of mp3 sound files. The Apple corporation has publicized its plan to stop selling music files in 2019, directing users instead to Apple Music, its audio streaming service.[32] Other subscription streaming services, including Spotify, Pandora, Amazon Music, and Google Play, are working hard to attract listeners. With **streaming** technology the digital audio may stay online and never be copied onto the user's device as a file; or the file may be "rented" for download and disappear automatically from the device after a short time. As a business model this move makes sense: on a subscription basis the record company can at least capture some **royalties** (payment) for the music that customers listen to online. These services create a more seamless experience: rather than tediously moving individual files onto devices, the user can order particular selections or styles of music from a single dashboard.

That seamlessness is strategic: it offers the user fewer chances to defy the system. According to the music theorist Eric Drott, streaming services have convinced copyright holders that streaming is a way to capture listeners, bringing them into a "**digital enclosure**" in which their behavior is more easily controlled. This business model takes away users' ownership over files and the means to alter or disseminate them. In a streaming system companies identify (authenticate) users as individuals; companies then deliver music encoded as streams of information rather than files that can be duplicated. The relationship between the rights-holders and the streaming services is negotiated by contract; for example, Spotify must pay 83 percent of its earnings to the rights-holders.[33]

The record companies' strategy of keeping listeners in the digital enclosure is aided by **convergence**: a few companies are now controlling more and more elements of our digital lives.[34] What used to be separate technologies— telephone and internet, audio publishing and distribution—increasingly operate over the same networks. Apple makes devices that store and play music, but the company also controls what software can be used to play music on its devices, and it sells access to music through its streaming service. Time-

Warner owns the copyright for many movies but may also serve as the customer's ISP and phone company. An ISP may even decide what content is permitted to flow to the customer.[35] The more integrated our electronic services become, the more power a few communications and content companies can exercise over user behavior.

Furthermore, the advent of streaming services enhances a little-noticed aspect of the streaming business model: rather than selling music to consumers, media companies strategically sell consumers to advertisers. This practice has a long history. In 1935 a radio show called *Your Hit Parade* broadcast lists of top songs of the week; in the 1940s fan magazines like *Billboard* began publishing charts of hit songs as a way of attracting people to their publications and thereby selling advertising to the music industry.[36] The Nielsen company, which had produced audience ratings of television programs since 1950, introduced SoundScan in 1991—a service that collected all sales data about every recording from retail outlets and sold that information to record companies. To assist in tracking, each recording is marked with a unique code.[37] Record companies, distributors, retailers, and people who manage concert venues pay Nielsen Music Sales Measurement for access to the sales data. Knowing how many of each kind of record they might expect to sell allows companies to make choices about what to pay artists for recording contracts.[38] More important, though, these systems allow detailed tracking of listener behavior.

Now, for example, as users access *Billboard* magazine's charts through the internet, there is an added component of data-gathering: *Billboard* tracks the users of that content and sells their information as well. If you visit *Billboard*'s website, *Billboard* reserves the right to "observe your behaviors and browsing activities over time across multiple websites or other platforms." That is, *Billboard* watches you not only when you are looking at its website but also thereafter. Furthermore, *Billboard* will then "serve you with interest-based or targeted advertising."[39] These ads do not only describe *Billboard* or its products: they can include ads from anyone *Billboard* has sold your browsing data to. Thus, *Billboard* is involved in a multidirectional flow of consumer data: consumer purchasing decisions produce the data that become its product (the charts), but consumers' attention to that product (measured in clicks and time spent online) also becomes a product to sell to advertisers.

In this way the music business has monetized listeners' attention. Eric Drott has described how the subscription streaming service Spotify sells its user data. According to Drott, Spotify issued a wide-ranging licensing agreement that would allow Spotify "to retrieve personal data held on third-party apps like Facebook; to access GPS and other sensors on mobile devices; to collect voice commands captured by built-in microphones; and to scan local media files on users' devices, including mp3 libraries, photo albums, and address books."[40] Spotify retracted this policy after user outcry in August of 2015. But the company still communicates user data to "advertising partners"; indeed, this data (not the music) is the company's principal asset. Because the data describes what users like, when they listen, and in the case of phones, where they listen—it reveals their personal habits in a way that advertisers can exploit.[41]

The ubiquity of these technologies, which accompany a person throughout the day, makes them strangely intimate: when the application solicits personal data, the user does not hesitate to give it. As we saw in chapter 6, this user is a flattered self—delighted to be attended to and catered to, and delighted to be asked. Spotify capitalizes on this sense of intimacy. Drott notes that when a user posted on Twitter that Spotify knows him well, "Like former-lover-who-lived-through-a-near-death experience-with-me well," Spotify began using this tweet when it marketed its services to record companies.[42] The tweet demonstrates how effectively Spotify draws the user into the service, making the user feel attended to and thereby concealing the unpleasant sensation of having one's data mined for personal details.

From the 1950s to today, then, record companies have gathered gradually more specific information about listeners—now achieving a stunning degree of particularity. Once clumsily used to sell advertising or prevent copying of physical media, this information is now deployed to encourage us to tell more and more and to allow the digital enclosure to meet our needs without our conscious awareness. Because this persuasive method is pleasing, it appears to be much more effective than any lawsuit in shaping user behavior toward streaming and diminishing the appeal of illegal sharing of music.

The International Cat-and-Mouse Game

Record companies find it particularly difficult to enforce their copyright across international borders. There is no such thing as "international copyright": international protection depends on the laws of each country. Not all nation-states agree on standards for intellectual property protections, and different nation-states may or may not be committed to spending resources on enforcement.[43] If one nation-state wants another to honor copyrights held by its citizens, that agreement must be secured by a treaty between the two governments. Many countries have worked on this problem for a long time. In 1886 a few countries signed a treaty called the Berne Convention, stating that each would honor the others' copyright laws, and these agreements have evolved over time.[44]

The founding of the United Nations (UN) in 1945 inspired a new sense of global cooperation in politics and trade. The UN encouraged newly decolonizing nations to join the Berne Convention, and in 1967 the UN funded the World International Property Organization (WIPO) to foster "balanced" worldwide policy about intellectual property. WIPO aimed to help newly decolonizing countries integrate into existing copyright treaties; in so doing, it connected private corporations with governments and governments with one another.

The World Trade Organization (WTO), formed by treaty in the mid-1990s as an entity separate from the UN, dealt with the regulation and enforcement of trade agreements, including intellectual property. Since 1995, all members of the WTO must sign the Agreement on Trade-Related Aspects of Intellectual Property Rights (TRIPS), which incorporated and expanded the Berne Convention. TRIPS required member nations to seek out and prosecute music piracy and to establish intellectual property laws in line with "international minimum standards."[45] The United States, Japan, and the European Union, which host the big media companies and own most of the world's copyrighted material, exerted pressure to get other countries to accept TRIPS. The WTO may punish its member states by sanctions if they do not follow the agreement.

The WTO permitted developing countries a "phase-in" period during which they would bring their practices in line with the TRIPS agreement, but the hurdles proved insurmountable. Enforcement costs money, and each country was supposed to bear the cost. To comply, some countries would have to revamp entire judicial and policing systems. Police were often reluctant to jail poor people who did not know the law merely to comply with an abstract international treaty.[46] Where states attempted to use local authorities for enforcement, the authorities and musicians associated with them have been assaulted by music vendors. In some cases police invented blackmail schemes in which they collected money from the sellers of illegal CDs and allowed them to keep their businesses open.[47]

Furthermore, most citizens in these countries were accustomed to their own ways of using music, so TRIPS would require changing citizen behavior on a vast scale. In Brazil, for example, entire livelihoods are built around the copying and sharing of recorded music. Since the 1990s, people near the city of Belém in northeastern Brazil have enjoyed *tecnobrega*, which means "cheesy" or "tacky" techno music. The DJs who mix this music in the studio use a computer to add a techno beat to an already existing song, usually one issued legally by a record label. The film in example 7.1 shows how, using the strategies of hip-hop and techno DJs, a tecnobrega DJ takes samples or loops from other copyrighted popular music as well.

> Example 7.1. Excerpt from Andreas Johsen, Ralf Christensen, and Henrik Moltke, *Good Copy Bad Copy* (Rosforth Films, 2007). Licensed under Creative Commons. YouTube.
> Link: https://doi.org/10.3998/mpub.9853855.cmp.114

Once enough songs are made to fill a CD, the disc is handed to a street vendor, who duplicates and sells copies at a low cost. The CD serves as an advertisement for a party, where thousands of people pay for entry and dance to the music mixed by the DJ. The party is the main revenue source: successful DJs can earn more than $1,000 at one party. The DJs include shout-outs to particular audience members to personalize the concert, and CDs and DVDs of that concert are sold that same evening as souvenirs.[48] If tecnobrega creators want to distribute their music through official channels, they may go to the trouble of licensing their work, but doing so is not the norm. There are numerous other instances of informal circulation in low-income countries: South Africa's *kwaito* music is another kind of creative studio work that takes preexisting music as its basis.[49]

Given the difficulty of changing citizen behavior and legal systems, many people in low-income countries began to criticize TRIPS as coercive and inappropriate. In states where basic needs such as food, literacy, and sanitation are not met, governments cannot and do not want to spend money to enforce the property rights of rich foreigners.[50] Nonetheless, Brazil made significant efforts to comply with TRIPS: officials implemented more restrictive copyright laws, destroyed four million pirated items, and closed more than 2,800 file-sharing websites. Yet in 2001, under threat of sanctions, Brazil was compelled to create a new government ministry to combat piracy, and international trade groups continued to lobby the US Trade Representative to place Brazil on a "priority watch list" for possible punishment.[51]

Adding insult to injury, musicians in lower-income countries have found frustration when they tried to gain representation by major record companies and participate in the legal market. Large record companies only market music they believe will sell very widely. Although Brazil has more than 200 million citizens, the companies treat low-income countries as consumers, not producers. Furthermore, the companies only pay royalties after a certain number of copies has been sold. Brazilian musicians report that the large international record labels are merely another form of piracy: they give up their music, the music sells well, but they receive no money in return. "I was pirated . . . by Sony!" exclaimed one musician, Marcílio Lisboa.[52] State officials have verified this claim: to evade paying taxes in countries where enforcement is lax, labels underreport the number of recordings sold, leaving musicians with no pay and no recourse. For this reason many musicians distribute their music through vendors via the informal economy. Rather than giving away their product to multinational companies, which will price the CDs too expensively and pay no royalties, they produce it themselves and offer it in the local market at a price people can pay.[53]

The situation is only more difficult for musicians in nation-states where the government suppresses music, for underground music is by definition difficult to regulate. In Iran, for example, rap music with socially critical lyrics is forbidden: musicians have been arrested and punished and illicit recording studios shut down.[54] Several musicians have left the country, but they still make their music in the Farsi language, so the largest market for their music remains in Iran. These musicians cannot openly sell or distribute their recordings in Iran, but they cannot sell their music as downloads or streaming from abroad, either: as a result of international sanctions, most Iranians cannot complete banking or credit card transactions with people outside the country. The musicians give their music away for free, putting it onto many different apps and file-sharing sites so that it can be streamed at private parties in Iran.[55] When the state cannot see the musical activity it is supposed to regulate, it is difficult to imagine how it could enforce copyright law.

Brazil: Changing the Rules of the Game

Thus, the rules of copyright enforcement, established by wealthy countries, did not at all match the reality of how people use music in low-income countries. Even while the Brazilian government attempted to comply with TRIPS, Brazilians developed an alternative model for thinking about intellectual property that challenged the WTO's model of cultural ownership. The Brazilian Ministry of Culture introduced a model called "Living Culture" (Cultura viva), based on a principle of shared resources rather than locked-down resources. Instead of encouraging a few products from outside the country to dominate the market, the ministry sought to provide avenues for many people, even poor people, to become creators. Gilberto Gil, who served as Brazil's minister of culture from 2003 to 2008, stated that his policy of "digital inclusion" was "inspired by the ethics of the *hacker*"—allowing remixing and even theft as means of participation.[56] Gil declared that citizens have a right to culture and that law should accommodate the real needs of citizens.[57] He hoped not only to revitalize the arts but also to support a cooperative model of citizenship that gave more people access to knowledge.[58]

Gil had been a famous singer and songwriter since the 1960s, and he resumed his career as a recording artist after leaving the Ministry of Culture in 2008. As a singer, he helped develop the Tropicália movement, which rejected efforts to create a Brazilian musical nationalism based solely on indigenous folk traits. Tropicália music emphasized internationalism and mixing: Afro-Brazilian elements blended with electric guitar or other elements imported from rock 'n' roll. In formulating their idea of mixture, Gil and the other Tropicálists drew on Brazilian theories of modernization from the 1920s. The Brazilian writer Oswald de Andrade believed that Brazil did not acquire its modern traits from being colonized by the Portuguese. Rather, as a proudly multiracial and multiethnic society, Brazil consumed and digested imported elements—in the manner of "cannibalism"—constantly producing something novel and meaningfully Brazilian.[59]

In 2005 Gil continued to claim "a mixture or a permanent recycling of values, references, sentiments, signs and races," as a principal feature of Brazilian society.[60] For Brazilians in the 2000s, that mixing also meant recirculation of ideas. Countries that could hardly afford to pay US or European prices for patented medications argued that these forms of intellectual property had to be loosened for humanitarian reasons. Likewise, the expense of purchasing software hampered efforts to improve industry in Latin America. Many viewed the high price of legal music purchases as a similar impediment. Copyright or no, in Gil's view adopting and remixing all these elements served the best interests of Brazil's citizens. Gil's project website offered a bold statement: "Copy, remix and distribute these files freely, you'll be doing a favor to cultural diversity and strengthening an autonomous network of free knowledge."[61] It is not surprising that the Brazilian affiliate of the IFPI strenuously opposed Gil's efforts.[62]

When Gil took office, few homes and schools had internet access.[63] Under Gil and his successor, Juca Ferreira, the Ministry of Culture established "Culture Hotspots" (Pontos de cultura), distributing technology resources such as internet access and free software. Many Culture Hotspots featured recording studios or other communications technology. The ministry did not manage the hotspots: maintaining local community control made it more likely that the hotspots would take on projects that reflected the interests of people in that community.[64] For instance, some communities produced documentaries and fiction films in indigenous languages, not the colonial language, Portuguese. The hotspots would never become financially viable, for the ministry placed many of them in the poorest communities. Rather, these state-funded enterprises aimed to create an educated and technologically savvy citizenry with a lively community spirit.[65] The emphasis on local production also served to emphasize the heterogeneity and diversity of Brazilian music and to publicize that heterogeneity as an alternative to imported music promoted by the global record labels. At the height of the program, hundreds of hotspots had opened all over the country.[66]

Apart from funding the technology and training, the Ministry of Culture also facilitated communication among the hotspots through online exhibitions and social media sites. The ministry hoped to produce a digital archive of Brazilian music, called Canto Livre (Free song), produced by citizens and reflecting their tastes and preferences. This archive would include digitized versions of Brazilian music that had entered the public domain and, with the artists' agreement, works produced at the Culture Hotspots. During its brief existence the archive aimed to promote artists and connect citizens who would otherwise never meet. The Canto Livre idea closely resembles Benedict Anderson's theory of nationhood: Gil wanted Brazilians of many ethnicities and places of origin to experience contact with each other, sympathize with each other, and gain a sense of fellow-feeling.[67]

Gil made common cause with the Electronic Frontier Foundation, which seeks to preserve individual rights against corporate intrusion. As of 2010, international music labels controlled 86 percent of the Brazilian market for legal CD purchases.[68] Gil encouraged Brazilians to embrace Creative Commons licensing, a form of copyright that allows the artist to choose whether and under what circumstances the work can be repurposed. Instead of reserving a whole bundle of rights for the copyright holder, Creative Commons offers a menu of separate rights. In choosing a license, the artist can decide to allow some kinds of reuse but not others. All Creative Commons licenses require that the author be given credit; other elements that the author can choose are prohibiting commercial use, prohibiting derivative works (like remixes), and requiring any derivative work to be issued under the same Creative Commons license as the original.[69] If an artist wants to allow remixing, a Creative Commons license easily accommodates that option.

During Gil's administration, the Ministry of Culture promoted Creative Commons licensing on its website and through its educational projects. This promotion directly challenged both strict Brazilian copyright laws and the premises of the TRIPS agreement, encouraging more open sharing of music and therefore diminishing the need to spend money on enforcement. Apart from pushing back at global corporations, Gil sought to embrace a copyright arrangement that fit how Brazilian people used music. A licensing scheme that allowed derivative works, for example, would legitimate tecnobrega and other forms of remixing that played important roles in Brazilians' lives. The ministry also hoped that the government's promotion of music would increase its circulation and allow musicians to earn more money through live performances.[70]

After 2011, with the election of a new president, a new minister of culture was appointed. Ana de Hollanda reversed the policies Gil had put into place. She revoked the Ministry of Culture's support for Creative Commons licenses. She vastly reduced the budgets for the Culture Hotspots and declined to meet with the hotspots' managers. The ministry has taken down the Canto Livre archives website and other sites associated with Gil's Culture Hotspots project. Several observers noted that Hollanda met frequently with representatives of the internationally affiliated trade groups that represented the recording industry: these observers attributed the ministry's abrupt change of course to her alliance with the industry.[71] Because the changeable will of governments affects both copyright law and international commitments to enforcement, efforts like Gil's remain fragile.

Copyright Enforcement and Global Power

The decline of Gil's Culture Hotspots happened around the same time as a shift in global corporations' strategy. Rather than waiting for the US Trade Representative and the WTO to act on piracy, the IFPI began to act more directly. The IFPI tracked illegal copies to their sources all over the world and asked local law enforcement officials to raid the producers, seizing the materials used to create the illegal copies.

For example, in August of 2008, in and around the market of the Tepito neighborhood in Mexico City, 375 police officers and 10 prosecutors from the Mexican Attorney General's office stormed 70 warehouses and 15 laboratories to seize pirated music and related equipment. The police seized approximately 410,000 recorded CD-Rs/DVDs, three million covers, and 850 CDR/DVD burners. The Mexican government had recently agreed to invest in intellectual property enforcement, and the government worked with the local industry antipiracy group APCM, which is affiliated with the IFPI, to carry out the raids.[72]

Also in 2012, the IFPI coordinated an international effort to close the torrent website Demonoid, asking INTERPOL, an organization that coordinates police forces across borders, to intervene. Ukrainian police seized computer servers and closed down the site, and Mexican authorities arrested several people. John Newton, who led INTERPOL's Trafficking in Illicit Goods Sub-Directorate, explained that "international police cooperation is the key to ensuring that the illegal activities of transnational organised criminals are stopped."[73] This case involved police from multiple countries, coordinated and informed by the agenda of the music industry.

Global music corporations are using the policing and military resources of their own and foreign governments to enforce their (private) rights and set the norms by which people live. According to the sociologist Saskia Sassen this is not an isolated incident but an arrangement characteristic of our times: "It has become increasingly common for rules originated by private actors to be eventually enacted by governments."[74] The private and public spheres are blurred together: where earlier the IFPI may have taken offenders to court in a particular nation-state and waited for the government of that nation-state to intervene, it now engages directly with police forces to carry out its aims. Increasingly, no one can hold the IFPI accountable because the organization is acting across international borders and using agents who are presumed to be enforcing the law.[75]

The idea that what is good for industry is good for the public at large is known as **neoliberalism**—"liberal" in the sense of allowing corporations to have liberty to pursue their interests.[76] The IFPI's efforts to make copyright enforcement global and require restrictions favorable to the United States are a form of neoliberalism that aligns with the popular notion of "globalization." With the support of world institutions like the WTO, international corporations and national governments have extended their reach around the world, shaping faraway events. Whereas the governments of nation-states formerly set the rules for corporations within their borders, the corporations are now dictating to governments what the rules should be and even intervening directly in other countries, disregarding borders. For this reason many thinkers say that globalization has made the nation-state less important and the corporation more important.[77]

Yet the effort to globalize the IFPI's and the WTO's concept of copyright enforcement is not exclusively imposed by powerful corporations. Many economists who specialize in development believe that the way to distribute the world's wealth more equally is to monetize existing resources—to bring these resources into the economy by assigning them exchange value. A monetized economy facilitates trade and connects the local economy to that of the rest of the world. Some economists and some commentators, including many in lower-income countries, believe that this connectedness would offer better livelihoods for citizens in those countries and contribute to stability and security of "the world order."[78] The UN's WIPO organization aims to support lower-income countries in entering the world's intellectual property economy. This argument is founded on the idea that even if the economy is structured in a way that favors large international corporations, participation in the economy still offers better opportunities than nonparticipation.

Some musicians and record industry executives in lower-income countries echo this sentiment. When the IFPI list of influential music markets for 2013 did not include Nigeria, for instance, music blogger and writer Ayomide Tayo blamed the lack of a "functioning music industry." Tayo observed that "the revenue that this so called industry of ours is making has been cut short by piracy, traditional media and the internet. We need to aggressively battle these monsters before we can start making serious revenue in this country."[79] An entertainment lawyer quoted in the same article advocated for stricter intellectual property laws, which would support the monetization of music.

Likewise, in many parts of the world, music industry executives and government officials subscribe to the IFPI's claim that piracy is bad for music, for musicians, and for economies. In Thailand, music industry officials claim that trade in pirated goods costs billions of dollars and takes away artists' and music corporations' incentive to make music.[80] Recognizing that the World Trade Organization's regulations did a poor job of meeting the needs of people in lower-income countries, the World Bank has joined the Senegalese government and musicians to create "The Africa Music Project," "an ongoing effort by World Bank staff to help Africans to advance the business and cultural potential of their music." The project's authors raised the possibility that "the legal environment should not be imposed from outside," but the platform calls for the institution of copyright tracking, elimination of piracy, and legal reform.[81]

These musicians are in a bind: if they do not accede to the WTO's copyright model, they may not receive payment for their work, and their music may not be protected from theft. According to Brazilian musician Gilson Neto, "In 1998, one CD that costs two dollars to make, and I sold for seven dollars. And the profit for my recording label was five dollars per CD sold. Today in 2002, the pirate is the one who sells the most of my CDs."[82] If they do accede, however, they face uncertainties. Will their legal recordings sell well enough to generate royalties? Will the laws be applied fairly? How will existing modes of music-making respond to the disruption caused by enforcement actions? Many musicians in lower-income countries face all these challenges. According to the ethnomusicologist Ryan Skinner, musicians in Mali want their nation-state to protect their work by law and to bring about an order that facilitates their livelihoods.[83] In an environment where nation-states do not deliver on the promise of order, though, and the "big three" music corporations favor a few highly successful artists and neglect others, most musicians do not feel the benefit of the promises made by the IFPI, WIPO, and the WTO.[84]

The choice to participate in the global distribution system may enable artists to market music on a worldwide scale, but because many have been left in obscurity by large record companies, they have little reason to trust this system. Recent evidence suggests that in an uncertain climate for intellectual property rights, musicians and labels are trying many different alternative tactics. In Brazil, for example, some are signing recording contracts with major labels or their affiliates, and some are signing on with independent labels that seek to control the pipeline from recordings to concerts in the manner of tecnobrega. Some are designing their own online platforms to sell individual tracks via mobile phone, and some are licensing their music primarily to film companies rather than trying to sell it as stand-alone work.[85] A variety of intermediaries have sprung up: e-commerce sites that sell music from multiple labels, shops where one can buy mp3s in exchange for a low monthly subscription fee, and streaming services. Many of these intermediaries exist for only a short while because their business models have proved unsustainable.[86] Even as Brazilian musicians and distributors seek access to global markets, they are also competing with each other for that access: this competition can intensify already existing rivalries between cities or musical styles.[87]

The large international record companies have named streaming as the future of their industry—not only in countries where these services are well established but also in countries where today's music industry is not within their reach. In a 2014 speech IFPI official Adrian Strain observed that streaming services have grown fast, from a handful of markets to worldwide in just a few years, and that they might be especially important in world regions where copyright protection has historically been weak.[88] The cost of legal CDs in Brazil has been so high that stores have offered installment plans so that customers can make payments over time to buy even a single disc.[89] With the advent of streaming, which reduces the likelihood of illegal copying, the IFPI plans to make price adjustments that will make the legal product affordable and guide people into the regulated digital enclosure.[90]

The anthropologist Anna Tsing has called the idea of globalization a "dream space" where ambitions have free play: for the people leading international corporations a global market appears to be a vast opportunity for expanding sales and profits.[91] From this perspective it is easy to imagine music moving effortlessly from place to place. It is also easy to imagine a uniform enforcement network that ensures that each customer, anywhere in the world, pays equally for the music they use.

When we look more closely, though, we see that the global free market does not operate smoothly; as Tsing points out, there is friction in the network. Some of this friction is created by practical obstacles. A minority of musicians—most of them from the US, Europe, or East Asia—can access global channels of distribution and copyright protection. Most cannot. A significant number of nation-states cannot enforce the supposedly global trade agreements that protect copyright, and listeners, artists, and vendors resist when the rules of ownership defined in those agreements do not protect their interests.

Disagreements of principle create further friction. Not everyone shares the vision of the digital enclosure. Those who have enjoyed music as a shared public good may find that use diminished or cut off by the monetization of their music.[92] As representatives of Brazil, Argentina, and many other countries have pointed out, the TRIPS agreement favors copyright holders, not the makers, users, or remixers of music.[93] If one cares about music for its use value, and wants to be able to share it with others, this balance may seem unfair: it certainly takes the control of music away from the many to place it in the hands of the few. This arrangement perpetuates the social inequalities that long plagued the colonized world: the TRIPS agreement appears to ensure continuing economic inequality by affirming the dominance of corporations' rights over musicians' interests.

While the effortless and well-regulated ideal of a global music market exists in the "dream space," the actual practice of regulating copyright internationally remains neither stable nor orderly. Under the neoliberal model the corporate copyright holders of the US, Europe, and Japan hold a great deal of power: they collaborate closely with the governments of wealthy nation-states to protect their interests, and these governments negotiate international agreements that set the rules for everyone. Many in the developing world have challenged this model, but for now, copyright holders seem to have the upper hand in controlling how music moves.

8 Localizations

Mediated Selves Mixing Musics

We have seen throughout this book that through migration and media, people have moved musics and blended them into new combinations. Instances of border-crossing or musical borrowing are more norm than exception. The terms people use to discuss global movements of people and music, like **deterritorialization** (moving the music out of its place of origin) and **localization** (settling the music into a new location), can make this movement sound like an orderly process, like snipping out a patch of fabric and sewing it on somewhere else.

These terms also tend to leave the individual out of the frame, treating the movement of music as a by-product of global forces. The impersonal nature of these terms reflects the tendency, prevalent since World War II, to see the world as a "system" and to think about its workings using technological language. The idea of modernization—bringing all world systems into efficient alignment—predates this period, but the worldwide institutions that support modernization came into existence during the United Nations era. The engagement of international corporations in creating and maintaining "labor forces" that serve their purposes, the remaking of persons as "consumers," and measurements of economic productivity all manifest this kind of thinking. Likewise, by conveying information to vast audiences, our communications systems incorporate individuals into larger wholes, whether those be nations, states, political parties, or other groups. This top-down, system-oriented view may suggest that technologies such as broadcasting, the digital music file, and the internet cause music to move along paths made by globalized states and corporations.[1]

The idea of a UN-style showcase of "cultures," discussed in chapter 5, also manifests "world systems" thinking. It presents an orderly picture of the world in which each group of people is distinct, known, and valued. The United

Nations has long encouraged the view that each country has "the right and the duty" to safeguard both tangible works of art and **intangible cultural heritage**—that is, "oral traditions, performing arts, social practices, rituals, festive events, knowledge and practices concerning nature and the universe or the knowledge and skills to produce traditional crafts."[2] As we saw with Mexico's Ballet Folklórico in chapter 5, in the UN era states and peoples have made it standard practice to represent themselves by performing heritage. Furthermore, the United Nations has urged its member states to make laws that discourage alteration of musical traditions and to found institutes for their preservation. Nation-states have embraced this idea: many have honed their individual brands by packaging their heritage for consumption by others through media or tourism. Although the UN system promotes the "**modernization**" that would bring many nations into similar forms of governance, at the same time it also fosters this well-contained traditionalism.[3]

The idea of modernization is troubling, since it involves comparing all the world's peoples to Europe or the United States and finding them lacking.[4] Seeing the world as a system in this way can also lead us to think in rigid ways about groups of people. The philosopher Kwame Anthony Appiah notes that early in the United Nations era, in 1954, a number of countries signed an agreement ensuring the protection of "cultural property" during wartime (the Hague Convention). Many works of art had been destroyed during World War II. The countries that signed the convention promised to try to preserve the arts rather than destroying them. The Hague Convention says that "*each people* makes its contribution to the cultures of the world." Appiah observes:

> That sounds like whenever someone makes a contribution, his or her "people" makes a contribution, too. And there's something odd, to my mind, about thinking of Hindu temple sculpture or Michelangelo and Raphael's frescos in the Vatican as the contribution of a people rather than the contribution of the individuals who made (and, if you like, paid for) them. . . . This is clearly the wrong way to think about the matter. The right way is to take not a national but a trans-national perspective—to ask what system of international rules about objects of this sort will respect the many legitimate human interests at stake.[5]

As Appiah sees it, we lose something important when we think of a work of art as belonging mainly or only to its country or people of origin. Often, especially in a mediated world, art has meaning not only for the group to which the art's maker belongs but also for many people outside that group. Appiah believes that these art lovers, too, should be taken into consideration.

Appiah's observation points to the complexity of individuals' artistic practices and attachments in a mediated world. When individuals make music, they may or may not be thinking about representing their own groups, whether national, ethnic, or otherwise. As we have seen (chapter 6), musical allegiances may be inherited, but they can also be chosen. People have personal wishes for how music should sound; they connect to a variety of traditions; they respond to their local markets and the desires of audiences. It is tricky to understand what is going on here: to get a grip on worldwide phenomena, like colonialism or globalization, it is useful to see the big picture. At the same time, the only way to know what those phenomena mean is to see how they play out in the lives of individuals or neighborhoods.

This chapter introduces some diasporic Korean people whose individual musical choices reflect a variety of artistic allegiances. We will also meet musicians from South Africa, Morocco, and Egypt who have adopted hip-hop from afar. These people are globally connected, yet their music-making also offers us insight into their specific local and personal situations. In thinking about these individuals and their particular kinds of connectedness in a diasporic and mediated world, we will see that heritage and tradition become flexible concepts. Members of diasporas relate to their histories and their families' historic places of origin in complicated ways. They may travel or learn a language to reconnect with their families' places of origin, study genealogy, take up a musical practice that is also valued in the place of origin, change their inherited music to fit a new context, or seek to assimilate in their current homes. We will also see that, in a mediated world, individuals may, for their own reasons, become deeply attached to music originating elsewhere, and that attachment may itself generate further long-distance contacts through travel or media.

The anthropologist Nestór García Canclini can help us understand all this complex motion. He defines "hybridization" as a strategic process in which people choose to blend practices that used to be separate, generating something new. This process can include the adoption of an existing musical practice by new people or the purposeful blending of styles. According to Canclini the mixing of musics does not result from an impersonal global process but from individual and group creativity. People change their artistic practices, affiliating themselves with unfamiliar musical traditions or renovating heritage to tell a new story about the present day.[6]

Whether it happens by taking up a new kind of music or by making a mixture of musics, that change in practice is a form of appropriation—the "taking to oneself" of music that was not originally one's own. In Canclini's view, when individuals creatively reuse or adapt music, that process need not be regarded as theft. Rather, Canclini calls those reuses "strategies for entering and leaving modernity." By *modernity* Canclini means the European vision of cosmopolitan modernity developed during the long era of colonialism, for that idea has had enormous influence in many places. Like the self-concept of the Europeans who visited the Paris Exposition in 1889, this vision of the modern may include an industrialized economy, the use of ever-advancing science and technology, a well-functioning administrative state, and styles of music that change rapidly in their movement toward the "new." Whereas Europeans used this idea to separate themselves from peoples they deemed "primitive" (chapter 1), many non-Europeans also adopted the "modern" as a standard by which to measure their own lives and societies (chapter 5). Like the idea of **race** or the concept of **authenticity**, this idea of what is "modern" has no basis in fact: it is a story people have told to create, enforce, and explain social divisions among groups of people.

Canclini sees that people in formerly colonized parts of the world routinely apply the categories of the modern (universal, global, changing) and the traditional (particular, local, unchanging—"the folk"). Yet in the **postcolonial** world people's experiences are neither "all modern" or "all traditional": most lives encompass some combination of the two. By adapting or adopting music, individuals can participate in what feels new, or what feels like heritage, or both. Through art artists define their own positions with respect to other art—which can mean choosing styles that represent a particular perspective as universal or local, modern or traditional.[7] The many people who live in that "in between" or mixed state use music to define and express the complexity of their situations. More broadly, any time we see appropriation, we may want to ask, When this artist mixes musics, what kind of world is the artist entering (or creating), and what is she or he leaving behind? Appropriations and mixes are commonplace and not always abusive; these practices can embody a host of emotions and perspectives.

A Mediated Diaspora: Koreans and Korean Americans

We can see some of that complexity in the musical lives of **diasporic** Koreans. According to the US 2010 census, 1.7 million people of Korean descent live in the United States; another 100,000 live in Canada (fig. 8.1).[8] The migration of Koreans to the United States is closely tied to the history of military, political, and religious connections between the two countries. Protestant Christian missionaries from the United States began to arrive in Korea in 1884, introducing their church music along with their religion. Between 1901 and 1905 the missionaries encouraged emigration to the US. They recommended that sugar planters conscript Korean people and bring them to the US colony of Hawaii as low-wage laborers. Korean Christians also came to the mainland US in search of education. During the Japanese colonial occupation of Korea (1910–45) the occupiers took many Koreans by force or deception to work in Japan, especially during wartime (1939–45). Only a small number of Korean people came to the United States during this period. Between 1945 and the end of the Korean War (1953), the United States military occupied the southern part of Korea, the Soviet Union the northern part: these occupations established political and musical relationships that supported later travel and migration patterns.[9]

After the Korean War about 100,000 Korean women and children entered the country as family members of American soldiers. Afraid that South Korea would turn toward communism, the United States continued to provide aid for economic development, including bank loans and support for building a capitalist economy based on manufacturing. US officials also offered unofficial support for Christianity in South Korea, as they believed religion was a safeguard against the secularism of communism: today, about 30 percent of South Koreans practice Christianity. These business and religious relationships developed countless collaborative ties between US and Korean people, introducing a steady stream of international travel for university students, venture capitalists, managers, church pastors, and choral directors.[10]

In 1965 a new law, the Immigration and Nationality Act, changed how US government officials decided which **immigrants** to admit. Because racial discrimination had become an embarrassment for the United States in world public opinion, the act disallowed discrimination on the basis of race and national origin. Before 1965, US law purposefully gave white western and northern Europeans priority, but the new law used categories like professional training, close family relationships, and refugee status to establish immigration quotas. With this new protection in place many Koreans—especially doctors and others with in-demand skills—migrated to the United States in search of better opportunities.[11] Still, some experienced a significant decline in wealth and social status on arrival in the United States.[12]

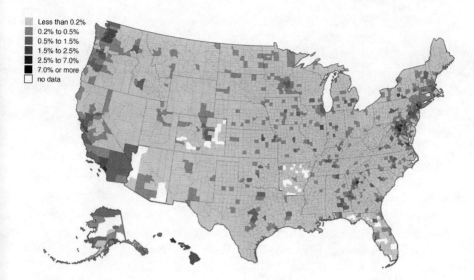

Fig. 8.1. *Music on the Move:* Korean population of the United States. This map by Eric Fosler-Lussier, based on an original map by Matt Stiles in the *Daily Viz*, illustrates the percentage of people in each county who identified themselves as Korean in the 2010 US Census. Overall, 1.7 million people in the United States claimed Korean identity. (See https://doi.org/10.3998/mpub.9853855.cmp.116)

Today, some Korean Americans live in ethnic enclaves—that is, areas where a high concentration of Korean people live and work in close proximity, often doing business in the Korean language and retaining a strong ethnic identity that separates them from the surrounding community.[13] Others have partly or fully **assimilated**, absorbing the language and practices of other US communities around them. One cannot assume that Asian Americans, or any other diasporic group, hold a primary allegiance to their Asian homelands; indeed, in the past this assumption has led to unjust persecution of loyal US citizens.[14] There are probably as many approaches to being Korean American as there are Korean Americans: patriotism for the United States may be mixed with experiences of racial discrimination, nostalgia or curiosity about Korea, a variety of chosen and inherited musical preferences, and much more. While acknowledging the diversity of these experiences, we can observe some practices that are common among this diasporic population and shared with other diasporic groups as well.

Classical Circuits

The world of European-style **concert music** (or "classical" music) has long consisted of international circuits. We have seen that colonialism and modernization efforts took this music to new places. Since the 1700s, it has been possible for performers of concert music to make international reputations by traveling widely.[15] After World War II these circuits became more geographically inclusive, and they have been shaped by political alliances. During the Cold War, Soviet Russia supplied North Korean, Chinese, and Eastern European orchestras with financial support, conductors, and soloists. The United States cultivated similar relationships with Japan, Korea, the Philippines, and Western Europe. And both the US and the USSR sought to build connections with nonaligned countries.[16]

According to the musicologist Hye-jung Park, European classical music was one way the United States strengthened its relationship with Korea. The US occupation government in South Korea sponsored a European-style orchestra. Korean educators and the US occupation government worked to include European-style concert music in new Korean school curricula. In fact, until recently, a Korean child could easily grow up with an extensive education in European concert music but no familiarity with Korean traditional music.[17] Korean composers began to compose music to be performed by Western-style orchestras. In addition US officials offered individual Korean musicians grants that allowed them to visit the United States for training. Teachers and students remained in contact across the Pacific, reinforcing firm connections between Korean arts institutions and schools of music in the United States. For South Korean musicians, travel to famous music schools like the Juilliard School in New York became a mark of prestige. Grace Wang, an American studies scholar, writes that for many Asian and Asian American parents, participation in European classical music is a mark of inclusion in a prestigious and globally valued practice, as well as a sign of education and hard work.[18]

Even though Korea has excellent teachers of Western concert music, many young musicians have continued to travel to the United States. For decades the arrival of talented and meticulously trained musicians from Asia has aroused considerable media attention in the West. One of the earliest instances of international fame was the Chung family. Siblings Kyung Wha Chung, Myung Wha Chung, and Myung Whun Chung moved to New York with their parents in the 1960s to continue their musical training. They gained great fame, performing as a trio and as soloists. Kyung Wha Chung, who had already been famous as a child prodigy on the violin in Korea, studied at the Juilliard School from her early teens and at age 19 won a major international competition. In her early 20s she performed as a violin soloist with major orchestras in Europe and the United States. Her sister, the cellist Myung Wha Chung, developed an international career as a performer and teacher: she has taught at the Mannes College of Music in New York and the Korean National University of the Arts in Seoul.

Their brother, Myung Whun Chung, built an international career as a conductor, traveling to lead major orchestras in Europe, the United States, and Asia. He served as principal conductor of the Radio France Philharmonic Orchestra in Paris, and for ten years he was the music director of the Seoul Philharmonic. During his tenure in Seoul the German record company Deutsche Grammophon granted the orchestra a large recording contract. The Seoul Philharmonic was the first Asian orchestra to receive this much attention from a Western recording company. Chung's response to the record deal was revealing: in an interview he said he hoped the deal would become a "footing for Seoul Philharmonic to become a world class orchestra."[19] Although Asian musicians have attained celebrity status throughout the international circuit, and Asian orchestras have performed very well for decades, a hierarchy persists. As the European tradition did not originate with Asian performers, people in the West have typically not regarded them as equal participants. The effort to "become" world-class has been part of Asian conversations about concert music for more than 60 years.[20]

Indeed, despite their conspicuous successes, many of these musicians have experienced discrimination. Some critics still make the racist charge that Asian performers may have technical merit but cannot understand or perform European music as a person of European descent can.[21] Asian musicians' adoption of European concert music seems to be one of Canclini's strategies for "entering modernity," but that entry is sometimes challenged. Blind auditions, in which judges hear musicians play but cannot see them, have increased access to orchestra jobs for members of racial minorities and women.[22] Yet most performing opportunities cannot happen behind a screen. Although participants in classical music continue to view music as a meritocracy, slurs and stereotypes persist. Even in the age of globalization, music does not flow unhindered among peoples: race-based exclusion is one form of friction in the system.[23]

Despite the continuing bias against Asian musicians, Asia has become a vital site for the cultivation and preservation of the European concert music tradition. When an interviewer asked the Korean American violinist Sarah

Chang about declining ticket sales for classical music in the United States, Chang responded, "I'm actually not too worried about this at all. Take my concerts in Hong Kong: they're sold out."[24] The white American violinist Joshua Bell likewise reports tremendous audience enthusiasm in Asia for European-style concert music: "Whenever I play in Korea, I feel like I'm at a rock concert."[25] Some critics in the US and Europe who value European-style concert music have mourned the demographic shift of interest in it to Asia, seeing it as a marker of decline of education and "values" in the West. Some talk about the "death" or "decline" of classical music, even though the music is evidently flourishing.[26] Like the racist critiques of Asian performers, this mourning invokes the idea of heritage. Does classical music belong to Europeans and their genetic heirs, exclusively? Or should this tradition be passed along to anyone who wants to invest the time and effort, just as any tradition can be handed down?

If these questions were really about the past, we might note that European concert music was never a unified tradition, ethnically or otherwise. But like other arguments about heritage these questions are not really about the past or about ascertainable historical facts. Rather, they reflect a use of the past by present-day people who are concerned about their place in the present-day world. To be sure, vestiges of the colonial past linger in the values of the present. As we saw in the cases of Japan and Turkey, in the 1800s and 1900s people outside Europe sought entry to the tradition because Europe seemed modern and powerful. Today, when people make the unfounded assertion that Asian musicians' performances lack an undefined "special something" compared to white peers, they are protecting their exclusive connection to the prestigious music by policing others' access to that music. When critics mourn the "death" of a music that is still living, they choose to ignore the contributions of Asian musicians and many others. The idea that concert music is a **heritage** that Europeans or European Americans can have, but Asians cannot quite fully possess, relies on the manufacture of an artificial difference between peoples.[27]

Participation in **traditions** is not inert or value-neutral. According to Canclini joining a tradition or combining traditions is a strategic act that places people into particular roles. A person can gain access to a tradition or be excluded from it; a person can take up a tradition or abandon it; a person can be made to feel superior or subordinate through their participation in a tradition. The very idea of prestige implies that only some people have access: and opening a tradition to anyone who wants it changes that social hierarchy, placing people into new and possibly uncomfortable roles. Thus, a discussion about heritage is one way that social differences can be maintained and conflicts can be played out: a place where the friction is visible.[28]

As Canclini has pointed out, though, attempts to draw firm boundaries separating "cultures" or groups are futile.[29] Music undergoes "continuous processes of transculturation," which the anthropologist Renato Rosaldo defines as "two-way borrowing and lending."[30] Seen from this perspective, the Asian adoption of Western music is a normal outcome of transnational interactions spanning more than 100 years. If people want to sustain the musical tradition, they might rejoice to see its worldwide adoption. But if they are invested in maintaining prestige or difference, they might instead continue to insist on using heritage or racial claims to draw boundaries. Because migration and media have deterritorialized and reterritorialized music, the relationships between the traditional and the modern, or between the central and the peripheral, are in flux.[31] The transnational aspect of European classical music is no longer a footnote to its history: it is central to the tradition's development in the 20th and 21st centuries. This destabilization of value and perspective, and the conflicts and frictions that come with it, are part of what people mean when they talk about globalization.

These conflicts and frictions also shape the work of composers of concert music. Hyo-Shin Na (1959–) is a Korean-born composer based in San Francisco, California. After studying piano and composition in Korea, she attended the Manhattan School of Music and the University of Colorado. She has traveled back to Korea repeatedly; there, she took up the study of Korean traditional music and East Asian music more generally. She maintains an active career in the San Francisco Bay area, and many organizations in that region have paid her commissions to compose pieces of music. She has won awards for her compositions on both sides of the Pacific.

Na has defined her Asian American identity with care. According to a recent liner note, Na has said, "I am no longer trying to write Korean music; nor am I trying not to write Korean music."[32] We can hear what Na means by listening to a piece entitled "Koto, Piano II," composed in 2016. As the title implies, the music is a duet between a Japanese instrument, the *koto*, which is played by plucking and scraping the strings, and a European instrument, the piano, which strikes its internal strings with felt hammers. Each instrument offers a resonant quality, as the vibration of the strings takes a while to decay. Yet the different sound qualities of plucking and striking mean that this piece is never quite unified: the two instruments retain their identities as they coexist. For those who are familiar with Japanese music, or have heard it in films, the sound of the koto is strongly associated with Japan, and listeners may bring this association with them as they approach the piece.

This music, heard in example 8.1, encourages the two performers to listen very closely to each other and to play in close synchronization: for the first minute of the piece, they play nearly (but not quite) in **unison**. Next, they begin to play separately but echoing each other's phrases, sometimes coming back together for a short while. At timepoint 1:34, and again at 2:47, they play a short refrain, a recurring section, in which their parts are not identical but fit together well. At timepoint 5:58 they play in unison again, then move apart once more as the piece comes to a close.

Example 8.1. Hyo-Shin Na, "Koto, Piano II," performed by Shoko Hikage, koto, and Thomas Schultz, piano, in 2017. YouTube.
Link: https://doi.org/10.3998/mpub.9853855.cmp.117

By the end of the piece the listener is accustomed to the interplay of sound qualities and may forget that the two instruments represent different musical traditions; the musicians perform as equals throughout the piece, and their play of sameness and difference seems to be amicable and cooperative.

Na's paradox—not trying to write music marked as "Asian," and not trying to *not* write such music—rings true for this work. The Asian instrument here (Japanese, not Korean) is integrated not as an exotic sound but simply as a way to make sound of equal importance to the chosen Western instrument, cooperating but not blending. The tuning of the koto means that its scale patterns will predominate, but the two instruments adapt to each other throughout. Like some of the examples of "next-generation mediated selves" we met in chapter 6, this music models a form of integration in which the origin of the instruments is less important than the sounds they make.

The transnational composer faces audience expectations that make all her compositional choices a little harder. If Hyo-Shin Na composes music that audiences find "stereotypically Korean," she may run the risk of limiting her audience, being labeled as a specialty composer who only writes for Korean or Asian audiences. Yet the story line of "uncovering one's heritage" or "returning to one's roots" has become a powerful marketing tool that has demonstrated appeal for audiences—another use of the heritage idea in the present day. This story line takes the "difference" that many in US audiences still attribute to Asian people and converts it into an asset by marking this music as distinctive or authentic as compared to all other new compositions. Composing music that does not draw on the expected heritage could mean losing this useful branding device.[33]

Throughout her career Na's strategy as a composer has been to create many kinds of music. The composition called *Ten Thousand Ugly Ink Blots* (example 8.2) bears no obvious markers of Asian identity. This piece, composed for a string quartet (two violins, viola, and cello), belongs to the genre called experimental music or **New Music**. (Though the genre is no longer new, its participants value modern novelty.) At the beginning of the piece the notes are separated from each other so that they sound like isolated points rather than a melody.

Example 8.2. Excerpt from Hyo-shin Na, "Ten Thousand Ugly Ink Blots."
All the Noises (New World Records, 2008).
Link: https://doi.org/10.3998/mpub.9853855.cmp.118

This strategy echoes modern Austrian music of the 1930s, such as Anton Webern's String Quartet opus 28. Other pieces, like *That Old Woman*, rely more prominently on Asian musical instruments—used sometimes in traditional ways, sometimes unconventionally. Na has made herself hard to pigeonhole by offering many different approaches to music-making. She freely uses her own strategies for entering and leaving the Asian traditional music world and the New Music world. Sometimes she stands in the doorway between the two.

Na's history is marked not only by assimilation of the musical practices of Euro-America but also by conscious and careful mixing of traditions, crafting a sensibility of multiple possible selves. This kind of cross-cultural thinking is not something that just happened to Na as a result of her migration; rather, it is a personal strategy for understanding and working with the challenges and opportunities that come with such a move.[34]

Traditional Music in the Global Flow

The ongoing relationship between some diasporic Koreans and the nation-state of South Korea has been cultivated by the South Korean government through music and heritage practices, with assistance from the US government and the United Nations. In the late 1940s the US occupation government in Korea sponsored a festival of Korean traditional music—that is, folk music. The festival helped reestablish a style of Korean percussion band music that had been suppressed during the Japanese occupation of Korea. Once called *nongak*—"farmer's music"—the music is now more often called **p'ung-mul**, reflecting the fact that it is no longer primarily a rural music.[35] The devastation of the Korean War temporarily halted the music's restoration, but after the war some Korean scholars and performers reinvigorated the tradition. They founded the National Center for Korean Traditional Performing Arts to support research into old practices and courses in which people could learn to perform traditional music.[36] As a revival of heritage, this new cultivation of p'ungmul did not precisely recreate what had come before; rather, it drew on the past in ways that made sense in the present. Whereas p'ungmul had once been an art practiced only by men, after 1958 the revival included all-female and mixed troupes. Since that time educational institutions have adopted p'ungmul into their curricula, protest movements have taken the music up as a populist symbol, tourist agencies have promoted it, and the South Korean government has supported its propagation through cultural institutions in Korea and abroad.[37]

P'ungmul originated as rural processional music involving drums, gongs, and wind instruments. The performers wear colorful costumes and festive hats, and they carry their instruments with them as they dance in circular, spiral, or zigzag patterns. The music is organized as a sequence of different rhythmic patterns, moving from slower patterns to faster ones. Both in Korea and in Korean American communities p'ungmul has been associated with festivals: the Lunar New Year, the May festival, the conclusion of the weeding of the rice in July, and the harvest in October.[38]

Between 1961 and 1979 the South Korean military government of Chung-Hee Park took stringent actions toward modernization of villages, abolishing a variety of village community rituals as "superstition." At the same time, though, the state took steps to preserve "cultural heritage," passing a Cultural Asset Preservation Law that supported further restoration of art forms the Japanese occupation had suppressed. These restoration efforts paralleled and were supported by the work of the United Nations. In 1972 UNESCO (the United Nations Educational, Scientific and Cultural Organization) issued a *Convention Concerning the Protection of World Cultural and Natural Heritage*. Nation-states could apply to the UN for special status and funding that would aid the preservation of art forms that seemed in danger of dying out. UN recognition also brought the preserved art forms to the attention of tourists. Thus, the Korean government had an incentive to preserve at least some elements of older music.[39]

Official state recognition of "Important Intangible Cultural Assets" in Korea led to the institutionalization of p'ungmul and the sponsorship of national competitions that showcased it. P'ungmul performances became more standardized across the country. When a regional style gained national recognition, sometimes groups in other regions adopted that style, even though it did not originate in their region. By law, however, the government officially recognizes and cultivates five distinct regional styles of p'ungmul.[40]

One Korean p'ungmul group, called Rumbling Sound (Sori Ulrim), recorded this concert performance of p'ungmul in 2012 (example 8.3).[41] This is a staged performance of p'ungmul: you can see the audience in the background, seated around the stage. The words on the backdrop say "Our Melody, Our Courtyard," pointing to the traditional setting for p'ungmul: the wording is purposefully antiquated, directing the listener to notice the traditional nature of this performance.

Example 8.3. Excerpt from Sori Ulrim (Rumbling Sound), p'ungmul performance at the Daejeon Culture & Arts Center in 2012. YouTube.
Link: https://doi.org/10.3998/mpub.9853855.cmp.119

The first performers to enter after the banner play *soe*, small handheld gongs. Their part moves fast and articulates a rhythm based on fast groupings of three pulses. The players alternate between different patterns within that overall plan of pulses, so the crashing sound of the soe fills the air all the time (see fig. 8.2). The lead soe player directs the music-making of the entire p'ungmul group and decides when they should change to a different rhythmic pattern. Next in line we see two players carrying *ching* (larger gongs); their part simply marks the first beat of each cycle of pulses. The players who follow play the *changgo*—hourglass-shaped drums—with thin sticks. Then come the *puk*: circular, deeper-sounding drums that keep the beat. Several *sogo* players enter next. The sogo is a small, double-headed drum held by a handle; it contributes some sound to the pattern but largely serves as a dance prop. Difficult to see but easy to hear is the *hojŏk*, a cone-shaped wind instrument with a reedy tone. The hojŏk plays a nearly continuous and emphatic melody that lines up with the rhythmic pattern set out by the rest of the ensemble.[42] The groupings of three pulses within each beat are especially effective, as they coincide with the circular swinging of the ribbons draped from the players' hats. The overall effect, cheerful and celebratory, is suitable for a parade.

Once the entire group is onstage, at timepoint 0:54, the entire rhythmic

groups of three pulses											
1	**2**	**3**	**4**	**5**	**6**	**7**	**8**	**9**	**10**	**11**	**12**
soe	/	/		/	/		/		/	/	/
soe	/		/		/		/		/	/	/
ching	/										
changgo	/		/	/	/	/	/	/	/		/	/ (frequently "off the beat")
puk	/		/	/							
sogo	/			/				/			

Fig. 8.2. Rhythmic pattern featured in performance of the Sori Ulrim (Rumbling Sound) ensemble.

pattern changes: the new pattern is based on groups of two rather than three. A p'ungmul performance typically consists of several sections lasting between one and 10 minutes, each with distinct music and dance. A piece structured in this way is flexible: sections of music can be extended as long as necessary, and new sections can be added as needed. This flexibility makes the music suitable for neighborhood performance: a piece of music may last as long as it takes to walk to the next destination. As the performance continues, the ensemble moves into different formations, and the dancers perform more athletic steps and leaps, as well as more intricate maneuvers with the ribbons.

In Seoul the National Center for Korean Traditional Performing Arts is now part of the government's Ministry of Culture and Tourism. This agency seeks to popularize p'ungmul within Korea, sponsoring a variety of performances and educational events. A revived form of p'ungmul is also practiced by urban clubs in Seoul.[43] Since the 1970s, the Korean state has also fostered the practice of traditional Korean music in the United States.[44] The Ministry of Culture and Tourism operates two cultural centers in the United States, one in New York City and one in Los Angeles; these cities feature large enclaves known as "Koreatowns." These cultural centers mediate Korean music to people in the United States. With a primary aim of encouraging tourism among the general public, the Korean Cultural Center in Los Angeles conveys a selection of "heritage" practices: traditional music, dress, martial arts, and cooking. Jiwon Ahn, a scholar of film, has called this selection a "standardized" and "touristy" image of Korea.[45] At the same time, the center also offers programs that support the Korean American community, including concerts and exhibitions. Second- and third-generation Korean Americans learn the Korean language at the center, as do interested people who are not of Korean descent.

The practice of Korean music extends into the communities around the cultural centers. The ethnomusicologist Soojin Kim has described p'ungmul performances in New York and Los Angeles Koreatowns. Some of these performances purposefully preserve the ritual quality of village p'ungmul. Kim observes that collegiate p'ungmul groups in Southern California come together at the Lunar New Year and follow a tradition called *chishinbalkki*, which the Park regime marginalized in rural Korea. The group parades to local Korean-owned businesses (fig. 8.3). They perform p'ungmul at each shop they visit, and they give the shop owners a *pokjori*, made from two bamboo ladles, a symbol of luck to be hung on a wall. The performers also ask for donations to be used for projects benefiting the Korean community. Regardless of their ability to speak Korean, the students also learn to say New Year's greetings in a traditional dialect so they can greet community members. These US college students offer a variety of reasons for their participation in the New Year's ritual: community building, having fun in a group, supporting the Korean community, bringing good fortune to others, and experiencing or expressing a connection to Korean heritage.[46]

Other p'ungmul performances in the United States and Korea do not share this ritual function, although they may serve as entertainment, build community, or display elements of Korean heritage for non-Korean people. Every October in New York, a Korean newspaper sponsors an annual Korean parade and festival along Broadway, in which p'ungmul performers play. A similar parade takes place in Los Angeles: "a variety of Korean American associations, churches, community organizations, Korean bank branches, companies, and performing arts clubs have a procession through the street."[47] Kim has also documented a p'ungmul Christmas party in New Jersey and visits to schoolchildren that offer p'ungmul as an introduction to Korea.

In the village practice of the 1800s in Korea, p'ungmul was taught as oral tradition, passed down in memorized form from teacher to student. Today, it is much more commonly learned in classes and collegiate clubs or through textbooks and audiovisual media.[48] P'ungmul cultivates tourism: many p'ungmul practitioners in the United States, especially American-born Korean people, travel to Korea to attend workshops and performances. It is also difficult to acquire Korean instruments in the United States; therefore, US performers have an incentive to go to Korea to select instruments. Korean p'ungmul experts also travel to give intensive workshops in the United States.[49]

As teachers of p'ungmul are comparatively few in the United States, the circulation of media provides essential support for Korean American p'ung-

Fig. 8.3. A *chishinbalkki* performance by college *p'ungmul* clubs in front of a Korean grocery store in Los Angeles, 2007. Photograph by Soojin Kim. Used by permission.

mul performers. Korean media circulate through Korean ethnic enclaves in the United States: grocery stores in these enclaves sell compact discs and DVDs, and Korean Americans use the internet to watch Korean TV and movies. Some report a wish to maintain a connection, a feeling of "keeping up" with Korea as a homeland. Members of the Korean diaspora are numerous and form an important audience for media produced in Korea.[50]

In the global circulation of p'ungmul we can see how individual desires and institutional supports make possible a transnationally connected form of diaspora for Koreans and Korean Americans. Through media and travel, participants on both sides of the Pacific Ocean take part in this musical tradition. That the chosen music is village (folk) music is not coincidental. The efforts of the Korean government and the United Nations have encouraged individuals to connect to village music as heritage—a reuse of the past that is meaningful to them in the present day. In p'ungmul Korean Americans can participate in an imagined heritage by entering into a folk practice or, in Canclini's terms, "leaving modernity." At the same time, the transformation of p'ungmul and related genres into an international business supported by the South Korean nation-state suggests that the music has become a way of entering the show-case of global modernity envisioned by the United Nations.[51]

Hip-Hop as a "World Music"

The emergence of rap music as a global form has similar strategic qualities. Beginning in the 1970s, African American and Latinx youth in New York developed an expressive style of spoken-word music—**rap**—that articulated their experiences in a compelling way. The rap artist, or MC, often speaks from a first-person perspective. Sometimes the MC's words make stories of hardship, conflict, or violence feel genuine and immediate, while also insisting that the speaker has the strength and resourcefulness to survive and even flourish; sometimes rap music is celebratory. In the words of political scientist Lakeyta Bonnette, "Rap music continues the cultural tradition of using the power of the spoken word to discuss political and social issues, advance attitudes, raise consciousness, and assert a political voice."[52] Rap is part of a larger set of practices called **hip-hop** that set these musicians apart: hip-hop artists choose particular styles of gesture and dance, typically wear baggy clothes and backward caps, practice turntablism, and may even incorporate graffiti into their routines, using spray paint to write on neighborhood walls. All these elements identify hip-hop participants as outsiders to a white mainstream society in the United States. This music offers a strong sense of voice: telling a variety of stories from a clearly defined and purposefully local point of view.[53]

Queen Latifah's "Just Another Day," from her 1993 album *Black Reign*, exemplifies that sense of voice. The song describes specific problems in troubled neighborhoods in New York—citing the neighborhoods by address so that the listener recognizes the singer's precise place.[54] Ironic quotation from the children's show *Mr. Rogers' Neighborhood* ("Well, it's a beautiful day in the neighborhood, a beautiful day in the neighborhood") contrasts painfully with mention of a child killed by a stray bullet. Latifah celebrates the neighborhood with a sense of ownership and claims it as beautiful despite its perils. Latifah's narration also asserts mastery over the situation: "I come with the real life perspective and rule / Me and my peoples from around the way remain cool" (example 8.4). Coupled with Latifah's strong stage presence, the song conveys a sense of survival in the face of difficulty and seems to speak from the local (the neighborhood) toward the rest of the world through audio and video mediation.

Example 8.4. Excerpt from Queen Latifah, music video for "Just Another Day" from *Black Reign* (Motown, 1994). YouTube.
Link: https://doi.org/10.3998/mpub.9853855.cmp.122

Once rap gained a foothold in the national and international media, African Americans were able to convey powerful words about their experiences to people unfamiliar with their neighborhoods. Rap also became a means to demand political recognition and change. Through art, rap has often corrected the misunderstanding and misrecognition of African Americans and constructed a better representation of their lives. This representation is not just a matter of image: it has real consequences. States and other legal entities choose how they recognize groups by counting them in the census, granting or withholding rights, and deciding whom to police. By making their voices audible and by claiming a social perspective not acknowledged by powerful authorities, rap artists sought not assimilation but recognition.[55] Bonnette has pointed out that although urban youth do not have access to the means of political change, music allows them to enter public space as entertainers and then use that media presence as a springboard to political participation.[56]

African American music became a transnational project with the support of Cold War networks of power. From the 1940s to the 1980s the government of the Soviet Union engaged in intensive propaganda campaigns that publicized the continuing violence against black people in the United States. Worldwide, newspapers published frightful photographs of abuse and described continuing violent conflicts about school desegregation.[57] To combat this publicity, the US government sent books, pamphlets, and films about prominent African Americans all over the world. One pamphlet described black Americans' "constant progress towards full enjoyment of the rights and privileges of free men."[58] Many people abroad took an interest in this drama and felt an imagined connection to African Americans. **Pan-African** activists cultivated this empathy, encouraging the travel of African American intellectuals to Africa. Both the US and Soviet governments sponsored international travel by African artists and political leaders to their respective countries, as well. In the 1960s postcolonial activists all over the world linked the struggle for African American civil rights to their own struggles for equal rights and self-determination.[59]

With this engagement as a backdrop, it is not surprising that the emergence of hip-hop in the 1970s sparked a global movement that continues to the present day. The sociologist Sujatha Fernandes has pointed out that although pan-Africanism has motivated some people outside the United States to adopt hip-hop, others find a connection in the genre's tradition of commenting on urban conditions, especially poverty.[60] The performance of this music involves highly animated speech, so it is no surprise that groups whose speech has been marginalized have seized on rap as a way to give voice to their perspectives. As in the tradition of rap in the United States, MCs from other parts of the world offer commentary on particulars of their situations, stating what needs to change.[61] Here I take up just a few examples, with an eye toward examining the nature and purposes of this appropriation.

Yugen Blakrok is an MC from South Africa whose work is densely woven and poetic. Blakrok frequently makes reference to images from **Afro-futurism**, an artistic movement that blends pan-African themes with themes from science fiction, presenting images of alternative future worlds as a means of criticizing the existing world.[62] The song "DarkStar," on Blakrok's album *Return of the Astro-Goth*, flits between very brief criticism of social problems and images of flight and cosmic wisdom:

At night-time while the homeless lie awake in insomniac states
I've spat on God's face for the lives he wouldn't take
Saw we're suffering for suffering's sake
Birdbrains stuck wingless in a cage
Hallucinating warped perverted images in the shape of the snake
I have read between the lines of historic fallacies
And now disappear in mists with no chances of you finding me
Turn the pages and learn the end of each age is
Preceded by the most inspired works of the sages
One day I'll lace a verse in 365 takes
Then launch my sound body into space
Where my food for the soul will be served on a cosmic plate
And occupy minds through invisible sound-waves.[63]

Blakrok cites Queen Latifah, Public Enemy, and other US musicians of the 1990s as her biggest influences, and her lyrics invoke the socially critical tradition and content of US rap music.[64] In particular, the words of "DarkStar" complain of homelessness, entrapment, the "mark of the slave," and police violence: how "cops know the flows blow holes through bulletproof vests."

The problems Blakrok describes are not localized: they could be the problems of any city. Blakrok's appropriation of rap alters the sense of the "local" that was so present in New York hip-hop of the 1980s and 1990s; instead of arguing that the speaker is surviving despite the rigors of a particular neighborhood, the speaker in Blakrok's song engages in fantastic escapist thoughts—"food for the soul . . . served on a cosmic plate"—that contrast with the social problems she names. The mix of social critique and self-assertion is present here, as it was in Queen Latifah's rap, but the balance and subject matter have tipped toward a fantastical escape into outer space, in keeping with Afro-futurism.

Blakrok's style of rapping is remarkable for its rhythmic flexibility. Part of the appeal of the genre is that the rapper's words pull away from the beat for a while, coming between beats rather than on them, until at last a key word lands on a strong beat. Sometimes Blakrok raps for long stretches before her words coordinate with the underlying pulse. This effect gives her music a breathless and floating feeling that matches the imagery in the song's music video, in which Blakrok's face floats through outer space in an old-fashioned television set (example 8.5).

Example 8.5. Yugen Blakrok, "Darkstar Animatron," music video for the song "DarkStar," animated by Kanif Sebright. *Return of the Astro-Goth* (Iapetus Records, 2014). Used by permission. YouTube.
Link: https://doi.org/10.3998/mpub.9853855.cmp.124

Also remarkable are the aspects of rap that Blakrok adopts selectively. Some women MCs choose suggestive costumes to resemble the female dancers in US rap videos. Blakrok is more likely to be seen in a hoodie sweatshirt and baggy pants, clothing associated with a male MC in the United States. Sometimes she uses costume and special effects to create an otherworldly persona (as in her "House of Ravens" video; see fig. 8.4). One of the standard stories people tell about globalization is that American corporations are wiping out differences, making all the available music more alike. But the sound of Blakrok's rapping is distinctively her own, as is the visual style of her videos. Blakrok's performance presents an Afro-futurist vision of modern Africa: she adopts the subject matter of hip-hop selectively to suit her own purposes.[65] Hip-hop is not the same all over the world, but individual musicians find power in drawing on the idea of a worldwide community of musicians in solidarity—an imagined community spanning several continents.[66] And as Okon Hwang has pointed out in another context, people are not required to

Fig. 8.4. Still from Yugen Blakrok, "House of Ravens," *Return of the Astro-Goth*, music video directed by Nic Hester (Iapetus Records, 2014). You-Tube: https://www.you tube.com/watch?v=N-HkBxjbXEAY

regard any repertory as the possession of a particular group or nation. Individuals who appropriate music from elsewhere typically perceive their musical choices as personal, not group, expression.[67]

In the Arab world MCs have experienced a broad range of responses to their work—from enthusiastic public acceptance to state suppression and exile. At the northwestern edge of Africa, Morocco is a kingdom with a history of authoritarian repression. The monarchy limits free speech, and although citizens may criticize other parts of the government, they may not criticize the king.[68] Yet the music of Youssra Oakuf, who raps under the name Soultana, is infused with social critique. As a Muslim teenager who began to get involved in hip-hop in the early 2000s, Soultana risked her reputation by attending the clubs that host hip-hop performances.[69] Some Moroccan music fans remain unwilling to accept female rappers, and Soultana's willingness to speak openly about poverty and prostitution has also troubled her listeners. Nonetheless, Soultana has been prominent on the Casablanca rap scene for more than a decade.

In a rap called "The Voice of Women" from 2010 (example 8.6) Soultana condemned poverty and the harassment of women on the street. The lyrics accuse Muslim men of hypocrisy, saying that they pretend to be devout but also use women as prostitutes and shame them:

> You looked at her like she was a cheap thing.
> She saw in your face what she wanted to be.
> You looked at her, a look of humiliation.
> She's selling her body because you are the buyer.
> And when she's walking by, you act all Muslim.[70]

Soultana links her motive for getting into hip-hop to the status of women in Morocco: "All I was searching for was not fame or money or something like that—I was searching for respect from people."[71]

Example 8.6. Excerpt from Soultana, "Sawt Nssa" (The Voice of Women), music video by Masta Flow. YouTube.
Link: https://doi.org/10.3998/mpub.9853855.cmp.125

Soultana delivers "The Voice of Women" in an emphatic and clearly spoken style, making every syllable audible. According to the ethnomusicologist Kendra Salois, this clarity is important, for Soultana's success has depended on her ability to draw in listeners who are not used to contemporary rap or its fast pace. This mode of delivery is a form of teaching and community building: Soultana frequently explains aspects of the hip-hop tradition or the meanings of specific songs before she performs them and even checks with the audience to make sure they have understood. Addressing her fans, she has said that "the culture of hip-hop is in our blood"—helping the audience to feel part of the transnational tradition of socially conscious hip-hop.[72]

Much like African American rappers, Soultana uses rap as a means for Moroccans to talk about important issues: poverty, harassment, gender discrimination. Yet there are limits to this criticism: Moroccan MCs may make remarks about "the government," but they dare not attribute social problems to the king's poor leadership. Whether or not they disagree with the present ruler, to voice such criticism would be a punishable offense.[73] Instead, when talking to the audience from the stage, Soultana and other Moroccan rappers couch their social criticism within the language of personal responsibility. This language is rooted in the Muslim traditions of virtue and citizenship, and MCs make reference to these principles when talking to audiences. As a political strategy, assigning personal responsibility for social problems means that the MCs' criticism of the status quo does not challenge the state's leadership. Rather, Salois writes, the focus is "transforming Moroccans into a certain kind of citizen."[74]

Since 2010, Western interest in MCs from the Arab world has been fueled in part by a region-wide conversation about personal and artistic freedoms. From late 2010 to mid-2012 popular demonstrations and uprisings took place throughout much of North Africa and the Middle East. Known as the Arab Spring, these demonstrations reflected a variety of forms of discontent. Protesters spoke out against political corruption, income inequality, and resentment against rule by dictators or monarchs. Many of the demonstrators also demanded more democratic forms of government. The protests sparked a civil war in Syria, and rulers of several countries were forced from power. Even so, only in Tunisia did the demonstrations result in a substantive change in government.

These dramatic circumstances focused Western attention on dissenters. When the Egyptian rapper Mayam Mahmoud appeared on the TV show *Arabs Got Talent* in 2013, her head covered with a hijab (head scarf), her performance set off a flurry of media interest in Western countries (example 8.7).

Example 8.7. Mayam Mahmoud, performance on *Arabs Got Talent* (2013).
Link: https://doi.org/10.3998/mpub.9853855.cmp.126

Mahmoud's lyrics, which come from the tradition of Arabic spoken-word poetry as well as from rap, call for women's freedom. In the song "It's My Right" Mahmoud's refrain addresses the men in the audience, assigning them the responsibility for respecting the freedom of women: "Even before it's my right, my freedom is your duty." Mahmoud goes still further, outlining the freedoms she claims for women:

I have the right to complete my education until I'm fully satisfied.
I have the right to show myself to the world. I don't want to
    disappear.
I have the right to choose my own partner and not my family's choice
to share the road with me and to help me complete my journey.
I have the right to have my brother respect me and not attack me.
Don't tell me, "Freedom's in other countries" or tell me to hush.[75]

Like Soultana, Mahmoud denounces a great deal of behavior in the everyday context in which she lives, but she is not calling for revolution: she does not claim opposition to society as a whole or to the religious principles by which her society is led. These performances do not criticize Islam; rather, they are based on core Islamic principles.[76]

By choosing rap as a mode of expression, musicians from the Islamic world become entangled in the international media. Salois observes that Western journalists often ask Muslim hip-hop artists to repudiate Islamic fundamentalism or overemphasize the extent to which they are breaking norms in their countries. To those who are both devout in their faith and calling for particular kinds of change, questions about these topics can seem like a trap: "if a Muslim artist reaches a certain level of visibility, eventually she will be asked to choose a side in a discourse whose terms she can't control."⁷⁷ These artists recognize that they may be misrepresented in stereotypical terms as religious extremists or radical pro-Western reformers—portrayals that do not match the complexity of their daily reality.

Both state policies and global music companies may restrict what speech makes it out into the wider world. As Salois points out, musicians find themselves in a double bind. Although what they want to say may or may not conform to the expectations of the state and the marketplace, in order to have their voices promoted enough to be heard, they must conform to those expectations, at least to some extent.⁷⁸ The nature of those constraints differs from place to place: they may include censorship of public or mediated performances, limits on what media can circulate in the artist's environment, and access to sponsorship that would bring the artist into broader public awareness. As the ethnomusicologist Ali Colleen Neff has described it, female rappers in the West African nation-state of Senegal face "an exploitative tourism industry, corruption in the national government, self-serving world music promoters, parasitic European corporate interest in the Senegalese telecommunications, power, and banking industries, [and] persistent prohibitions on women's divorce and inheritance rights."⁷⁹ All artists experience some constraints, and for many the constraints are severe enough to threaten their ability to be heard.

Many MCs from lower-income countries affiliate with foreign music companies to achieve wider publicity and distribution. For example, Yugen Blakrok is represented by the German record label Iapetus. Rap artists outside the United States can gain some attention by their presence on "top 10 artists from [any country] you should hear" lists on the internet, many of which are paid advertisements published by third-party promoters. The marketing of rap music from outside the United States to North Americans resembles the "world beat" phenomenon, which demonstrated a mixture of genuine musical interest and the pursuit of ever more novelties to sell in the marketplace.

If the musicians attract enough attention, recording companies may sponsor professionally made video biographies—short videos that allow the musicians to introduce themselves. Like the performances of national folk-dance troupes, these videos have a fairly standard format. The artist speaks in brief interview segments about personal history and local circumstances. That footage is interspersed with performance video, which often appears to be filmed in the artist's neighborhood of origin, aiming to demonstrate some special qualities of that scene. This sense of being **local** is tactical: as the literary scholar Stephen Greenblatt points out, art that seems to be original or rooted in place may attract special attention because it seems authentic.[80] At the same time, these videos explain the artist's personality in a way that engages Western audiences. In a promotional video that explains her music to an English-speaking audience, for example, Soultana explained: "Hip hop taught me how to be strong, how to face men"—emphasizing the feminist aspect of her Moroccan rap that may appeal to women in the West.[81] To make a connection, statements like these may gloss over the strategic differences between Soultana's self-presentation and that of Western artists.

Thus, many musicians adapt their music and their self-presentation to make their music marketable. Is this adaptation a threat to other musical practices? Possibly so, for as musicians accommodate themselves to the demands of the marketplace, they may choose some traditions and abandon others. As Appiah has pointed out, though, each musician should have the right to decide what kind of music to make: "telling other people what they ought to value in their own traditions" is neither productive nor appropriate.[82] Canclini also notes that global corporations can coerce or limit artists because they cater so much to the desires of people in the United States, Europe, and Japan. Cooperation with music distributors may also place artists into exploitative financial relationships.[83] Artists may or may not resent these trade-offs. Abdoulaye Niang, who has worked for the United Nations Economic Commission in West Africa, has explained that the Senegalese MCs he knows want to represent their "specific cultural and social aspirations" while participating in larger systems.[84] Yet the initiative to decide on the pros and cons of participation must remain with the individual musician. Indeed, the power to mix musics also means the power to decide how one is represented to the world. According to Canclini, blending traditions can free musicians from feeling obligated to represent a single traditional identity, allowing them to express new or mixed identities that better reflect the particulars of their situations.[85]

Examining these extensions of the rap tradition, we might ask with Canclini: what world are these artists entering (or creating), and what are they leaving behind? The adoption of rap by people outside the United States allows them to enter a global music marketplace, as well as regional and international conversations about social concerns. This borrowing grows not from a desire to take others' music but rather from a sense of affinity and shared experience. At the same time, many MCs from outside North America do not talk about their musical style as borrowed: they recognize the roots of rap in the United States, but they understand their music as their own creation. Like the later generation of mediated selves discussed in chapter 6, the MCs discussed here have a great variety of musical styles and techniques at their disposal; their art feels like an integrated and novel whole, not like a mere borrowing or copy. The Moroccan and Egyptian rappers discussed here have not left their own sense of self behind; rather, they have made music to represent themselves, defining their own places in the world.[86]

The anthropologists John Kelly and Martha Kaplan have argued that people need representation in two senses: metaphorical representation, having the feeling of being heard, seen, or recognized; and literal representation, as in a democracy that grants and protects their rights.[87] Artists who create blended musics engage in metaphorical representation, ensuring that they can be recognized as they wish. If we look only from the perspective of the "world system" or the other large-scale systems in which artists live, we might not recognize the individuality of their contributions or the meaningfulness of their music to them personally: their mixing of musics may look like the product of global forces. If we listen closely to the artists, however, we can hear them; they exert individual creativity to shape the music around them, and they purposefully add their voices to a broader conversation about how the world should be.

Conclusion

*Violence, Difference, and Peacemaking
in a Globalized World*

Writing in 1970, the American sociologist Philip Rieff (1922–2006) stated that for the sake of stability, "cultures" should have clear and definite boundaries. According to Rieff the "members of a culture learn, through their membership, how to narrow the range of choices otherwise open. Safely inside their culture—more precisely, the culture safely inside them—members of it are disposed to enact only certain possibilities of behavior while refusing even to dream of others. . . . Members of the same culture can expect each other to behave in certain ways and not others."[1] In Rieff's view the purpose of a culture is to instill those social norms. Indeed, Rieff believed that a culture—conceived of as a bounded, unitary entity that teaches and defends norms—could "prevent disorganizing questions from arising."[2]

In Rieff's time there were many "disorganizing questions," among them challenges to prevailing social norms governing gender and race and worldwide protests against colonialism and war. The 21st century has witnessed an intensification of those questions. Processes of migration and mediation have accelerated. In the past few decades large numbers of people have been deterritorialized. As guest workers, immigrants, deployed members of the military, or refugees, they dwell in countries where they may not have the rights traditionally granted by nation-states. They may bring customs and practices that cause friction with populations that were already there. Local schools, houses of worship, and other institutions may accommodate these deterritorialized people or resist doing so; either way, the presence of these populations ties distant places to each other and changes how people live. Their presence also makes the population in many places more heterogeneous and challenges the idea of nationhood as a particular people tied to a particular geographical place.[3]

In today's world, then, we should pay attention to the people who move, the people who stay in place, and the contacts between them. According to the literary scholar Stephen Greenblatt, "Mobility is often perceived as a threat—a force by which traditions, rituals, expressions, beliefs are decentered, thinned out, decontextualized, lost. In response to this perceived threat, many groups and individuals have attempted to wall themselves off from the world or, alternatively, they have resorted to violence."[4] Precipitated by mobility, feelings of loss or change can make it harder for people to live together.

According to the anthropologist Arjun Appadurai, in addition to the changes caused by large-scale migration, mediated entertainments (music videos, movies, television) have also changed how people think about each other. Media from afar offer people images of lives different from their own. Through television, Appadurai notes, lower-income people witness theatrical versions of how wealthier people live. When they see that prosperity is impossible within the financial system in their neighborhoods, that comparison offers them new information that shapes their own expectations for what is possible, prompting them to develop new "scripts for possible lives."[5] Likewise, some activists have found the media helpful in cultivating a growing worldwide awareness of human rights and in raising the expectations of women or minority groups that they, too, can assert those rights.[6] If, in Benedict Anderson's terms, a nation is one kind of imagined community, mediated communication allows individuals to be networked at a distance into much larger imagined communities, in which people might share some norms or values. No one is linked with everyone, but many people are linked with others internationally, and that connection changes what these people know about the rest of the world.

Appadurai calls these moments of clashing information, in which individuals' knowledge about faraway people or situations conflicts with local knowledge, **disjunctures**. In Appadurai's view, living with many kinds of conflicting information is now commonplace because global phenomena may create new conflicts on the local level.[7] Furthermore, different elements of the social landscapes people experience in their everyday lives may conflict; for example, the music people want to receive from afar may not be available owing to financial constraints, or the values of an ethnic minority may conflict with those of the nation-state that rules over that minority group. Different individuals, neighborhoods, or nation-states may experience a variety of disjunctures and be challenged by a variety of conflicts and constraints, for it is the interaction between social forces at different scales that produces the conflict.

The existence of disjunctures is not new. We saw in chapters 1 through 3 that as people have moved through processes of migration, colonialism, and diaspora, conflicts have arisen between the "local" phenomena and the "from elsewhere" that change how people think, live, and make music. As we saw in Turkey and Japan in chapter 5, the impulse to "modernize" a nation or a nation-state stems from a process of comparison: a judgment about a group of people in relation to others and the desire to impose standards from elsewhere on the judged people. As mediated communication increased and travel became safer and easier, opportunities for disjuncture multiplied.[8] As when Laura Boulton made a recording of the Iñupiat singer Joseph Sikvayugak, the encounter of audio recording often brought together people with different expectations of what their encounter might mean—for Sikvayugak, preserving his people's music in a time of change; for Boulton, material for publication and earnings. This encounter changed the Iñupiat people's idea of their own heritage over the decades following Boulton's visit.

Even as the era of globalization has produced economic growth and feelings of connectedness, it has also produced clashes related to those social changes. Recent decades have witnessed more and more conflicts that target specific groups of people with the intent of destroying them completely.[9] In Indonesia, Cambodia, Rwanda, Bosnia, Chechnya, Sudan, and Syria, among other places, brutal attacks have targeted persons belonging to specific identity groups. Appadurai believes this hardening of divisions among groups is closely aligned with the anxiety and instability caused by globalization. In recent decades it has become less clear who is in charge, who defines the terms and sets the rules for how people live. As we saw in chapter 7, in a globalized world not only nation-states make these decisions; corporations, international organizations, and military or police forces may also exert control over what everyday people can or cannot do. As we saw in the case of Brazil's copyright enforcement, actions across international borders also disrupt the power of nation-states, making them less able to control what happens inside their borders.[10]

Appadurai points out that not only is globalization unevenly distributed; the resources for understanding it are also unevenly distributed. For instance, individuals may know that jobs are being added or disappearing in their town, without direct knowledge of the global forces that cause these shifts. Likewise, they may see that their usual business of buying and selling audio recordings on the street is disrupted, without knowledge of the international agreements that caused the disruption. Whether they want to or not, everyone is participating in globalization, but not everyone has control over their participation, leaving people feeling afraid or confused as they try to master their situations. Appadurai notes that minority groups often become a target of violent acts because their presence heightens these uncertainties for the majority population. The presence of different languages or customs may threaten the coherence of social and educational systems. And because the minority is close at hand, as a neighbor, their presence may make the instabilities and challenges caused by global forces feel personal.[11]

The widespread circulation of media has not solved the old problems of displaced populations or unequal opportunity, but it has added layers of complexity to those problems. As we saw in chapter 6, many people in the mediated world have used music to define themselves and to distinguish themselves from others, individually or in groups. In an environment where mediated sounds are abundant, people feel free to choose from and blend a wide array of musics.

At the very same time, contradicting this freedom of choice, struggles over the ownership and control of music have become more and more pervasive. Arguments about appropriation have taken on urgency: many listeners are insisting on clear definitions of "ours" and "theirs," calling for a hardening of the lines between groups of people and kinds of music. On one hand, members of a minority group may believe it important to monitor that boundary to guard against appropriation. On the other hand, members of a majority may define a minority's "culture" as a tactic of exclusion, accompanied by criticism of others or restrictions on others' rights. Policing the boundary between groups only increases the feeling of separation and conflict.[12] Yet in a time when unseen global forces are changing local practices, it is not surprising that people might want to avoid "disorganizing questions" in favor of certainty.

The use of music to define the boundaries between groups can be benign—a mere matter of taste—but it can also do harm. During the recent wars in Afghanistan and Iraq US military personnel brought their music with them. They listened constantly, whether to generate excitement before missions or remind themselves of home with personalized mixtapes.[13] But according to the musicologist Suzanne Cusick, US military personnel also used music to break the will of prisoners. As part of a larger interrogation plan that routinely put prisoners under intense stress, US soldiers frequently chose music that they knew would be offensive to Muslim prisoners. In some Islamic traditions entertainment or frivolous music is forbidden. To prisoners who held these beliefs, being forced to listen to popular music with explicit lyrics or performed by women put them in a morally objectionable position from which they could not escape. The soldiers also used very loud music, especially heavy metal music, to keep prisoners awake for extended periods of time. In this setting music became a way of drawing a sharp distinction between "us" and "them," supporting the selfhood of the soldiers while tearing down that of prisoners.[14] This wartime situation is another disjuncture in which a global conflict becomes localized, changing the lives of individual persons.

We have also seen that local conflicts can become meaningful global forces. Rap music emerged from the disjuncture felt by African American and Latinx youth: living in cities of dramatically unequal circumstances, they have used music to address unfair differences in economic and social opportunity. The worldwide appropriation of this once-local music allows a disjuncture felt in one place to become an international convention for representing frustration and demanding social justice.[15] Thus, disjunctures do not only originate in global circumstances; they can also emerge from local concerns.

When Philip Rieff developed his theory about the norms that make up a "culture," he described two ways of understanding the world that were in direct conflict with one another. Rieff imagined the old model, on which Western cultural values were based, as a vertical scale of value, in which the top is better than the bottom (fig. 9.1). Rieff developed many analogies for this model. Based on the monotheist idea of "one God," this hierarchy privileges oneness, unity, and wholeness, and it devalues multiplicity or changeableness. This model pertains not only to religious values but also to artistic and scientific thinking. Consider the example of the pop singer Lady Gaga, or anybody else who is considered to be too changeable: having many identities, being multiple, automatically bestows a lack of "integrity" or authenticity. Musically, this scale of value means that some music has to be judged more valuable than other music and that all members of the "culture" must acknowledge that judgment as true.

Rieff's second model, in contrast, was a horizontal, nonhierarchical model (fig. 9.2). It closely resembles Thomas de Zengotita's idea of mediated thinking, for in this model all options are equally valid. No one is entitled to say that some are better or worse than others. Rieff wrote his essay to criticize the writer Oscar Wilde, who delighted in overturning social hierarchies. Wilde believed that the "true personality" of humankind "will not be always meddling with others, or asking them to be like itself. It will love them because they will be different."[16] Wilde envisioned a society that resembled Rieff's second model, allowing many individual identities and commitments to flourish.

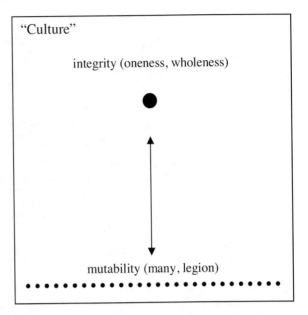

"Culture"

integrity (oneness, wholeness)

mutability (many, legion)

Fig. 9.1. Schematic of
Philip Rieff's "vertical
of authority."

In contrast, Rieff believed that the mediated selves who thrive in this environment destabilized society: if everyone has a god's-eye view, and flits from one
identity to the next, it is difficult for a society to maintain a sense of ordered
values where some identities are clearly preferred.[17]

Rieff believed firmly in the necessity of his first model: the hierarchical,
vertical order. Without a hierarchy that would allow us to make judgments, he
reasoned, we would live in a lawless society: "everything could be expressed
and nothing would be true."[18] In the world Rieff sketched out, difference was
a private matter, kept to oneself: one's public identity was based on common
ground with other people, and those commonalities preserved unity and
order.[19]

To be sure, having clear universal standards for judging whether some
music is better than other music offers listeners a guidepost for deciding what
to listen to and making claims about what music has value. The European
concert music tradition is marked by the existence of a **canon**—a recognized
and valued subset of musical works. (In the case of European music these are
the works that often appear on course syllabi and on the programs of large arts
institutions like symphony orchestras and opera houses: works by Ludwig van
Beethoven, Giuseppe Verdi, and so forth.) In the history of the United States,
too, the music of empowered groups has been marked with more prestige.

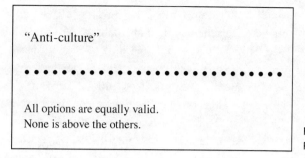

Fig. 9.2. Schematic of Rieff's "anti-culture."

Some European Americans took for granted that European concert music was good and dismissed other types of music as mere noise.

The habit of assigning prestige extends to many kinds of music: jazz fans may make their case for the superiority of particular styles or players, and so may fans of country music. Not all musical genres lend themselves to the formation of a canon.[20] But in our day, processes of preserving and conveying heritage have often led to the selection and canonization of particular performances or works. Creating canons reinforces a vertical standard of value. Music selected for the heritage treatment gains prestige, and it travels farther and more easily than the music not selected. Challenges to a canon—purposeful attention to musical practices outside the valued collection—correspond to Rieff's second model, in which people may assign value to many different musical customs, treating each as worthy of respect.

Since Rieff's time, other thinkers have offered support for a less hierarchical model, one that might allow for more diverse lifeways within a single society. The sociologist Craig Calhoun points out that the idea of a constitutional democracy—a framework of laws that guide social relationships and ensure rights—establishes norms but does not require judgments that some ways of life are better than others. In practice the history of the United States reveals tensions between the vertical dominance of citizens of European origin and the horizontal "nation of immigrants" ideal of heterogeneity—and between Euro-American concert music and other American musics. Yet Calhoun imagines a functioning democracy in which difference is recognized but does not define citizenship, a society that has a commitment both to rational discourse and to social equality.[21] Calhoun's theory does not answer all the questions; but it does describe a way in which the equality of Rieff's second model could exist without the lawlessness Rieff predicted.

Rieff's second model did not replace the first: these two models coexist and compete, sometimes in paradoxical ways. Many of the social conflicts of our time stem from differences between religious fundamentalism (vertical) and pluralist secularism (horizontal).[22] Once people become aware of many optional identities and practices, it is harder to make them cooperate with a vertical authority that forbids some of those practices, and governments or other actors sometimes eliminate options by force. Scientists tend to seek one coherent explanation (vertical); people who argue against evolutionary theory use a "hear all sides of the debate" argument (horizontal). One person can switch back and forth between these two models of thinking, and most of us do so without conscious thought. It is not clear whether one model is gaining dominance over the other, but it is clear that the difference between them is driving significant conflicts in the United States and elsewhere.

The solutions Appadurai offers to the conflicts the world faces combine the second model that Rieff describes—the nonhierarchical one—with a legal system, like Calhoun's, that would secure basic rights for all people. Appadurai believes that the only way out of the horrifying cultural violence that so much of the world is now experiencing is to encourage everyone to embrace mediatedness and the mixed traditions that come with it. Appadurai suggests that governments should cut the link between ethnicity and citizenship, making it easier to be a citizen of a place without belonging to the major ethnicity or nation historically associated with that place. States should accommodate minorities and allow dual or multiple citizenship so that fewer people remain stateless or lack basic rights. In Appadurai's imagined peaceful world nationalism could still exist, but it would be framed multiculturally: group identities would be forged based on principles of openness and mixture rather than authenticity, exclusion, or purity. Access to media would be widespread, and people would use the media to promote cultural mixing as a social norm.[23]

Canclini agrees with Appadurai to a great extent: he says that artistic mixing that comes from genuine engagement among people produces greater understanding. At the same time, however, he notices some dangers. He believes that encouraging mixing may dissolve "weakened" social groups or practices: if groups with unequal resources collide, the customs of the weaker group often adapt to those of the stronger. Kwame Anthony Appiah has already dispensed with this objection: no one can choose whether the weaker group should change except the members of that group.[24] But for people living under duress, others' attempts to use their music to make hybrids can feel threatening to their sense of self. If white musicians borrow black spirituals (chapter 3), historical and continuing inequities between the two groups make this borrowing a potentially offensive appropriation. The particulars of the relationships around the music's making will shape listeners' reactions, but it is reasonable to assume that because of the power differential, this form of borrowing carries some risk.

For Canclini the biggest ethical and aesthetic risk of mixing musics is that it makes the musics that have been merged appear to be equal partners, masking inequalities of power.[25] This false appearance of equality may include instances of **tokenism**, in which representations of inclusiveness may hide continuing inequality, as when people of various skin colors appear on posters for a program that serves minority groups poorly. This strategy may make members of the majority group feel good by depicting friendship or closeness. Yet the various people involved in a project may not all experience their participation that way; even as one party feels friendly to the other, another might feel forced or participate only for practical gain. The debates about Paul Simon's *Graceland* (chapter 6) address this risk without resolving it. As outsiders to the *Graceland* situation, we cannot really know how the interplay of power, fame, money, and music felt to all participants, but it would be naive to believe that differences in power played no role in their work. Canclini urges us not to mistake market forces for real affection and to consider carefully what inequalities may be masked by hybrids.[26]

Likewise, on the largest scale, Canclini believes that the idea of "planetary reconciliation" represented by the United Nations–style "showcase of cultures" (chapter 5) presents a distorted image of reality. The UN showcase makes it seem as though "the world" values every nation's presentation of its own art equally, that all groups stand on the same footing. Yet experience suggests that profound asymmetries persist in economic and political relations among nations. The nation may also serve its citizens unequally: state officials may do a poor job of showcasing minority musics or even suppress them (chapters 5 and 7). Canclini wants artists to retain the power to criticize unfair situations or refuse to participate in them. He fears that if the global marketplace takes too much control over artists' lives, they might no longer be able to stand apart from it. For Canclini, mixing is good only if artists choose it, and they must also have the option to make music that blends poorly with other musics—refusing to mix.[27] As we have seen (chapters 7 and 8), participation in the global music market requires economic and personal trade-offs.

As we saw in chapter 3, individual people may feel constrained when others lock them into fixed categories. The music scholar Jairo Moreno advocates a "principled indifference to difference": he finds it unnecessary that "difference-based identities, particularly those of oppressed peoples and societies, must be constantly proclaimed and relentlessly performed in order to resist or subvert the status quo."[28] In Moreno's study of the jazz saxophonist Miguel Zenón, Moreno praises Zenón for creating situations that allow people to participate in music together, regardless of their expertise or past experience. Acknowledging that each relationship between people, groups, or nations has its own power relations, Moreno argues that we can create situations that suspend hierarchies, allowing us to connect with each other without our differences becoming a primary focus.[29]

To some extent Moreno's approach resembles Rieff's second, nonhierarchical model of society, but it leaves room for people to connect in the public sphere based on their common interests, an element of Rieff's first model. Moreno's idea also resembles recent theories about how to create a stable democracy that includes diverse peoples: stability requires finding a way to build feelings of solidarity and social commitment among people who share a geographical space, regardless of their ancestry, history, or musical preferences.[30] Moreno argues that in the moment of musical performance, individuals may find a point of meaningful contact regardless of their background or heritage. Appiah calls this kind of value a "project-dependent value." That is, people who hold differing religious principles or opposing political positions may still come together and agree on particular ideas for a time—that torture is wrong or that the blues are beautiful—and those ideas offer a place to begin.[31] Participation in music provides both a point of personal contact and a shared value as a starting point.

Like Moreno, Craig Calhoun believes that the public sphere can be a setting where people choose to develop social solidarity with one another. We know that people value tradition and heritage; and, for different reasons, they also value novelty.[32] As individuals, we choose which traditions to foster, which to join, which to create anew, and participation with other people can help us imagine who we are in new ways. Human groupings of any kind are not set in stone; indeed, our social choices, including our music-making, form and reform our groupings as we are brought into contact with each other.[33] In Calhoun's view, "the nature of life together is chosen as it is constructed."[34] In other words, the choices we make about how to relate on a micro level, how we make music together or invite others to share our music, are not a result of our social order; these choices build our social order. By deciding to use music in ways that connect us with our neighbors, we may build solidarity and community.

As I mentioned at the end of chapter 8, the anthropologists John Kelly and Martha Kaplan make the case that people need representation in two senses: metaphorical representation, having the feeling of being heard, seen, or recognized; and literal representation, as in a democracy that grants and protects meaningful rights.[35] As we saw in the case of Hyo-shin Na, for many individuals the mixing and remixing of music may address that first sense: the mix may help them define and express their places in the world or help them connect with others. Music alone cannot accomplish the second, literal kind of representation; only political action can extend and protect human rights. Indeed, there is nothing magical about music; it can be used for harm as well as for good. But, at least in concept, musical mixing might ease the way for the political project of inclusion. Canclini writes that blended artistic practices can help societies "work democratically with differences": respect for another person's music may serve as a smaller-scale demonstration of respect for that person's personal autonomy.[36]

Oscar Wilde wrote, "Literature always anticipates Life." Or, as present-day activists have argued more colloquially, "If you can't see it, you can't be it."[37] Artistic representations do not fix the world's problems, but they do help us to imagine what is possible for our own lives. By articulating the challenges and joys of lives lived in a globalized and mediated world, hybrid musical experiences allow individuals to make new identities for themselves or blend old identities with others'. As Appiah has written, "if we care *about* others who are not part of our political order—others who may have commitments and beliefs that are unlike our own—we must have a way to talk *to* them"—and they to us. Shared artistic experiences allow people to establish these contacts, often mediated over distance.[38] As we saw in the case of rap musicians on the African continent (chapter 8), this form of solidarity need not mean giving up one's own voice, but it may mean demonstrating care for another's tradition. That sense of attachment seems important, for extending care may entangle people in relationships of respect, perhaps even of obligation.[39]

Thomas de Zengotita has warned that the constant mixing, remixing, quotation, and mediation of words, sounds, and images may lead to "a certain point of mass meaninglessness"; that is, awash in a sea of representations, we may stop judging, shrug, and simply turn away.[40] Yet we have encountered many recent examples in which the particular elements of the mix, and the way they are mixed, matter very much to musicians and listeners. The musicologists Olivia Bloechl and Melanie Lowe suggest that "what we do with what we know . . . discloses *who* we are and with whom we are in community."[41] The signaling of identity and connectedness through musical borrow-ing suits the mediated self, which eagerly declares its positions and alliances (chapter 6). This signaling has all the positive and negative traits of mediated behavior: it is hard for us to discern what is real and what is put on for show, and a single choice may be some of each.

At the time of this writing, "disorganizing questions" remain unavoidable. Since the 1960s, various groups all over the world have challenged dominant standards of value in their societies: refusing their assigned roles, asserting civil rights, or seeking equality under law. Disagreements within the borders of countries are at least as heated as those between countries.[42] The mixing of musics disrupts the tidy categories of "nation" and "culture," and it may seem like a further element of disorganization. Yet, as a musicians' strategy, musical mixing may promote not disorganization but reorganization: migrants and mediated persons finding ways to relate to one another and convey their expe-riences. In Canclini's view these strategic mixes "help us make the world more translatable, which is to say more cohabitable in the midst of differences."[43] It is possible—and much to be hoped—that these translations might create points of contact that encourage respectful relations among the citizens of the world.

Notes

Preface

1. Arjun Appadurai, *Modernity at Large: Cultural Dimensions of Globalization* (Minneapolis: University of Minnesota Press, 1996), 18.

Introduction

1. Conversation with Anthony Sheppard and Tamara Levitz, UCLA, April 2017; Grace Wang, *Soundscapes of Asian America: Navigating Race through Musical Performance* (Durham: Duke University Press, 2015), 158–64.

2. Christopher Small, *Musicking: The Meanings of Performing and Listening* (Hanover, NH: University Press of New England, 1998), 13–14.

3. Miniwatts Marketing Group, "Internet World Stats," www.internetworldstats.com/stats.htm; World Bank Group, *World Development Report 2016: Digital Dividends Overview*, document 102724, https://openknowledge.worldbank.org/handle/10986/23347

4. John Tomlinson, *Globalization and Culture* (Chicago: University of Chicago Press, 1999), 9.

5. Tomlinson, 2; Arjun Appadurai, "Disjuncture and Difference in the Global Cultural Economy," *Theory, Culture & Society* 7 (1990): 296.

6. Anna Tsing, *Friction: An Ethnography of Global Connection* (Princeton: Princeton University Press, 2005), 9, 85.

7. David Harvey, "Time-Space Compression and the Postmodern Condition," in *The Global Transformations Reader*, ed. David Held and Anthony McGrew (Cambridge, UK: Polity Press, 2000), 82–91.

8. Saskia Sassen, *Territory—Authority—Rights: From Medieval to Global Assemblages* (Princeton: Princeton University Press, 2006), 299, 302–3.

9. This description of definitions is based on Bryan S. Turner, "Theories of Globalization: Issues and Origins," in *The Routledge International Handbook of Globalization Studies*, ed. Bryan S. Turner (New York: Routledge, 2010), 3–10.

10. Arjun Appadurai, *Modernity at Large: Cultural Dimensions of Globalization* (Minneapolis: University of Minnesota Press, 1996), 18, 178–99.

11. Danielle Fosler-Lussier, "Music Pushed, Music Pulled: Cultural Diplomacy, Globalization, and Imperialism," *Diplomatic History* 36, no. 1 (2012): 53–64.

12. Tsing, *Friction*, 4, 5.

13. Benedict Anderson, *Imagined Communities: Reflections on the Origin and Spread of Nationalism*, rev. ed. (1983; New York: Verso, 1991), 5–7.

14. Seyla Benhabib, *The Claims of Culture: Equality and Diversity in the Global Era* (Princeton: Princeton University Press, 2002), ix, 4. For a map that shows when geographic boundaries were established, see https://c1.staticflickr.com/5/4596/24556520177_d5a5b-6d97a_o.png

15. Edward Said, *Orientalism* (1978; New York: Vintage, 1994), 4–9, 54–63, and esp. 72–73.

16. Stephen Blum, "Music in an Age of Cultural Confrontation," in *Music-Cultures in Contact: Convergences and Collisions*, ed. Margaret J. Kartomi and Stephen Blum (Basel, CH: Gordon and Breach, 1994), 255.

17. Frantz Fanon, "Racism and Culture," in *Toward the African Revolution*, trans. Haakon Chevalier (New York: Grove Press, 1967), 34–35.

18. Gregory H. Stanton, "The 8 Stages of Genocide," paper presented to the US Department of State, 1996, www.genocidewatch.org/images/8StagesBriefingpaper.pdf; summary available at www.genocidewatch.org/aboutgenocide/8stagesofgenocide.html

19. Arjun Appadurai, *Fear of Small Numbers: An Essay on the Geography of Anger* (Durham: Duke University Press, 2006), 42–45.

20. Benhabib, *The Claims of Culture*, 6–10.

21. Henry Spiller, *Gamelan: The Traditional Sounds of Indonesia* (Santa Barbara: ABC-CLIO, 2004), xix.

22. Peter Howard, "The Heritage Discipline," *International Journal of Heritage Studies* 1, no. 1 (2007): 3–5.

23. Barbara Kirshenblatt-Gimblett, "Theorizing Heritage," *Ethnomusicology* 39, no. 3 (Autumn 1995): 373–79.

24. Seyla Benhabib, *The Claims of Culture: Equality and Diversity in the Global Era* (Princeton: Princeton University Press, 2002), 10.

25. Esther de Bruijn, "'What's Love' in an Interconnected World? Ghanaian Market Literature for Youth Responds," *Journal of Commonwealth Literature* 43, no. 3 (Sept. 2008): 11, 15, 18–21.

26. Maruša Pušnik and Kristina Sicherl, "Relocating and Personalising Salsa in Slovenia: To Dance Is to Communicate," *Anthropological Notebooks* 16, no. 3 (2010): 107–23.

27. Howard J. Ross, *Everyday Bias: Identifying and Navigating Unconscious Judgments in Our Daily Lives* (Lanham, MD: Rowman and Littlefield, 2014), 6–7.

28. Stuart Hall, "Race: The Floating Signifier," transcript, p. 8, Media Education Foundation, https://shop.mediaed.org/race-the-floating-signifier-p173.aspx. See also Benhabib, *The Claims of Culture*, 13; Nestór García Canclini, *Hybrid Cultures: Strategies for Entering and Leaving Modernity*, trans. Christopher L. Chiappari and Silvia L. López (Minneapolis: University of Minnesota Press, 1995), xxvi.

29. "West Coast Story, I. Frontiers of New Music," BBC TV, 29 Nov. 1986, as quoted in Neil Sorrell, *A Guide to the Gamelan* (London: Amadeus Press, 1990), 12.

30. See Ingrid Monson, *Saying Something: Jazz Improvisation and Interaction* (Chicago: University of Chicago Press, 1996), esp. 125–32.

Introduction to Part I

1. Russell King, ed., *Atlas of Human Migration* (Buffalo, NY: Firefly Press, 2007), 16, 20–21, 28, 42, 48–49.

2. Jeremy Waldron, "Indigeneity? First Peoples and Last Occupancy," *New Zealand Journal of Public and International Law* 1 (2003): 55–82; Francesca Merlan, "Indigeneity: Global and Local," *Current Anthropology* 50, no. 3 (June 2009): 303–33.

3. See, for example, the case studies in Jason Toynbee and Byron Dueck, eds., *Migrating Music* (New York: Routledge, 2011).

4. Saskia Sassen, *Territory—Authority—Rights: From Medieval to Global Assemblages* (Princeton: Princeton University Press, 2006), 40.

5. Sassen, 277–86; Arjun Appadurai, *Fear of Small Numbers: An Essay on the Geography of Anger* (Durham: Duke University Press, 2006), 3–7, 49–50; James Minahan, *Encyclopedia of the Stateless Nations: Ethnic and National Groups around the World* (Westport, CT: Greenwood Press, 2002); John Torpey, *The Invention of the Passport: Surveillance, Citizenship, and the State* (Cambridge: Cambridge University Press, 2000), 1–17.

6. Sassen, *Territory—Authority—Rights*, 287.

7. Appadurai, *Fear of Small Numbers*, 8, and chap. 4; Richard Wike, Bruce Stokes, and Katie Simmons, "Europeans Fear Wave of Refugees Will Mean More Terrorism, Fewer Jobs," Pew Research Center, 11 July 2016, www.pewglobal.org/2016/07/11/europeans-fear-wave-of-refugees-will-mean-more-terrorism-fewer-jobs

8. Benhabib, *The Claims of Culture*, xiii; Elsadig Elsheikh and Hossein Ayazi, "Moving Targets: An Analysis of Global Forced Migration," Research Report, Haas Institute for a Fair and Inclusive Society, University of California, Berkeley (June 2017), 5, http://haasin stitute.berkeley.edu/sites/default/files/haasinstitute_moving_targets_globalmigrationre port_publish_web.pdf

9. Sassen, *Territory—Authority—Rights*, 290–98.

10. Manuel Peña, *The Texas-Mexican Conjunto: History of a Working-Class Music* (Austin: University of Texas Press, 1985); Alejandro L. Madrid, ed., *Transnational Encounters: Music and Performance at the U.S.-Mexico Border* (New York: Oxford University Press, 2011).

11. James Fernandez, "Andalusia on Our Minds: Two Contrasting Places in Spain as Seen in a Vernacular Poetic Duel of the Late 19th Century," *Cultural Anthropology* 3, no. 1 (Feb. 1988): 21–35.

12. Alejandro Madrid, *Nor-tec Rifa! Electronic Dance Music from Tijuana to the World* (New York: Oxford University Press, 2008), 26.

13. Sassen, *Territory—Authority—Rights*, 82–83.

14. Susan Thomas, "Music, Conquest, and Colonialism," in *Musics of Latin America*, ed. Robin Moore (New York: W.W. Norton, 2012), 25–50; Robert Stevenson, "Mexico City Cathedral Music: 1600–1750," *The Americas* 21, no. 2 (Oct. 1964): 113–15, 130–33.

Chapter 1

1. Jane Burbank and Frederick Cooper, *Empires in World History: Power and the Politics of Difference* (Princeton: Princeton University Press, 2010), 5, 149–56; and Eric R. Wolf, *Europe and the People without History* (1982; Berkeley: University of California Press, 1997), 195–97.

2. Jean Gelman Taylor, *The Social World of Batavia: Europeans and Eurasians in Colonial Indonesia* (Madison: University of Wisconsin Press, 2009), 7–8, 11–19.

3. Burbank and Cooper, *Empires in World History*, 8; Saskia Sassen, *Territory—*

Authority—Rights: From Medieval to Global Assemblages (Princeton: Princeton University Press, 2006), 79–96.

4. The two foregoing paragraphs are a gloss on Burbank and Cooper, *Empires in World History*, 159–61.

5. Frans H. Winarta, "No More Discrimination against the Chinese," in *Ethnic Chinese in Contemporary Indonesia*, ed. Leo Suryadinata (Singapore: Chinese Heritage Centre and Institute of Southeast Asian Studies, 2008), 57–58.

6. J. C. M. Warnsinck, ed., *Reisen van Nicolaus de Graaf gedaan naar alle gewesten des werelds, beginnende 1639 tot 1687 incluis* ('s-Gravenhage: M. Nijhoff, 1930), 8, quoted in Taylor, *The Social World of Batavia*, 53.

7. Taylor, *The Social World of Batavia*, 57–59, 61–66, 238n16.

8. Taylor, 61.

9. Henry Spiller, *Gamelan: The Traditional Sounds of Indonesia* (Santa Barbara: ABC-CLIO, 2004), 25–26, 58–59, 70–74.

10. Franki S. Notosudirdjo, "Music, Politics, and the Problems of National Identity in Indonesia" (PhD diss., University of Wisconsin, Madison, 2001), 29–38, 74–85.

11. Franki S. Notosudirdjo, "European Music in Colonial Life in 19th-Century Java: A Preliminary Study" (MM thesis, University of Wisconsin, 1990), 12–14.

12. Notosudirdjo, "Music, Politics," 40.

13. Notosudirdjo, 37–40, 54–58, 85–94.

14. Notosudirdjo, 36.

15. I first learned about tanjidor from Sumarsam, who taught at the National Endowment for the Humanities Summer Institute for Ethnomusicology, Wesleyan University, 2011. See Sumarsam, *Javanese Gamelan and the West* (Rochester, NY: University of Rochester Press, 2013), 17–19; Notosudirdjo, "European Music in Colonial Life," 9.

16. Ernst Heins, "Kroncong and Tanjidor—Two Cases of Urban Folk Music in Jakarta," *Asian Music* 7, no. 1 (1975): 27–29.

17. Philip Yampolsky, liner notes to *Betawi and Sundanese Music of the North Coast of Java* (Washington, DC: Smithsonian Folkways 40421, 1994 [recorded 1990]), 10–12.

18. Nicholas B. Dirks, introduction to *Colonialism and Culture*, ed. Nicholas B. Dirks (Ann Arbor: University of Michigan Press, 1992), 3.

19. Jonathan D. Martin, "'The Grandest and Most Cosmopolitan Object Teacher': *Buffalo Bill's Wild West* and the Politics of American Identity, 1883–1899," *Radical History Review* 66 (1996): 95–97.

20. Annegret Fauser, "New Media, Source-Bonding, and Alienation: Listening at the 1889 Exposition Universelle," in *French Music, Culture, and National Identity, 1870–1939*, ed. Barbara L. Kelly (Rochester, NY: University of Rochester Press, 2008), 40–57.

21. Sindhumathi K. Revuluri, "On Anxiety and Absorption: Musical Encounters with the *Exotique* in Fin-de-siècle France" (PhD diss., Princeton University, 2007), 33–36. This section is based largely on Revuluri's work.

22. Otis T. Mason, "Anthropology in Paris during the Exposition of 1889," *American Anthropologist* 3, no. 1 (1890): 31. *Smithsonian Collections Online*, tinyurl.galegroup.com/tinyurl/5DbpLX

23. Sumarsam, *Javanese Gamelan and the West*, 92.

24. Mason, "Anthropology in Paris," 35; Dirks, *Colonialism and Culture*, 3.

25. Revuluri, "On Anxiety and Absorption," 24–33, 50; Sumarsam, *Javanese Gamelan and the West*, 82–84; Annegret Fauser, *Musical Encounters at the 1889 Paris World's Fair* (Rochester, NY: University of Rochester Press, 2005), 158–65; Edward Said, *Orientalism* (1978; New York: Vintage Books, 1994), 233–40.

26. Arjun Appadurai, *Modernity at Large: Cultural Dimensions of Globalization* (Minneapolis: University of Minnesota Press, 1996), 1–2, 9–11.

27. Revuluri, "On Anxiety and Absorption," 55, 39, 45.

28. Sumarsam, *Javanese Gamelan and the West*, 92–106; Revuluri, "On Anxiety and Absorption," 26, 55–56, 73, 90. See also Neil Sorrell, *A Guide to the Gamelan*, 2; and Fauser, *Musical Encounters*, 163–77.

29. Revuluri, "On Anxiety and Absorption," 76–77.

30. Fauser, *Musical Encounters*, 177–83; Jann Pasler, "Sonic Anthropology in 1900: The Challenge of Transcribing Non-Western Music and Language," *Twentieth-Century Music* 11, no. 1 (2014): 14; Richard Mueller, "Javanese Influence on Debussy's *Fantaisie* and Beyond," *19th Century Music* 10, no. 2 (Fall 1986): 162–66.

31. Revuluri, "On Anxiety and Absorption,"104–14, 99.

32. Said, *Orientalism*, esp. 4–8.

33. E. Monod, *L'Exposition Universelle de 1889*, 3:136–37, quoted in Revuluri, "On Anxiety and Absorption," 59.

34. Monod, *L'Exposition Universelle de 1889*, 2:565, quoted in Revuluri, "On Anxiety and Absorption," 56.

35. Debussy (1913), quoted in Edward Lockspeiser, *Debussy: His Life and Mind* (London: Cassell, 1962), 1:115. See also Richard Mueller, "Javanese Influence," 158.

36. Said, *Orientalism*, 12.

37. Sylvia Parker, "Claude Debussy's Gamelan," *College Music Symposium* 52 (2012): http://dx.doi.org/10.18177/sym.2012.52.sr.22

38. Claude Debussy, *Debussy on Music*, ed. François Lesure, trans. and ed. Richard Langham Smith (New York: Knopf, 1977), 16. Quoted in Mueller, "Javanese Influence," 179.

39. Richard Middleton notes the link between authenticity and modernity in "The Real Thing? The Spectre of Authenticity in Modern Musical Thought," in *Frispel: Festskrift till Olle Edström*, ed. Alf Björnberg (Göteborg: Institutionen för musikvetenskap, 2005), 477, 479–80.

40. Mueller, "Javanese Influence," 179–81.

41. Notosudirdjo, "Music, Politics," 94.

42. Homi Bhabha, *The Location of Culture* (New York: Routledge, 1994), 122 (Bhabha's italics). Cited in Sindhumathi K. Revuluri, "Maurice Ravel's *Chants populaires* and the Exotic Within," in *Rethinking Difference in Music Scholarship*, ed. Olivia Bloechl, Melanie Lowe, and Jeffrey Kallberg (New York: Cambridge University Press, 2015), 255–56.

43. Revuluri, 256–59.

44. Revuluri, "On Anxiety and Absorption," 115–16.

45. I Wayan Dibia, *Kecak: The Vocal Chant of Bali* (Denpasar, Indonesia: Hartanto Art Books Studio, 1996), 4–5. Kendra Stepputat attests to the rarity of the sacred form in her

"Performing *Kecak*: A Balinese Dance Tradition between Daily Routine and Creative Art," *Yearbook for Traditional Music* 44 (2012): 54.

46. Dibia, *Kecak*, 4, 10–16; Stepputat, "Performing *Kecak*," 70.

47. Dibia, *Kecak*, 20–24.

48. Plot summary in Dibia, 37.

49. Dibia, 7–8; Kendra Stepputat, "*Kecak* behind the Scenes—Investigating the *Kecak* Network," in *Dance Ethnography and Global Perspectives: Identity, Embodiment, Culture*, ed. Linda E. Dankworth and Ann R. David (Basingstoke: Palgrave Macmillan, 2014), 117.

50. Tantri Yuliandini, "Limbak, Rina: Two Generations of 'Kecak' Dancers," *Jakarta Post*, 18 May 2002, cited in Stepputat, "Performing *Kecak*," 54.

51. Ronaldo Morelos, "Angels of Bali: The Sanghyang Dedari Trance Performance Tradition," in *Intercultural Music: Creation and Interpretation*, ed. Sally Macarthur, Bruce Crossman, and Ronaldo Morelos (Grosvenor Place: Australian Music Centre, 2007): 90–100; personal communication from Jeremy Grimshaw, 9 Feb. 2018.

52. Stepputat, "Performing *Kecak*," 54.

53. Like the Indian version of the epic, the Indonesian version dramatizes the conflict between good and evil. It includes different deities than does the Indian text, and it is used for both moral instruction and entertainment.

54. Michel Picard, *Bali: Cultural Tourism and Touristic Culture*, trans. Diana Darling (Singapore: Archipelago Press, 1996), 20–23.

55. Picard, 25–28.

56. Kendra Stepputat, "Kecak Ramayana: Tourists in Search for the 'Real Thing,'" in *Hybridity in the Performing Arts of Southeast Asia*, ed. Mohd. Anis Md. Nor, Patricia Matusky, Tan Sooi Beng, Jacqueline-Pugh Kitingan, and Felicidad Prudente (Kuala Lumpur: Nusantara Performing Arts Research Centre, 2011), 43; Dibia, *Kecak*, 8–9; Stepputat, "Performing *Kecak*," 56–57.

57. Stepputat, "*Kecak* behind the Scenes," 118–19.

58. Mark Aarons, "Justice Betrayed: Post-1945 Responses to Genocide," in *The Legacy of Nuremberg: Civilising Influence or Institutionalized Vengeance?* ed. David A. Blumenthal and Timothy L. H. McCormack (Leiden: Martinus Nijhoff, 2008), 79–82; Picard, *Bali*, 40–42.

59. Stepputat, "Performing *Kecak*," 58–60.

60. Stepputat, "*Kecak* behind the Scenes," 121–22. On music in the New Order see Margaret Kartomi, "Music, Dance, and Ritual in Ternate and Tidore," in *Culture and Society in New Order Indonesia*, ed. Virginia Matheson Hooker (Kuala Lumpur: Oxford University Press, 1993), 187–89, 206–7.

61. Dibia, *Kecak*, 30, 57–58; Stepputat, "Performing *Kecak*," 58–60; Stepputat, "*Kecak* behind the Scenes," 127–28.

62. Stepputat, "*Kecak* behind the Scenes," 121–24.

63. Eric Hobsbawm, "Introduction: Inventing Traditions," in *The Invention of Tradition*, ed. Eric Hobsbawm and Terence Ranger (Cambridge: Cambridge University Press, 1983), 4–6, 9, 12, 13.

64. R. H. Bruce Lockhart, *Return to Malaya* (New York: G. P. Putnam's Sons, 1936), 345.

65. Barbara Kirshenblatt-Gimblett, "Theorizing Heritage," *Ethnomusicology* 39, no. 3 (Autumn 1995): 373–79.

66. "Animal Instinct," broadcast on National Geographic Channel, 1996, quoted in Stepputat, "Kecak Ramayana," 43.

67. Maria Mendonça, "Gamelan Performance Outside Indonesia 'Setting Sail': Babar Layar and Notions of 'Bi-musicality,'" *Asian Music* 42, no. 2 (Summer/Fall 2011): 57; Sumarsam, *Javanese Gamelan and the West*, 77–114.

68. David Ruffer, "Gamelan Alun Madu . . ." *Seleh Notes* 8, no. 3 (2001): 12, as cited in Maria Mendonça, "Gamelan in Britain: Communitas, Affinity, and Other Stories" (PhD diss., Wesleyan University, 2002), 291; Judith Becker, "One Perspective on Gamelan in America," *Asian Music* 15, no. 1 (1983): 81–89.

69. Mendonça, "Gamelan in Britain," 283–94; Sumarsam, *Javanese Gamelan and the West*, 106–14.

70. Anna Tsing, *Friction: An Ethnography of Global Connection* (Princeton: Princeton University Press, 2005), 4–5.

71. Laurie Margot Ross, *The Encoded Cirebon Mask: Materiality, Flow, and Meaning along Java's Islamic Northwest Coast* (Leiden: Brill, 2016), 64–67.

72. Sumarsam, *Javanese Gamelan and the West*, xiii.

73. Sumarsam, 6.

74. Andrew Weintraub, *Dangdut Stories: A Social and Musical History of Indonesia's Most Popular Music* (New York: Oxford University Press, 2010), 177, 194–96.

75. On tradition and novelty see Sumarsam, *Javanese Gamelan and the West*, 42–53.

Chapter 2

1. Lev Tcherenkov and Stéphane Laederich, *The Rroma* (Basel: Schwabe, 2004), 1:16–17, 72; Angus Fraser, *The Gypsies* (Oxford: Blackwell, 1992), 11–44.

2. Stephen Berman, "Gypsies: A National Group or a Social Group?" *Refugee Survey Quarterly* 13, no. 4 (Dec. 1994): 51–61.

3. Fraser, *The Gypsies*, 57, 109–12.

4. Tcherenkov and Laederich, *The Rroma*, 1:8, 118–40.

5. Fraser, *The Gypsies*, 257–70; see also "Genocide of European Roma (Gypsies), 1939–1945," United States Holocaust Memorial Museum, https://encyclopedia.ushmm.org/content/en/article/genocide-of-european-roma-gypsies-1939-1945; "Roma Victims of the Holocaust: Roma in Auschwitz," Jewish Virtual Museum, www.jewishvirtuallibrary.org/roma-gypsies-in-auschwitz; Petra Gelbart and Aleisa Fishman, *Voices on Antisemitism*, a podcast series of the United States Holocaust Memorial Museum, www.ushmm.org/m/audio/voa_20140306.mp3

6. I owe this information to Lynn Hooker. For detailed updates, see www.errc.org

7. For the material about Romungro and Vlach Roma musicians throughout this section, I am indebted to a set of teaching notes given to me by Lynn Hooker. My thanks to Professor Hooker for sharing them.

8. David E. Schneider, *Bartók, Hungary, and the Renewal of Tradition: Case Studies in the Intersection of Modernity and Nationality* (Berkeley: University of California Press, 2006), 26.

9. Lynn M. Hooker, "Turks, Hungarians, and Gypsies on Stage: Exoticism and Auto-Exoticism in Opera and Operetta," *Hungarian Studies* 27, no. 2 (2013): 295–97. See also

Lynn M. Hooker, *Redefining Hungarian Music from Liszt to Bartók* (New York: Oxford University Press, 2013), 35–45.

10. Hooker, "Turks, Hungarians, and Gypsies," 295–97; Schneider, *Bartók, Hungary,* 15–26.

11. Gábor Mátray, quoted in Bálint Sárosi, *Gypsy Music* (Budapest: Corvina, 1978), 144; and Jonathan Bellman, *The* Style Hongrois *in the Music of Western Europe* (Boston: Northeastern University Press, 1993), 178. This section of my chapter draws on Hooker, *Redefining Hungarian Music,* 78–94.

12. Hooker, *Redefining Hungarian Music,* 133–40, 150–53.

13. Hooker, *Redefining Hungarian Music,* 82–88.

14. See Katalin Kovalcsik, "The Music of the Roma in Hungary," *Rombase,* Sept. 2003, 1–3, http://rombase.uni-graz.at/cd/data/music/countries/data/hungary.en.pdf

15. Other Vlach Roma groups elsewhere in Europe have their own musical styles that do include instruments. See Tcherenkov and Laederich, *The Rroma,* 2:709–11.

16. Translation from the liner notes to *Gypsy Folk Songs from Hungary,* collected and edited by Rudolf Víg (Hungaroton SLPX18028-29, 1976).

17. Hungarian lyrics translated by the author.

18. A video example is available in Jeremy Marre's film *The Romany Trail* (Harcourt Films, 1981), part 2, timepoint 1:18:29.

19. Lynn Hooker, "Controlling the Liminal Power of Performance: Hungarian Scholars and Romani Musicians in the Hungarian Folk Revival," *Twentieth-Century Music* 3, no. 1 (March 2007): 51–72.

20. Philip V. Bohlman, *World Music: A Very Short Introduction* (New York: Oxford University Press, 2002), xiv–xv, 143–50.

21. See Miriam Whaples, "Early Exoticism Revisited," in *The Exotic in Western Music,* ed. Jonathan Bellman (Boston: Northeastern University Press, 1998), 3–25; and Catherine Mayes, "Turkish and Hungarian-Gypsy Styles," in *The Oxford Handbook of Topic Theory,* ed. Danuta Mirka (New York: Oxford University Press, 2014), 214–37.

22. According to Jonathan Bellman this may be the first example of the Romungro "music for listening" style to appear in Viennese classical music. Bellman, *The* Style Hongrois, 49.

23. Bálint Sárosi, *Gypsy Music,* trans. Fred Macnicol (Budapest: Corvina, 1978), 62–65.

24. Matthew Head, "Haydn's Exoticisms: Difference and the Enlightenment," in *The Cambridge Companion to Haydn,* ed. Caryl Clark (Cambridge: Cambridge University Press, 2011), 79.

25. See Bellman, *The* Style Hongrois, 69–92.

26. Franz Liszt, *The Gipsy in Music,* trans. Edwin Evans, 2 vols. (London: W. Reeves, 1926), 1:82.

27. Liszt, 2:306.

28. Frantz Fanon, "Racism and Culture," in *Toward the African Revolution,* trans. Haakon Chevalier (New York: Grove Press, 1967), 34–35; Jonathan Bellman, introduction to *The Exotic in Western Music* (Boston: Northeastern University Press, 1998), ix.

29. Ralph Locke, *Musical Exoticism: Images and Reflections* (Cambridge: Cambridge University Press, 2009), esp. 1–2, 8–12.

30. I owe this idea to Lynn Hooker; personal communication with the author, 15 May 2018.

31. Dana Gooley, *The Virtuoso Liszt* (Cambridge: Cambridge University Press, 2004), 129–30, 140–51.

32. Alaina Lemon, *Between Two Fires: Gypsy Performance and Romani Memory from Pushkin to Post-Socialism* (Durham: Duke University Press, 2000), 1–5. Lynn Hooker notes that the "Gypsy punk" band Gogol Bordello makes an identical point in their song "Break the Spell," from *Trans-Continental Hustle* (American Recordings, 2010).

33. Stuart Hall, "Race: The Floating Signifier," transcript, 9. Media Education Foundation, https://shop.mediaed.org/race-the-floating-signifier-p173.aspx

34. Jewish Telegraphic Agency, "Roma, Jews in Hungary Laud Gypsy Singer's Eurovision Progress," 12 May 2017, www.jta.org/2017/05/12/culture/gypises-jews-in-hungary-celebrate-roma-singers-progress-in-eurovision-song-contest

35. Paul Jordan, "The 2017 Eurovision Song Contest Reaches Over 180 Million Viewers," 23 May 2017, https://eurovision.tv/story/Eurovision-2017-reaches-more-than-180-million; "Eurovision Song Contest: Facts and Figures," Eurovision Song Contest website, https://eurovision.tv/about/facts-and-figures

36. Elise Morton, "Eurovision 2017: Why This Mix of Camp and Nationalism Still Matters," *Calvert Journal* (London), 11 May 2017, www.calvertjournal.com/opinion/show/8260/eurovision-2017-nationalism-russia-ukraine

37. Carol Silverman, *Romani Routes: Cultural Politics and Balkan Music in Diaspora* (New York: Oxford University Press, 2012), 172–74.

38. Bernard Rorke, "10 Things They Said about Roma in Hungary," European Roma Rights Centre Blog, 27 Oct. 2015, www.errc.org/blog/10-things-they-said-about-roma-in-hungary/83. See also Emily L. Mahoney, "It's Hard to Be a Gypsy in My Town," Cronkite News Borderlands Project, 11 July 2016, https://cronkitenews.azpbs.org/buffett/hungary/roma-village

39. Helena Nilsson, "Joci Pápai Is Hungary's Choice for Eurovision 2017," Eurovision Song Contest website, 18 Feb. 2017, https://eurovision.tv/story/joci-papai-is-hungary-s-choice-for-eurovision-2017; "Hungary in the Eurovision Song Contest 2017," Wikipedia, https://en.wikipedia.org/wiki/Hungary_in_the_Eurovision_Song_Contest_2017

40. Silverman, *Romani Routes*, 241.

41. Paul Jordan, "Ukraine Is Ready to Celebrate Diversity in 2017," Eurovision Song Contest website, 30 Jan. 2017, https://eurovision.tv/story/ukraine-is-ready-to-celebrate-diversity-in-2017

42. Quoted in Yulia Kryvinchuk, "What Does Celebrate Diversity Mean?" Eurovision Song Contest website, 10 May 2017, https://eurovision.tv/story/meaning-of-celebrate-diversity-2017

43. "22 Pictures Show How Eurovision Is Changing Kyiv," *Hromadske International* (Ukraine), English version, 26 April 2017, https://en.hromadske.ua/posts/how-eurovision-is-changing-kyiv

44. Sergey Movchan, "The Reconstruction of Kyiv for Eurovision and the Tradition of Potemkin Villages," trans. Roksolana Mashkova and Rebekah Switala, *Political Critique: Krytyka Polityczna & European Alternatives*, 8 May 2017, http://politicalcritique.org/cee/ukraine/2017/reconstruction-kyiv-eurovision-potemkin

45. Arkadiy Bushchenko, Ukrainian Helsinki Human Rights Union, "Official Appeal to Volodymir Hroisman Due with Cleansing of the Roma Settlements during the Preparation of the 2017 Eurovision Song Contest," 18 April 2017, https://helsinki.org.ua/en/appeals/official-appeal-to-volodymir-hroisman-due-with-cleansing-of-the-roma-settlements-during-the-preparation-of-the-2017-eurovision-song-contest

46. Movchan, "The Reconstruction of Kyiv."

47. The "old-style" folk song, identified by the composer and folk-song collector Béla Bartók, was characterized by an open-ended formal pattern, without repeated music to close the verse. See Bartók, "Hungarian Peasant Music" (1933), in *Béla Bartók Essays*, ed. Benjamin Suchoff (New York: St. Martin's, 1976), 80–102.

48. "Interview: Joci Pápai on One-Man Shows, Singing in the Shower and the Value of a Romani Boy from Hungary." *Good Evening Europe*, 21 Feb. 2017, www.goodeveningeurope.net/2017/02/21/interview-joci-papai-on-the-importance-of-being-alone-singing-in-the-shower-and-being-a-romani-boy-from-hungary

49. My analysis here is indebted to refinements from Lynn Hooker; personal communication with the author, 15 May 2018.

50. See Carol Silverman, "Trafficking in the Exotic with 'Gypsy' Music: Balkan Roma, Cosmopolitanism, and 'World Music' Festivals," in *Balkan Popular Culture and the Ottoman Ecumene*, ed. Donna A. Buchanan (Lanham, MD: Scarecrow Press, 2007), 348–52; Reuters, "Croatia's 'Mr. Voice' and Hungarian Gypsy Singer among Eurovision Finalists," 12 May 2017, www.reuters.com/article/us-music-eurovision/croatias-mr-voice-and-hungarian-gypsy-singer-among-eurovision-finalists-idUSKBN1881BE

51. Anikó Imre, "Roma Music and Transnational Homelessness," *Third Text* 22, no. 3 (May 2008): 325–36.

52. Imre, 333–36; Silverman, *Romani Routes*, 174–75.

53. Silverman, *Romani Routes*, 236.

54. Peter Vermeersch, "Roma Mobilization and Participation: Obstacles and Opportunities," in *Realizing Roma Rights*, ed. Jacqueline Bhabha, Andrzej Mirga, and Margareta Matache (Philadelphia: University of Pennsylvania Press, 2017): 200–213; "Who We Are," European Roma Rights Centre website, www.errc.org/about-us-overview

55. Valeriu Nicolae and Hannah Slavik, *Roma Diplomacy* (New York: International Debate Education Association, 2007), x.

56. Adriana Helbig, "'Play for Me, Old Gypsy': Music as Political Resource in the Roma Rights Movement in Ukraine" (PhD diss., Columbia University, 2005), 3–15, 25–34, 159–75.

57. Lynn Hooker, "Dancing on the Edge of a Volcano: East European Roma Performers Respond to Social Transformation," *Hungarian Studies* 25, no. 2 (2011): 295–99.

Chapter 3

1. More than 12 million Africans were sent to the Americas, but only 10 million survived the brutally difficult journey. These figures are from Peter Stearns, *Cultures in Motion: Mapping Key Concepts and Their Imprints in World History* (New Haven: Yale University Press, 2001), 66–73. Estimates of lives lost in the slave trade have been controversial: see "Introduction: Gainers and Losers in the Atlantic Slave Trade," in *The Atlantic Slave Trade:*

Effects on Economies, Societies, and Peoples in Africa, the Americas, and Europe, ed. Joseph E. Inikori and Stanley L. Engerman (Durham: Duke University Press, 1992), 5–7; Gwendolyn Midlo Hall, *Slavery and African Ethnicities in the Americas* (Chapel Hill: University of North Carolina Press, 2005), xiii–xv; *Trans-Atlantic Slave Trade Database*, ed. David Eltis, www.slavevoyages.org; and Eric R. Wolf, *Europe and the People without History* (1982; Berkeley: University of California Press, 1997), 131–35, 149–57, 195–231.

2. Henry Louis Gates, "Editor's Introduction: Writing 'Race' and the Difference It Makes," *Critical Inquiry* 12, no. 1 (Autumn 1985): 2–9. Brian Currid has compared the situations of racialized Romani and African American musicians; see Brian Currid, "'Gypsy Violins' and 'Hot Rhythms': Race, Popular Music, and Governmentality," in *Western Music and Race*, ed. Julie Brown (Cambridge: Cambridge University Press, 2007): 37–48.

3. Katrina Dyonne Thompson, *Ring Shout, Wheel About* (Urbana: University of Illinois Press, 2014), 8–9, 42–68.

4. Dena Epstein, "African Music in British and French America," *Musical Quarterly* 59, no. 1 (1973): 64–67, 79–89; Thompson, *Ring Shout*, 99–128.

5. Gerhard Kubik, *Africa and the Blues* (Jackson: University Press of Mississippi, 1999), 12, 15–20; Dena Epstein, "The Folk Banjo: A Documentary History," *Ethnomusicology* 19, no. 3 (1975): 347–71. The material in this section draws on Kubik's book, and the music examples are drawn from the recording that accompanies the book.

6. Gwendolyn Midlo Hall argues that some groups of people were able to remain together; see Hall, *Slavery and African Ethnicities*, 22–79, 165–72.

7. Paul E. Lovejoy, "The African Diaspora: Revisionist Interpretations of Ethnicity, Culture and Religion under Slavery," *Studies in the World History of Slavery, Abolition and Emancipation* 2, no. 1 (1997): n.p. Ronald Radano has critiqued the idea of "survivals" in *Lying Up a Nation: Race and Black Music* (Chicago: University of Chicago Press, 2003), 5–13, 55–63.

8. V. Kofi Agawu, *The African Imagination in Music* (Oxford: Oxford Scholarship Online, 2016), 308.

9. Jeff Todd Titon, *Early Downhome Blues: A Musical and Cultural Analysis* (Urbana: University of Illinois Press, 1977), 44.

10. Mississippi Matilda Powell, Sonny Boy Nelson, and Willie Harris Jr., "Hard Workin' Woman," originally issued as Bluebird B6812 (78 rpm), 1936.

11. Kubik, *Africa and the Blues*, 82–93.

12. Kubik, 74–75.

13. Kubik, 200–203.

14. Thompson, *Ring Shout*, esp. 2–7 and chap. 3; Karen Sotiropoulos, *Staging Race: Black Performers in Turn of the Century America* (Cambridge, MA: Harvard University Press, 2006), 1.

15. Peter C. Muir, *Long Lost Blues: Popular Blues in America, 1850–1920* (Urbana: University of Illinois Press, 2010); Paige A. McGinley, *Staging the Blues: From Tent Shows to Tourism* (Durham: Duke University Press, 2014), 1–127; Elijah Wald, *Escaping the Delta: Robert Johnson and the Invention of the Blues* (New York: Harper Collins, 2004), 4–42.

16. McGinley, *Staging the Blues*, 129–75; Danielle Fosler-Lussier, *Music in America's Cold War Diplomacy* (Oakland: University of California Press, 2015), 148–52.

17. See, e.g., Resolution of the Writers' Union of Canada (1992), quoted in Bruce Ziff and Pratima V. Rao, "Introduction to Cultural Appropriation: A Framework for Analysis," in *Borrowed Power: Essays on Cultural Appropriation*, ed. Bruce Ziff and Pratima V. Rao (New Brunswick, NJ: Rutgers University Press, 1997), 1.

18. Rupert Till, "The Blues Blueprint: The Blues in the Music of the Beatles, the Rolling Stones, and Led Zeppelin," in *Cross the Water Blues: African American Music in Europe*, ed. Neil A. Wynn (Jackson: University Press of Mississippi, 1997), 195–97; Susan Oehler Herrick, "Performing Blues and Navigating Race in Transcultural Contexts," in *Issues in African American Music: Power, Gender, Race, Representation*, ed. Portia K. Maultsby and Mellonee V. Burnim (London: Routledge, 2017), 20–23.

19. It is difficult to pin down a source for this widely quoted statement. It is unattributed in "Muddy Waters," *The Penguin Encyclopedia of Popular Music*, ed. Donald Clarke (London: Viking, 1989), 1217.

20. Ulrich Adelt, "Trying to Find an Identity: Eric Clapton's Changing Conception of Blackness," *Popular Music and Society* 31, no. 4 (Oct. 2008): 433–52.

21. Leon F. Litwack, *Trouble in Mind: Black Southerners in the Age of Jim Crow* (New York: Alfred A. Knopf, 1998), 452, quoted in Christian O'Connell, *Blues, How Do You Do? Paul Oliver and the Transatlantic Story of the Blues* (Ann Arbor: University of Michigan Press, 2015), 3.

22. Mike Baker and John Pidgeon, "'It Takes a Great Deal of Studying and Discipline for Me to Sing the Blues" [1994], in *Guitar Player Presents: Clapton Beck Page*, ed. Michael Molenda (New York: Backbeat Books, 2010), 66.

23. Stuart Hall, "The Spectacle of the 'Other,'" in *Representation: Cultural Representations and Signifying Practices*, ed. Stuart Hall (Milton Keynes: Open University, 1997), 243–49; O'Connell, *Blues*, 2–9.

24. See Martin Stokes, introduction to *Ethnicity, Identity, and Music: The Musical Construction of Place* (Oxford: Berg, 1994), 6–7.

25. Titon, *Early Downhome Blues*, 31.

26. Lynn Abbott and Doug Seroff, *Ragged but Right: Black Traveling Shows, "Coon Songs," and the Dark Pathway to Blues and Jazz* (Jackson: University Press of Mississippi, 2007). On "discovery" by the revival see Jeff Todd Titon, "Reconstructing the Blues: Reflections on the 1960s Blues Revival," in *Transforming Tradition: Folk Music Revivals Examined*, ed. Neil V. Rosenberg (Urbana: University of Illinois Press, 1993), 222–23; Herrick, "Performing Blues," 24–42; and Titon, *Early Downhome Blues*, 50–51.

27. Robert M. W. Dixon and John Godrich, *Recording the Blues* (New York: Stein and Day, 1970); Sandra R. Lieb, *Mother of the Blues: A Study of Ma Rainey* (Amherst: University of Massachusetts Press, 1981), 1–48.

28. Titon, *Early Downhome Blues*, 45–51.

29. Portia K. Maultsby, "The Politics of Race Erasure in Defining Black Popular Music Origins," in Maultsby and Burnim, *Issues in African American Music*, 20–23.

30. Hall, "The Spectacle of the 'Other,'" 257–64.

31. The term is associated with the theorist Gayatri Spivak, who has since disavowed its use. See Sara Danius, Stefan Jonsson, and Gayatri Chakravorty Spivak, "An Interview with Gayatri Chakravorty Spivak," *boundary 2* 20, no. 2 (Summer 1993): 24–50.

32. LeRoi Jones [Amiri Baraka], *Blues People: Negro Music in White America* (New York: William Morrow, 1963), 148.

33. Amiri Baraka, "The Great Music Robbery," in Amiri Baraka and Amina Baraka, *The Music: Reflections on Jazz and Blues* (New York: William Morrow, 1987), 331.

34. Radano, *Lying Up a Nation*, 39–42, 168–69.

35. Amiri Baraka, "Jazz and the White Critic" (1963), in *Black Music* (New York: Apollo, 1968), 13, quoted in Joel Rudinow, "Race, Ethnicity, Expressive Authenticity: Can White People Sing the Blues?" *Journal of Aesthetics and Art Criticism* 52, no. 1 (Winter 1994): 135.

36. See Nancy Fraser, "Redistribution or Recognition? A Critique of Justice Truncated," in *Redistribution or Recognition? A Political-Philosophical Exchange*, ed. Nancy Fraser and Axel Honneth (London: Verso, 2003), 9–26; and Briahna Joy Gray, "The Question of Cultural Appropriation," *Current Affairs*, 6 Sept. 2017, www.currentaffairs.org/2017/09/the-question-of-cultural-appropriation

37. Kwame Anthony Appiah, "Whose Culture Is It, Anyway?" in *Cultural Heritage Issues: The Legacy of Conquest, Colonization, and Commerce*, ed. James A. R. Nafziger and Ann M. Nigorski (Leiden: Martinus Nijhoff, 2010), 210.

38. Thomas DeFrantz, "American Traditions in Dance and Its Study," lecture given at Ohio State University, 5 Feb. 2019.

39. Dena Epstein, *Sinful Tunes and Spirituals: Black Folk Music to the Civil War* (Urbana: University of Illinois Press, 1977), 100–111, 217–37; Eileen Southern, *The Music of Black Americans: A History*, 3rd ed. (New York: Norton, 1997), 35–41, 71–80; Sylvia R. Frey and Betty Wood, *Come Shouting to Zion: African American Protestantism in the American South and British Caribbean to 1830* (Chapel Hill: University of North Carolina Press, 1998), 65–79.

40. Jon Cruz, *Culture on the Margins: The Black Spiritual and the Rise of American Cultural Interpretation* (Princeton: Princeton University Press, 1999), 67–69.

41. Southern, *The Music of Black Americans*, 71–84.

42. John F. Watson, *Methodist Error*, in *Readings in Black American Music*, ed. Eileen Southern, 2nd ed. (New York: W.W. Norton, 1983), 63. See also Epstein, *Sinful Tunes and Spirituals*, 196–99.

43. William T. Dargan, *Lining Out the Word: Dr. Watts Hymn Singing in the Music of Black Americans* (Berkeley: University of California Press and Columbia College Chicago: Center for Black Music Research, 2006), 103–19.

44. Henry Russell, *Cheer, Boys, Cheer!* (1895), 85, quoted in Portia Maultsby, "Traditional Music: African-American," USA, §2, 2, Grove Music Online. https://doi.org/10.1093/gmo/9781561592630.article.28794

45. Bernice Johnson Reagon, *If You Don't Go, Don't Hinder Me: The African American Song Tradition* (Lincoln: University of Nebraska Press, 2001), 68.

46. Lawrence Levine, "The Antebellum Period: Communal Coherence and Individual Expression," in Maultsby and Burnim, *Issues in African American Music*, 411, 412, 415.

47. For selection of the examples in this section I am indebted to the unpublished research of Tracie Parker.

48. Charles Keil, "Participatory Discrepancies and the Power of Music," *Cultural Anthropology* 2, no. 3 (August 1987): 275–83.

49. Alan Lomax, liner notes to *The Gospel Ship: Baptist Hymns & White Spirituals from the Southern Mountains* (1977; New World Records 80294, 1994).

50. George Pullen Jackson, *White and Negro Spirituals: Their Life Span and Kinship* (New York: J. J. Augustin, 1943), 260–69; Reagon, *If You Don't Go*, 77–82.

51. Reagon, *If You Don't Go*, 78.

52. Radano, *Lying Up a Nation*, 4.

53. Radano, 168–69.

54. H. H. Wright, "Jubilee Songs at Chapel Exercises," quoted in Sandra Jean Graham, *Spirituals and the Birth of a Black Entertainment Industry* (Champaign-Urbana: University of Illinois Press, 2017), 30.

55. Ella Sheppard Moore, "Historical Sketch," 43; as quoted in Graham, *Spirituals*, 31.

56. Graham, *Spirituals*, 62–73. This section relies throughout on Graham's history.

57. Graham, xiii, 51–72, 83–100.

58. Graham, 48.

59. Graham, 50, 74.

60. Graham, 74–81.

61. See Marva Griffin Carter, "The 'New Negro' Choral Legacy of Hall Johnson," in *Chorus and Community*, ed. Karen Ahlquist (Urbana: University of Illinois Press, 2006), 185–201.

62. Gates, "Editor's Introduction," 12–15.

63. Zora Neale Hurston, "Spirituals and Neo-spirituals," in *The Sanctified Church* (Berkeley, CA: Turtle Island, 1981), 80. See also Shelley Eversley, *The Real Negro: The Question of Authenticity in Twentieth-Century African American Literature* (London: Routledge, 2004), 26.

64. Marti K. Newland, "Sounding 'Black': An Ethnography of Racialized Vocality at Fisk University" (PhD diss., Columbia University, 2014), 40–73.

65. See Olly Wilson, "Negotiating Blackness in Western Art Music," in Maultsby and Burnim, *Issues in African American Music*, 66–67, 72–74.

Chapter 4

1. Jonathan Sterne, *MP3: The Meaning of a Format* (Durham: Duke University Press, 2012), 9–11. On the mediation of concert music see the essays in *Consuming Music: Individuals, Institutions, Communities, 1730–1830*, ed. Emily H. Green and Catherine Mayes (Rochester, NY: University of Rochester Press, 2017).

2. Mark Katz, *Capturing Sound: How Technology Has Changed Music* (Berkeley: University of California Press, 2004), 74. This chapter originated in lessons taught from Katz's book; I am broadly indebted to his thinking throughout.

3. Tan Sooi Beng, "The 78 RPM Record Industry in Malaya prior to World War II," *Asian Music* 28, no. 1 (Fall/Winter 1996–97): 1.

4. Geoffrey Jones, "The Gramophone Company: An Anglo-American Multinational," *Business History Review* 59, no. 1 (Spring 1985): 77; Ali Jihad Racy, "Record Industry and Egyptian Traditional Music: 1904–1932," *Ethnomusicology* 20, no. 1 (Jan. 1976): 27–28; Tan, "The 78 RPM Record Industry," 3. Christina Lubinski and Andreas Steen, "Traveling Entrepreneurs, Traveling Sounds: The Early Gramophone Business in India and China," *Itinerario* 41, no. 2 (2017): 275–303.

5. Paul Vernon, "Odeon Records: Their Ethnic Output," www.mustrad.org.uk.proxy. lib.ohio-state.edu/articles/odeon.htm; Bruno Sébald, "L'édition du disque," *Revue de la BNF* 3, no. 33 (2009): 34, www.cairn.info/revue-de-la-bibliotheque-nationale-de-france-2009-3-page-30.html; Lubinski and Steen, "Traveling Entrepreneurs," 290.

6. Tan, "The 78 RPM Record Industry," 4, 10.

7. Wolfgang Bender, "Modern African Music—An Autonomous Music," in *Sounds of Change—Social and Political Features of Music in Africa*, ed. Stig-Magnus Thorsén (Stockholm: Sida, 2004): 89–90; Lubinski and Steen, "Traveling Entrepreneurs," 284.

8. Drago Kunej, "Intertwinement of Croatian and Slovenian Musical Heritage on the Oldest Gramophone Records," *Croatian Journal of Ethnology and Folklore Research* 51, no. 1 (2014): 148–49.

9. Tan, "The 78 RPM Record Industry," 3, 23, 7.

10. Hinda Ouijjani, "Le fonds de disques 78 tours Pathé de musique arabe et orientale donné aux Archives de la Parole et au Musée de la Parole et du Geste de l'Université de Paris: 1911–1930" (The collection of Pathé 78 rpm discs of Arab and Oriental music given to the Archives de la Parole and the Musée de la Parole et du Geste of the University of Paris, 1911–1930), *Sonorités (Bulletin de l'AFAS)* 38 (2012): 1–14; and 39 (2013): 2–9, http://afas.revues.org/2835

11. Ali Jihad Racy, "Sound Recording in the Life of Early Arab-American Immigrants," *Revue des traditions musicales des mondes Arabe et Méditerranéen* 5 (2011): 43–44.

12. Racy, "Record Industry and Egyptian Traditional Music," 41–42.

13. Pekka Gronow, "Ethnic Recordings: An Introduction," in American Folklife Center, *Ethnic Recordings in America: A Neglected Heritage* (Washington, DC: Library of Congress, 1982), 1–31; William Howland Kenney, *Recorded Music in American Life: The Phonograph and Popular Memory, 1890–1945* (New York: Oxford University Press, 1999), 65–87.

14. Drago Kunej and Rebeka Kunej, *Music from Both Sides: Gramophone Records Made by Matija Arko and the Hoyer Trio* (Ljubljana: Založba ZRC, 2017), 33–57; and Richard K. Spottswood, ed., *Ethnic Music on Records: A Discography of Ethnic Recordings Produced in the United States, 1893 to 1942* (Urbana: University of Illinois Press, 1990).

15. Emilie Da Lage-Py, "Les collections de disques de musiques du monde entre patrimonialisation et marchandisation" (Collections of music records of the world between heritage and marketing), *Culture & musées*, no. 1 (2003): 89–90.

16. Darius Milhaud, "Chronique des disques" (Chronicle of recordings), *Art et décoration: Revue mensuelle d'art moderne* (Oct. 1930): 8.

17. Percy Grainger, "Collecting with the Phonograph," *Journal of the Folk-Song Society* 3, no. 12 (May 1908): 147.

18. Graham Freeman, "'That Chief Undercurrent of My Mind': Percy Grainger and the Aesthetics of English Folk Song," *Folk Music Journal* 9, no. 4 (2009): 608–11.

19. "Special General Meeting," *Journal of the Folk-Song Society* 8, no. 35 (Dec. 1931): x–xi.

20. On the threat of homogenization see Katz, *Capturing Sound*, 13–14. See also Matthew Gelbart, *The Invention of "Folk Music" and "Art Music"* (New York: Cambridge University Press, 2007), 272–77.

21. Bruno Nettl, "Hanging On for Dear Life: Archives and Preservation," in *The Study*

of Ethnomusicology: Thirty-One Issues and Concepts (Champaign: University of Illinois Press, 2005), 167; Graham Freeman, "'It Wants All the Creases Ironing Out': Percy Grainger, the Folk Song Society, and the Ideology of the Archive," *Music and Letters* 92, no. 3 (2011): 412–16; Martin Stokes, introduction to *Ethnicity, Identity, and Music: The Musical Construction of Place* (Oxford: Berg, 1994), 6–7; Barbara Kirshenblatt-Gimblett, "Theorizing Heritage," *Ethnomusicology* 39, no. 3 (Autumn 1995): 373–79.

22. Nestór García Canclini, *Hybrid Cultures: Strategies for Entering and Leaving Modernity*, trans. Christopher L. Chiappari and Silvia L. López (Minneapolis: University of Minnesota Press, 1995), 223–24; Diana Taylor, *The Archive and the Repertoire: Performing Cultural Memory in the Americas* (Durham: Duke University Press, 2003), 18–22; Nathaniel G. Lew, "'Words and Music That Are Forever England': *The Pilgrim's Progress* and the Pitfalls of Nostalgia," *Vaughan Williams Essays* (2002): 175–206; Freeman, "'It Wants All the Creases Ironing Out,'" 412.

23. Meltem Ahiska, "Occidentalism: The Historical Fantasy of the Modern," *South Atlantic Quarterly* 102, no. 2/3 (Spring–Summer 2003): 351–79.

24. Ziya Gökalp, *The Principles of Turkism*, ed. and trans. Robert Devereux (Leiden: Brill, 1968), 99, quoted in Erol Koymen, "A Musical Minefield: Composing the Turkish Nation-State," paper delivered at the Joint Conference of the AMS-Southwest Chapter and SEM-Southern Plains Chapter, http://ams-sw.org/Proceedings/AMS-SW_V3Spring 2014Koymen.pdf. See also Martin Stokes, *The Arabesk Debate: Music and Musicians in Modern Turkey* (Oxford: Clarendon, 1992), 21–49.

25. Orhan Tekelioğlu, "The Rise of a Spontaneous Synthesis: The Historical Background of Turkish Popular Music," *Middle Eastern Studies* 32, no. 2 (1996): 196–98, 205–7; Edward Said, *Orientalism* (1978; New York: Vintage, 1994), esp. 4–8.

26. Eric Hobsbawm, "Introduction: Inventing Tradition," in *The Invention of Tradition*, ed. Eric Hobsbawm and Terence Ranger (Cambridge: Cambridge University Press, 1983), 4–6, 9, 12, 13.

27. Robert C. Lancefield, "Musical Traces' Retraceable Paths: The Repatriation of Recorded Sound," *Journal of Folklore Research* 35, no. 1 (Jan.–April 1998): 47.

28. See Resolution of the Writers' Union of Canada (1992), cited in Bruce Ziff and Pratima V. Rao, "Introduction to Cultural Appropriation: A Framework for Analysis," in *Borrowed Power: Essays on Cultural Appropriation*, ed. Bruce Ziff and Pratima V. Rao (New Brunswick, NJ: Rutgers University Press, 1997), 1.

29. Aaron Fox, "Repatriation as Reanimation through Reciprocity," in *The Cambridge History of World Music*, ed. Philip V. Bohlman (Cambridge: Cambridge University Press, 2013), 533–34, 537.

30. Lancefield, "Musical Traces' Retraceable Paths," 53–54.

31. Fox, "Repatriation as Reanimation," 533–35; Lancefield, "Musical Traces' Retraceable Paths," 54.

32. Lancefield, "Musical Traces' Retraceable Paths," 48.

33. This paragraph and the next two are based on Aaron Fox, "Repatriation as Reanimation," 522–54.

34. "Rare Indigenous Music Recordings Go Home Again," Columbia University News, https://vimeo.com/68637578

35. See also Thomas R. Hilder, "Repatriation, Revival and Transmission: The Politics of a Sámi Musical Heritage," *Ethnomusicology Forum* 21, no. 2 (August 2012): 170.

36. Katz, *Capturing Sound*, 100–101.

37. Mezz Mezzrow with Bernard Wolfe, *Really the Blues* (London: Flamingo, 1993), 325–26, quoted in Albin J. Zak III, *The Poetics of Rock: Cutting Tracks, Making Records* (Berkeley: University of California Press, 2001), 7.

38. Michael Khoury, "A Look at Lightning: The Life and Compositions of Halim El-Dabh," in *The Arab Avant-Garde: Music, Politics, Modernity*, ed. Thomas Burkhalter, Kay Dickinson, and Benjamin J. Harbert (Middletown, CT: Wesleyan University Press, 2013), 171–72.

39. Brian Kane, *Sound Unseen: Acousmatic Sound in Theory and Practice* (New York: Oxford University Press, 2014), 4–6.

40. Walter Benjamin, "The Work of Art in the Age of Mechanical Reproduction," in *Illuminations*, ed. Hannah Arendt, trans. Harry Zohn (New York: Schocken Books, 1968), 218–24; Luis-Manuel Garcia, "On and On: Repetition as Process and Pleasure in Electronic Dance Music," *Music Theory Online* 11, no. 4 (Oct. 2005), para. 3.1, www.mtosmt.org/issues/mto.05.11.4/mto.05.11.4.garcia.pdf; Jonathan Sterne, *The Audible Past: Cultural Origins of Sound Reproduction* (Durham: Duke University Press, 2003), 25–26, 217–22.

41. Jean Baudrillard, *The Ecstasy of Communication*, trans. Bernard and Caroline Schutze (Brooklyn, NY: Autonomedia, 1988), 11.

42. Steven Feld, *Sound and Sentiment: Birds, Weeping, Poetics, and Song in Kaluli Expression*, 3rd ed. (Durham: Duke University Press, 2012), xiv–xix.

43. Steven Feld, "Voices of the Rainforest," *Public Culture* 4, no. 1 (Fall 1991): 131–40.

44. Umberto Eco, *Travels in Hyperreality: Essays*, trans. William Weaver (1973; San Diego: Harcourt Brace, 1983), 43.

45. Feld, "Voices of the Rainforest," 137–38.

46. Katz, *Capturing Sound*, 114–36; Mark Katz, *Groove Music: The Art and Culture of the Hip Hop DJ* (New York: Oxford University Press, 2012), esp. 51–69, 127–52.

47. Katz, *Capturing Sound*, 137–57.

48. Luis-Manuel Garcia, "'Can You Feel It, Too?': Intimacy and Affect at Electronic Dance Music Events in Paris, Chicago, and Berlin" (PhD diss., University of Chicago, 2011), 50–51.

49. The Black Madonna at Lente Kabinet Festival 2017, https://soundcloud.com/dkmntl/the-black-madonna-at-lente-kabinet-festival-2017. Fans often try to identify tracks through social media. For a list of tracks identified in the Lente Festival set, see www.mixesdb.com/w/2017-05-27_-_The_Black_Madonna_@_Lente_Kabinet,_Het_Twiske,_Amsterdam

50. Metro Area, "Miura," www.youtube.com/watch?v=jT9IPPuNDyg

51. Garcia, "'Can You Feel It, Too?'" 40.

52. Garcia, 43.

53. Marea Stamper, "Artist of the Year: The Black Madonna on the Beautiful Paradox of Being a Catholic DJ," *Thump*, 29 Dec. 2016, https://thump.vice.com/en_us/article/kb5pkn/artist-of-the-year-the-black-madonna-catholic-faith-essay

54. Garcia, "'Can You Feel It, Too?'" 35, 53, 246–47, 329–32.

55. "This Is Pirotecnia," http://thisispirotecnia.com/inspiration/fernanda-arrau/. For an example of Arrau's music, entitled "Talk Talk," see https://soundcloud.com/pirotecnia/talk-talk-fernanda-arrau

56. Michael Scott Barron, "Meet Shuja Rabbani, the Afghan Producer on a Mission to Bring EDM to Kabul," *Thump*, 26 Jan. 2016, https://thump.vice.com/en_us/article/9avkaa/meet-shuja-rabbani-the-afghan-producer-on-a-mission-to-bring-edm-to-kabul. For an example of Rabbani's music, entitled "Dark Lights Playlist," see https://soundcloud.com/shuja-rabbani/dark-lights-playlist-volume-1

57. Sarah Weiss, "Listening to the World but Hearing Ourselves: Hybridity and Perceptions of Authenticity in World Music," *Ethnomusicology* 58, no. 3 (Fall 2014): 509.

58. Martin Stokes, "Globalization and the Politics of World Music," in *The Cultural Study of Music: A Critical Introduction*, ed. Martin Clayton, Trevor Herbert, and Richard Middleton (New York: Routledge, 2003), 107–9; see also Simon Frith, "The Discourse of World Music," in *Western Music and Its Others*, ed. Georgina Born and David Hesmondhalgh (Berkeley: University of California Press, 2000), 305–22.

59. Donna A. Buchanan, *Performing Democracy: Bulgarian Music and Musicians in Transition* (Chicago: University of Chicago Press, 2006), 360–72, 418–25.

60. A collection of articles describing the technique can be found at "Friends of Tuva," www.fotuva.org/music/theory.html

Chapter 5

1. Saskia Sassen, *Territory—Authority—Rights: From Medieval to Global* (Princeton: Princeton University Press, 2006), 76–82; Dilip Parameshwar Gaonkar, "Toward New Imaginaries: An Introduction," *Public Culture* 14, no. 1 (Winter 2002): 8.

2. See Benedict Anderson, *Imagined Communities: Reflections on the Origins and Spread of Nationalism*, rev. ed. (1983; London: Verso, 1991).

3. Arjun Appadurai, *Fear of Small Numbers: An Essay on the Geography of Anger* (Durham: Duke University Press, 2006), 3–7, 49–50; James Minahan, *Encyclopedia of the Stateless Nations: Ethnic and National Groups around the World* (Westport, CT: Greenwood Press, 2002).

4. Anderson, *Imagined Communities*, 5–7.

5. Kelly M. Askew, *Performing the Nation: Swahili Music and Cultural Politics in Tanzania* (Chicago: University of Chicago Press, 2002), 10–13; Lisa Gilman, *The Dance of Politics: Gender, Performance, and Democratization in Malawi* (Philadelphia: Temple University Press, 2009), 16–19, 26–47.

6. Mark Ravina, *To Stand with the Nations of the World: Japan's Meiji Restoration in World History* (New York: Oxford University Press, 2017), 6–13. On "pushing" and "pulling" music, see Danielle Fosler-Lussier, "Music Pushed, Music Pulled: Cultural Diplomacy, Globalization, and Imperialism," *Diplomatic History* 36, no. 1 (2012): 53–64.

7. Edward A. Shils, "Political Development in the New States," draft (c. 1958), as quoted in Nils Gilman, *Mandarins of the Future: Modernization Theory in Cold War America* (Baltimore: Johns Hopkins University Press, 2003), 2.

8. Edward Said, *Orientalism* (1978; New York: Vintage, 1994), 7; Liping Bu, *Public Health and the Modernization of China, 1865–2015* (Abingdon: Routledge, 2017), 1–4.

9. Bruce M. Knauft, introduction to *Critically Modern: Alternatives, Alterities, Anthro-*

pologies (Bloomington: Indiana University Press, 2002), 18; Ury Eppstein, *The Beginnings of Western Music in Meiji Era Japan* (Lewiston, NY: Edward Mellen, 1994), 3–4.

10. Eppstein, *Beginnings of Western Music*, 10–15.

11. William Malm, "Modern Music of Meiji Japan," in *Tradition and Modernization in Japanese Culture*, ed. Donald H. Shively (Princeton: Princeton University Press, 2015), 259–65; Kōichi Nomura, "Occidental Music," in Toyotaka Komiya, *Japanese Music and Drama in the Meiji Era*, trans. and adapted by Edward G. Seidensticker and Donald Keene (Tokyo: Ōbunsha, 1956), 451–58.

12. Nomura, "Occidental Music," 460.

13. Nomura, 465–66; Bonnie Wade, *Composing Japanese Musical Modernity* (Chicago: University of Chicago Press, 2014), 15–32; Judith Ann Herd, "Western-Influenced 'Classical' Music in Japan," in *The Ashgate Research Companion to Japanese Music*, ed. Allison McQueen Tokita and David W. Hughes (Aldershot: Ashgate, 2008), 364–65.

14. Yamada's given name is sometimes spelled Kosçak. For biographical information see Luciana Galliano, *Yōgaku: Japanese Music in the Twentieth Century*, trans. Martin Mayes (Lanham, MD: Scarecrow Press, 2002), 43–51; and liner notes to the recording of this work by the Tokyo Metropolitan Symphony Orchestra conducted by Takuo Yuasa (Naxos 8.557971, 2007).

15. M. Şükrü Hanioğlu, *Atatürk: An Intellectual Biography* (Princeton: Princeton University Press, 2017), 199–201.

16. Hanioğlu, 202–19.

17. Emre Araci, "The Turkish Music Reform: From Late Ottoman Times to the Early Republic," in *Turkey's Engagement with Modernity: Conflict and Change in the Twentieth Century*, ed. Celia Kerslake, Kerem Öktem, and Philip Robins (Basingstoke: Palgrave Macmillan, 2010), 336–38. See also Araci, "Giuseppe Donizetti at the Ottoman Court: A Levantine Life," *Musical Times* 143, no. 1880 (Autumn 2002): 49–56.

18. Hanioğlu, *Atatürk*, 219–21; Ayhan Erol, "Music, Power and Symbolic Violence: The Turkish State's Music Policies during the Early Republican Period," *European Journal of Cultural Studies* 15, no. 1 (2015): 45. Experts were skeptical of these changes: see Emre Araci, "The Life and Works of Ahmed Adnan Saygun" (PhD diss., University of Edinburgh, 1999), 36.

19. Martin Stokes, *The Arabesk Debate: Music and Musicians in Modern Turkey* (Oxford: Clarendon, 1992), 21–49.

20. The analysis of Saygun's *Yunus Emre* here and in subsequent paragraphs is based on Araci, "The Life and Works," 135–63.

21. Araci, 136, 146.

22. Saygun was a protégé of Béla Bartók, and these strategies are similar to Bartók's. See Béla Bartók, "The Relation between Contemporary Hungarian Art Music and Folk Music," in *Béla Bartók Essays*, ed. Benjamin Suchoff (Lincoln: University of Nebraska Press, 1976), 351–52.

23. Araci, "The Life and Works," 151n53.

24. See Jennifer L. Campbell, "Creating Something Out of Nothing: The Office of Inter-American Affairs Music Committee (1940–1941) and the Inception of a Policy for

Musical Diplomacy," *Diplomatic History* 36, no. 1 (Jan. 2012): 29–39; and Carol Hess, *Representing the Good Neighbor: Music, Difference, and the Pan-American Dream* (New York: Oxford University Press, 2013).

25. Hye-jung Park, "From World War to Cold War: Music in US-Korea Relations, 1941–1960" (PhD diss., Ohio State University, 2019), chap. 1; Or Rosenboim, *The Emergence of Globalism: Visions of World Order in Britain and the United States, 1939–1950* (Princeton: Princeton University Press, 2017), 1–15.

26. John D. Kelly and Martha Kaplan, *Represented Communities: Fiji and World Decolonization* (Chicago: University of Chicago Press, 2001), 1–22, 59; Gaonkar, "Toward New Imaginaries," 8; Bruce Jones, Thomas Wright, et al., "The State of the International Order," Brookings Institution Policy Paper no. 33 (Feb. 2014), 3–7, www.brookings.edu/wp-content/uploads/2016/07/intlorder_report.pdf

27. Stephen Kotkin, *Magnetic Mountain: Stalinism as a Civilization* (1995; Berkeley: University of California Press, 1997), 11–17, 29–35.

28. Shils, "Political Development in the New States," quoted in Gilman, *Mandarins of the Future*, 1; Gilman, *Mandarins of the Future*, 1–23.

29. Andrey Olkhovsky, *Music under the Soviets: The Agony of an Art* (New York: Frederick A. Praeger, 1955), 282, 284; Laurel Fay, *Shostakovich: A Life* (New York: Oxford University Press, 2000), 155–65.

30. Marina Frolova-Walker, "'National in Form, Socialist in Content': Musical Nation-Building in the Soviet Republics," *Journal of the American Musicological Society* 51, no. 2 (1998): 332–39.

31. Sheila Fitzpatrick, "Everyday Stalinism: Ordinary Life in Extraordinary Times," in *Stalinism: The Essential Readings*, ed. David L. Hoffmann (Oxford: Blackwell, 2003), 164–77.

32. Viktor Suslin, "The Music of Spiritual Independence: Galina Ustvolskaya," in *Ex oriente: Ten Composers from the USSR*, ed. Galina Grigorieva and Valeriia Tsenova, trans. Carolyn Dunlop (Berlin: E. Kuhn, 2002), 102–3, 114.

33. Pierre Boulez, "Nécessité d'une orientation esthétique (II)" [Necessity of an aesthetic orientation II], *Canadian University Music Review* 7 (1986): 61.

34. Richard Taruskin, *Music in the Late Twentieth Century*, vol. 5 of *Oxford History of Western Music* (Oxford: Oxford University Press, 2010), 27–38; Leslie A. Sprout, "The 1945 Stravinsky Debates: Nigg, Messiaen, and the Early Cold War in France," *Journal of Musicology* 26, no. 1 (Winter 2009): 89.

35. Sprout, "The 1945 Stravinsky Debates," 88–90.

36. Martin Brody, "'Music for the Masses': Milton Babbitt's Cold War Music Theory," *Musical Quarterly* 77, no. 2 (Summer 1993): 163–64; Joseph N. Straus, "The Myth of 'Serial Tyranny' in the 1950s and 1960s," *Musical Quarterly* 83, no. 3 (Autumn 1999): 305–21; and Anne C. Shreffler, "The Myth of Empirical Historiography: A Response to Joseph N. Straus," *Musical Quarterly* 84, no. 1 (Spring 2000): 30–39.

37. Peter J. Schmelz, *Such Freedom, but Only Musical: Unofficial Soviet Music during the Thaw* (Oxford: Oxford University Press, 2009), 7–10; Danielle Fosler-Lussier, *Music Divided: Bartók's Legacy in Cold War Culture* (Berkeley: University of California Press, 2007): 164–65.

38. Kiril Tomoff, *Virtuosi Abroad: Soviet Music and Imperial Competition during the Early Cold War, 1945–1958* (Ithaca: Cornell University Press, 2015), 1–19, 116–45.

39. Anthony Shay, *Choreographic Politics: State Folk Dance Companies, Representation, and Power* (Middletown, CT: Wesleyan University Press, 2002), 57–81; and Anthony Shay, "The Spectacularization of Soviet/Russian Folk Dance: Igor Moiseyev and the Invented Tradition of Staged Folk Dance," in *Oxford Handbook of Dance and Ethnicity*, ed. Anthony Shay and Barbara Sellers-Young (Oxford: Oxford University Press, 2016), 236–54.

40. This paragraph and the following three are a gloss of Danielle Fosler-Lussier, *Music in America's Cold War Diplomacy* (Oakland: University of California Press, 2015).

41. Mark Katz, "The Case for Hip-Hop Diplomacy," *American Music Review* 46, no. 2 (Spring 2017): 1–5, www.brooklyn.cuny.edu/web/aca_centers_hitchcock/AMR_46-2_ Katz.pdf; and performer comments in Zach Christy, Tim Scholl, and Ben Jones, *Tour of Tours: The 1964 Oberlin College Choir in the Soviet Union* (film), 2015, https://vimeo. com/122021714

42. Gerald Horne, *Paul Robeson: The Artist as Revolutionary* (London: Pluto Press, 2016), 112, 57–64.

43. Horne, 84–85, 91; Dorothy Butler Gilliam, *Paul Robeson: All-American* (Washington, DC: New Republic, 1976), 71–80.

44. Horne, *Paul Robeson*, 101, 104–8, 114–15, 221n81; Paul Robeson Jr., *The Undiscovered Paul Robeson: Quest for Freedom, 1939–1976* (Hoboken, NJ: John Wiley and Sons, 2010), 142–50; Gilliam, *Paul Robeson*, 137–43.

45. Shana Redmond, *Anthem: Social Movements and the Sound of Solidarity in the African Diaspora* (New York: New York University Press, 2013), 122–24; Horne, *Paul Robeson*, 121–25; Gilliam, *Paul Robeson*, 145–54; and Tony Perucci, *Paul Robeson and the Cold War Performance Complex: Race, Madness, Activism* (Ann Arbor: University of Michigan Press, 2012), 95–111.

46. Horne, *Paul Robeson*, 120, 140; Gilliam, *Paul Robeson*, 155–59, 163.

47. Redmond, *Anthem*, 124–30; Horne, *Paul Robeson*, 126–27; Kate Baldwin, *Beyond the Color Line and the Iron Curtain* (Durham: Duke University Press, 2002), 202–51.

48. Redmond, *Anthem*, 136–39; Horne, *Paul Robeson*, 145; Gilliam, *Paul Robeson*, 173.

49. Baldwin, *Beyond the Color Line*, 218.

50. Horne, *Paul Robeson*, 131–35, 147–50, 164.

51. Baldwin, *Beyond the Color Line*, 227–35; Robert Robinson, *Black on Red: My 44 Years inside the Soviet Union* (Washington, DC: Acropolis Books, 1988), 319; Martin Duberman, *Paul Robeson* (New York: Knopf, 1988), 352, 468.

52. BBC Wales, NJN Public Television, and NVC Arts, *Speak of Me as I Am: The Rise and Fall of an American Legend* (1998; DVD: Kultur, 2007), from 23:45.

53. Robeson had known of Soviet crimes since 1949, if not earlier. See Lauren McConnell, "Understanding Paul Robeson's Soviet Experience," *Theatre History Studies* 30 (2010): 147–51.

54. Uta G. Poiger, *Jazz, Rock, and Rebels: Cold War Politics and American Culture in a Divided Germany* (Berkeley: University of California Press, 2000), 132–36, 150–67; Fosler-Lussier, *Music in America's Cold War Diplomacy*, 85–87, 145.

55. Jie Chen and Peng Deng, *China since the Cultural Revolution: From Totalitarianism to Authoritarianism* (Westport, CT: Praeger, 1995), 16–26.

56. Anthony Fung, "Deliberating Fandom and the New Wave of Chinese Pop: A Case Study of Chris Li," *Popular Music* 32, no. 1 (Jan. 2013): 81.

57. Chen and Deng, *China since the Cultural Revolution*, 24–25.

58. Hao Huang, "Voices from Chinese Rock, Past and Present Tense: Social Commentary and Construction of Identity in *Yaogun Yinyue*, from Tiananmen to the Present," *Popular Music and Society* 26, no. 2 (2003): 186–87.

59. Andrew F. Jones, *Like a Knife: Ideology and Genre in Contemporary Chinese Music* (Ithaca: Cornell University East Asia Program, 1992), 18–34.

60. My thanks to Dan Jurafsky for translating this song from Cantonese.

61. Anthony Y. H. Fung, "The Emerging (National) Popular Music Culture in China," *Inter-Asia Cultural Studies* 8, no. 3 (2007): 427–31.

62. Translation by Dennis Rea, *Live at the Forbidden City: Musical Encounters in China and Taiwan* (Lincoln, NE: iUniverse, 2006), 105.

63. Jeroen de Kloet, *China with a Cut: Globalisation, Urban Youth and Popular Music* (Amsterdam: Amsterdam University Press, 2010), 25–36; Schmelz, *Such Freedom*, 13–21. See also Jolanta Pekacz, "Did Rock Smash the Wall? The Role of Rock in Political Transition," *Popular Music* 13, no. 1 (1994): 41–49.

64. Huang, "Voices from Chinese Rock," 187. See also Rea, *Live at the Forbidden City*, 114–19.

65. Louisa Lim, *The People's Republic of Amnesia: Tiananmen Revisited* (New York: Oxford University Press, 2014), esp. 3, 6, 85–88, 182–201.

66. Jeroen de Kloet, "Rock in a Hard Place: Commercial Fantasies in China's Music Industry," in *Media in China: Consumption, Content, and Crisis*, ed. Stephanie Hemelryk Donald, Michael Keane, and Yin Hong (London: Routledge Curzon, 2002), 101–2; Dennis Rea, "Ambushed from All Sides: Rock Music as a Force for Change in China," in *The Routledge History of Social Protest in Popular Music*, ed. Jonathan C. Friedman (New York: Routledge, 2013), 380–81.

67. Fung, "Deliberating Fandom," 80; Jeroen de Kloet, "Popular Music and Youth in Urban China: The *Dakou* Generation," *China Quarterly* 183 (Sept. 2005): 611–15.

68. Barbara Kirshenblatt-Gimblett, "Intangible Heritage as Metacultural Production," *Museum International* 56, no. 1–2 (2004): 52–65.

69. Dipesh Chakrabarty, "The Legacies of Bandung: Decolonization and the Politics of Culture," in *Making a World after Empire: The Bandung Moment and Its Political Afterlives*, ed. Christopher J. Lee (Athens: Ohio University Press, 2010), 53–55. See also Barbara Kirshenblatt-Gimblett, *Destination Culture: Tourism, Museums, and Heritage* (Berkeley: University of California Press, 1988), 65; and Rob Kroes, "American Empire and Cultural Imperialism: A View from the Receiving End," *Diplomatic History* 23, no. 3 (1999): 467.

70. Penelope Harvey, *Hybrids of Modernity: Anthropology, the Nation-State, and the Universal Exhibition* (London: Routledge, 1996), 53–59.

71. Askew, *Performing the Nation*, 11.

72. Kelly and Kaplan, *Represented Communities*, 18–26, 139–42. See also Connie McNeely, *Constructing the Nation-State: International Organization and Prescriptive Action* (Westport, CT: Greenwood Press, 1995), 21–26, 35–36.

73. Sulwyn Lewis, "Principles of Cultural Co-operation," *Reports and Papers on Mass*

Communication, no. 61 (Paris: UNESCO, 1970), 11–12; James W. Fernandez, "Andalusia on Our Minds: Two Contrasting Places in Spain as Seen in a Vernacular Poetic Duel of the Late 19th Century," *Cultural Anthropology* 3, no. 1 (1988): 21–35; Kirshenblatt-Gimblett, *Destination Culture*, 65; Lisa McCormick, *Performing Civility: International Competitions in Classical Music* (Cambridge: Cambridge University Press, 2015), 53–82; Askew, *Performing the Nation*, 190.

74. This paragraph and the next are based on Shay, *Choreographic Politics*, 82–107.

75. The framing of these performances resembles the Soviet treatment of national minorities. See Greg Castillo, "Peoples at an Exhibition: Soviet Architecture and the National Question," in *Socialist Realism without Shores*, ed. Thomas Lahusen and Evgeny Dobrenko (Durham: Duke University Press, 1997), 91–119; and Askew, *Performing the Nation*, 217–18.

76. Kwame Anthony Appiah, *The Ethics of Identity* (Princeton: Princeton University Press, 2005), 256; Philip Kotler and David Gertner, "Country as Brand, Product, and Beyond: A Place Marketing and Brand Management Perspective," *Brand Management* 4, no. 5 (2002): 249–61; Margaret Mead, "The Importance of National Cultures," in *International Communication and the New Diplomacy*, ed. Arthur S. Hoffman (Bloomington: Indiana University Press, 1968), 89–105.

Chapter 6

1. Marshall McLuhan, *Understanding Media: The Extensions of Man* (1964; Cambridge, MA: MIT Press, 1994), 20, 59, 47, 5.

2. McLuhan, 73, 92–93.

3. Thomas de Zengotita, *Mediated: How the Media Shapes Your World and the Way You Live in It* (New York: Bloomsbury, 2005), 1–11.

4. This paragraph and the next are based on de Zengotita, 7–9, 13–25, 227–29.

5. This paragraph and the next are based on de Zengotita, 10–11, 46–48, 75–80, 115–32.

6. De Zengotita, 13–32, 259–64.

7. De Zengotita, 28–32.

8. De Zengotita, ix, 13–14.

9. I use *generation* here to give a general sense of the progression of time, but as Yayoi Uno Everett has suggested, a range of models of appropriation and synthesis have been in place since the 1950s. See Yayoi Uno Everett, "Intercultural Synthesis in Western Art Music: Historical Contexts, Perspectives, and Taxonomy," in *Locating East Asia in Western Art Music*, ed. Yayoi Uno Everett and Frederick Lau (Middletown, CT: Wesleyan University Press, 2004), 16–21.

10. United Nations resolution, "Policies of Apartheid of the Government of South Africa," 17 Dec. 1981, www.un.org/documents/ga/res/36/a36r172.htm

11. On the Reagan administration's reasoning for this abstention, presented under the guise of "constructive engagement," see Justin Elliott, "Reagan's Embrace of Apartheid South Africa," *Salon*, 5 Feb. 2011, www.salon.com/2011/02/05/ronald_reagan_apartheid_south_africa; and for a contemporaneous critique of the policy see Sanford J. Ungar and Peter Vale, "South Africa: Why Constructive Engagement Failed," *Foreign Affairs* 64, no. 2 (Winter 1985): 234–58.

12. Bakithi Kumalo, interview by Christina Roden, RootsWorld, www.rootsworld.com/rw/feature/kumalo.html

13. Louise Meintjes, "Paul Simon's *Graceland*, South Africa, and the Mediation of Musical Meaning," *Ethnomusicology* 34, no. 1 (1990): 43–48.

14. *Classic Albums: Paul Simon Graceland* (DVD, Eagle Rock Entertainment/Isis Productions, 1997), 31:44–32:29. Available online at www.youtube.com/watch?v=ncagXen fUKQ

15. *Classic Albums: Paul Simon Graceland*, 4:01–10:10.

16. Veit Erlmann, "Notes on World Beat," *Public Culture Bulletin* 1, no. 1 (Fall 1988): 31–37; Veit Erlmann, "'Africa Civilised, Africa Uncivilised': Local Culture, World System, and South African Music," *Journal of Southern African Studies* 20, no. 2 (June 1994): 175–79.

17. *Classic Albums: Paul Simon Graceland*, 1:30; Meintjes, "Paul Simon's *Graceland*," 41–49.

18. McLuhan, *Understanding Media*, 69.

19. Anahid Kassabian, "Would You Like Some World Music with your Latte? Starbucks, Putumayo, and Distributed Tourism," *Twentieth-Century Music* 1, no. 2 (Sept. 2004): 209–23; Philip V. Bohlman, *World Music: A Very Short Introduction* (Oxford: Oxford University Press, 2002), 41–46, 69–87, 143–50.

20. Terry Riley, personal website, www.terryriley.com, accessed 2006 (page no longer available).

21. Mark Alburger, "Terry Riley in the '70s," *21st-Century Music* 11, no. 3 (March 2004): 4–7.

22. See George E. Ruckert, *Music in North India: Experiencing Music, Expressing Culture* (New York: Oxford University Press, 2004), 56–61.

23. Leta E. Miller and Fredric Lieberman, *Lou Harrison: Composing a World* (New York: Oxford University Press, 1998), 141–55, 160–61; Henry Spiller, personal communication, 6 March 2019.

24. Maria Cizmic, "Composing the Pacific: Interviews with Lou Harrison," *Echo* 1, no. 1 (1999): www.echo.ucla.edu/Volume1-Issue1/cizmic/cizmic-interview.html

25. Miller and Lieberman, *Lou Harrison: Composing a World*, 57, 59, 160–61.

26. Dale A. Craig, "Transcendental World Music," *Asian Music* 2, no. 1 (1971): 2; Miller and Lieberman, *Lou Harrison: Composing a World*, 215–17; Leta E. Miller and Fredric Lieberman, *Lou Harrison* (American Composers) (Urbana and Chicago: University of Illinois Press, 2006), 97–103.

27. See Christopher Keyes, "Recent Technology and the Hybridization of Western and Chinese Musics," *Organized Sound* 10, no. 1 (April 2005): 51; Judy Tsou, "Composing Racial Difference in *Madama Butterfly*: Tonal Language and the Power of Cio-Cio-San," in *Rethinking Difference in Music Scholarship*, ed. Olivia Bloechl, Melanie Lowe, and Jeffrey Kallberg (New York: Cambridge University Press, 2015), 214–37.

28. Lou Harrison, liner notes to *The Music of Lou Harrison* (Phoenix CD 118, 1991).

29. Henry Spiller, *Javaphilia: American Love Affairs with Javanese Music and Dance* (Honolulu: University of Hawai'i Press, 2015), 152–82.

30. Christina Klein, *Cold War Orientalism: Asia in the Middlebrow Imagination, 1945–1961* (Berkeley: University of California Press, 2003), esp. 1–17.

31. Olly Wilson, quoted by Billy Taylor in liner notes to *Videmus* (New World Records/ Recorded Anthology of American Music 80423-2, 1992).

32. W. E. B. DuBois, *The Souls of Black Folk* (1903; New York: Fawcett, 1961), 16–17, quoted in Olly Wilson, "Composition from the Perspective of the African-American Tradition," *Black Music Research Journal* 16, no. 1 (Spring 1996): 43.

33. Wilson, "Composition," 50.

34. Olly Wilson, "The Heterogeneous Sound Ideal in African-American Music," in *New Perspectives on Music: Essays in Honor of Eileen Southern*, ed. Josephine Wright and Samuel A. Floyd Jr. (Warren, MI: Harmonie Park Press, 1992), 328–29.

35. Miller and Lieberman, *Lou Harrison* (American Composers), 108.

36. Kwame Anthony Appiah, *The Ethics of Identity* (Princeton: Princeton University Press, 2005), xv–xvi; de Zengotita, *Mediated*, 218–27.

37. Appiah, *The Ethics of Identity*, 62–71.

38. Frank J. Oteri, "Barbara Benary: Mother of Lion," *New Music Box*, 1 Feb. 2011, www.newmusicbox.org/articles/barbara-benary-mother-of-lion; Kyle Gann, liner notes to *Barbara Benary: Sun on Snow*, DRAM, www.dramonline.org/albums/barbara-benary-sun-on-snow/notes

39. Marcus Boon, liner notes to *The Complete Gamelan in the New World* (Folkways 31313, CD reissue by Locust Media, 2003).

40. Barbara Benary, "Gamelan Works Vol. 1: The Braid Pieces" ([New York]: Gamelan Son of Lion, 1993), American Gamelan Institute, www.gamelan.org/composers/benary/benary_vol1braid.pdf

41. Daniel Goode, "Braiding Hot Rolled Steel," *Musicworks* 56 (Fall 1993): 16–18.

42. Sumanth Gopinath, "Contraband Children: The Politics of Race and Liberation in the Music of Steve Reich" (PhD diss., Yale University, 2005), esp. 267–70, 283–306.

43. Asha Srinivasan, personal communication, 23 Feb. 2018; Asha Srinivasan, faculty webpage, www.lawrence.edu/conservatory/faculty/asha_srinivasan

44. The unison section is repeated three times: it is based on a *korvai* pattern. See David Paul Nelson, "Karnatak Tala," in *The Garland Encyclopedia of World Music*, vol. 5, *South Asia: The Indian Subcontinent*, ed. Alison Arnold (New York: Garland, 2000), 155–57. The composer explained that this section resembles the rhythmic and melodic climax that happens at the end of a *svara kalpana* (improvised) section. Asha Srinivasan, personal communication, 23 Feb. 2018.

45. Example 6.21 comes from a videotape in a personal collection. See https://crownpropeller.wordpress.com/2016/04/26/anthony-braxton-quartet-in-montreux-1975

46. Asha Srinivasan, Note to *Janani*, www.twocomposers.org/asha/works.php

47. Courtney Bryan, Twitter biography, https://twitter.com/cbryanmusic, as of 22 Feb. 2019.

Chapter 7

1. Mark Katz, *Capturing Sound: How Technology Has Changed Music* (Berkeley: University of California Press, 2004), 12–13.

2. IFPI, *Global Music Report 2017*, 6, www.ifpi.org/downloads/GMR2017.pdf

3. Statista, Mobile Phone User Penetration Worldwide, www.statista.com/statistics/470018/mobile-phone-user-penetration-worldwide

4. Christopher J. Arthur, *Marx's "Capital": A Student Edition* (London: Lawrence and Wishart, 1992), 3–7.

5. Sinéad Cantillon, "Property for Free? An Analysis of Music and Copyright in the Digital Age," *Hibernian Law Journal* 11 (2012): 37–39.

6. Adrian Strain, Speech at FILAIE / IFPI Latin America & Caribbean Annual Regional Meeting, Buenos Aires, 9 June 2014, www.ifpi.org/downloads/AS_speech_at_IFPI_FILAIE_event_Buenos_Aires_090614.pdf (italics in the original). See also Jonathan Sterne, *MP3: The Meaning of a Format* (Durham: Duke University Press, 2012), 184–226.

7. Jack Bishop, "Building International Empires of Sound: Concentrations of Power and Property in the 'Global' Music Market," *Popular Music and Society* 28, no. 4 (2005): 445–46; Glenton Davis, "When Copyright Is Not Enough: Deconstructing Why, as the Modern Music Industry Takes, Musicians Continue to Make," *Chicago-Kent Journal of Intellectual Property* 16, no. 2 (21 June 2017): 373–407.

8. IFPI, *Digital Music Report 2007*, 18, www.ifpi.org/content/library/digital-music-report-2007.pdf

9. See Mark Kirkeby, "The Pleasures of Home Taping," *Rolling Stone*, 2 Oct. 1980, 62–64. The term *piracy* had been used for illegal copying and republishing of printed music for at least 80 years prior to this date.

10. Cornell Copyright Information Center, "Copyright Term and the Public Domain in the United States," https://copyright.cornell.edu/publicdomain; US Copyright Office, "Orrin G. Hatch—Bob Goodlatte Music Modernization Act," www.copyright.gov/music-modernization

11. United States Copyright Office, "Copyright and the Music Marketplace" (Feb. 2015), 16–17, https://copyright.gov/docs/musiclicensingstudy/copyright-and-the-music-marketplace.pdf

12. Quoted in Gershon Legman, "Who Owns Folklore?" *Western Folklore* 21, no. 1 (Jan. 1962): 4.

13. Richard Jones, "Technology and the Cultural Appropriation of Music," *International Review of Law, Computers & Technology* 23, no. 1–2 (March–July 2009): 118; see also World Intellectual Property Organization, "Model Provisions of National Laws on the Protection of Expressions of Folklore" (1985), www.wipo.int/edocs/lexdocs/laws/en/unesco/unesco001en.pdf; and Kofi Agawu, *Representing African Music: Postcolonial Notes, Queries, Positions* (New York: Routledge, 2003), 218–20.

14. US Copyright Office, "More Information on Fair Use," www.copyright.gov/fair-use/more-info.html

15. US Copyright Office, "Copyright and the Music Marketplace," 13; US Copyright Office, "Orrin G. Hatch—Bob Goodlatte Music Modernization Act"; Corynne McSherry, "The Sony Digital Rights Management Debacle," Educause webinar, 28 Feb. 2005, https://library.educause.edu/resources/2006/1/the-sony-digital-rights-management-debacle-the-litigation-the-settlement-and-some-thoughts-on-the-future-of-drm. On selection taping see Rob Drew, "New Technologies and the Business of Music: Lessons from the 1980s Home Taping Hearings," *Popular Music and Society* 37, no. 3 (2014): 263–66.

16. United States Copyright Office, "Pre-1972 Sound Recordings: Executive Summary," www.copyright.gov/docs/sound/pre-72-exec-summary.pdf

17. Connie C. Davis, "Copyright and Antitrust: The Effects of the Digital Performance Rights in Sound Recordings Act of 1995 in Foreign Markets," *Federal Communications Law Journal* 52, no. 2, article 6 (2000): 415–16.

18. There used to be six companies: see Bishop, "Building International Empires," 447–52. Wikipedia tracks the frequent mergers and reorganizations of these media companies in the article "Music Industry," https://en.wikipedia.org/wiki/Music_industry

19. "WMG Makes Recorded-Music Market Share Gains, While Indies Extend Publishing Lead," Music and Copyright Blog, Informa Telecoms and Media, https://musicand copyright.wordpress.com/2017/05/12/wmg-makes-recorded-music-market-share-gains-while-indies-extend-publishing-lead. This figure has been estimated as high as 36 percent: see US Copyright Office, "Copyright and the Music Marketplace," 23.

20. IFPI, *Global Music Report 2017*, 11.

21. Center for Responsive Politics, "Recording Industry Assn. of America," www.open secrets.org/lobby/clientsum.php?id=D000000581

22. Drew, "New Technologies," 257–62.

23. Serona Elton, "A Survey of Graduated Response Programs to Combat Online Piracy," *MEIEA Journal* 14, no. 1 (2014): 95–97.

24. Timothy K. Anderson, "Digital Rights Management and the Process of Fair Use" (2006), University of Cincinnati, *Faculty Articles and Other Publications*, https://scholar ship.law.uc.edu/fac_pubs/146

25. Pamela Samuelson, "Digital Rights Management {and, or, vs.} the Law," *Communications of the ACM* 46, no. 4 (2003): 42.

26. Mitch Stoltz, "New Exemptions to DMCA Section 1201 Are Welcome, but Don't Go Far Enough," Electronic Frontier Foundation, 26 Oct. 2018, www.eff.org/deep links/2018/10/new-exemptions-dmca-section-1201-are-welcome-dont-go-far-enough

27. Elton, "Survey of Graduated Response Programs," 94–95.

28. Lisa Scott, "Lawyer Fights RIAA for Student Rights," *The Lantern* (Ohio State University), 28 Nov. 2007.

29. Elton, "Survey of Graduated Response Programs," 92–95.

30. Sarah McBride and Ethan Smith, "Music Industry to Abandon Mass Suits," *Wall Street Journal*, 19 Dec. 2008, www.wsj.com/articles/SB122966038836021137

31. Elton, "Survey of Graduated Response Programs," 94.

32. Paul Resnikoff, "Apple 'On Schedule' to Terminate Music Downloads by 2019," *Digital Music News*, 6 Dec. 2017, www.digitalmusicnews.com/2017/12/06/apple-termi nate-music-downloads

33. Eric Drott, "Music as a Technology of Surveillance," *Journal of the Society for American Music* 12, no. 3 (August 2018): 235–37; Mark Andrejevic, "Surveillance in the Digital Enclosure," *Communication Review* 10 (2007): 296, 298–99; Patrick Burkart, "Music in the Cloud and the Digital Sublime," *Popular Music and Society* 37, no. 4 (2014): 404–5.

34. Helge Rønning, "Systems of Control and Regulation: Copyright Issues, Digital Divides and Citizens' Rights," *Critical Arts: A South-North Journal of Cultural and Media Studies* 20, no. 1 (2006): 20.

35. "After Net Neutrality: Brace for Internet 'Fast Lanes,'" *New York Times*, 20 Dec. 2017.

36. Don Tyler, *Hit Songs, 1900–1955: American Popular Music of the Pre-Rock Era* (Jefferson, NC: McFarland, 2007), 2; David Brackett, *Categorizing Sound: Genre and Twentieth-Century Popular Music* (Berkeley: University of California Press, 2016), 142–43; "Billboard Media Kit 2019," www.billboard.com/files/media/bb_Media_Kit_2019.pdf; Robert G. Woletz, "Pop Music: Technology Gives the Charts a Fresh Spin," *New York Times*, 26 Jan. 1992.

37. Chuck Philips, "The Accidental Chart Revolution," *Los Angeles Times*, 30 May 1991, http://articles.latimes.com/print/1991-05-30/entertainment/ca-3677_1_market-research-system; Sound Exchange, "Reporting Requirements," www.soundexchange.com/service-provider/reporting-requirements

38. Woletz, "Pop Music."

39. Billboard, "About Our Ads," www.billboard.com/p/about-our-ads

40. Drott, "Music as a Technology of Surveillance," 233.

41. Drott, 237–39, 243–45; Colin J. Bennett and Christopher Parsons, "Privacy and Surveillance: The Multidisciplinary Literature on the Capture, Use, and Disclosure of Personal Information in Cyberspace," in *The Oxford Handbook of Internet Studies*, ed. William H. Dutton (Oxford: Oxford University Press, 2013), 492–93.

42. Dave Horwitz, Twitter post, 27 Oct. 2015, 12:09 p.m., http://twitter.com/Dave_Horwitz. I owe this source, along with many of the insights in this section, to Eric Drott. On this mode of address see Drott, "Why the Next Song Matters: Streaming, Recommendation, Scarcity," *Twentieth-Century Music* 15, no. 3 (2018): 325–57.

43. Christopher May, *The World Intellectual Property Organization: Resurgence and the Development Agenda* (New York: Routledge, 2007), 19.

44. May, *The World Intellectual Property Organization*, 20–21.

45. J. H. Reichman, "Universal Minimum Standards of Intellectual Property Protection under the TRIPS Component of the WTO Agreement," *International Lawyer* 29, no. 2 (Summer 1995): 351.

46. John Fredrick Bishop, "Who Are the Pirates? Power Relationships in a Globalized Music Market, Ethnomusicological Perspectives" (PhD diss., University of California, Los Angeles, 2005), 183, 235–37. See also K. E. Goldschmitt, *Bossa Mundo: Brazilian Music in Transnational Media Industries* (New York: Oxford University Press, 2019), 144–50.

47. Ryan Thomas Skinner, "Artists, Music Piracy, and the Crisis of Political Subjectivity in Contemporary Mali," *Anthropological Quarterly* 85, no. 3 (2012): 732–39; Bishop, "Who Are the Pirates?" 198–99.

48. Andreas Johnsen, Ralf Christensen, and Henrik Moltke, *Good Copy, Bad Copy* (Copenhagen: Rosforth Films, 2007); Helene Garcia-Solek, "Sampling as Political Practice: Gilberto Gil's Cultural Policy in Brazil and the Right to Culture in the Digital Age," *Volume!* 11, no. 1 (2015): 54–55; Samuel Howard-Spink, "The Political Economy of Music Networks and Glocal Hybrid Social Imaginaries: A Comparative Study of the United States, Canada, and Brazil" (PhD diss., New York University, 2012), 256–59; Goldschmitt, *Bossa Mundo*, 2–4.

49. Gavin Steingo, *Kwaito's Promise: Music and the Aesthetics of Freedom in South Africa* (Chicago: University of Chicago Press, 2016), esp. chap. 2. See also Tom Astley, "The People's Mixtape: Peer-to-Peer File Sharing without the Internet in Contemporary Cuba," in

Networked Music Cultures: Contemporary Approaches, Emerging Issues, ed. Raphaël Nowak and Andrew Whelan (London: Palgrave Macmillan, 2016), 13–30; and Noriko Manabe, "Streaming Music in Japan: Corporate Cultures as Determinants of Listening Practice," in Nowak and Whelan, 67–76.

50. Laurence R. Helfer, "Regime Shifting: The TRIPs Agreement and New Dynamics of Intellectual Property Lawmaking," *Yale Journal of International Law* 29, no. 1 (2004), 24.

51. Bishop, "Who Are the Pirates?" 180–81.

52. Bishop, 219–24.

53. Bishop, 224; Howard-Spink, "Political Economy of Music Networks," 250–55.

54. The government appears to have licensed individual artists with approved messages. Hailey Bondy, "YAS: Persian Rap Royalty," *MTV Iggy*, 14 Dec. 2011, https://archive.fo/20130427050730/http://www.mtviggy.com/articles/yas-persian-rap-royalty

55. Janine Di Giovanni, "Iranian Rap Music Flourishes Underground Despite Strict Religious Laws in Tehran," *Newsweek*, 16 August 2016, www.newsweek.com/2016/08/26/iran-rap-i-farsi-021-music-tehran-490762.html

56. Saulo Faria Almeida Barretto et al., "Digital Culture and Sharing: Theory and Practice of a Brazilian Cultural Public Policy," in *Information Resources Management: Global Challenges*, ed. Wai K. Law (Hershey, PA: Idea Group, 2007), 153.

57. Garcia-Solek, "Sampling as Political Practice," 56–57.

58. Francesco Nachira, Andrea Nicolai, Paolo Dini, Marion Le Louarn, and Lorena Rivera Leon, *Digital Business Ecosystems* (Luxembourg: Office for Official Publications of the European Communities, 2007), sec. 4, 187–88, www.digital-ecosystems.org/book

59. Andrade referred to this concept as "cultural cannibalism," or *antropofagia*. Howard-Spink, "Political Economy of Music Networks," 229.

60. Gilberto Gil, "Uma nova política cultural para o Brasil," *Revista Rio de Janeiro*, no. 15 (May 2005): 103–10, quoted in Garcia-Solek, "Sampling as Political Practice," 57.

61. Digital Culture Initiative website, http://estudiolivre.org (site no longer available).

62. Howard-Spink, "Political Economy of Music Networks," 248.

63. Nachira et al., *Digital Business Ecosystems*, sec. 4, 188.

64. Barbara Szaniecki and Gerardo Silva, "Rio et la politique de 'Pontos de Cultura'" (Rio and the Politics of 'Culture Hotspots'), *Multitudes*, no. 43 (2010): 75.

65. Szaniecki and Silva, 76–77.

66. Ronaldo Lemos, "A Legacy at Risk: How the New Ministry of Culture in Brazil Reversed Its Digital Agenda," *Freedom to Tinker*, Princeton University Center for Information Technology Policy, 14 March 2011, https://freedom-to-tinker.com/2011/03/14/legacy-risk-how-new-ministry-culture-brazil-reversed-its-digital-agenda; see also Barretto et al., "Digital Culture and Sharing," 158–59.

67. Barretto et al., "Digital Culture and Sharing," 153–56; Garcia-Solek, "Sampling as Political Practice," 57–58.

68. Howard-Spink, "Political Economy of Music Networks," 223, 332–33n209.

69. Creative Commons, "Licensing Types," https://creativecommons.org/share-your-work/licensing-types-examples; see also Michael W. Carroll, "Creative Commons as Conversational Copyright" (2007), Villanova University Charles Widger School of Law Digital Repository, http://digitalcommons.law.villanova.edu/wps/art71

70. Garcia-Solek, "Sampling as Political Practice," 57.

71. Lemos, "A Legacy at Risk"; Sergio Amadeu da Silveira, Murilo Bansi Machado, and Rodrigo Tarchiani Savazoni, "Backward March: The Turnaround in Public Cultural Policy in Brazil," *Media, Culture & Society* 35, no. 5 (2013): 560–61.

72. "'Tepito Market Raided Again" and "Customs Seizure in Mexico," IFPI *Right Track*, Feb. 2009, 8, www.ifpi.org/content/library/Right-Track-2.pdf

73. IFPI press release, "IFPI Welcomes Closure of Demonoid," 13 August 2012, http://top40-charts.com/news/Music-Industry/IFPI-Welcomes-Closure-Of-Demonoid/81085.html

74. Saskia Sassen, *Territory—Authority—Rights: From Medieval to Global Assemblages* (Princeton: Princeton University Press, 2006), 203, 412.

75. Sassen, 194.

76. Sassen, 195–97; Lisa Duggan, *The Twilight of Equality: Neoliberalism, Cultural Politics, and the Attack on Democracy* (Boston: Beacon Press, 2003), x–xiii; Wendy Brown, *Undoing the Demos: Neoliberalism's Stealth Revolution* (New York: Zone Books, 2015), 28–35.

77. Susan Strange, "The Declining Authority of States," in *The Global Transformations Reader*, ed. David Held and Anthony McGrew (Cambridge: Polity Press, 2000): 148–55.

78. Bruce Jones, Thomas Wright, et al., "The State of the International Order," Brookings Institution Policy Paper no. 33 (Feb. 2014), 5–6, www.brookings.edu/wp-content/uploads/2016/07/intlorder_report.pdf; Cameron McLoughlin and Noriaki Kinoshita, "Monetization in Low- and Middle-Income Countries," International Monetary Fund Working Paper 12/160 (June 2012), 3–4, 10, www.imf.org/en/Publications/WP/Issues/2016/12/31/Monetization-in-Low-and-Middle-Income-Countries-26010; Anand G. Chandavarkar, "Monetization of Developing Economies," Staff Papers (International Monetary Fund) 24, no. 3 (Nov. 1977): 665–70. For a feminist critique of monetization strategies see Anne Marie Goetz, "From Feminist Knowledge to Data for Development: The Bureaucratic Management of Information on Women and Development," *IDS Bulletin* 25, no. 2 (1994): 32.

79. Micheal Abimboye, "Nigeria Not Among World's Top 20 Music Markets—D'Banj Disagrees," *Premium Times* (Nigeria), 1 Nov. 2013, www.premiumtimesng.com/news/147676-nigeria-among-worlds-top-20-music-markets-dbanj-disagrees.html

80. Thai News Service (Bangkok), "Thailand: Fighting Intellectual Property Piracy Gets Harder," 25 May 2009, ProQuest Global Newsstream.

81. Frank J. Penna, Monique Thormann, and Michael Finger, "The Africa Music Project," in *Poor People's Knowledge: Promoting Intellectual Property in Developing Countries*, ed. J. Michael Finger and Philip Schuler (Washington, DC: World Bank and Oxford University Press, 2004), 95, 99.

82. Bishop, "Who Are the Pirates?" 226.

83. Skinner, "Artists, Music Piracy," 741–49; see also Heather MacLachlan, *Burma's Pop Music Industry: Creators, Distributors, Censors* (Rochester, NY: University of Rochester Press, 2011), 131–34.

84. Paul Resnikoff, "The Top 1% of Artists Earn 77% of Recorded Music Income, Study Finds," *Digital Music News*, 5 March 2014, www.digitalmusicnews.com/2014/03/05/topo nepercent; Natalia Linares and Francisco Perez, "'Despacito' Will Not Save Us," *Africa Is a*

Country, 27 August 2017, http://africasacountry.com/2017/08/despacito-will-not-save-us; Boima Tucker, "Sunday Read: Cultural Appropriation and Sugar Drinks," *Africa Is a Country*, 30 July 2017, http://africasacountry.com/2017/07/sunday-read-cultural-appropriation-revisited

85. K. E. Goldschmitt, "Mobile Tactics in the Brazilian Independent Music Industry," in *The Oxford Handbook of Mobile Music Studies*, vol. 1, ed. Sumanth Gopinath and Jason Stanyek (Oxford: Oxford University Press, 2014), 497–98, 503, 509–14.

86. Goldschmitt, 511–13; Leonardo de Marchi, "Structural Transformations of the Music Industry in Brazil, 1999–2009," in *Made in Brazil: Studies in Popular Music*, ed. Martha Tupinambá de Ulhôa, Cláudia Azevedo, and Felipe Trotta (New York: Routledge, 2015), 181–85.

87. K. E. Goldschmitt, "From Rio to São Paulo: Shifting Urban Landscapes and Global Strategies for Brazilian Music," in *Sounds and the City*, vol. 2, ed. Brett Lashua, Stephen Wagg, Karl Spracklen, and M. Selim Yavuz (London: Palgrave Macmillan, 2019), 103–22.

88. Strain, Speech at FILAIE, 2.

89. Bishop, "Who Are the Pirates?" 184–87.

90. Strain, Speech at FILAIE, 2; John Baldivia, "A Stream of Hope: Why Music Streaming Licenses Will Turn Around China's Music Industry in Spite of Rampant Piracy of Music," *Southwestern Journal of International Law* 22, no. 1 (2016): 180–87. See also Howard-Spink, "Political Economy of Music Networks," 232–37.

91. Anna Tsing, *Friction: An Ethnography of Global Connection* (Princeton: Princeton University Press, 2005), 9, 85, 4, 5.

92. Brown, *Undoing the Demos*, 9–11, 29–45; Bonnie Honig, *Public Things: Democracy in Disrepair* (New York: Fordham University Press, 2017), 4–7.

93. "WIPO Development Agenda: Background (2004–2007)," www.wipo.int/ip-development/en/agenda/background.html

Chapter 8

1. Donna Haraway, "A Cyborg Manifesto: Science, Technology, and Socialist-Feminism in the Late 20th Century," in *The International Handbook of Virtual Learning Environments*, ed. Joel Weiss, Jason Nolan, Jeremy Hunsinger, and Peter Trifonas (Dordrecht: Springer, 2006): 121–22, 128–32, 136–40; Néstor García Canclini, *Hybrid Cultures: Strategies for Entering and Leaving Modernity*, trans. Christopher L. Chiappari and Silvia L. López (Minneapolis: University of Minnesota Press, 1995), 8; Jonathan Sterne, *The Audible Past: Cultural Origins of Sound Reproduction* (Durham: Duke University Press, 2003), 6–8.

2. "What Is Intangible Cultural Heritage?" UNESCO, https://ich.unesco.org/en/what-is-intangible-heritage-00003

3. Thomas Beardslee, "Questioning Safeguarding: Heritage and Capabilities at the Jemaa el Fnaa" (PhD diss., Ohio State University, 2014), 3–8, 171–225; Canclini, *Hybrid Cultures*, 6–11.

4. John D. Kelly and Martha Kaplan, *Represented Communities: Fiji and World Decolonization* (Chicago: University of Chicago Press, 2001), 96–99.

5. Kwame Anthony Appiah, "Whose Culture Is It, Anyway?" in *Cultural Heritage Issues: The Legacy of Conquest, Colonization, and Commerce*, ed. James A. R. Nafziger and

Ann M. Nigorski (Leiden: Martinus Nijhoff, 2010), 217. See also Convention for the Protection of Cultural Property in the Event of Armed Conflict, preamble (14 May 1954), http://portal.unesco.org/en/ev.php-URL_ID=13637&URL_DO=DO_TOPIC&URL_SECTION=201.html

6. Canclini, *Hybrid Cultures*, xxv–xxvii.

7. Canclini, 6–13, 58–59; Renato Rosaldo, preface to Canclini, *Hybrid Cultures*, xii–xvi.

8. Elizabeth M. Hoeffel, Sonya Rastogi, Myoung Ouk Kim, and Hasan Shahid, "The Asian Population: 2010," US Census Bureau, Report no. C2010BR-11 (March 2012): 14.

9. In-Jin Yoon, "Migration and the Korean Diaspora: A Comparative Description of Five Cases," *Journal of Ethnic and Migration Studies* 38, no. 3 (March 2012): 424–25.

10. Hyun Kyong (Hannah) Chang, "Musical Encounters in Korean Christianity: A Trans-Pacific Narrative" (PhD diss., University of California, Los Angeles, 2014), 1–101.

11. Yoon, "Migration and the Korean Diaspora," 424–27; Mae M. Ngai, "'The Unlovely Residue of Outworn Prejudices': The Hart-Celler Act and the Politics of Immigration Reform, 1945–1965," in *Americanism: New Perspectives on the History of an Ideal*, ed. Michael Kazin and Joseph A. McCartin (Chapel Hill: University of North Carolina Press, 2006), 108–27; Muzaffar Chishti, Faye Hipsman, and Isabel Ball, "Fifty Years On, the 1965 Immigration and Nationality Act Continues to Reshape the United States," Migration Policy Institute, 15 Oct. 2015, www.migrationpolicy.org/article/fifty-years-1965-immigra tion-and-nationality-act-continues-reshape-united-states

12. Jiwon Ahn, "Signifying Nations: Cultural Institutions and the Korean Community in Los Angeles," in *The Sons and Daughters of Los: Culture and Community in L.A.*, ed. David E. James (Philadelphia: Temple University Press, 2003), 163–64.

13. Soo-Jin Kim, "Diasporic *P'ungmul* in the United States: A Journey between Korea and the United States" (PhD diss., Ohio State University, 2011), 11–15.

14. See Susan Kiromi Serrano and Dale Minami, "Korematsu v. United States: A Constant Caution in a Time of Crisis," *Asian American Law Journal* 10, no. 1 (2003): 37–50.

15. See, e.g., Benjamin Walton, "Italian Operatic Fantasies in Latin America," *Journal of Modern Italian Studies* 17, no. 4 (2012): 460–71.

16. Danielle Fosler-Lussier, *Music in America's Cold War Diplomacy* (Oakland: University of California Press, 2015), 47–76.

17. Hye-jung Park, "From World War to Cold War: Music in US-Korea Relations, 1941–1960" (PhD diss., Ohio State University, 2019), 78–94; Chang, "Musical Encounters in Korean Christianity," 1; Kim, "Diasporic *P'ungmul*," 27–28.

18. Grace Wang, *Soundscapes of Asian America: Navigating Race through Musical Performance* (Durham: Duke University Press, 2015), 4–5, 23–63.

19. Martin Cullingford, "Seoul Philharmonic Signs to DG," *Gramophone*, 13 April 2011, www.gramophone.co.uk/classical-music-news/seoul-philharmonic-signs-to-dg

20. Fosler-Lussier, *Music in America's Cold War Diplomacy*, 54.

21. Wang, *Soundscapes of Asian America*, 12–16; Mari Yoshihara, *Musicians from a Different Shore* (Philadelphia: Temple University Press, 2007), 5–6, 188–224.

22. Wang, *Soundscapes of Asian America*, 75–87, 98–100.

23. Canclini, *Hybrid Cultures*, xxxvii.

24. "Sarah Chang: CNN Interview, Part 2," www.youtube.com/watch?v=8o7laAIQeJw

25. Quoted in Michael Ahn Paarlberg, "Can Asians Save Classical Music?" *Slate*, 2 Feb. 2012, www.slate.com/articles/arts/culturebox/2012/02/can_asians_save_classical_music_.html

26. Leon Botstein, "Music of a Century," in *The Cambridge History of Twentieth-Century Music*, vol. 1, ed. Nicholas Cook and Anthony Pople, 48–49, 65–66; Norman Lebrecht, *The Life and Death of Classical Music* (New York: Anchor Books, 2007), 130–40; Lawrence Kramer, *Why Classical Music Still Matters* (Berkeley: University of California Press, 2007), vii.

27. See Canclini, *Hybrid Cultures*, 179; and Richard Taruskin, "The Musical Mystique," *New Republic*, 22 Oct. 2007, https://newrepublic.com/article/64350/books-the-musical-mystique

28. Linda Shaver-Gleason, "Who Wrote the Symphonies, and Why Should It Matter?" *Not another Music History Cliché!* (blog), 27 Sept. 2018, https://notanothermusichistorycliche.blogspot.com/2018/09/who-wrote-symphonies-and-why-should-it.html; Canclini, *Hybrid Cultures*, xxx, 135–37.

29. Canclini, *Hybrid Cultures*, xxviii–xxix.

30. Rosaldo, preface to Canclini, *Hybrid Cultures*, xv.

31. Canclini, *Hybrid Cultures*, 258.

32. Quoted in Boudewijn Buckinx, liner notes to *All the Noises* (New World Records 80674-2, 2008).

33. Wang, *Soundscapes of Asian America*, 90–96.

34. Canclini, *Hybrid Cultures*, xxxi.

35. Nathan Hesselink, *P'ungmul: South Korean Drumming and Dance* (Chicago: University of Chicago Press, 2006), 9–10, 15–16; Park, "From World War to Cold War," 94–99; Kim, "Diasporic *P'ungmul*," 69–70.

36. Byong Won Lee, "History," in *Music of Korea*, ed. Byong Won Lee and Yong-Shik Lee (Seoul: National Center for Korean Traditional Performing Arts, 2007), 11.

37. Katherine In-Young Lee, "The Drumming of Dissent during South Korea's Democratization Movement," *Ethnomusicology* 56, no. 2 (Spring/Summer 2012): 179–205; Hesselink, *P'ungmul*, 2, 11; Donna Lee Kwon, *Music in Korea: Experiencing Music, Expressing Culture* (New York: Oxford University Press, 2012), 79–82.

38. Kwon, *Music in Korea*, 71–79; Hesselink, *P'ungmul*, 94–95.

39. Jan Turtinen, "Globalising Heritage—On UNESCO and the Transnational Construction of a World Heritage," *SCORE Rapportserie* 2000, no. 12 (Stockholm: Stockholm Center for Organizational Research, 2000), 9–17.

40. Chang, "Musical Encounters in Korean Christianity," 107–15; Hesselink, *P'ungmul*, 12; Kim, "Diasporic *P'ungmul*," 103–8; Shingil Park, "Negotiated Identities in a Performance Genre: The Case of *P'ungmul* and *Samulnori* in Contemporary Seoul" (PhD diss., University of Pittsburgh, 2000), 65–68.

41. Sori Ulrim (Rumbling Sound), performance at the Daejeon Culture & Arts Center in 2012, www.youtube.com/watch?v=i8KFlJbRbus. My thanks to Hyun Kyong (Hannah) Chang for the translation and interpretation of the text in the video.

42. Hesselink, *P'ungmul*, 50–64; Park, "Negotiated Identities," 31–41.

43. Park, "Negotiated Identities," 70–141; "The National Center for Korean Traditional Performing Arts (NCKTPA)," Asia-Europe Foundation, 3 July 2011, https://culture360. asef.org/resources/national-center-korean-traditional-performing-arts-ncktpa

44. Kim, "Diasporic *P'ungmul*," 132–35, 148.

45. Ahn, "Signifying Nations," 159; Kim, "Diasporic *P'ungmul*," 58.

46. Kim, "Diasporic *P'ungmul*," 241–60; see also Park, "Negotiated Identities," 127–42.

47. Kim, "Diasporic *P'ungmul*," 63–64.

48. Nathan Hesselink, "Folk Music: Instrumental," in *Music of Korea*, ed. Byong Won Lee and Yong-Shik Lee (Seoul: National Center for Korean Traditional Performing Arts, 2007), 98.

49. Kim, "Diasporic *P'ungmul*," 165–67, 174–78.

50. Kim, 51–54, 160.

51. Katherine In-Young Lee, *Dynamic Korea and Rhythmic Form* (Middletown, CT: Wesleyan University Press, 2018), 61–131.

52. Lakeyta M. Bonnette, *Pulse of the People: Political Rap Music and Black Politics* (Philadelphia: University of Pennsylvania Press, 2015), 109.

53. Tricia Rose, *Black Noise: Rap Music and Black Culture in Contemporary America* (Middletown, CT: Wesleyan University Press, 1994), 2–3, 21–61.

54. Rose, 12.

55. Lisa Disch, "Representation," *Oxford Handbook of Feminist Theory* (Oxford: Oxford University Press, 2015), 782, 792–98; Charles Taylor, "The Politics of Recognition," in *Multiculturalism: Examining the Politics of Recognition*, ed. Amy Gutmann (Princeton: Princeton University Press, 1994), 25–73.

56. Bonnette, *Pulse of the People*, 109–12; Abdoulaye Niang, "Bboys: Hip-Hop Culture in Dakar, Sénégal," in *Global Youth? Hybrid Identities, Plural Worlds*, ed. Pam Nilan and Carles Feixa (New York: Routledge, 2006), 176.

57. Foundational accounts of this dynamic include Brenda Gayle Plummer, *Rising Wind: Black Americans and U.S. Foreign Affairs, 1935–1960* (Chapel Hill: University of North Carolina Press, 1996); Paul Gordon Lauren, "Seen from the Outside: The International Perspective on America's Dilemma," in *Window on Freedom: Race, Civil Rights, and Foreign Affairs, 1945–1988*, ed. Brenda Gayle Plummer (Chapel Hill: University of North Carolina Press, 2003), 21–43; Thomas Borstelmann, *The Cold War and the Color Line: American Race Relations in the Global Arena* (Cambridge, MA: Harvard University Press, 2001); and Laura Belmonte, *Selling the American Way: U.S. Propaganda and the Cold War* (Philadelphia: University of Pennsylvania Press, 2008), 159–77.

58. Melinda Schwenk-Borrell, "Selling Democracy: The US Information Agency's Portrayal of American Race Relations, 1953–1976" (PhD diss., University of Pennsylvania, 2004), 72–73, 136; Belmonte, *Selling the American Way*, 165–66.

59. Anne Garland Mahler, "The Global South in the Belly of the Beast: Viewing African American Civil Rights through a Tricontinental Lens," *Latin American Research Review* 50, no. 1 (2015): 95–116.

60. Sujatha Fernandes, *Close to the Edge: In Search of the Global Hip Hop Generation* (London: Verso, 2011), 2–3; see also Bonnette, *Pulse of the People*, 2–3.

61. See, for instance, Raquel Z. Rivera, "Rap in Puerto Rico: Reflections from the Mar-

gins," in *Globalization and Survival in the Black Diaspora*, ed. Charles Green (Albany: State University of New York Press, 1997), 109–27; Chiara Minestrelli, *Australian Indigenous Hip Hop* (New York: Routledge, 2017); *The Cambridge Companion to Hip-Hop*, ed. Justin A. Williams (Cambridge: Cambridge University Press, 2015); and *Global Noise: Rap and Hip-Hop Outside the USA*, ed. Tony Mitchell (Middletown, CT: Wesleyan University Press, 2001).

62. See George E. Lewis, "Foreword: After Afrofuturism," *Journal of the Society for American Music* 2, no. 2 (2008): 139–53; Susana M. Morris, "Black Girls Are from the Future: Afrofuturist Feminism in Octavia E. Butler's *Fledgling*," *WSQ: Women's Studies Quarterly* 40, no. 3–4 (Fall/Winter 2012): 152–56.

63. Yugen Blakrok, "DarkStar," from *Return of the Astro-Goth* (Iapetus Records, 2013).

64. Apocalypse, "Interview: Yugen Blakrok," *Lalelani*, 9 June 2016, https://lalelani.co.za/interview-yugen-blakrok (no longer accessible).

65. See Qiana Whitted, "'To Be African Is to Merge Technology and Magic': An Interview with Nnedi Okorafor," in *Afrofuturism 2.0: The Rise of Astro-Blackness*, ed. Reynaldo Anderson and Charles E. Jones (Lanham, MD: Lexington Books, 2016), 209.

66. Fernandes, *Close to the Edge*, 187. Mark Katz has emphasized the sense of ownership of the genre felt by hip-hop musicians. I am grateful for his comments, which have improved this section.

67. Okon Hwang, *Western Art Music in South Korea: Everyday Experience and Cultural Critique* (Saarbrücken: VDM, 2009), 202.

68. James N. Sater, "Morocco's 'Arab' Spring," Middle East Institute, 1 Oct. 2011, www.mei.edu/content/morocco's-"arab"-spring; Vish Sakthivel, "Six Years after the Arab Spring, Morocco Is Experiencing Its Own Unrest," *Washington Post*, 18 August 2017, www.washingtonpost.com/news/democracy-post/wp/2017/08/18/six-years-after-the-arab-spring-morocco-is-experiencing-its-own-unrest

69. Kendra Salois, "The Networked Self: Hip Hop Musicking and Muslim Identities in Neoliberal Morocco" (PhD diss., University of California, Berkeley, 2013), 74.

70. Soultana, "Sawt Nssa ('The Voice of Women')," trans. Sean O'Keefe, Revolutionary Arab Rap: The Index, 19 Feb. 2012, http://revolutionaryarabraptheindex.blogspot.com/2012/02/soultana-sawt-nssa-voice-of-women.html

71. Raja Felgata and Margo de Haas, *Soultana Raps for Change in Morocco*, YouTube (Dec. 20, 2013), www.youtube.com/watch?v=QTjM8wQ64nM

72. Salois, "The Networked Self," 153, 161, 165–69.

73. Salois, 80.

74. Salois, 180; see also 147, 167, 176–80.

75. Mayam Mahmoud, "It's My Right," trans. Sean O'Keefe, *Revolutionary Arab Rap Music: The Index* (blog), 6 June 2014, http://revolutionaryarabraptheindex.blogspot.com/2014/06/myam-mahmoud-its-my-right.html

76. Salois, "The Networked Self," 147, 157; Kendra Salois, "Jihad against Jihad against Jihad," *New Inquiry*, 17 Oct. 2012, https://thenewinquiry.com/jihad-against-jihad-against-jihad

77. Salois, "Jihad against Jihad against Jihad."

78. Salois, 177; see also Stephen Greenblatt, *Cultural Mobility: A Manifesto* (New York: Cambridge University Press, 2010), 251.

79. Ali Colleen Neff, "Roots, Routes, and Rhizomes: Sounding Women's Hip Hop on the Margins of Dakar, Senegal," *Journal of Popular Music Studies* 27, no. 4 (2015): 469.

80. Greenblatt, *Cultural Mobility*, 5.

81. Felgata and de Haas, *Soultana Raps for Change*.

82. Appiah, "Whose Culture Is It, Anyway?" 210.

83. Canclini, *Hybrid Cultures*, xli–xliv; Ashwani Sharma, "Sounds Oriental: The (Im) Possibility of Theorizing Asian Musical Cultures," in *Dis-Orienting Rhythms: The Politics of the New Asian Dance Music*, ed. Sanjay Sharma, John Hutnyk, and Ashwani Sharma (London: Zed, 1996), 22.

84. Niang, "Bboys," 176.

85. Canclini, *Hybrid Cultures*, xliii.

86. Marc D. Perry, "Global Black Self-Fashionings: Hip Hop as Diasporic Space," *Identities* 15, no. 6 (2008): 636–39; Reinhard Meyer-Kalkus, "World Literature beyond Goethe," trans. Kevin McAleer, in Greenblatt, *Cultural Mobility*, 120.

87. Kelly and Kaplan, *Represented Communities*, 27–28, 85–86, 98–99.

Conclusion

1. Philip Rieff, "The Impossible Culture: Wilde as a Modern Prophet" (1970), introduction to Oscar Wilde, *The Soul of Man under Socialism* (New York: Harper and Row, 1970), xv. A forthcoming biography by Benjamin Moser attributes some of Rieff's work from this period to his spouse, Susan Sontag.

2. Rieff, "The Impossible Culture," xxvii–xxviii.

3. Arjun Appadurai, *Fear of Small Numbers: An Essay on the Geography of Anger* (Durham: Duke University Press, 2006), 83.

4. Stephen Greenblatt, *Cultural Mobility: A Manifesto* (New York: Cambridge University Press, 2010), 252.

5. Arjun Appadurai, *Modernity at Large: Cultural Dimensions of Globalization* (Minneapolis: University of Minnesota Press, 1996), 3.

6. Appadurai, *Fear of Small Numbers*, 128.

7. Appadurai, *Modernity at Large*, 3–4.

8. Appadurai, 1–2.

9. Appadurai, *Fear of Small Numbers*, 1–3.

10. Saskia Sassen, *Territory—Authority—Rights: From Medieval to Global Assemblages* (Princeton: Princeton University Press, 2006), 200–203.

11. Appadurai, *Fear of Small Numbers*, 5–11, 44–47.

12. Appadurai, 53.

13. Lisa Gilman, *My Music, My War: The Listening Habits of U.S. Troops in Iraq and Afghanistan* (Middletown, CT: Wesleyan University Press, 2016), 4–9, 52–79.

14. Suzanne G. Cusick, "'You Are in a Place That Is Out of the World . . .': Music in the Detention Camps of the 'Global War on Terror,'" *Journal of the Society for American Music* 2, no. 1 (2008): 1–26.

15. Anthony Kwame Harrison, "Post-Colonial Consciousness, Knowledge Production,

and Identity Inscription within Filipino American Hip Hop Music," *Perfect Beat* 13, no. 1 (2012): 45.

16. Oscar Wilde, *The Soul of Man under Socialism*, 237.

17. Rieff, "The Impossible Culture," xviii.

18. Rieff, xv–xvi.

19. Rieff, xxi.

20. V. Kofi Agawu, *The African Imagination in Music* (New York: Oxford University Press, 2016), 23–24.

21. Craig Calhoun, "Imagining Solidarity: Cosmopolitanism, Constitutional Patriotism, and the Public Sphere," *Public Culture* 14, no. 1 (Winter 2002): 169–70. See also Charles Taylor, *Modern Social Imaginaries* (Durham: Duke University Press, 2004), 7–14.

22. Kwame Anthony Appiah, *The Ethics of Identity* (Princeton: Princeton University Press, 2005), 220–21.

23. Arjun Appadurai, "The New Territories of Culture: Globalization, Cultural Uncertainty and Violence," in *Keys to the 21st Century*, ed. Jérôme Bindé (New York: Berghahn, 2001), 138.

24. Appiah, *The Ethics of Identity*, 268.

25. Nestór García Canclini, "Toward Hybrid Cultures?" in *Keys to the 21st Century*, ed. Jérôme Bindé (New York: Berghahn, 2001), 143–44.

26. See also Olivia Bloechl with Melanie Lowe, "Introduction: Rethinking Difference," in *Rethinking Difference in Music Scholarship*, ed. Olivia Bloechl, Melanie Lowe, and Jeffrey Kallberg (New York: Cambridge University Press, 2015), 41–46.

27. Nestór García Canclini, *Hybrid Cultures: Strategies for Entering and Leaving Modernity*, trans. Bruce Campbell (Minneapolis: University of Minnesota Press, 1995), xli, xliv.

28. Jairo Moreno, "Difference Unthought," in *Rethinking Difference in Music Scholarship*, ed. Olivia Bloechl, Melanie Lowe, and Jeffrey Kallberg (New York: Cambridge University Press, 2015), 386.

29. Moreno, 391, 401, 415–16.

30. Philippe van Parijs, "Concluding Reflections: Solidarity, Diversity, and Social Justice," in *The Strains of Commitment: The Political Sources of Solidarity in Diverse Societies*, ed. Keith Banting and Will Kymlicka (Oxford: Oxford University Press, 2017), 424.

31. Appiah calls these points of practical agreement "project-dependent values" in *The Ethics of Identity*, 243, 253.

32. Calhoun, "Imagining Solidarity," 148.

33. Calhoun, 149, 154–58.

34. Calhoun, 171.

35. John D. Kelly and Martha Kaplan, *Represented Communities: Fiji and World Decolonization* (Chicago: University of Chicago Press, 2001), 27–28, 85–86, 98–99.

36. Canclini, *Hybrid Cultures*, xxxi.

37. Wilde quoted in Rieff, "The Impossible Culture," xi.

38. Appiah, *The Ethics of Identity*, 245. For examples of such interactions see Danielle Fosler-Lussier, *Music in America's Cold War Diplomacy* (Oakland: University of California

Press, 2015); and Mark Katz, *Build: The Power of Hip Hop Diplomacy in a Divided World* (New York: Oxford University Press, 2019).

39. Appiah, *The Ethics of Identity*, 226–28, 236.

40. De Zengotita, *Mediated*, 9, 14–18, 263; Philip Rieff, *My Life among the Deathworks* (Charlottesville: University of Virginia Press, 2006), xxii.

41. Bloechl with Lowe, "Introduction: Rethinking Difference," 52.

42. Appiah, *The Ethics of Identity*, 254–56.

43. Canclini, *Hybrid Cultures*, xliii.

Selected Bibliography

I list here the writings that have been of primary use in the writing of this book. Sources that do not appear here can be found in the endnotes, where those sources are cited in full.

Abbott, Lynn, and Doug Seroff. *Ragged but Right: Black Traveling Shows, "Coon Songs," and the Dark Pathway to Blues and Jazz.* Jackson: University Press of Mississippi, 2007.

Agawu, V. Kofi. *The African Imagination in Music.* Oxford: Oxford University Press, 2016.

Agawu, V. Kofi. *Representing African Music: Postcolonial Notes, Queries, Positions.* New York: Routledge, 2003.

Ahiska, Meltem. "Occidentalism: The Historical Fantasy of the Modern." *South Atlantic Quarterly* 102, no. 2/3 (Spring-Summer 2003): 351–79.

Ahn, Jiwon. "Signifying Nations: Cultural Institutions and the Korean Community in Los Angeles." In *The Sons and Daughters of Los: Culture and Community in L.A.*, edited by David E. James, 153–73. Philadelphia: Temple University Press, 2003.

American Folklife Center. *Ethnic Recordings in America: A Neglected Heritage.* Washington, DC: Library of Congress, 1982.

Anderson, Benedict. *Imagined Communities: Reflections on the Origin and Spread of Nationalism.* 1983. Rev. ed. New York: Verso, 1991.

Anderson, Reynaldo, and Charles E. Jones, eds. *Afrofuturism 2.0: The Rise of Astro-Blackness.* Lanham, MD: Lexington Books, 2016.

Andrejevic, Mark. "Surveillance in the Digital Enclosure." *Communication Review* 10 (2007): 295–317.

Appadurai, Arjun. "Disjuncture and Difference in the Global Cultural Economy." *Theory, Culture & Society* 7 (1990): 295–310.

Appadurai, Arjun. *Fear of Small Numbers: An Essay on the Geography of Anger.* Durham: Duke University Press, 2006.

Appadurai, Arjun. *Modernity at Large: Cultural Dimensions of Globalization.* Minneapolis: University of Minnesota Press, 1996.

Appiah, Kwame Anthony. *The Ethics of Identity.* Princeton: Princeton University Press, 2005.

Appiah, Kwame Anthony. "Whose Culture Is It, Anyway?" In *Cultural Heritage Issues: The Legacy of Conquest, Colonization, and Commerce*, edited by James A. R. Nafziger and Ann M. Nigorski, 209–21. Leiden: Martinus Nijhoff, 2010.

Aracı, Emre. "The Life and Works of Ahmed Adnan Saygun." PhD diss., University of Edinburgh, 1999.

Aracı, Emre. "The Turkish Music Reform: From Late Ottoman Times to the Early Republic." In *Turkey's Engagement with Modernity: Conflict and Change in the Twentieth Century*, edited by Celia Kerslake, Kerem Öktem, and Philip Robins, 336–45. Basingstoke:
Palgrave Macmillan, 2010.

Askew, Kelly M. *Performing the Nation: Swahili Music and Cultural Politics in Tanzania*.
Chicago: University of Chicago Press, 2002.

Baldwin, Kate. *Beyond the Color Line and the Iron Curtain*. Durham: Duke University
Press, 2002.

Banting, Keith, and Will Kymlicka, eds. *The Strains of Commitment: The Political Sources of
Solidarity in Diverse Societies*. Oxford: Oxford University Press, 2017.

Baraka, Amiri. *Black Music*. New York: Apollo, 1968.

Baraka, Amiri, and Amina Baraka. *The Music: Reflections on Jazz and Blues*. New York:
William Morrow, 1987.

Barretto, Saulo Faria Almeida, Renata Piazalunga, Dalton Martins, Claudio Prado, and
Célio Turino. "Digital Culture and Sharing: Theory and Practice of a Brazilian Cul-
tural Public Policy." In *Information Resources Management: Global Challenges*, edited by
Wai K. Law, 146–60. Hershey, PA: Idea Group, 2007.

BBC Wales, NJN Public Television, and NVC Arts. *Speak of Me as I Am: The Rise and Fall
of an American Legend*. 1998. DVD: Kultur, 2007.

Beardslee, Thomas. "Questioning Safeguarding: Heritage and Capabilities at the Jemaa el
Fnaa." PhD diss., Ohio State University, 2014.

Bellman, Jonathan. Introduction to *The Exotic in Western Music*, edited by Jonathan Bellman, ix–xiii. Boston: Northeastern University Press, 1998.

Bellman, Jonathan. *The Style Hongrois in the Music of Western Europe*. Boston: Northeastern University Press, 1993.

Belmonte, Laura. *Selling the American Way: U.S. Propaganda and the Cold War*. Philadelphia: University of Pennsylvania Press, 2008.

Benhabib, Seyla. *The Claims of Culture: Equality and Diversity in the Global Era*. Princeton:
Princeton University Press, 2002.

Benjamin, Walter. "The Work of Art in the Age of Mechanical Reproduction." In *Illuminations*, edited by Hannah Arendt, translated by Harry Zohn, 217–52. New York:
Schocken, 1968.

Berman, Stephen. "Gypsies: A National Group or a Social Group?" *Refugee Survey Quarterly* 13, no. 4 (Dec. 1994): 51–61.

Bhabha, Homi. *The Location of Culture*. New York: Routledge, 1994.

Bhabha, Jacqueline, Andrzej Mirga, and Margareta Matache, eds. *Realizing Roma Rights*.
Philadelphia: University of Pennsylvania Press, 2017.

Bindé, Jérôme, ed. *Keys to the 21st Century*. New York: Berghahn, 2001.

Bishop, Jack. "Building International Empires of Sound: Concentrations of Power and
Property in the 'Global' Music Market." *Popular Music and Society* 28, no. 4 (2005):
443–71.

Bishop, John Fredrick. "Who Are the Pirates? Power Relationships in a Globalized Music
Market, Ethnomusicological Perspectives." PhD diss., University of California, Los
Angeles, 2005.

Bloechl, Olivia, Melanie Lowe, and Jeffrey Kallberg, eds. *Rethinking Difference in Music Scholarship*. New York: Cambridge University Press, 2015.

Blum, Stephen. "Music in an Age of Cultural Confrontation." In Kartomi and Blum, *Music-Cultures in Contact*, 250–77.

Bohlman, Philip V. *World Music: A Very Short Introduction*. New York: Oxford University Press, 2002.

Bonnette, Lakeyta M. *Pulse of the People: Political Rap Music and Black Politics*. Philadelphia: University of Pennsylvania Press, 2015.

Born, Georgina, and David Hesmondhalgh, eds. *Western Music and Its Others*. Berkeley: University of California Press, 2000.

Brown, Julie, ed. *Western Music and Race*. Cambridge: Cambridge University Press, 2007.

Buchanan, Donna A. *Performing Democracy: Bulgarian Music and Musicians in Transition*. Chicago: University of Chicago Press, 2006.

Burbank, Jane, and Frederick Cooper. *Empires in World History: Power and the Politics of Difference*. Princeton: Princeton University Press, 2010.

Calhoun, Craig. "Imagining Solidarity: Cosmopolitanism, Constitutional Patriotism, and the Public Sphere." *Public Culture* 14, no. 1 (Winter 2002): 147–71.

Campbell, Jennifer L. "Creating Something Out of Nothing: The Office of Inter-American Affairs Music Committee (1940–1941) and the Inception of a Policy for Musical Diplomacy." *Diplomatic History* 36, no. 1 (Jan. 2012): 29–39.

Canclini, Néstor García. *Hybrid Cultures: Strategies for Entering and Leaving Modernity*. Translated by Christopher L. Chiappari and Silvia L. López. Minneapolis: University of Minnesota Press, 1995.

Cantillon, Sinéad. "Property for Free? An Analysis of Music and Copyright in the Digital Age." *Hibernian Law Journal* 11 (2012): 35–62.

Carter, Marva Griffin. "The 'New Negro' Choral Legacy of Hall Johnson." In *Chorus and Community*, edited by Karen Ahlquist, 185–201. Urbana: University of Illinois Press, 2006.

Castillo, Greg. "Peoples at an Exhibition: Soviet Architecture and the National Question." In *Socialist Realism without Shores*, edited by Thomas Lahusen and Evgeny Dobrenko, 91–119. Durham: Duke University Press, 1997.

Chakrabarty, Dipesh. "The Legacies of Bandung: Decolonization and the Politics of Culture." In *Making a World after Empire: The Bandung Moment and Its Political Afterlives*, edited by Christopher J. Lee, 45–68. Athens: Ohio University Press, 2010.

Chang, Hyun Kyong (Hannah). "Musical Encounters in Korean Christianity: A Trans-Pacific Narrative." PhD diss., University of California, Los Angeles, 2014.

Craig, Dale A. "Transcendental World Music." *Asian Music* 2, no. 1 (1971): 2–7.

Cusick, Suzanne G. "'You Are in a Place That Is Out of the World . . .': Music in the Detention Camps of the 'Global War on Terror.'" *Journal of the Society for American Music* 2, no. 1 (2008): 1–26.

Da Lage-Py, Emilie. "Les collections de disques de musiques du monde entre patrimonialisation et marchandisation." *Culture & musées*, no. 1 (2003): 89–107.

Davis, Connie C. "Copyright and Antitrust: The Effects of the Digital Performance Rights in Sound Recordings Act of 1995 in Foreign Markets." *Federal Communications Law Journal* 52, no. 2, article 6 (2000): 411–27.

Davis, Glenton. "When Copyright Is Not Enough: Deconstructing Why, as the Modern Music Industry Takes, Musicians Continue to Make." *Chicago-Kent Journal of Intellectual Property* 16, no. 2 (21 June 2017): 373–407.

de Kloet, Jeroen. *China with a Cut: Globalisation, Urban Youth and Popular Music*. Amsterdam: Amsterdam University Press, 2010.

de Kloet, Jeroen. "Popular Music and Youth in Urban China: The *Dakou* Generation." *China Quarterly* 183 (Sept. 2005): 609–26.

de Marchi, Leonardo. "Structural Transformations of the Music Industry in Brazil, 1999–2009." In *Made in Brazil: Studies in Popular Music*, edited by Martha Tupinambá de Ulhôa, Cláudia Azevedo, and Felipe Trotta, 173–86. New York: Routledge, 2015.

de Zengotita, Thomas. *Mediated: How the Media Shapes Your World and the Way You Live in It*. New York: Bloomsbury, 2005.

Dibia, I Wayan. *Kecak: The Vocal Chant of Bali*. Denpasar, Indonesia: Hartanto Art Books Studio, 1996.

Drew, Rob. "New Technologies and the Business of Music: Lessons from the 1980s Home Taping Hearings." *Popular Music and Society* 37, no. 3 (2014): 253–72.

Drott, Eric. "Music as a Technology of Surveillance." *Journal of the Society for American Music* 12, no. 3 (August 2018): 233–67.

Drott, Eric. "Why the Next Song Matters: Streaming, Recommendation, Scarcity." *Twentieth-Century Music* 15, no. 3 (2018): 325–57.

Dutton, William H., ed. *The Oxford Handbook of Internet Studies*. Oxford: Oxford University Press, 2013.

Eltis, David, ed. *Trans-Atlantic Slave Trade Database*. www.slavevoyages.org

Elton, Serona. "A Survey of Graduated Response Programs to Combat Online Piracy." *MEIEA Journal* 14, no. 1 (2014): 89–122.

Eppstein, Ury. *The Beginnings of Western Music in Meiji Era Japan*. Lewiston, NY: Edward Mellen Press, 1994.

Epstein, Dena. "African Music in British and French America." *Musical Quarterly* 59, no. 1 (1973): 61–91.

Epstein, Dena. *Sinful Tunes and Spirituals: Black Folk Music to the Civil War*. Urbana: University of Illinois Press, 1977.

Erlmann, Veit. "'Africa Civilised, Africa Uncivilised': Local Culture, World System, and South African Music." *Journal of Southern African Studies* 20, no. 2 (June 1994): 165–79.

Erlmann, Veit. "Notes on World Beat." *Public Culture Bulletin* 1, no. 1 (Fall 1988): 31–37.

Erol, Ayhan. "Music, Power and Symbolic Violence: The Turkish State's Music Policies during the Early Republican Period." *European Journal of Cultural Studies* 15, no. 1 (2015): 138–61.

Everett, Yayoi Uno, and Frederick Lau, eds. *Locating East Asia in Western Art Music*. Middletown, CT: Wesleyan University Press, 2004.

Eversley, Shelley. *The Real Negro: The Question of Authenticity in Twentieth-Century African American Literature*. London: Routledge, 2004.

Fanon, Frantz. *Toward the African Revolution*. Translated by Haakon Chevalier. New York: Grove Press, 1967.

Fauser, Annegret. "New Media, Source-Bonding, and Alienation: Listening at the 1889 Exposition Universelle." In *French Music, Culture, and National Identity, 1870–1939*, edited by Barbara L. Kelly, 40–57. Rochester, NY: University of Rochester Press, 2008.

Fay, Laurel. *Shostakovich: A Life*. New York: Oxford University Press, 2000.

Felgata, Raja, and Margo de Haas. *Soultana Raps for Change in Morocco*. YouTube, Dec. 20, 2013. www.youtube.com/watch?v=QTjM8wQ64nM

Fernandes, Sujatha. *Close to the Edge: In Search of the Global Hip Hop Generation*. London: Verso, 2011.

Finger, J. Michael, and Philip Schuler, eds. *Poor People's Knowledge: Promoting Intellectual Property in Developing Countries*. Washington, DC: World Bank and Oxford University Press, 2004.

Fosler-Lussier, Danielle. *Music Divided: Bartók's Legacy in Cold War Culture*. Berkeley: University of California Press, 2007.

Fosler-Lussier, Danielle. *Music in America's Cold War Diplomacy*. Oakland: University of California Press, 2015.

Fosler-Lussier, Danielle. "Music Pushed, Music Pulled: Cultural Diplomacy, Globalization, and Imperialism." *Diplomatic History* 36, no. 1 (2012): 53–64.

Fox, Aaron. "Repatriation as Reanimation through Reciprocity." In *The Cambridge History of World Music*, edited by Philip V. Bohlman, 522–54. Cambridge: Cambridge University Press, 2013.

Freeman, Graham. "'It Wants All the Creases Ironing Out': Percy Grainger, the Folk Song Society, and the Ideology of the Archive." *Music and Letters* 92, no. 3 (2011): 410–36.

Freeman, Graham. "'That Chief Undercurrent of My Mind': Percy Grainger and the Aesthetics of English Folk Song." *Folk Music Journal* 9, no. 4 (2009): 581–617.

Friedman, Jonathan C., ed. *The Routledge History of Social Protest in Popular Music*. New York: Routledge, 2013.

Frolova-Walker, Marina. "'National in Form, Socialist in Content': Musical Nation-Building in the Soviet Republics." *Journal of the American Musicological Society* 51, no. 2 (1998): 331–71.

Fung, Anthony. "Deliberating Fandom and the New Wave of Chinese Pop: A Case Study of Chris Li." *Popular Music* 32, no. 1 (Jan. 2013): 79–89.

Fung, Anthony Y. H. "The Emerging (National) Popular Music Culture in China." *Inter-Asia Cultural Studies* 8, no. 3 (2007): 425–37.

Galliano, Luciana. *Yōgaku: Japanese Music in the Twentieth Century*. Translated by Martin Mayes. Lanham, MD: Scarecrow, 2002.

Gaonkar, Dilip Parameshwar. "Toward New Imaginaries: An Introduction." *Public Culture* 14, no. 1 (Winter 2002): 1–19.

Garcia, Luis-Manuel. "'Can You Feel It, Too?': Intimacy and Affect at Electronic Dance Music Events in Paris, Chicago, and Berlin." PhD diss., University of Chicago, 2011.

Garcia, Luis-Manuel. "On and On: Repetition as Process and Pleasure in Electronic Dance Music." *Music Theory Online* 11, no. 4 (Oct. 2005): www.mtosmt.org/issues/mto.05.11.4/mto.05.11.4.garcia.pdf

Garcia-Solek, Helene. "Sampling as Political Practice: Gilberto Gil's Cultural Policy in Brazil and the Right to Culture in the Digital Age." *Volume!* 11, no. 1 (2015): 51–63.

Gates, Henry Louis. "Editor's Introduction: Writing 'Race' and the Difference It Makes." *Critical Inquiry* 12, no. 1 (Autumn 1985): 1–20.

Gilliam, Dorothy Butler. *Paul Robeson: All-American.* Washington, DC: New Republic, 1976.

Gilman, Lisa. *The Dance of Politics: Gender, Performance, and Democratization in Malawi.* Philadelphia: Temple University Press, 2009.

Gilman, Lisa. *My Music, My War: The Listening Habits of U.S. Troops in Iraq and Afghanistan.* Middletown, CT: Wesleyan University Press, 2016.

Goldschmitt, K. E. "From Rio to São Paulo: Shifting Urban Landscapes and Global Strategies for Brazilian Music." In *Sounds and the City,* vol. 2, edited by Brett Lashua, Stephen Wagg, Karl Spracklen, and M. Selim Yavuz, 103–22. London: Palgrave Macmillan, 2019.

Gooley, Dana. *The Virtuoso Liszt.* Cambridge: Cambridge University Press, 2004.

Gopinath, Sumanth. "Contraband Children: The Politics of Race and Liberation in the Music of Steve Reich." PhD diss., Yale University, 2005.

Gopinath, Sumanth, and Jason Stanyek, eds. *The Oxford Handbook of Mobile Music Studies.* Vol. 1. New York: Oxford University Press, 2014.

Graham, Sandra Jean. *Spirituals and the Birth of a Black Entertainment Industry.* Champaign-Urbana: University of Illinois Press, 2017.

Grainger, Percy. "Collecting with the Phonograph." *Journal of the Folk-Song Society* 3, no. 12 (May 1908): 147–62.

Gray, Briahna Joy. "The Question of Cultural Appropriation." *Current Affairs,* 6 Sept. 2017, www.currentaffairs.org/2017/09/the-question-of-cultural-appropriation

Green, Emily H., and Catherine Mayes, eds. *Consuming Music: Individuals, Institutions, Communities, 1730–1830.* Rochester, NY: University of Rochester Press, 2017.

Greenblatt, Stephen, ed. *Cultural Mobility: A Manifesto.* New York: Cambridge University Press, 2010.

Hall, Stuart. "Race: The Floating Signifier." Transcript. Media Education Foundation, https://shop.mediaed.org/race-the-floating-signifier-p173.aspx

Hall, Stuart, Jessica Evans, and Sean Nixon, eds. *Representation: Cultural Representations and Signifying Practices.* Milton Keynes: Open University, 1997.

Harrison, Anthony Kwame. "Post-Colonial Consciousness, Knowledge Production, and Identity Inscription within Filipino American Hip Hop Music." *Perfect Beat* 13, no. 1 (2012): 29–48.

Harvey, David. "Time-Space Compression and the Postmodern Condition." In Held and McGrew, *The Global Transformations Reader,* 82–91.

Harvey, Penelope. *Hybrids of Modernity: Anthropology, the Nation-State, and the Universal Exhibition.* London: Routledge, 1996.

Head, Matthew. "Haydn's Exoticisms: Difference and the Enlightenment." In *The Cambridge Companion to Haydn,* edited by Caryl Clark, 77–92. Cambridge: Cambridge University Press, 2011.

Helbig, Adriana. "'Play for Me, Old Gypsy': Music as Political Resource in the Roma Rights Movement in Ukraine." PhD diss., Columbia University, 2005.

Held, David, and Anthony McGrew, eds. *The Global Transformations Reader.* Cambridge: Polity Press, 2000.

Hess, Carol. *Representing the Good Neighbor: Music, Difference, and the Pan-American Dream*. New York: Oxford University Press, 2013.

Hesselink, Nathan. *P'ungmul: South Korean Drumming and Dance*. Chicago: University of Chicago Press, 2006.

Hilder, Thomas R. "Repatriation, Revival and Transmission: The Politics of a Sámi Musical Heritage." *Ethnomusicology Forum* 21, no. 2 (August 2012): 161–79.

Hobsbawm, Eric, and Terence Ranger, eds. *The Invention of Tradition*. Cambridge: Cambridge University Press, 1983.

Hooker, Lynn M. "Dancing on the Edge of a Volcano: East European Roma Performers Respond to Social Transformation." *Hungarian Studies* 25, no. 2 (2011): 287–302.

Hooker, Lynn M. *Redefining Hungarian Music from Liszt to Bartók*. New York: Oxford University Press, 2013.

Hooker, Lynn M. "Turks, Hungarians, and Gypsies on Stage: Exoticism and Auto-Exoticism in Opera and Operetta." *Hungarian Studies* 27, no. 2 (2013): 291–311.

Horne, Gerald. *Paul Robeson: The Artist as Revolutionary*. London: Pluto Press, 2016.

Howard-Spink, Samuel. "The Political Economy of Music Networks and Glocal Hybrid Social Imaginaries: A Comparative Study of the United States, Canada, and Brazil." PhD diss., New York University, 2012.

Huang, Hao. "Voices from Chinese Rock, Past and Present Tense: Social Commentary and Construction of Identity in *Yaogun Yinyue*, from Tiananmen to the Present." *Popular Music and Society* 26, no. 2 (2003): 183–202.

Hurston, Zora Neale. *The Sanctified Church*. Berkeley, CA: Turtle Island, 1981.

Hwang, Okon. *Western Art Music in South Korea: Everyday Experience and Cultural Critique*. Saarbrücken: VDM, 2009.

Imre, Anikó. "Roma Music and Transnational Homelessness." *Third Text* 22, no. 3 (May 2008): 325–36.

Johnsen, Andreas, Ralf Christensen, and Henrik Moltke. *Good Copy, Bad Copy*. Copenhagen: Rosforth Films, 2007.

Jones, Andrew F. *Like a Knife: Ideology and Genre in Contemporary Chinese Music*. Ithaca: Cornell University East Asia Program, 1992.

Jones, Geoffrey. "The Gramophone Company: An Anglo-American Multinational." *Business History Review* 59, no. 1 (Spring 1985): 76–100.

Jones, LeRoi [Amiri Baraka]. *Blues People: Negro Music in White America*. New York: William Morrow, 1963.

Jones, Richard. "Technology and the Cultural Appropriation of Music." *International Review of Law, Computers & Technology* 23, no. 1–2 (March–July 2009): 109–22.

Kartomi, Margaret J., and Stephen Blum, eds. *Music-Cultures in Contact: Convergences and Collisions*. Basel, CH: Gordon and Breach, 1994.

Kassabian, Anahid. "Would You Like Some World Music with Your Latte? Starbucks, Putumayo, and Distributed Tourism." *Twentieth-Century Music* 1, no. 2 (Sept. 2004): 209–23.

Katz, Mark. *Build: The Power of Hip Hop Diplomacy in a Divided World*. New York: Oxford University Press, 2019.

Katz, Mark. *Capturing Sound: How Technology Has Changed Music*. Berkeley: University of California Press, 2004.

Katz, Mark. "The Case for Hip-Hop Diplomacy." *American Music Review* 46, no. 2 (Spring 2017): 1–5, www.brooklyn.cuny.edu/web/aca_centers_hitchcock/AMR_46-2_Katz. pdf

Katz, Mark. *Groove Music: The Art and Culture of the Hip Hop DJ.* New York: Oxford University Press, 2012.

Keil, Charles. "Participatory Discrepancies and the Power of Music." *Cultural Anthropology* 2, no. 3 (August 1987): 275–83.

Kelly, John D., and Martha Kaplan. *Represented Communities: Fiji and World Decolonization.* Chicago: University of Chicago Press, 2001.

Kim, Soo-Jin. "Diasporic *P'ungmul* in the United States: A Journey between Korea and the United States." PhD diss., Ohio State University, 2011.

Kirshenblatt-Gimblett, Barbara. *Destination Culture: Tourism, Museums, and Heritage.* Berkeley: University of California Press, 1988.

Kirshenblatt-Gimblett, Barbara. "Intangible Heritage as Metacultural Production." *Museum International* 56, no. 1–2 (2004): 52–65.

Kirshenblatt-Gimblett, Barbara. "Theorizing Heritage." *Ethnomusicology* 39, no. 3 (Autumn 1995): 367–79.

Klein, Christina. *Cold War Orientalism: Asia in the Middlebrow Imagination, 1945–1961.* Berkeley: University of California Press, 2003.

Komiya, Toyotaka, ed. *Japanese Music and Drama in the Meiji Era.* Translated and adapted by Edward G. Seidensticker and Donald Keene. Tokyo: Ōbunsha, 1956.

Kotler, Philip, and David Gertner. "Country as Brand, Product, and Beyond: A Place Marketing and Brand Management Perspective." *Brand Management* 4, no. 5 (2002): 249–61.

Kovalcsik, Katalin. "The Music of the Roma in Hungary." *Rombase*, Sept. 2003, 1–10. http://rombase.uni-graz.at/cd/data/music/countries/data/hungary.en.pdf

Koymen, Erol. "A Musical Minefield: Composing the Turkish Nation-State." Paper delivered at the Joint Conference of the AMS-Southwest Chapter & SEM-Southern Plains Chapters. http://ams-sw.org/Proceedings/AMS-SW_V3Spring2014Koymen.pdf

Kroes, Rob. "American Empire and Cultural Imperialism: A View from the Receiving End." *Diplomatic History* 23, no. 3 (1999): 463–77.

Kubik, Gerhard. *Africa and the Blues.* Jackson: University Press of Mississippi, 1999.

Kunej, Drago. "Intertwinement of Croatian and Slovenian Musical Heritage on the Oldest Gramophone Records." *Croatian Journal of Ethnology and Folklore Research* 51, no. 1 (2014): 131–53.

Kunej, Drago, and Rebeka Kunej. *Music from Both Sides: Gramophone Records Made by Matija Arko and the Hoyer Trio.* Ljubljana: Založba ZRC, 2017.

Kwon, Donna Lee. *Music in Korea: Experiencing Music, Expressing Culture.* New York: Oxford University Press, 2012.

Lancefield, Robert C. "Musical Traces' Retraceable Paths: The Repatriation of Recorded Sound." *Journal of Folklore Research* 35, no. 1 (Jan.–April 1998): 47–68.

Lee, Byong Won, and Yong-Shik Lee, eds. *Music of Korea.* Seoul: National Center for Korean Traditional Performing Arts, 2007.

Lee, Katherine In-Young. "The Drumming of Dissent during South Korea's Democratization Movement." *Ethnomusicology* 56, no. 2 (Spring/Summer 2012): 179–205.

Lee, Katherine In-Young. *Dynamic Korea and Rhythmic Form*. Middletown, CT: Wesleyan University Press, 2018.

Legman, Gershon. "Who Owns Folklore?" *Western Folklore* 21, no. 1 (Jan. 1962): 1–12.

Lemon, Alaina. *Between Two Fires: Gypsy Performance and Romani Memory from Pushkin to Post-Socialism*. Durham: Duke University Press, 2000.

Lewis, George E. "Foreword: After Afrofuturism." *Journal of the Society for American Music* 2, no. 2 (2008): 139–53.

Lim, Louisa. *The People's Republic of Amnesia: Tiananmen Revisited*. New York: Oxford University Press, 2014.

Locke, Ralph. *Musical Exoticism: Images and Reflections*. Cambridge: Cambridge University Press, 2009.

MacLachlan, Heather. *Burma's Pop Music Industry: Creators, Distributors, Censors*. Rochester, NY: University of Rochester Press, 2011.

Madrid, Alejandro. *Nor-tec Rifa! Electronic Dance Music from Tijuana to the World*. New York: Oxford University Press, 2008.

Madrid, Alejandro L., ed. *Transnational Encounters: Music and Performance at the U.S.-Mexico Border*. New York: Oxford University Press, 2011.

Mahler, Anne Garland. "The Global South in the Belly of the Beast: Viewing African American Civil Rights through a Tricontinental Lens." *Latin American Research Review* 50, no. 1 (2015): 95–116.

Malm, William. "Modern Music of Meiji Japan." In *Tradition and Modernization in Japanese Culture*, edited by Donald H. Shively, 259–65. Princeton: Princeton University Press, 2015.

Maultsby, Portia K., and Mellonee V. Burnim, eds. *Issues in African American Music: Power, Gender, Race, Representation*. London: Routledge, 2017.

May, Christopher. *The World Intellectual Property Organization: Resurgence and the Development Agenda*. New York: Routledge, 2007.

Mayes, Catherine. "Turkish and Hungarian-Gypsy Styles." In *The Oxford Handbook of Topic Theory*, edited by Danuta Mirka, 214–37. New York: Oxford University Press, 2014.

McConnell, Lauren. "Understanding Paul Robeson's Soviet Experience." *Theatre History Studies* 30 (2010): 139–53.

McCormick, Lisa. *Performing Civility: International Competitions in Classical Music*. Cambridge: Cambridge University Press, 2015.

McGinley, Paige A. *Staging the Blues: From Tent Shows to Tourism*. Durham: Duke University Press, 2014.

McLuhan, Marshall. *Understanding Media: The Extensions of Man*. 1964. Cambridge, MA: MIT Press, 1994.

Meintjes, Louise. "Paul Simon's *Graceland*, South Africa, and the Mediation of Musical Meaning." *Ethnomusicology* 34, no. 1 (1990): 37–73.

Mendonça, Maria. "Gamelan in Britain: Communitas, Affinity, and Other Stories." PhD diss., Wesleyan University, 2002.

Mendonça, Maria. "Gamelan Performance Outside Indonesia 'Setting Sail': Babar Layar and Notions of 'Bi-musicality.'" *Asian Music* 42, no. 2 (Summer/Fall 2011): 56–87.

Merlan, Francesca. "Indigeneity: Global and Local." *Current Anthropology* 50, no. 3 (June 2009): 303–33.

Miller, Leta E., and Fredric Lieberman. *Lou Harrison.* Champaign: University of Illinois Press, 2006.

Miller, Leta E., and Fredric Lieberman. *Lou Harrison: Composing a World.* New York: Oxford University Press, 1998.

Muir, Peter C. *Long Lost Blues: Popular Blues in America, 1850–1920.* Urbana: University of Illinois Press, 2010.

Neff, Ali Colleen. "Roots, Routes, and Rhizomes: Sounding Women's Hip Hop on the Margins of Dakar, Senegal." *Journal of Popular Music Studies* 27, no. 4 (2015): 448–77.

Nettl, Bruno. *The Study of Ethnomusicology: Thirty-One Issues and Concepts.* Champaign: University of Illinois Press, 2005.

Newland, Marti K. "Sounding 'Black': An Ethnography of Racialized Vocality at Fisk University." PhD diss., Columbia University, 2014.

Ngai, Mae M. "'The Unlovely Residue of Outworn Prejudices': The Hart-Celler Act and the Politics of Immigration Reform, 1945–1965." In *Americanism: New Perspectives on the History of an Ideal,* edited by Michael Kazin and Joseph A. McCartin, 108–27. Chapel Hill: University of North Carolina Press, 2006.

Nilan, Pam, and Carles Feixa, eds. *Global Youth? Hybrid Identities, Plural Worlds.* New York: Routledge, 2006.

Notosudirdjo, Franki S. "European Music in Colonial Life in 19th-Century Java: A Preliminary Study." MM thesis, University of Wisconsin, 1990.

Notosudirdjo, Franki S. "Music, Politics, and the Problems of National Identity in Indonesia." PhD diss., University of Wisconsin, Madison, 2001.

Nowak, Raphaël, and Andrew Whelan, eds. *Networked Music Cultures: Contemporary Approaches, Emerging Issues.* London: Palgrave Macmillan, 2016.

Olkhovsky, Andrey. *Music under the Soviets: The Agony of an Art.* New York: Frederick A. Praeger, 1955.

Oteri, Frank J. "Barbara Benary: Mother of Lion." *New Music Box,* 1 Feb. 2011, www.newmusicbox.org/articles/barbara-benary-mother-of-lion

Ouijjani, Hinda. "Le fonds de disques 78 tours Pathé de musique arabe et orientale donné aux Archives de la Parole et au Musée de la Parole et du Geste de l'Université de Paris: 1911–1930." *Sonorités (Bulletin de l'AFAS)* 38 (2012): 1–14; and 39 (2013): 2–9, http://afas.revues.org/2835

Park, Hye-jung. "From World War to Cold War: Music in US-Korea Relations, 1941–1960." PhD diss., Ohio State University, 2019.

Park, Shingil. "Negotiated Identities in a Performance Genre: The Case of *P'ungmul* and *Samulnori* in Contemporary Seoul." PhD diss., University of Pittsburgh, 2000.

Pekacz, Jolanta. "Did Rock Smash the Wall? The Role of Rock in Political Transition." *Popular Music* 13, no. 1 (1994): 41–49.

Perry, Marc D. "Global Black Self-Fashionings: Hip Hop as Diasporic Space." *Identities* 15, no. 6 (2008): 635–64.

Racy, Ali Jihad. "Record Industry and Egyptian Traditional Music: 1904–1932." *Ethnomusicology* 20, no. 1 (Jan. 1976): 23–48.

Racy, Ali Jihad. "Sound Recording in the Life of Early Arab-American Immigrants." *Revue des traditions musicales des mondes Arabe et Méditerranéen* 5 (2011): 41–52.

Radano, Ronald. *Lying Up a Nation: Race and Black Music.* Chicago: University of Chicago Press, 2003.

Rea, Dennis. "Ambushed from All Sides: Rock Music as a Force for Change in China." In Friedman, *The Routledge History of Social Protest in Popular Music,* 373–86.

Reagon, Bernice Johnson. *If You Don't Go, Don't Hinder Me: The African American Song Tradition.* Lincoln: University of Nebraska Press, 2001.

Redmond, Shana. *Anthem: Social Movements and the Sound of Solidarity in the African Diaspora.* New York: New York University Press, 2013.

Reichman, J. H. "Universal Minimum Standards of Intellectual Property Protection under the TRIPS Component of the WTO Agreement." *International Lawyer* 29, no. 2 (Summer 1995): 345–88.

Revuluri, Sindhumathi K. "On Anxiety and Absorption: Musical Encounters with the *Exotique* in Fin-de-siècle France." PhD diss., Princeton University, 2007.

Rieff, Philip. "The Impossible Culture: Wilde as a Modern Prophet." Introduction to Oscar Wilde, *The Soul of Man under Socialism.* New York: Harper and Row, 1970.

Rose, Tricia. *Black Noise: Rap Music and Black Culture in Contemporary America.* Middletown, CT: Wesleyan University Press, 1994.

Rosenboim, Or. *The Emergence of Globalism: Visions of World Order in Britain and the United States, 1939–1950.* Princeton: Princeton University Press, 2017.

Ruckert, George E. *Music in North India: Experiencing Music, Expressing Culture.* New York: Oxford University Press, 2004.

Rudinow, Joel. "Race, Ethnicity, Expressive Authenticity: Can White People Sing the Blues?" *Journal of Aesthetics and Art Criticism* 52, no. 1 (Winter 1994): 127–37.

Said, Edward. *Orientalism.* 1978. New York: Vintage, 1994.

Salois, Kendra. "Jihad against Jihad against Jihad." *New Inquiry,* 27 Oct. 2012. https://the newinquiry.com/jihad-against-jihad-against-jihad

Salois, Kendra. "The Networked Self: Hip Hop Musicking and Muslim Identities in Neoliberal Morocco." PhD diss., University of California, Berkeley, 2013.

Samuelson, Pamela. "Digital Rights Management {and, or, vs.} the Law." *Communications of the ACM* 46, no. 4 (2003): 41–45.

Sárosi, Bálint. *Gypsy Music.* Budapest: Corvina, 1978.

Sassen, Saskia. *Territory—Authority—Rights: From Medieval to Global Assemblages.* Princeton: Princeton University Press, 2006.

Schmelz, Peter J. *Such Freedom, but Only Musical: Unofficial Soviet Music during the Thaw.* Oxford: Oxford University Press, 2009.

Sharma, Sanjay, John Hutnyk, and Ashwani Sharma, eds. *Dis-Orienting Rhythms: The Politics of the New Asian Dance Music.* London: Zed Books, 1996.

Shay, Anthony. *Choreographic Politics: State Folk Dance Companies, Representation, and Power.* Middletown, CT: Wesleyan University Press, 2002.

Shay, Anthony, and Barbara Sellers-Young, eds. *Oxford Handbook of Dance and Ethnicity.* Oxford: Oxford University Press, 2016.

Silveira, Sergio Amadeu da, Murilo Bansi Machado, and Rodrigo Tarchiani Savazoni. "Backward March: The Turnaround in Public Cultural Policy in Brazil." *Media, Culture & Society* 35, no. 5 (2013): 549–64.

Silverman, Carol. *Romani Routes: Cultural Politics and Balkan Music in Diaspora*. New York: Oxford University Press, 2012.

Silverman, Carol. "Trafficking in the Exotic with 'Gypsy' Music: Balkan Roma, Cosmopolitanism, and 'World Music' Festivals." In *Balkan Popular Culture and the Ottoman Ecumene*, edited by Donna A. Buchanan, 335–61. Lanham, MD: Scarecrow Press, 2007.

Skinner, Ryan Thomas. "Artists, Music Piracy, and the Crisis of Political Subjectivity in Contemporary Mali." *Anthropological Quarterly* 85, no. 3 (2012): 723–53.

Small, Christopher. *Musicking: The Meanings of Performing and Listening*. Hanover, NH: University Press of New England, 1998.

Sorrell, Neil. *A Guide to the Gamelan*. London: Amadeus, 1990.

Sotiropoulos, Karen. *Staging Race: Black Performers in Turn of the Century America*. Cambridge, MA: Harvard University Press, 2006.

Southern, Eileen. *The Music of Black Americans: A History*. 3rd ed. New York: Norton, 1997.

Southern, Eileen, ed. *Readings in Black American Music*. 2nd ed. New York: W.W. Norton, 1983.

Spiller, Henry. *Gamelan: The Traditional Sounds of Indonesia*. Santa Barbara: ABC-CLIO, 2004.

Spiller, Henry. *Javaphilia: American Love Affairs with Javanese Music and Dance*. Honolulu: University of Hawai'i Press, 2015.

Spottswood, Richard K., ed. *Ethnic Music on Records: A Discography of Ethnic Recordings Produced in the United States, 1893 to 1942*. Urbana: University of Illinois Press, 1990.

Steingo, Gavin. *Kwaito's Promise: Music and the Aesthetics of Freedom in South Africa*. Chicago: University of Chicago Press, 2016.

Stepputat, Kendra. "*Kecak* behind the Scenes—Investigating the *Kecak* Network." In *Dance Ethnography and Global Perspectives: Identity, Embodiment, Culture*, edited by Linda E. Dankworth and Ann R. David, 116–32. Basingstoke: Palgrave Macmillan, 2014.

Stepputat, Kendra. "Kecak Ramayana: Tourists in Search for the 'Real Thing.'" In *Hybridity in the Performing Arts of Southeast Asia*, edited by Mohd. Anis Md. Nor, Patricia Matusky, Tan Sooi Beng, Jacqueline-Pugh Kitingan, and Felicidad Prudente, 43–49. Kuala Lumpur: Nusantara Performing Arts Research Centre, 2011.

Stepputat, Kendra. "Performing *Kecak*: A Balinese Dance Tradition between Daily Routine and Creative Art." *Yearbook for Traditional Music* 44 (2012): 49–70.

Sterne, Jonathan. *The Audible Past: Cultural Origins of Sound Reproduction*. Durham: Duke University Press, 2003.

Sterne, Jonathan. *MP3: The Meaning of a Format*. Durham: Duke University Press, 2012.

Stokes, Martin. *The Arabesk Debate: Music and Musicians in Modern Turkey*. Oxford: Clarendon, 1992.

Stokes, Martin. "Globalization and the Politics of World Music." In *The Cultural Study of Music: A Critical Introduction*, edited by Martin Clayton, Trevor Herbert, and Richard Middleton, 107–16. New York: Routledge, 2003.

Stokes, Martin. Introduction to *Ethnicity, Identity, and Music: The Musical Construction of Place*, edited by Martin Stokes, 1–27. Oxford: Berg, 1994.

Sumarsam. *Javanese Gamelan and the West*. Rochester, NY: University of Rochester Press, 2013.

Suslin, Viktor. "The Music of Spiritual Independence: Galina Ustvolskaya." In *Ex oriente: Ten Composers from the USSR*, edited by Galina Grigorieva and Valeriia Tsenova, translated by Carolyn Dunlop, 99–114. Berlin: E. Kuhn, 2002.

Szaniecki, Barbara, and Gerardo Silva. "Rio et la politique de 'Pontos de Cultura.'" *Multitudes*, no. 43 (2010): 70–77.

Tan, Sooi Beng. "The 78 RPM Record Industry in Malaya prior to World War II." *Asian Music* 28, no. 1 (Fall/Winter 1996–97): 1–41.

Taylor, Charles. *Modern Social Imaginaries*. Durham: Duke University Press, 2004.

Taylor, Charles. "The Politics of Recognition." In *Multiculturalism: Examining the Politics of Recognition*, edited by Amy Gutmann, 25–73. Princeton: Princeton University Press, 1994.

Taylor, Jean Gelman. *The Social World of Batavia: Europeans and Eurasians in Colonial Indonesia*. Madison: University of Wisconsin Press, 2009.

Tcherenkov, Lev, and Stéphane Laederich. *The Rroma*. 2 vols. Basel, CH: Schwabe, 2004.

Tekelioğlu, Orhan. "The Rise of a Spontaneous Synthesis: The Historical Background of Turkish Popular Music." *Middle Eastern Studies* 32, no. 2 (1996): 194–215.

Thomas, Susan. "Music, Conquest, and Colonialism." In *Musics of Latin America*, edited by Robin Moore, 25–50. New York: W.W. Norton, 2012.

Thompson, Katrina Dyonne. *Ring Shout, Wheel About*. Urbana: University of Illinois Press, 2014.

Thorsén, Stig-Magnus, ed. *Sounds of Change—Social and Political Features of Music in Africa*. Stockholm: Sida, 2004.

Titon, Jeff Todd. *Early Downhome Blues: A Musical and Cultural Analysis*. Urbana: University of Illinois Press, 1977.

Tomlinson, John. *Globalization and Culture*. Chicago: University of Chicago Press, 1999.

Tomoff, Kiril. *Virtuosi Abroad: Soviet Music and Imperial Competition during the Early Cold War, 1945–1958*. Ithaca: Cornell University Press, 2015.

Toynbee, Jason, and Byron Dueck, eds. *Migrating Music*. New York: Routledge, 2011.

Tsing, Anna. *Friction: An Ethnography of Global Connection*. Princeton: Princeton University Press, 2005.

Turner, Bryan S., ed. *The Routledge International Handbook of Globalization Studies*. New York: Routledge, 2010.

Turner, Bryan S. "Theories of Globalization: Issues and Origins." In Turner, *Routledge International Handbook*, 3–10.

Turtinen, Jan. "Globalising Heritage—On UNESCO and the Transnational Construction of a World Heritage." *SCORE Rapportserie* 2000, no. 12 (Stockholm: Stockholm Center for Organizational Research, 2000).

Wade, Bonnie. *Composing Japanese Musical Modernity*. Chicago: University of Chicago Press, 2014.

Wald, Elijah. *Escaping the Delta: Robert Johnson and the Invention of the Blues*. New York: Harper Collins, 2004.

Waldron, Jeremy. "Indigeneity? First Peoples and Last Occupancy." *New Zealand Journal of Public and International Law* I (2003): 55–82.

Wang, Grace. *Soundscapes of Asian America: Navigating Race through Musical Performance.* Durham: Duke University Press, 2015.

Weiss, Sarah. "Listening to the World but Hearing Ourselves: Hybridity and Perceptions of Authenticity in World Music." *Ethnomusicology* 58, no. 3 (Fall 2014): 506–25.

Wilde, Oscar. *The Soul of Man under Socialism.* New York: Harper and Row, 1970.

Wilson, Olly. "Composition from the Perspective of the African-American Tradition." *Black Music Research Journal* 16, no. 1 (Spring 1996): 43–51.

Wilson, Olly. "The Heterogeneous Sound Ideal in African-American Music." In *New Perspectives on Music: Essays in Honor of Eileen Southern*, edited by Josephine Wright and Samuel A. Floyd Jr., 327–38. Warren, MI: Harmonie Park Press, 1992.

Wolf, Eric R. *Europe and the People Without History.* 1982; Berkeley: University of California Press, 1997.

Yoon, In-Jin. "Migration and the Korean Diaspora: A Comparative Description of Five Cases." *Journal of Ethnic and Migration Studies* 38, no. 3 (March 2012): 413–35.

Yoshihara, Mari. *Musicians from a Different Shore.* Philadelphia: Temple University Press, 2007.

Ziff, Bruce, and Pratima V. Rao. "Introduction to Cultural Appropriation: A Framework for Analysis." In *Borrowed Power: Essays on Cultural Appropriation*, edited by Bruce Ziff and Pratima V. Rao, 1–27. New Brunswick, NJ: Rutgers University Press, 1997.

Index

Note: Page numbers for audio examples are in **boldface**; page numbers in *italics* refer to figures and maps.